KV-648-767

Contemporary issues and debates in EU policy

The European Union and international relations

edited by
Vassiliki N. Koutrakou

Manchester University Press
Manchester and New York

distributed exclusively in the USA by Palgrave

Copyright © Manchester University Press 2004

While copyright in the volume as a whole is vested in Manchester University Press, copyright in individual chapters belongs to their respective authors, and no chapter may be reproduced wholly or in part without the express permission in writing of both author and publisher.

Published by Manchester University Press
Oxford Road, Manchester M13 9NR, UK
and Room 400, 175 Fifth Avenue, New York, NY 10010, USA
www.manchesteruniversitypress.co.uk

Distributed exclusively in the USA by
Palgrave, 175 Fifth Avenue, New York,
NY 10010, USA

Distributed exclusively in Canada by
UBC Press, University of British Columbia, 2029 West Mall,
Vancouver, BC, Canada V6T 1Z2

British Library Cataloguing-in-Publication Data
A catalogue record for this book is available from the British Library

Library of Congress Cataloging-in-Publication Data applied for

ISBN   0 7190 6418 X   *hardback*
       0 7190 6419 8   *paperback*

First published 2004

11 10 09 08 07 06 05 04   10 9 8 7 6 5 4 3 2 1

Typeset in Minion
by Action Publishing Technology Ltd, Gloucester
Printed in Great Britain
by Bell & Bain Ltd, Glasgow

To my father

Contents

Tables and figures

Tables

Figures

Contributors

Hazel Dawe is senior lecturer in law at London Guildhall University. She is currently working on a PhD on the Austrian Nuclear Prohibition Law and Austria's membership of the Atomic Community. Her research is interdisciplinary and draws on politics as well as law and with Austria as a starting point, also touches on the EU's eastward expansion.

Steve Dawe teaches social sciences and environmental policy for the Open University.

Jenny Fairbrass is Senior Research Associate at the Centre for Economic and Social Research on the Global Environment (CSERGE) at the University of East Anglia. She is currently working on the impact of devolution on environmental decision-making at the subnational, national, European Union and wider international levels. She has published primarily on British and EU environmental policy in a number of academic journals and books.

Geoffrey D. Gooch is Jean Monnet Professor of European Political Integration at Linköping University, Sweden, publishing on regional municipal co-operation, and on the implementation of Agenda 21 in Europe. He is now organiser of a major project examining environmental administration and politics on the Estonian–Russian border.

Andrew Jordan is lecturer in Environmental Politics at the University of East Anglia and a member of UEA's CSERGE, with an involvement in several research projects. Recent publications include: *Re-interpreting the Precautionary Principle* (Cameron and May, 2001), *Environmental Policy in the EU* (London: Earthscan, 2002), and *The Europeanisation of British Environmental Policy* (New York: Palgrave, 2002).

Vassiliki Koutrakou is lecturer in European Studies and Director of the Centre for Research in European Studies (CREST) at the University of East Anglia, Norwich. Recent publications include: *Technological Collaboration for Europe's Survival* (Avebury, 1995); *European Union and Britain: Debating the Challenges Ahead* (with L. A. Emerson, eds) (Basingstoke: Macmillan, 2000).

Jonathan Luckhurst is completing his doctoral research on globalisation, using Foucauldian concepts for problematising the concept and employing the Palestinian situation as a 'case study'. Recent publications include (with V. Koutrakou): 'The Globalisation versus Regionalisation Paradox and the European Union' (RIEAS Special Strategic Paper No. 81, 2000).

Barbara Marshall is lecturer in European Studies at the University of East Anglia, Norwich. Recent publications include: *Willy Brandt – A Political Biography* (London: Macmillan, 1996), 'British and German Refugee Policies in the European Context' (RIIA Discussion Paper, 1997); *The New Germany and Migration in Europe* (Manchester: Manchester University Press, 2001).

Nicola Murrell is an analyst in Ovum's Asia-Pacific analyst team, after having spent five years in Europe at Ovum's London headquarters, at Nortel Networs GSM and other IT companies. Specialising in wireless and digital media sectors, she currently follows developments in Asia-Pacific markets and regularly contributes to telecoms publications.

Paul G. Nixon is senior lecturer in European Politics at HEBO, Haagse Hogeschool, Netherlands. He is a member of an EU COST 14 working group on new social movements and ICTs. He has published a number of articles around the broad themes of e-democracy and e-government. He is an editorial board member of the international journal *Information, Communication and Society*.

Caroline Nolan has worked in a series of NGOs, as Deputy Director for the Kurdish Human Rights Project (KHRP), the West Belfast Economic Forum, and the West Belfast Economic Partnership and is currently working on a doctoral research project on human rights at Queen's University, Belfast.

John M. Nomikos is Director of the Research Institute for European and American Studies (RIEAS), in Athens, Greece. He is also the Director of the educational committee of AHEPA (American Hellenic Educational Progressive Association) in Athens, Greece.

Tim O'Riordan is Professor of Environmental Sciences at the University of East Anglia and a member of UEA's CSERGE. He has edited a number of books on the institutional aspects of global environmental change policy and practice, and led two international research projects on the transition to sustainability in the European Union (1995–99). He is also executive editor of *Environment* magazine, and of *Risk Assessment: An Institutional Journal*.

Sabine S. Saurugger is lecturer in Politics at the Institut d'Etudes Politiques de Grenoble and Research Fellow at the CIDSP. Recent publications include (with E. Grossman and B. Irondelle) *Les Mots de l'Europe* (Presses de Science Po, 2001); (with Neill Nugent) 'Organisational structuring: the case of the European Commission and its external policy responsibilities', *Journal of European Public Policy*, 9:3 (2002), pp. 345–64 and 'L'expertise: une forme de participation des groupes d'intérêt au processus décisionnel communautaire', *Revue française de science politique*, 52:4 (2002), pp. 367–93. She is editor of the journal *Politique européenne*.

Michael E. Smith, is Assistant Professor at the Department of Political Science, in Georgia State University, Atlanta, USA. Recent publications include: 'The quest for coherence: institutional dilemmas of external action from Maastricht to Amsterdam', in Alec Stone Sweet, Neil Fligstein and Wayne Sandholtz (eds), *The Institutionalization of Europe* (Oxford: Oxford University Press, 2001).

Tarja Väyrynen is Research Director at Tampere Peace Research Institute in Finland. Her most recent publications include *Culture and International Conflict Resolution* (Manchester: Manchester University Press, 2001).

James H. Wyllie is Senior Lecturer in International Relations, and Director of the Conflict and Security Studies Programme at the University of Aberdeen. Recent publications include 'European Security Realities and the Influence of Cold War Institutions', *European Security*, 3:2 (Summer 1994); *European Security in the New Political Environment* (London: Longman, 1997).

Acknowledgements

This book would not have happened without the sponsorship of the 3rd CREST Conference by the European Commission; therefore my first thanks are due to the EU, which we are analysing and dissecting throughout this volume. Secondly, my gratitude turns to the talented and good-humoured contributors of chapters, all of whom shared the same enthusiasm for this project, gave their best to make this a rich and interesting collection and responded eagerly and promptly to all questions or comments raised by myself or the reviewers, making my editing task rewarding and trouble free. I most sincerely wish to thank all those who contributed to the completion of this volume, either through their encouragement and advice, such as my family and my friends, particularly my dad and Richard Deswarte, or through their calming and cheerful hands-on secretarial assistance, such as Carol Curtis, Rachel Lunness and Scott Wright. Last but not least, thanks are due to everyone at Manchester University Press for believing in the book and for showing more than a little patience. Finally, I should like this book to also honour the memory of Gordon John Lake who was Principal Administrator at the European Parliament's DG for Research. John was responsible for the 2002 study on the Euratom Treaty (ENER 114 EN, Energy and Research Series). He attended the 3rd CREST conference of his own initiative and proved a valuable source of lively and informed contributions to panel discussions, and subsequently maintained an interest in the progress of the book project. He passed away recently but was much appreciated and will be missed.

Introduction

Vassiliki N. Koutrakou

The inspiration for this volume came from the third annual conference held by the Centre for Research in European Studies (CREST) in the spring of 2000, at the University of East Anglia, in Norwich. The title of the conference was 'European Perspectives on Interdependence and Co-operation in Current International Relations', and most of the contributors to this book were part of it. The timing of the conference, at the start of a new century, and the innovative angles employed by several of the participants, gave rise to lively and continued informal debate for some time after the end of the conference, which explored the transition between old and new agendas in global developments, key pervasive themes, and the direction of EU policy within them. When complemented by insightful contributions by several other friends of CREST, that initial event and continued discussions instigated this latest project and composed the backbone of the present book.

The primary purpose of this work is to cast a penetrative look at a broad – if not exhaustive – range of fiercely debated contemporary issues which are shaping the policy-making agenda in international relations and particularly European affairs in the politico-economic world order of the early twenty-first century.

The Cold War and East–West/North–South perceptions from the 1970s and 1980s, as well as the euphoria of the immediate post-Cold War era were quickly left well behind. Economic crises, wars and social problems occur no less than before, nor are they easier than before to resolve, and the European continent, and even more specifically, the European Union, finds itself intricately involved, sometimes directly, sometimes less so.

Since the late 1980s, the EU has faced the collapse of communism in Eastern Europe and the former Soviet bloc in general, followed by more than a dozen new applications for membership; the re-unification of Germany; variable ethnic conflicts and instability threats, coupled with costly economic demands by a reforming but volatile East in its efforts to return to the 'European family'. A fragmenting Yugoslavia and the dramas of Bosnia and Kosovo were accompanied by rising waves of refugees and immigration. The world, with only one remaining overbearing military superpower, the United States, is also a world where economic wealth is centred upon a core-triangle, with the EU itself as one of its poles together with the USA and Japan. A new powerful international institution, the WTO, is stamping its authority and making whole new sets of waves in the relations between these biggest economic competitors, while protesters among the triangle's outsiders and non-governmental lobby groups cause ripples of their own. The era of the Internet and faster, fiercer global interactions reside alongside widespread social debates, spear-headed by environmental concerns, but at the same time, galloping advances in high technologies and telecommunications. The troublesome completion of a Monetary Union and the introduction of a challenging single currency, the euro, was successful even if it had to be without everyone together on board. Finally, there are demands for a stronger out-of-area response in conflicts such as Iraq and the Arab–Israeli conflict, and the immensely laborious efforts to formulate a Common Foreign and Security Policy, as well as to co-ordinate to some extent, immigration, anti-drug-trafficking, anti-terrorism and other policies.

Such new circumstances are redefining politico-economic power balances and demand intensified scrutiny.

Most of the theoretical analyses employed today diverge little from Cold War, or even pre-Cold War models. Realism, or neo-realism, liberalism, neo-liberalism, world society are still predominant and adapting in their interpretations and attempts at predicting the factors shaping international relations. However, they appear to only partially, and inadequately, cover the impact of a succession of the new and fast-changing parameters, such as environmental concerns, immigration, terrorism or human rights, and international responses to these. Perhaps this has always been the case, even in traditional international relations (IR), with theory racing to keep up with world events, but the perception is that the shape of the new world order has changed at a much more accelerated pace since the late 1980s. The impact of all this upon the continuing integration in Europe and upon its frameworks of governance and policy-making is understandably analogous.

In view of this, it is interesting to consider perceptions and policy changes in traditional areas of politics, economics and security, while at the same time paying attention to a range of relatively 'younger' issues and concerns which, rather than being peripheral, have become a central part of current IR in their own right. These include the pervasiveness of high technology in governance and its vital importance in economic prosperity; the changing competences and impact of telecommunications upon global interactions; striking the right balance between improving cross-border transport for easier trade and tightening and maintaining effective border controls; the treatment of increasing waves of refugees, asylum seekers and economic migrants in the face of proliferating immigration legislation; responding to global environmental degradation and a need for energy conservation when this may mean compromising economic development; tackling atomic energy management; dealing with the uneasy awareness and regulation of biotechnology; legislating on human rights in view of endless disputes on the right to intervene to safeguard them in violation of state sovereignty; rethinking Third World development as it finds itself juxtaposed to the growing pressures of globalisation; and similar issues which are indisputably central today.

In this volume we look at the interaction of certain EU politico-economic structures with a variety of internal but also international actors on the above broad range of global issues. For example, we look at issues of European security in the light of a changing NATO role. We look at proposals for more effective sharing of intelligence between the EU and other parts of the world, an issue which appears to have assumed a new urgency and centrality since the terrorist attacks of the 11 September 2001 in the United States. We analyse the behaviour of the EU in contributing to, and at defending its interests from, the ultimate, full trade-liberalisation policies of the World Trade Organisation. In all this, we try not to neglect the 'domestic' actors and processes which determine EU policy formulation at any one point, and the difficulties and conflicts frequently faced in reaching the common positions required for the EU's global interactions.

In studying the above, a number of key themes, popular contemporary buzzwords, inevitably show through, and form threads running through the entire volume. Globalisation, liberalisation, interdependence, co-operation, fragmentation, are but a few examples, which, although not new, seem to dominate political, economic and social discourse nowadays, probably more than ever. None of these in isolation can explain or codify the direction which EU policy response is taking on the range of issues we are dealing with. They are however useful methodologically, in combination, to enhance insight. They are therefore considered in the book, in part theoretically, and to a large extent empirically, through our case studies and illustrations as, chapter by chapter, we run through some of the main areas of debate in Europe today.

The volume is divided into three parts: Part I deals with issues of security, defence and conflict. After a general review, in chapter 1, of the theoretical discourse on interdependence and fragmentation theories as they transcend the early post-Cold War era, it looks at international and European manifestations of conflict and the constantly evolving approaches in conflict resolution. The specific case study of Kosovo, demonstrating the functionality and dysfunctionality of the European response to conflict, is picked up in chapter 2. The uneasy relationship with NATO is highlighted as it began to search for a new role, reinventing and reasserting itself throughout the 1990s. Persevering in the quest for a Common Foreign and Security Policy, as well as the co-ordination of Justice and Home Affairs, the two new pillars which, together with the old European Community shaped the new European Union at Maastricht in 1991, the EU is looking for ways in which to become a more substantial international actor, and respond more effectively in future to conflicts, both at its doorstep, such as the former Yugoslavia, and further afield. It also tries to tackle the increased dangers of freer drug trafficking, crime and terrorism, which have been benefiting from the lowering of intra-European barriers to movement, through better co-ordination domestically, and more co-operation with international bodies and agencies. Chapter 3 explores the organised exchange of intelligence in the EU, to meet the above needs, and its potential impact both internally and internationally. Given these considerations, chapters 4 and 5 look at two of the most crucial, prominent and most fiercely debated spin-offs of world conflict and insecurity, human rights and migration, and developments in the EU's institutional and policy handling of these issues.

Part II explores issues akin to economic development. It begins, in chapter 6, with an overview of EU institutional economic policy-making structures and processes within the context of the world system. There follows a critical review of the theory for and against globalisation, as expressed in the neo-liberal capitalist policies of the developed world and the World Trade Organisation, and the impact of such trends in the world system on contemporary and future EU policy-making. EU trade relations with its main economic competitors/partners, the United States and Canada, Japan and South-East Asia , but also the other world regions, are broadly mentioned in this chapter. However, the following one concentrates most particularly upon the re-evaluation in EU perceptions and changes in policy towards the Third World, which have developed, partly by choice, and partly as a result of unrelenting pressures from its competitors via WTO channels, and the promises and tensions which these changes in policy are heralding. There follows three more specific case-studies of EU economic policy-making. Chapters 8, 9, 10 and 11 explore institutional transborder co-operation between EU regions and their neighbouring Eastern European or former Soviet neighbours; environmental sustainability, nuclear energy – a highly contentious source of energy – and cross-border transport as four areas, which cause considerable economic and environmental concern, not to mention administrative headaches in the relations between EU member states, and between the EU and non-member states, particularly Eastern European countries, and impact heavily upon negotiations for continued EU enlargement. Chapter 12 closes this part by focusing more closely upon Euro-firms and Euro-groups and their behaviour and interaction with EU institutional structures and processes within the European market as it aspires to act as an ever-more effective springboard for European companies on to the world scene.

Part III concentrates on high technology and innovation, areas not always at the forefront of international negotiations per se, yet underlining almost all major developments in international relations from the way wars are waged to the foundations of economic globalisation. Chapter 13 revisits nuclear energy and EURATOM, but this time from an European institutional and technological empowerment perspective in relation to high-level international relations. Chapter 14 examines the diverse approaches to biotechnology policy, an area of contention which generates friction with respect to international trade between the USA and Europe, and how these approaches translate into policy orientation. Telecommunications has been one of the most versatile areas in international joint ventures, and certainly one of the corner-stones of globalisation, and chapter 15 describes the complexity of recent developments in this industry and their particular reverberations across Europe. The final chapter of the book revisits the subject of European governance through the prism of recent developments in high technology, which matter not only in terms of products, services and competitiveness for the region, but underpin all areas of EU politics and which have enabled, and promise to further enable, increased hands-on participation by European citizens in many aspects of EU policy-making processes at both the domestic and international levels.

Part I

Conflict and foreign and security policy approaches

This part explores issues which figure heavily in the current international agenda on political and security considerations.

The foundations are set by Väyrynen who explores generally the theories of conflict, interdependence, co-operation and fragmentation, which affect policy-making at national, regional and international levels, and she seeks out manifestations on the European and international stages. The interdependence and fragmentation theories, which she focuses on, present very interesting analyses as to the relative significance of different actors in conflict resolution. For example, she evaluates the role of nation-states, as international actors, and of processes, which remain predominant in interdependence theories, as opposed to communities, based on perceptions of identity, which tend to prevail among fragmentation theories. To illustrate, she considers several cases of contemporary conflict resolution, where it is rarely possible to make progress without a multi-pronged approach, in other words with just state-level diplomacy and negotiation to the exclusion of a host of other actors, including local communities, specific interest-representing lobbies, international and regional organisations, non-governmental actors, etc.

A dynamic form of conflict resolution using force – a post-Cold war phenomenon which made its appearance in Europe with the NATO strikes in Bosnia and Kosovo, and created many question marks regarding the future of European defence – is evaluated by Wyllie in the second chapter. By 1990 NATO had won the Cold War. A cohesive, robust deterrent posture defeated the clear danger posed by the Soviet bloc to the national security of all the alliance members. The EU was struggling to put together a coherent, yet also flexible, basis for a common foreign and security policy. Reluctant to abandon an international organisation which had served its members so well, the major Western powers sought a new justification and role for NATO in the post-Cold War world. Since the early 1990s the policy of twin enlargement – members and mission – has transformed the Atlantic alliance from the deterrence-based, defensive organisation, which its members previously valued, and with which public opinion largely felt comfortable, into an expansive organisation based on military compellance in pursuit of political objectives beyond its own borders. The summer of 1999 saw the new NATO win its first military campaign, but in the process seriously erode its reputation as a law-abiding, non-offensive, efficacious military alliance in permanent occupation of the moral high ground. NATO's Kosovo intervention exacerbated extant strains in the European security regime, not least in US–West European defence relations and NATO–Russian relations.

Building on the discussion in the previous two chapters, Nomikos re-examines the mechanisms for responding to conflict at EU borders, and proposes a European Union Intelligence Agency (EUIA), to codify and regularise the exchange of intelligence between member states. He argues that this is necessary, particularly in view of the urgency for more global co-operation since the 11 September 2001 terrorist attacks on the United States and the United

Nations' determination for concerted efforts to tackle it. More specifically, he identifies problems 'closer to home' for the EU, with actual and simmering ethnic conflicts and successive waves of immigration and crime in Eastern Europe and the Mediterranean. He speculates that an EUIA could operate along similar lines to the US independent Central Intelligence Agency (CIA), despite the obvious organisational peculiarities, and theorises as to the shape and feasibility of such a venture.

Marshall picks up on the issue of immigration and examines national and European strategies for addressing the problems. She assesses the magnitude of the problems and the approaches taken by different European countries, the factors which affect these approaches and the changes over time. Although the member states have committed to co-operation in Justice and Home Affairs, one of the two intergovernmental pillars introduced at Maastricht and further by the Amsterdam Treaty, there are still significant differences between the member states' policies, and different views on the urgency for a coherent policy, as some, the 'front-line' states, face the effects more than others. Nevertheless to a degree a unified approach is more and more urgent if the freedom of movement and Schengen are ever to function fully within the EU area. The most prominent proposed solutions, stricter controls at external borders, burden-sharing with respect to asylum-seeking applications and others, are analysed in depth.

Combining considerations of conflict resolution and the growing problem of refugees with the increasingly entrenched international post-Cold War norm – though not necessarily law – which tends towards justifying international intervention, over-riding state sovereignty, at least selectively, to uphold causes such as human rights, Nolan examines international law and European legislation underpinning responses in this area. International law, she argues, has a chequered history. It seems to exist to provide moral justification for states' actions and at the same time it seems to be honoured more in its breach than its observance. In chapter 5 she seeks to determine the role of international law in the international relations arena and looks at the different perspectives in which it can be viewed. She then considers the implications of these perspectives when seeking to assess the influence of international law in the decision-making processes of state actors.

Interdependence and fragmentation: the articulations of political space in the discourses of integration and ethnic conflict

Tarja Väyrynen

The terms 'ethnic conflict' and 'interdependence' are at the centre of the study of international relations (IR) and to an extent determine policy-making at national, regional and international levels. The former is seen to imply fragmentation, whereas the common sense understanding of the latter suggests integration. In the post-Cold War world conceptions such as 'security', 'nation-state' and 'territoriality' are more difficult to define than they used to be in the interdependent world of the 1970s. The tension between the co-existent discourses of fragmentation and interdependence can be interpreted to illustrate a move from modern to post-modern politics and space. The aim of this chapter is to examine the articulations of global politics and political space in these two discourses. The emphasis is on such issues as the role of the nation-state, the emergence of multiple actors in international relations and the rationality of conflict and conflict resolution.

Two discourses

Although interdependence may be essentially a contested, intrinsically controversial, concept in IR, there seems to be a sufficient general understanding of what interdependence means and what kind of phenomena it can be employed to explain. Importance is attached to global issues such as the fate of the planet, economic and ecological interdependence and mass communications. Interdependence theorists believe that the mosaic of interconnections between governments, inter-governmental organisations and individuals has been neglected by the realist school of IR. The obsession of the realist paradigm with the behaviour of unitary state actors has not allowed it to see the reality of web-like transnational relations. Even neo-functionalism, neo-liberalism and other contemporary theoretical strands trying to explain and codify interdependence and regional integration arrangements such as the European Union, persist in utilising the nation-state as the central actor-unit of reference.

Whether interdependence implies conflict or peace is a disputed view. It has been associated with both of them. It has been argued that increasing interdependence in international relations is necessary if major conflict is to be avoided. Shared interests facilitate conflict management at an early stage of conflict, and war is an unlikely phenomenon between interdependent actors, be those states or nations, in the international system. This was the primary rationale behind integration theories which underpinned the creation of the European Community in the aftermath of the Second World War. On the other hand, it has been claimed that conflict may arise out of the interdependence of interests, because actors tend to compete for the same resources in a tightly integrated system.

Coexistent with the agenda set by the interdependence theorists is the discourse on global politics which points towards the fragmentative tendencies in the post-Cold War world. Many states experience dissidence in the name of ethnic or cultural autonomy. The 'politics of soil' expressed by a variety of ethnic groups is founded on the image of small communities.[1] The politics of soil suggests that there is a need for a re-articulation of local identities. The criticism is levelled particularly at the existing nation-states as the limited and exclusive sources of collective identities. In other words, ethnic groups claim to seek alternative ways to organise community relations, and see the modern territorial state as a provider of hegemonic national identities.

Turkey's relations with its own Kurdish population and with the Kurdish population in neighbouring countries illustrate both articulations of global politics through which the meaning of, for example, state sovereignty, integration, fragmentation and co-operation are ultimately interpreted. Turkey has conducted military operations against the separatist Kurdistan Workers' Party for several decades, and some of the offensives have extended inside the territory of Iraq. Turkey has justified these operations by arguing that the Kurdistan Workers' Party is using northern Iraq as a springboard in its fight for a homeland in Turkey.[2] Four themes arise from the case.

Firstly, the actions of Turkey, which have been legitimised by the national security needs of the state, have had influence on another state, namely, Iraq. Secondly, the actions demonstrate that the Kurds (i.e. the Kurdistan Workers' Party) are perceived to possess the type of qualities and to be able to carry out the type of actions, which make them important political actors at least at the regional level. Thirdly, it is unlikely that Turkey alone could generate a lasting solution for the conflict, which arises from the demands of the Kurdish population in the region and from the demands of 'societal security',[3] which is about the survival of a social collective rather than of a state. In other words, there is a need for regional or international co-operation, which creates a framework capable of tackling issues related to societal security. Furthermore, any lasting solution of the Kurdish conflict will require co-operative actions, which involve states and other actors. This co-operation may, in turn, strengthen the interdependence of the actors included. It will strengthen interdependence of 'independent social actors, who wish to preserve their identity, but who are also structurally affected by one another's behaviour (whether they like it or not)'.[4]

Fourthly, the political mobilisation of Kurdish population in the area, which transcends the borders of three states (Turkey, Iraq and Iran) and consists of small enclaves within the territory of two more states (Armenia and Syria), can be seen to demonstrate the fragmentative tendencies of an international system understood to be composed of nation-states. The Kurdish political movements call into question the state-system based on territoriality and sovereignty by demanding ethnic re-territorialisation.

Models of interdependence

Four decades ago a feeling emerged that a world system composed of sovereign states cannot deal with the most pressing issues which humankind faces in a world of increasing transactions and interconnections. Such issues as nuclear annihilation, hunger, over-population and environmental degradation were proved not to respect state boundaries, and it was argued that individual states are, in fact, poorly equipped to deal with these problems, which require co-operation at a transnational level. Similarly, it was argued that sovereign states may not be capable of satisfying all fundamental human needs and, therefore, the contribution of non-state actors to the fields of human welfare should be welcomed. The Report of the Club of Rome, titled *Limits to Growth* (1972), reinforced the feeling of urgency by reaching some disturbing conclusions as a result of an attempt to use global modelling. The report declared that if present growth trends in world population, industrialisation, pollution, food production and resource depletion continue unchanged, the limits of growth on this planet would be reached sometime within the next one hundred years. The increased prominence of this urgency most notably led to the launching of regional and global policies on the environment, such as the European Community's environmental policy 'Towards Sustainability' and the United Nations' Environment Programme (UNEP).

At the same time, the study of international relations became witness to a renewed attention to interdependence in world politics. The first wave of inter-dependent scholars (for example, John Burton, Karl Deutsch, David Mittrany and James Rosenau) had paved the way some 20 years earlier for theorising on interdependence in IR. It was no longer taken as axiomatic that the starting-point for explaining any global phenomena must be the state. Robert Keohane's and Joseph Nye's *Trans-national Relations and World Politics* and *Power and Interdependence* set the renewed agenda for the examination of interdependence and transnationalism.[5]

Keohane and Nye referred by interdependence in general to 'situations characterised by reciprocal effects among countries or actors in different countries'.[6] The main characteristics of 'complex interdependence' are that (1) societies are connected by multiple channels of communication, (2) there is an absence of hierarchy among political issues and the distinction between domestic and foreign issues becomes blurred and (3) military force is not used by governments toward other governments when complex interdependence prevails. Interdependence refers also to sensitivity and vulnerability of the parties concerned. Sensitivity involves the speed and the extent to which changes in one country or actor entail costly changes in another country or actor. Vulnerability concerns the relative availability and cost of alternatives to having to accept the burdens imposed by the sensitivity of the second country.[7]

Keohane's and Nye's interdependence and transnational agenda pointed out most particularly the neglect of transnational actors in the study of IR, and delineated their role in different issue areas. The agenda challenged the notion that the state is the unitary and major actor in international relations. Their work did not deny the importance of states, but it encouraged research on non-state actors. In other words, neither supranational and transnational (e.g. the EU's Parliament and the Pan-African movement) nor non-state actors (e.g. the Palestine Liberation Organisation (PLO) and the Kosovars) can be ignored in the study of international relations. In a similar vein, Burton questioned the role of the state in world politics. For Burton, linkages and transactions shape the 'world society' within which the behaviour of individuals, groups, nations and states occur. According to Burton, 'the behaviour of one part of a society affects the behaviour of others'. In other words, 'increased interdependence, which is the consequence of increased specialisation, industrialisation and trade, leads to change everywhere when there is change anywhere'.[8] Burton, thereby, hinted in his conception of interdependence at the principle, which has recently come to symbolise an understanding of chaos theory: a flap of butterfly wings in the Amazon 'causes' a snowstorm in Europe; or an Al Qaeda terrorist attack on some of the most potent symbols of the United States' military and economic might (the Pentagon and the World Trade Center) embroils much of Europe in a war to topple the Al Qaeda-harbouring Taliban government of Afghanistan.

In Burton's 'cobweb model' of international relations the emphasis was put on transactions to the extent that the basic unit of analysis was considered to be a set of patterned interactions. Many important systems of transactions transcend state boundaries in ways that are not amenable to governmental control. These can be institutionally based, such as the EU's supranational authorities which, despite their inter-governmental nature of decision-making, ultimately override the power of the member states, or they can be of non-codified forms. A contemporary manifestation of the latter, with a hint of the former, on EU soil, is Catalonia. Its relations with Spanish authorities within the general context of Spain have at times been strained, yet it is now taking advantage of the facilitation of cross-border co-operation under the EU umbrella and the creation of euro-regions to forge closer – transnational – relations with Provence in the south of France, in preference to neighbouring Spanish provinces. Moreover, non-governmental organisations play an important global role, which often escapes the control of their member states. Given that the unit of analysis is a set of patterned interactions, the level of analysis (e.g. interstate, intra-state and individual) varies according to the issue area. Key elements in patterned interactions also vary. It is, thus, possible to consider Malays, Chinese or nationalists as key elements in some patterned interaction and the Israeli Air Force in another.[9]

In the world cobweb-type relations conflicts have often an internal origin, but they easily spill over on to a regional or international level.[10] Spill-over demonstrates that there is a degree of interdependence among different actors: it is characterised by a set of complex effects among countries and different actors. For example, the dissolution of Yugoslavia rapidly created a clear situation of interdependence in the Balkans. There were at least ten actors (e.g. Slovenia, Croatia, Serb Republic of Krajina, Yugoslavia, Kosovo, the former Yugoslav Republic of Macedonia, Bosnia-Herzegovina, Turkey, Bulgaria, Albania and Greece) which had capability in the conflict in the early 1990s, which were mutually interdependent and which had a 'say' in the attempt to find a lasting solution for the complex conflict system of the Balkans.[11]

Interdependence and political space

The observation that the state is not the sole actor in international transactions does not remove the state 'as a spatial container in which political community can occur'[12] from the centre of the interdependence discourse. The emergence of non-state and transnational actors does not change the political space created by states: the space within which the logic of the state system prevails. The border between what is 'inside' the state and what is 'outside' it may be blurred in the interdependence agenda, but it does not imply giving up territoriality and sovereignty as the organising principles of global politics. In other words, the assumption that there are 'transnational relations', that is 'contacts, coalitions and interactions across state boundaries that are not controlled by the central foreign policy organs of governments',[13] does not question the actual existence of the boundaries between 'inside' and 'outside'. These boundaries are the source of the entire constitutive logic of the modern state system.

The interdependence discourse gives politics a definition, which derives from a specific – and narrow – understanding of power. Politics and power are seen to be intimately linked, and refer, according to Keohane and Nye, to 'relationships in which at least one actor consciously employs resources, both material and symbolic, including the threat or exercise of punishment, to induce other actors to behave differently than they would otherwise behave'.[14] The view of power differs from that advocated by some political realists; the emphasis is not on measurable, for example military and economic, power. The focus is, rather, on a spectrum of resources employable in a variety of relationships. Resources form a continuum from ordinary arguments and persuasion through economic or diplomatic pressures to final use of military force.[15] In sum, the political space is maintained by power, and power lies in relationships and is manifest in the control of behaviour. Politics is ultimately reducible to behavioural aspects.

The logic behind the behaviour of actors in the world of interdependence derives from the assumed utilitarian nature of actors. The interdependent world is subject to the universalising principles of modern life, and modern life is characterised by utilitarian self-interest. Relations, marked by utilitarian interests, are characterised by tensions, conflict and struggle for power. Relations of strong asymmetry, and thus a net dependence, are a source of conflict. In the cases of symmetry, on the other hand, conflicts exist, for example, about the distribution of the involved costs and benefits. The example of the much debated EU's Common Foreign and Security Policy (CFSP) and its more-recent cobweb of endless bargaining, dispute and uneasy compromises over European foreign policy priorities versus US ones on the issue of the war on Iraq to name but one instance, or, on the purpose, remit and composition of the European Army, is an obvious case at hand. The state system as such is thought to be governed by 'Westphalian rationality',[16] and by logic that takes a particular state as the given guarantee for security. Security is interdependent due to the cross-cutting interests, transactions and communications. Moreover, security can be guaranteed by institutional arrangements between the states. A 'security community' can emerge, if there are integrative processes and mutual leaning resulting in minimal probability of war and positive expectations of peaceful management of change.[17] If conflict arises, it is assumed to be tractable. Given the suggested universalistic logic underlying the behaviour of different actors, conflicting interests are negotiable. Negotiations, based ultimately on a shared rationality, are a plausible means to solve conflicts. The interdependent world is, by and large, a 'zone of peace'.

Ethnic conflicts and interdependence agenda

The idea that the human being has a need for identity seems to be widely incorporated into the most recent academic discourse on ethnic conflicts. It is suggested that ethnic conflicts, evolving around the need for ethnic identity, have replaced interstate wars as the dominant form of contemporary political violence. However, the emphasis on ethnicity and ethnic identity raises the question of whether there is a tendency to 'over-ethnicise' conflicts and global politics. Are we just witnessing the latest of the periodic waves of ethnic nationalism, as Anthony Smith seems to argue?[18]

Particularly in the field of International Conflict Analysis and Peace Research, ethnicity is gaining more and more attention. For example, Ted Robert Gurr examines in his 'Minorities at Risk' project ethnic identities and ethno-political conflicts in which groups that define themselves using ethnic criteria make claims on behalf of their collective interests against the state, or against other political actors.[19] Gurr's interest in the topic is legitimised by the statistics, which show that, for example, between 1989 and 2000 there were 111 armed conflicts of which only seven were inter-state conflicts. Others were intra-state conflicts consisting of variety of actors, often ethno-political groups. Through the period more than 200 non-governmental actors were identified.[20]

Although it was possible to argue, in the optimist spirit of modernisation theory, that the growing integration and interdependence would break down peoples' parochial, local identities with ethnic kindred and replace them with loyalties to larger communities, as with the EU member states' national identities being gradually replaced by any kind of European – or EU – identity, a counter-argument has been posed. The increase in the amount of communal conflicts can be seen to be a trend indicating the growing importance of the politics of soil that began in the 1960s and continued through the 1990s. The discussion on ethnic conflicts follows to an extent the interdependence and transnationalist agenda by producing studies on ethnic or ethno-national groups as non-state actors. There are studies on, for example, the Palestinian national movement and the Kurds, which show the importance of ethnic groups in politics at the regional level. Helena Lindholm Schulz demonstrates how the institution building of the PLO reached such a level that it could be perceived as the foundation of state building.[21] Following Gurr's definition, the Palestinian national movement has became a politically significant group, because it has collectively suffered from systematic discriminatory treatment vis-à-vis other groups in Israel and it has been the 'focus of political mobilisation and action in defence or promotion of the group's self-defined interests'.[22] Similarly, the Kurds can be seen to form an ethno-political group, because they 'consider themselves to be a distinct ethnic group with a distinct language, common origins, a shared historical experience, a common shared culture and, to a certain extent, a common destiny and set of aspirations'.[23]

Ethno-political conflicts are seen to be difficult, but not impossible, to solve, for they often form regional conflict complexes, as the case of the Kurdish conflict demonstrates.[24] It is suggested that there is a need for regional and international co-operation in conflict resolution, which will further strengthen the ties of interdependence and, thereby, promote co-operation. Since nation-states are thought to be at the centre of the problems created by ethnic conflicts, they have difficulties in finding tools for ethno-political conflict resolution. Indeed, one can stretch the point to argue that international organisations, composed of nation-states and based still on the predominance of the state actor and despite their different ways of codifying co-operation as in the European Union and the United Nations, may manage to stem conflict but find it almost equally difficult to achieve actual ethno-political conflict resolution. In other words, it is argued that state-based and state-centric solutions are likely to be ineffective, because the Westphalian state system is an integral part of the whole problematique of intra-state conflicts.[25]

The disintegration of nation-states is thought to lead to regional security crises, due to the structures of interdependence, where the distinction between internal and external security can no longer be maintained. The Balkan crisis, triggered by the dissolution of Yugoslavia, is an example of the disintegration of the state that has spilled over causing a security crisis in the region. Given the spill-over tendency of domestic conflicts, regional or international engagements in conflict resolution are expected to be preferable. Similarly, various – almost therapeutic – means that provide psychological and communal remedies are assumed to be needed in order for peace-building to be successful. It is claimed that ethno-political conflicts consist of non-negotiable value issues, and that, therefore, non-traditional means of conflict resolution (e.g. track-two diplomacy) are better equipped to transform them than traditional negotiations which often just reflect the interest of the most powerful parties.[26]

In sum, there is an optimistic conviction that it is possible to solve ethnic conflicts. It may be difficult to create an universal theory of conflict resolution applicable to all cases, but there are several arrangements, which can be successfully employed in order to tackle ethnic issues. Ethnic conflict resolution may require the development of indigenous (local) means of conflict resolution, but this is not thought to imply that conflict resolution is based on irrationality or arationality.[27] The examples of the rivalry of Somali warlords, the genocide in Rwanda or Serbian war-leaders are not seen to challenge the belief in the possibility of rationally solving these conflicts. Neither are they seen to challenge the universal logic of interaction, which the interdependence models suggest.

Identity conflicts and fragmentation

The discourse on ethnic conflict is by no means homogeneous. An interesting starting-point for the study of fragmentation can be found in the critique of the nation-state embedded in the discourse. Just as the interdependence and transnationalism discourse examines critically the role of the state, and particularly the 'nation-state project', so does the most recent discussion on ethno-political fragmentation. The emphasis in the former discourse is on the transactions, which escape the state control, and in the latter on the disintegration of the 'nation-state project'. For example, Björn Hettne evokes a powerful metaphor of 'black holes' while discussing the international system. According to Hettne, several nation-states are becoming black holes. Black holes create 'zones of war' in which states disintegrate from within as a result of a challenge put forward by the dissident groups.[28]

The politics of soil of ethno-political groups does not found the identities of the group in the state. Rather, they derive their identities from the image of the existence of *Gemeinshaft* (community) which does coincide with the *Geschellshaft* (society) of the state. The question of identities and identity formation constitutes one of the core issues which the most recent studies on ethnic conflicts examine. The movement from modern to post-modern is expressed particularly through the notion of changing, floating and multi-dimensional identities. Identities are not thought to be given or fixed entities; they are seen to be formed according to the situation the social actor finds himself or herself.

The normative question of the exclusion of some identities from social arrangements is also asked in the discourse.

There seems to be an agreement that ethnic identity does not derive from such 'objective' criteria as language, religion, race, culture, customs and traditions, territory and a common history. Ethnic identity is not a category which is objectively recognisable. Rather, ethnic groups are, as Frederic Barth argues, categories of ascription and identification by the actors themselves, and they organise interaction between people.[29] In other words, ethnic groups are inter-subjectively 'imagined communities' which are constructed and invented; there is nothing fixed or given about them.[30] Ethnic identity implies, in this view, a series of roles a person draws from his or her 'identity budget' according to the situations and interactions in the social world.

Identities may be multi-dimensional, but through their politicisation they can come firmly anchored to, for example, nationalist symbols. An ethnic group may drive for a 'nation-state project', which challenges an existing state. It may claim for the re-territorialisation of the existing territorial state. There are also ethnic groups which do not possess nationalistic identity. However, in both cases, a political space is created where local loyalties, which are tied to the particular ethnie (as a self-ascribed category), are prioritised over loyalty to the state. Pierre Hassner calls the phenomena a return to the Middle Ages when, in contrast to the modern nation-state and its monopoly of violence, order was based on a variety of actors, of authorities, territorial or not territorial, of loyalties and rivalries.[31] Although the Christian Commonwealth of Europe formed with regional institutional arrangements, such as the Hanseatic League, overarching frameworks of actors, a variety of actors capable of violence existed in the Middle Ages. Hassner's argument can be seen to point towards the fragmentation of reason, which was thought to be universal in the Westphalian state system. The logic of means–ends rationality does not penetrate all spaces in the neo-medieval world.

Where does power lie in the neo-medieval world and what does politics look like in fragmented spaces? There is politics in every encounter between human beings, and politics always indicates power. Power springs up between human beings when they act together. In other words, power is what keeps the public realm in existence. It is always a power potential, not an unchangeable, measurable, reliable entity like force or strength. Neither is power totally dependent on material factors nor the number of means. Violence, on the other hand, can destroy power, but never become a substitute for it, as Hanna Arendt argues.[32] If power unites men, violence does the opposite. Violent behaviour derives from an extreme exclusion of a dehumanised 'Other', and indicates the end of politics. The 'zone of war' in the neo-medieval world is characterised by complex formations of conflicts; some violent, some not. Conflict can be seen to be endemic in human condition, and it can even be seen to satisfy some fundamental existential human needs. In fragmented spaces, where local loyalties are emphasised, conflict resolution cannot derive from a rationality, which transcends local loyalties and rivalries. Since there is no universal logic and reason governing human relations, some violent conflicts remain intractable. They remain intractable at least by the means suggested in Western thinking, which is founded upon Westphalian – territorially oriented and state-centred – solutions.

Security cannot be guaranteed solely by institutional means in the fragmented world. The concept of societal security is suggested to grasp the security of identity groups, as argued earlier. The focus is, then, on the security which arises from threats perceived by societies in identity terms. As Ole Waever legitimises the use of the concept, 'societal security is relevant in itself and not only as an element of state security, because communities (that do not have a state) are also significant political realities, and their reactions to threats against their identity will be politically significant'.[33] State security has sovereignty as its ultimate criterion, whereas societal security is about identity, about the survival and politics of an identity group. In many cases there is a mutual relationship between societal and national security, as with Greek Cypriots and the Republic of Cyprus. Especially when an identity group – defined for example by an assumed shared ethnic origin – is mobilised in the name of the nation-state project, the insecurity of the nation (or nations) increases the insecurity of the state.

In sum, the issue of the political community is at the core of the discourse on fragmentation. If several nation-states are seen to be on the verge of collapsing into black holes, the question of the 'sovereign state as a problematic form of political community' – to use Andrew Linklater's phrase – needs to be asked.[34] It is argued that the principle of state sovereignty codifies a historically specific answer to historically specific questions about political community. The answer is articulated in the context of an attempt to fix a political community within spatial categories.[35]

Concluding remarks

The discourses of interdependence and fragmentation introduced in this chapter present simplified versions of complex arguments, but they do underline some of the themes, which are prominent in the current study of IR and which impact on policy-making at national, regional and international levels. Interdependence theorists place the focus on transactions and actors, which transcend state boundaries and, thereby, produce the loosening of the distinction between domestic and foreign issues. The fragmentation agenda, on the other hand, sets the question of domestic and foreign realms in terms of identities. The discourse questions the sustainability of the modern Westphalian nation-state projects. It is argued that from the point of view of an identity group (for example, ethnic group) the question about domestic and foreign environment does not arise in terms of territoriality and sovereignty. Rather, the politics of soil of ethno-political groups emerges from parochial ties, which in

many cases transcend state boundaries. The political space created by the interdependence agenda is governed by an universalistic logic and reason. Modern
life penetrating all relationships is thought to be characterised by a means–ends
rationality. In the interdependent world, the actors behave in order to maximise
interests. For the fragmentation agenda, such an universalistic reason does not
exist. In the neo-medieval world reason has disintegrated, and the political space
is founded also on parochial loyalties and rivalries.

The discourse on fragmentation as expressed in the study of ethnic conflicts
is not coherent: it re-produces the interdependence agenda and, at the same
time, questions its foundations. Nor is the discourse of interdependence coherent. Some accounts of interdependence start with the analysis of the
internationalisation of production, and speak of the transformation of the state
under specific historic conditions. States appear as historically determinate and
variable forms of political communities. In this form, the discourse comes close
to the arguments presented in the fragmentation discourse. Nation-states are
seen to be challenged from both fronts: ethno-national movements challenge
them from within and transnational transactions from outside.

Notes

1 P. Hassner, 'Beyond nationalism and internationalism: ethnicity and world order',
   Survival, 35: 2 (1993), 49.
2 For a major offensive see, e.g., *International Herald Tribune*, 8–9, 11, 13 and 18 April,
   1995.
3 On security see, e.g., O. Waever, B. Buzan, M. Kelstrup and P. Lemaitre, *Identity,
   Migration and the New Security Agenda in Europe* (London: Frances Pinter, 1993). B.
   Buzan, O. Waever and J. de Wilde, *Security: A New Framework for Analysis* (London:
   Lynne Rienner Publishers, 1998). B. McSweeney, *Security, Identity and Interests: A
   Sociology of International Relations* (Cambridge: Cambridge University Press, 1999).
4 J. de Wilde, *Saved from Oblivion: Interdependence Theory in the First Half of the 20th
   Century: A Study on the Causality between War and Complex Interdependence*
   (Aldershot, Brookfield USA, Hong Kong, Singapore, Sydney: Dartmouth, 1991),
   p. 17.
5 R. Keohane and R. Nye Jr (eds), *Trans-national Relations and World Politics*
   (Cambridge, MA: and London: Harvard University Press, 1971); R. Keohane and R.
   Nye Jr, *Power and Interdependence: World Politics in Transition* (Boston, MA: Little
   Brown, 1977). See also R. Mansbach, Y. Ferguson and D. Lampert, *The Web of World
   Politics: Nonstate Actors in the Global System* (Englewood Cliffs, NJ: Prentice-Hall,
   1976). D. Singer, 'The global system and its sub-system', in J. Rosenau (ed.), *Linkage
   Politics: Essays on the Convergence of National and International System* (New York:
   Free Press, 1969), pp. 21–43.
6 Keohane and Nye *Power and Interdependence*, p. 8.
7 Keohane and Nye, Jr., *Power and Interdependence*, pp. 11–25.
8 J. Burton, *World Society* (Cambridge: Cambridge University Press, 1972), pp. 4–5.
9 Burton, *World Society*, pp. 35–51. For summaries of the model see C. R. Mitchell,
   'World society as cobweb', in M. Banks (ed.), *Conflict in World Society* (Brighton:

Wheatsheaf, 1984), pp. 59–77. W. Olson and A. J. R. Groom, *International Relations Then and Now: Origins and Trends in Interpretation* (London: HarperCollins Academic, 1991), pp. 204–10.

10 Burton, *World Society*, p. 142.

11 For the actors and their interests see H. Wiberg, 'Divided states and divided nations as a security problem – the case of Yugoslavia', Working Papers 14/1992, Centre for Peace and Conflict Research, Copenhagen, 1992, pp. 16–25.

12 J. B. R. Walker, 'Sovereignty, identity, community: reflections on the horizons of contemporary political practice', in R. B. J. Walker and S. Mendlowitz (eds), *Contending Sovereignties, Redefining Political Community* (Boulder, CO and London: Lynne Rienner Publishers, 1990), p. 176.

13 Keohane and Nye (eds), *Trans-national Relations*, p. xi.

14 *Ibid.*, p. xxiv.

15 See also Burton, *World Society*, pp. 58–9 and 70.

16 B. Hettne, 'Regional conflict management: an analytical framework', a paper prepared for the Nordic–Baltic Peace Conference, Lohusalu, Estonia, 28 June–2 July 1995, p. 1.

17 For a recent debate on security community see 'Symposium on Security Community', *Co-operation and Conflict* 35: 3 (2000), 288–329. The debate is inspired by E. Adler's and M. Barnett's book *Security Communities* (Cambridge: Cambridge University Press, 1998).

18 A. Smith, *National Identity* (Reno, Las Vegas, NY and London: University of Nevada Press, 1991).

19 T. Gurr, *Minorities at Risk: A Global View of Ethnopolitical Conflicts* (Washington, DC, United States Institute of Peace Press, 1993). Also T. Gurr, 'Peoples against states: ethnopolitical conflict and the changing world system', *International Studies Quarterly*, 38: 3 (1994), 347–77. T. Gurr, 'Ethnic warfare on wane', *Foreign Affairs*, 79: 3 (2000), 52–64. T. Gurr *et al.* 'Minorities at risk', database, www.bsos.umd.edu/cidcm/mar/.

20 P. Wallensteen and M. Sollenberg, 'States in armed conflict, 1989–2000', Research Report no. 60, Department of Peace and Conflict Research, Uppsala University, 2001, pp. 7–39.

21 H. Lindholm Schulz, *The Reconstruction of Palestinian Nationalism: Between Revolution and Statehood* (Manchester: Manchester University Press, 1999).

22 Gurr, 'Peoples against states', p. 349.

23 O. Sheikhmous, 'The Kurdish question in regional politics: possible peaceful solutions', in K. Rupesinghe (ed.), *Internal Conflict and Governance* (Houndmills and London: Macmillan Press, 1992), p. 132.

24 Wallensteen and Sollenberg, 'States in armed conflict', p. 11. They refer to Barry Buzan's conceptualisation of conflict complex.

25 T. Väyrynen, 'On the border of disorder: ethnopolitical identification and modern territorial state', in T. Seppä and J. Holma (eds), *Knowledge, Power and World Politics, Scripta in honorem professoris Osmo Apunen sexagesimum annum completins* (Tampere: Tampere University, Department of Politics and International Relations, 1998), pp. 449–64.

26 See, e.g., K. Rupesinghe, 'Theories of conflict resolution and protracted ethnic conflict', PRIO Report no. 1/1988, PRIO, Oslo, 1988. R. Väyrynen, *Towards a Theory of Ethnic Conflicts and their Resolution* (Notre Dame, IN: The Joan B. Kroch Institute

for International Peace Studies, 1994). R. Väyrynen and J. Leatherman, 'Conflict theory and conflict resolution, directions for collaborative research', *Co-operation and Conflict*, 30: 1 (1995), 53–82.

27 For indigenous conflict resolution see, e.g., K. Avruch, B. Black and J. Scimecca (eds), *Conflict Resolution: Cross-cultural Perspectives* (New York, Westport, CT and London: Greenwood Press, 1991). P. Wehr and P. Lederach, 'Mediating conflict in Central America', in J. Bercovitch (ed.), *Resolving International Conflicts, The Theory and Practice of Mediation* (Boulder, CO and London: Lynne Rienner Publishers, 1996), pp. 55–74.

28 B. Hettne, 'The dynamics of ethnic conflict', in H. Lindholm (ed.), *Ethnicity and Nationalism, Formation of Identity and Dynamics of Conflict in the 1990s* (Göteborg: Nordnes, 1993), pp. 68–89. Hettne, 'Regional conflict', p. 4.

29 F. Barth, 'Introduction', in *Ethnic Groups and Boundaries: The Social Organisation of Culture Differences* (Oslo, Bergen, Tromso: Universitetsforslaget, 1969), pp. 9–38.

30 On 'imagined communities' and nationalism see B. Anderson, *Imagined Communities: Reflections on the Origins and Spread of Nationalism* (London: Verso, 1983).

31 Hassner, 'Beyond nationalism', p. 53.

32 H. Arendt, *The Human Condition* (New York: Doubleday Anchor, 1958), pp. 178–84.

33 Waever *et al.*, *Identity, Migration*, p. 27.

34 A. Linklater, 'Dialogue, dialectic and emancipation in international relations at the end of the post-war age', *Millennium: Journal of International Studies*, 23: 1 (1994), 129.

35 Walker, 'Sovereignty, identity, community', p. 173.

[handwritten annotation:] there have been a variety of declarations and treaties such as human rights & arms defense but no power to back it up.

2

The Kosovo intervention and European security: NATO's pyrrhic victory

James H. Wyllie

By 1990 the North Atlantic Treaty Organisation (NATO) had won the Cold War. A cohesive, robust deterrent posture defeated the clear danger posed by the Soviet bloc to the national security of all the alliance members. Reluctant to abandon an international organisation which had served its members so well, the major Western powers sought a new justification and role for NATO in the post-Cold War world. Over the last decade the policy of twin enlargement – members and mission – has transformed the alliance from the deterrence-based, defensive organisation, which its members previously valued, and with which public opinion largely felt comfortable, into an expansive organisation based on military compellence in pursuit of political objectives beyond its own borders.

The summer of 1999 saw the new NATO win its first military campaign, but in the process seriously erode its reputation as a law-abiding, non-offensive, efficacious military alliance in permanent occupation of the moral high ground. NATO's Kosovo intervention exacerbated extant strains in the European security regime, not least in US–West European defence relations and NATO–Russian relations, and mired NATO in a role for which it was neither designed nor equipped and which has little future beyond costly, long-term, coercive crisis containment in south-east Europe. The security of the rest of Europe and contiguous regions has been poorly served by NATO's Balkan venture.

In November 1990 the Charter of Paris for a New Europe declared the Cold War to be over.[1] The European security regime which had evolved over the previous 45 years, partly by design and partly by default, became obsolete. Since then a new European security regime has emerged, but there is one clear constant between the old and the new – the dominant role played by NATO. Between 1949 and 1990 NATO was the bedrock of the Western half of the framework of European security which emerged during the Cold War. NATO was the primary security institution in the West. Under its security umbrella and patronage other, secondary security institutions emerged – the West European Union (WEU), the Conference on Security and Co-operation in Europe (CSCE) and, insofar as it reinforced close, integrative relations between old West European enemies, the European Community (EC) – but none had NATO's influence, nor could they deliver the security dividend produced by NATO's military strength.

Since 1990 NATO has been the dominant security institution across Europe as never before, and the cornerstone of the continent's security framework. Now it straddles the Euro-Atlantic region, from Canada to Poland. It has 19 members, is on the verge of acquiring more, and its forces are deployed out-of-area in the Balkans. WEU (most of whose functions have been assumed by the EU during 2001–2), the Organisation for Security and Co-operation in Europe (OSCE), replacing CSCE in 1994, and the European Union (EU) are clearly secondary in the European security business.[2] However, NATO in the new century is very different from NATO in 1990. In the early 1990s, for a variety of reasons, most NATO members wished the Alliance to remain the viable, leading European security institution. The United States perceives NATO as a vital link to Europe. It is the sole international organisation which contains only the North American states and most West European states. This organisation is an excellent platform for US influence throughout the European continent, and the NATO area is contiguous with the Middle East – a region of profound strategic importance for the United States. It is also hoped that NATO will provide partners for the US role in global security. So far, this is a major source of disappointment in Washington as only the United Kingdom appears to be willing to take on this role with any seriousness of purpose. However, as the United States demonstrated in the incident of Franco-German-Belgian opposition to the war on Iraq in 2003, that if it cannot get its way through NATO, it is prepared to bypass it, if the need arises, in other words if other top European allies present opposition and frustrate the channeling of US interests through the organisation.

For the United Kingdom, NATO is a vehicle for, and manifestation of, the Anglo-American Special Relationship. NATO is also valued as a co-operative international organisation, not integrative. As such, whatever the British political rhetoric of the moment, NATO provides a valuable obstacle to a purely European defence organisation which, by its very nature, would require to be much more integrative than co-operative. For decades the national security culture of Britain has been strongly Atlanticist. It will remain so for some time to come. Current official support for the concept of an EU defence force is predicated upon the new entity being co-operative, not integrative, and not posing any challenge to NATO's primacy in European security.[3] In addition, NATO is valuable to London because it is the UK's most favoured international organisation. In NATO Britain is at least the second most important power, and in terms of 'NATO Europe' Britain is the most important power. In other international organisations, for example the United Nations Security Council or the European Union, Britain is not number two but is perhaps number four, five or even six. For Germany NATO provides reassurance to its neighbours, not least Poland, Hungary and the Czech Republic which joined NATO in 1999. NATO also inhibits any re-nationalisation of European defence policies, which would not be in the new Germany's political or strategic interests, and it allows effective European continental defence at a relatively low price. As a proportion of GDP, Germany's defence budget is currently less than half that of the United States, and between 2000 and 2004 there will be defence cuts every year.[4] Without the security provision provided by NATO it is unlikely that Germany would contemplate such a low defence budget, and without the NATO structure there would be the possibility that the inherent strength of unified Germany could alarm many of its neighbours. Hence, as NATO serves the particular interests of many members it was deemed worthwhile that NATO re-invent itself.

Enlargement – in two modes – was the mechanism pursued to reinvigorate and sustain NATO as a viable European security institution. The first mode was enlargement of mission. The 1991 Rome NATO summit gave early warning of the Alliance's intentions. NATO was tasked with 'the establishment of a just and peaceful order in Europe'.[5] There were clear signals that NATO was looking for an out-of-area role. The use of NATO airpower in Bosnia four years later, in 1995, and the subsequent deployment of the NATO Implementation Force (IFOR) in 1996, under the remit of the Dayton Accords, illustrated that NATO was fully embarked on a mission beyond collective defence of its own territory. This mission reached its apogee, or nadir, with the Kosovo intervention of 1999. This action was ratified by NATO Council during the campaign in the Alliance's 'new strategic concept' at the April 1999 Washington NATO summit. 'To engage actively in crisis management' and to undertake 'active crisis response' in 'non-Article 5' situations, in the 'Euro-Atlantic area' was clearly seen as NATO's primary, core role – and raison d'être – in the new century.[6]

The second mode has been the enlargement in numbers. Orthodox alliance theory says that successful alliances are those that continue only as long as the prime objective remains, that sustain a prime objective common to all members, that stay geographically compact and that limit numbers to those who really need to be members.[7] NATO, in the 1990s, has broken all those inter-related rules, not least the final rule. After initial prevarication, NATO decided to enlarge. At the Brussels summit of January 1994 President Clinton decided, largely for domestic political reasons, that enlargement was a matter of when, not if.[8] The cumbersome 16-member decision-making machinery was to be expanded; and the notion of 'strategic partnership' with Russia – albeit a very uneven partnership – was to be abandoned in favour of a NATO security imperium over East Europe. In 1997 NATO decided to increase to 19 members in 1999; and in 2002 seven more countries, Bulgaria, Estonia, Latvia, Lithuania, Romania, Slovakia and Slovenia, were invited to accession talks. It will also be very difficult for NATO in the next few years to deny membership to long-standing European democracies such as Finland, Sweden, Austria and perhaps even Ireland, if such countries should decide to apply for full membership of the Alliance. That could easily take NATO to 25 or 30 members, and render decision-making even more problematical. The 1997 NATO–Russia Founding Act has proved ineffective in soothing Moscow's feelings of betrayal, even though NATO enlargement makes the Alliance much more like the ponderous collective security organisation Moscow would like NATO to be, rather than the relatively sharper, more alert, single-minded collective defence organisation NATO used to be.[9] Collective security, as an alternative to military alliance (collective defence) posits the notion that each state shares responsibility for each other state's security. All are supposed to act together against any aggressive behaviour by any other members. The collective interest ought to be protected against the narrow self-interests of one. But in practice such a worthy concept is usually found to be wanting. Not all states will agree on what constitutes aggression, or who is the culpable aggressor. How, where and when action should be taken and who should bear the cost can reduce decisions to that which is least unacceptable to the members, and put cohesion and goodwill under severe strain.[10] However, politics is not logic and, even though NATO enlargement does move the Alliance closer towards a collective security organisation, there is a sense of betrayal running across the whole spectrum of Russian politics over the NATO policy to enlarge. There is a conviction in Moscow that part of the deal ending the Cold War was that a peaceful withdrawal of Soviet armies from East Europe would not lead to formal NATO enlargement to incorporate former Warsaw pact members, except the former East Germany as an integral part of the unified Germany.

At the end of the first post-Cold War decade the bedrock of European security remains NATO – a multilateral military alliance of good pedigree which, in order to save itself, is slowly committing suicide.[11] It has assumed a mission for which it was never designed, is ill-equipped and which it spent all of the Cold War trying to avoid. This is a mission which has created expectations that NATO can meet its rhetoric of the past decade, and bring peace and harmony throughout the ill-defined Euro-Atlantic area and its periphery. Decision-making during the Cold War was difficult enough with 12, 15 and then 16 members, even in the face of the clear and present danger which was the Soviet threat. Differences over nuclear strategy, arms control, burden-sharing and out-of-area responsibilities, periodically posed major threats to the political cohesion of the Alliance between 1949 and 1990. Now, with 19 members and rising, all in the Alliance for different reasons, and a permanent Russian mission in NATO headquarters as a consequence of the 1997 Founding Act, a recipe for virtual decision-making paralysis has been created. The Kosovo operation has painfully demonstrated that NATO, with a new mission and bloated numbers, ill-serves European security.

Strategic and military ramifications

There are campaigns and there are wars. Clearly NATO won the 1999 March–June military campaign in the Balkans. Air power, largely alone but with the growing prospect of some kind of land war, obliged the Serbs to abandon their province of Kosovo in June 1999. The June armistice was met within NATO by a sense of distinct relief and only limited celebration. There was an inner knowledge that NATO's military campaign was not textbook, and but for Russian diplomatic intervention NATO would have had to mount a land campaign which would have been politically very difficult to hold together.[12] There was also a sense that this was a war NATO was ill-advised to embark upon, and given the chance to start all over again it would not go down that route. In many official quarters, there is the discreet realisation that NATO won the military campaign but, at best, achieved only a pyrrhic victory in the war. NATO's problems escalated the day bombing began. On 24 March NATO's strategic doctrine was practically transformed from one derived from deterrence to one based on compellence. Deterrence is about preventing a prospective enemy from beginning an attack against you or close allies. Compellence is about changing or undoing a policy under way and inducing a new policy. Deterrence may be described as 'a threat made passively to persuade the other to remain passive', while compellence is a threat 'made actively to stop the other being active'.[13] Effective military power is demonstrated best by influence, not coercion. The prospect of engagement ought to persuade the enemy to amend behaviour. For over 40 years that is how deterrence worked for NATO. The prospect of denial of victory and devastating punishment was enough to inhibit any attack from the Soviet bloc against NATO territory. The track record of NATO compellence is much less illustrious. Against Yugoslavia coercion had to be used; the threat was not enough. And to compound the failure of military power, the coercion that was utilised was the lowest common denominator that could hold the Alliance together – bombing from 15,000 feet and taking every precaution to avoid NATO casualties while accepting the increased risk of Serb and Kosovan non-combatant casualties on the ground.[14] Apparently, the Kosovars required a Western crusade to save them from a perceived humanitarian disaster of Biblical proportions, but only if no NATO casualties were suffered in the process. Consequently a small state of eight million people with, at best, a 'second world' army, was seen to withstand history's most powerful alliance for over 70 days. Yugoslavia did not capitulate in three or four days, but persevered for over ten weeks. Rather than reinforcing NATO's strategic credibility, the war was a severe embarrassment to NATO's reputation. It was as if a world heavyweight boxing champion took 15 rounds to defeat, narrowly on points, an unknown lightweight.

Another unfortunate ramification of the campaign is that, in the eyes of the world, NATO appeared to make strategic bombing again respectable. During the campaign NATO deliberately attacked many targets which only in the broadest terms could be defined as military.[15] As Yugoslavia's resistance persisted in the weeks following the outbreak of the conflict, NATO began to target bridges, factories and even television stations inside Serbia in an effort to bring a Serb withdrawal from Kosovo. As much care as possible was taken by

NATO to avoid collateral damage, but inevitably there were many non-combatant casualties and much of Yugoslavia's industrial and transport infrastructure
was severely damaged. Within three weeks of the cessation of NATO bombing
of Yugoslavia in June 1999, Israel, for the first time in ten years, directly bombed
Beirut. This was in response to attacks by Hezbollah, the Islamic terrorist group
opposing Israel's presence in the narrow security zone in south Lebanon, against
Israeli soldiers in the zone. The response of Washington, London and Paris to
the Israeli use of high altitude bombing as a punishment for the inability of the
Lebanese government to control Hezbollah was extremely muted. In February
2000 Israel again attacked Beirut in an effort to persuade the Lebanese government to exert stronger control over Hezbollah. Amongst other things, Lebanese
power stations were on the target list. Prime Minister Barak announced a policy
of Israeli military withdrawal from the security zone in south Lebanon in July
2000. He made it clear that any attack from south Lebanon against towns in
north Israel would be met by deploying strategic air power against targets within
Lebanon. Prime Minister Sharon, the victor in the elections of 2001 and 2003,
concurs with this policy. Clearly Israel thinks it is again respectable to use strategic air power in a national security role, rather than risking forces on the
ground.[16] During the winter of 1999–2000 Russia waged a brutal campaign in
Chechyna against the rebels that were refusing to accept Moscow's sovereignty
over the territory. In contrast to the earlier war in 1994–96, the Russian military
decided to use as much firepower as they possibly could from as safe a distance
as possible before deploying ground forces. The Russian campaign was
extremely harsh, yet the Western powers that had been so critical of the earlier
Russian campaign in Chechnya were constrained in their condemnation of the
tactics employed by the Russians, no doubt because of the resemblance to the
tactics employed by NATO in the Balkans a few months earlier and the Russian
readiness to denounce NATO criticism as rank hypocrisy.[17] By 2002, the time of
the US–UK bombings of Afghanistan to oust the Taliban regime, the practice,
albeit selective, was beginning to become commonplace.

   Throughout the 1990s one of NATO's self-declared objectives was to inhibit
the proliferation of weapons of mass destruction.[18] If one compares the West's
treatment of Yugoslavia with the relative 'kid-glove' treatment of, for instance,
North Korea, China and more recently Russia, then it could suggest that to
avoid an attack, or indeed very heavy pressure, from the West, potential target
states should acquire weapons of mass destruction. A lesson from the Yugoslav
conflict of 1999 for smaller powers which do not conform to Western values,
but which seek some kind of level playing field in world affairs, is that if you do
not have weapons of mass destruction then you are liable to suffer an attack
from the Western powers. There is a strong argument that if Yugoslavia had
possessed a secure and credible nuclear deterrent then NATO would not have
taken the risk of actually bombing Belgrade. One unforeseen consequence of the
NATO intervention of 1999 has been to sustain the arguments of those who
suggest that one way to stem the tide of Western imperialism is to acquire

weapons of mass destruction. Another consequence of the NATO intervention has been a deepening of Russian and Chinese cynicism towards NATO, and US, long-term strategic policies. The distrust and the profound sense of betrayal produced by NATO enlargement has been compounded by the military intervention in the Balkans. Since 1997, in response to NATO enlargement and the assumption of a power-projection strategy, Russia and China have agreed upon a degree of strategic co-operation, with the clear, primary purpose of checking and balancing US influence across the globe.[19] There is the common determination that the USA should not be allowed to think it can pursue its policies wherever it wants and whenever it wishes without encountering any opposition, particularly in the regions contiguous to Russia and China. Despite the terrorist attacks on the US in 2001 temporarily watering down this determination, it was quickly reaffirmed when, after the inconclusive results and dubious legitimacy of the Afghanistan campaign, the US and the UK embarked on an even more bizarre campaign against Iraq, which did not only irritate Russia and China, but also core European allies such as Germany and France. The Middle East is a sensitive region, and a major diplomatic offensive by Russia has been under way since the mid 1990s.[20] Russia has become a major arms supplier to Iran, and has been reviving relations with old Soviet client states such as Libya, Syria and Iraq. There is a clear realisation in Moscow that Russia cannot return to the level of influence and power in the Middle East that the Soviet Union enjoyed in the 1960s, the 1970s and into the 1980s. However, there is scope for a revival of some level of Russian influence within the region, if only as a potential alternative to the overweening influence that Washington exerts throughout the Middle East. Local states who will not readily conform to the US blueprint for the region at least see in Moscow some kind of non-ideological, competitive power centre, and Moscow, given its disappointments in East Europe, is prepared to exploit that potential discontent. The Kosovo intervention has encouraged those in Moscow, across Russian political life, who wish to seek foreign policy compensation for the loss of influence within Europe in other strategically important parts of the world.[21]

A major strategic repercussion of the Kosovo intervention, not in NATO's best interest, has been the reaction of some of the leading EU states to the whole operation. Humiliated over the low level of military capabilities that could be devoted by NATO Europe to the Kosovo intervention, the EU has decided to move the prospect of some kind of European defence force with power projection capabilities up the EU political agenda. Prior to Kosovo the intention was to look seriously at a common European defence policy after other major issues such as the bedding down of the Euro, the reform of EU finances, enlargement to the East and reform of agricultural policies had been settled.[22] However, given the experience in the Balkans in 1999, the EU has moved the common defence question to the top of the agenda. At the Helsinki EU summit of December 1999 it was decided that by 2003 an EU military force 60,000 strong, deployable within 60 days and sustainable for one year, should be developed.[23] At the core

of this force would be an Anglo-French military partnership, emanating from
the 1998 St Malo Agreement and subsequent developments.[24] However, such an
arrangement would, if implemented, pose a major threat to NATO's primacy in
European security, and has exacerbated some of the anxieties and tensions
about US–West European security relations ever-present in the US Congress
and parts of the national security establishment in Washington. But, an even
greater worry is that such ambitious objectives are so unlikely to be met that
confusion and a loss of morale amongst NATO Europe is a probable outcome.
Britain and France have different images of what this force should be like.
Britain, following tradition, supports the notion of a co-operative force, which
would work within the NATO framework. The French ambition is to have a
much more integrative force, with a European general staff, which would parallel NATO but be autonomous of the Alliance. In addition to a potentially
damaging political competition between NATO and a new EU defence entity,
and strategic dispute between Britain and France over the nature of this entity,
there is the big question of whether the entity is operationally and financially
viable at all over the next few years.[25] There is a major question mark over the
funding of such a force. Defence budgets across NATO Europe are under
considerable pressure, and countries such as Germany and Spain are undertak-
ing a long-term programme of real defence cuts. Many European countries may
support the rhetoric of a separate European defence entity, but actually funding
it would be deeply problematic. To procure the long-range transport, communications capabilities, intelligence facilities and all the integrated military
equipment required for a coalition force will be so expensive that one can anticipate bitter political debates within the major NATO European states.

Moral, legal and political repercussions

In Kosovo, NATO lost the moral and legal high ground it had enjoyed since
1949. For over 40 years NATO had been a deterrent, defensive alliance. NATO
supported the status quo; it was peace-loving; it would never attack anyone
unless it was attacked first. It was not imperialistic; its purpose was not to force
its values on anyone else. NATO's own public, and the world at large, could feel
comfortable with NATO. Given its size and power, such a reputation was
deemed essential, both for internal alliance cohesion and wider, international
calm. Yugoslavia was not a strategic threat to NATO; it had not attacked any
NATO member. Yet, NATO attacked Yugoslavia; not just its military capabilities but also its capital city, its bridges, its factories and its television stations.
Throughout the campaign in 1999, no NATO country was ever attacked by
Yugoslavia. NATO's moral high ground has been abandoned. 'Foreign policy as
social work' carries such paradoxical costs and consequences.[26]

    When in doubt over the moral quality of military action, many look to inter-
national law for guidance. International law can be disputatious, as it is based
upon a flexible evolutionary mix of custom and statute. While custom is always

in the process of some kind of change, presently it remains the legal convention that sovereignty is sacrosanct, and that one state should not interfere in the affairs of another state unless invited.[27] That custom was broken and statutory international law was also broken. Article 2(4) of the UN Charter was clearly broken. This Article prohibits 'the threat or use of force against the territorial integrity or political independence of any state'. There are two exceptions. Under Article 51 individual or collective self defence allows intervention in another state's sovereignty when the interventionary state is the victim of aggression. Under Chapter 7, Article 39, intervention is allowed when the Security Council decides that there is a threat to the peace, breach of the peace, or act of aggression. However, even if the Security Council does invoke Article 39 it does not automatically trigger military action. Under Article 42 the UN Security Council has to authorise coercive measures explicitly. Article 2(4) was clearly broken; Article 51 did not apply as Yugoslavia had not attacked any other states; Articles 39 and 42 were not invoked. Since 1945 the UN Charter has been accepted as the fundamental legal basis for international order. The Western democracies have frequently extolled it as such, for instance in the Gulf conflict of 1990–91. NATO may claim high moral and political justification, and appeal to secondary international conventions, such as the 1948 Genocide Convention and the 1949 European Convention on Human Rights, but the 'current international legality of the use of force is determined by the UN Security Council ...'.[28] Even if one wishes to consider secondary conventions or legislation as legal justification for the attack on Yugoslavia, there are problems. In 1986 the International Court of Justice in the case of Nicaragua versus the US affirmed the 1970 UN General Assembly Resolution 2625 that assistance to either party in a civil war is prohibited.

For decades the NATO treaty has been acclaimed as a defensive treaty, becoming operational only when NATO is attacked. While there is no clause explicitly preventing NATO, if it collectively chooses, from attacking another country, that has not been the spirit or the custom of the NATO treaty until now. Indeed, one could even venture that the letter of the NATO treaty prevents such an attack as that on Yugoslavia in 1999. In the Preamble and Article 1 of the NATO treaty, the Alliance pledges itself to the 'principles and purposes' of the UN Charter. In addition, Article 7 of the NATO treaty recognises that it is the primary purpose of the UN Security Council to maintain international peace and security.[29] UN Security Council Resolutions 1199 and 1203 of September and October 1998 did acknowledge a NATO interest in Kosovo, but did not authorise force. However, these resolutions made it clear that NATO would need to return to the UN Security Council for the authorisation of any use of force. Indeed, this was the basis on which Russia and China supported these resolutions. The broad consensus of the international law community is that NATO broke international law, which makes it difficult for NATO to invoke international law to its assistance in the future as it used to do, so effectively, for much of the previous 40 years.

In February and March 1999, before the NATO attack on Yugoslavia, efforts had been made to come to an agreement with Belgrade over the future of Kosovo. The conditions that NATO wished to impose on Belgrade have become known as the Rambouillet terms. These were named after the location, outside Paris, of the conference between the Yugoslav government, NATO and representatives of the Kosovo Albanians. These terms called for, amongst other things, the withdrawal from Kosovo of Serb forces, the free entry of NATO forces into Kosovo, the unimpeded right of NATO forces to manoeuvre, bivouac and patrol throughout all of Yugoslavia and the implementation of a referendum within three years on the political future of the Kosovo province of Yugoslavia. Within these terms there was no UN role in Kosovo, and Kosovo was to become effectively a NATO protectorate.[30] It was the rejection of these terms which NATO used to justify its military coercion against Yugoslavia. The June 1999 Agreement, detailed in UN Security Council Resolution 1244, which brought the campaign to an end, required the withdrawal of Serb forces, with provision for the later return of limited forces; the political future of Kosovo was to be in the hands of the UN Security Council with no commitment to a referendum; NATO and other forces, including Russian forces, were to be in Kosovo under UN Security Council mandate; no NATO or KFOR (Kosovo force) forces were permitted elsewhere in Yugoslavia; and Kosovo, while having substantial autonomy, should remain part of Federal Yugoslavia.[31] The oft-repeated NATO objectives of achieving the Rambouillet terms were not met, not least in having non-NATO forces as part of KFOR and giving Russia and China, via the UN Security Council, a leading role in determining Kosovo's future. There is a very strong argument that politically NATO's war in Kosovo was not completely successful as its own self-declared terms were not met.

The overarching goal of the NATO attack on Yugoslavia was to prevent a humanitarian disaster. In the winter of 1998–99 over 200,000 Kosovars had been displaced, internally, as a consequence of the crude Serbian counter-insurgency campaign against the Kosovo Liberation Army (KLA). NATO action was claimed to be essential to prevent such Serbian behaviour. The NATO attack resulted in nearly one million extra refugees being driven into the Former Yugoslav Republic of Macedonia (FYROM) and Albania, and the destruction of over one-third of all the housing stock and much of the power and water infrastructure in Kosovo.[32] In addition to NATO attacks on Kosovo (including thousands of unexploded cluster bomblets dropped from 15,000 feet rather than the required 2,000–3,000 feet),[33] the war provided the pretext and the cover for Serbian depredation. Most refugees have returned, but to poor conditions. There is little power, limited accommodation, rampant criminality and widespread ethnic murder against the remaining Serbs and gypsies. The KFOR, all 40,000 troops, may protect the province against Serb military invasion, but KFOR cannot effectively police the province or induce multi-ethnic harmony.[34] Municipal elections were eventually held in October 2000, but the overall government of Kosovo will remain in the hands of the UN administrator for some time to come.

The 'something must be done' lobby in London, Paris and Washington made matters much worse for most Kosovars. This lobby fell into the trap prepared for it by the KLA. Whenever an insurgency force is faced by a superior enemy it is good asymmetrical strategy – assuming a ruthless attitude towards one's own population – to create or portray adverse humanitarian conditions. Aware of perceptions in Western governments, the KLA was pushing at an open door and managed to entice Western intervention. In 1998 the KLA had succeeded in internationalising the Kosovo conflict by having it considered by the United Nations. In 1999 the West became entrapped by the actual conflict, to the benefit of the KLA.[35]

Kosovo is being administered by the UN, but the whole exercise has not enhanced the UN's reputation. UN aid provision is in a mess. About $500 million have been allocated, but nearly two-thirds of the allocation is used up in UN administration costs. The average UN worker in Kosovo is paid over $50,000 a year plus extra danger money. While the UN has raised about $500 million for Kosovo, it struggles to raise $4 million for West Africa, yet there are 400,000 refugees in Liberia and Sierra Leone.[36]

Prospect

The post-Cold War security regime in Europe is a delicate and unpredictable creature; it requires, sensitive, sophisticated and light management. During the Cold War the West became familiar with a design for European security with which they felt reasonably comfortable. However, the Cold War years, in the context of European history, were actually an aberration and not the norm. The norm is for a fluid, flexible continent where many different value systems coexist with each other. An attempt to impose one particular value system across the continent inevitably leads to political strains within the continent and, indeed, within the Atlantic Alliance itself. Many of the consequences of NATO action in Kosovo were foreseen, and NATO was warned. NATO, which is so valuable to European security, has damaged itself seriously, and perhaps irretrievably, by its misguided Balkan venture. The Kosovo intervention clearly demonstrated the limits of NATO political cohesion and war-fighting options beyond the collective defence of NATO territory. This large, sophisticated alliance, limited to a lowest common denominator military strategy in its new crisis management and peacemaking mission, achieved an embarrassing, inglorious and very costly victory over Yugoslavia.

NATO's reputation as a non-aggressive, law-abiding international organisation was seriously compromised in the eyes of the rest of the world. The deep suspicions and cynicism about United States objectives and behaviour were reinforced across the political spectrum in Russia, Europe's largest state and still the world's second nuclear power, and also in China, potentially the world's next superpower.

Predictably, within two years of the 1999 Kosovo war, civil conflict broke out between ethnic Albanian rebels and government forces in the Former Yugoslav Republic of Macedonia, and this is by no means the end to instability in the region.[37] NATO and EU efforts to create a peaceful settlement are inhibited by real limits to the pressure that NATO may apply to the insurgents, often recruited from and largely supplied by Kosovo Albanian nationalists. NATO resources are limited, and the Alliance must consider the security of KFOR – which is hostage to the good behaviour of almost two million Kosovo Albanians.

Where, and with what strategy, NATO will next intervene with force in any significant manner, north, east or south of Kosovo is difficult to foresee. Even if the military capabilities were to hand, it is highly unlikely that 19, or soon more, members could agree on realistic and realisable objectives and military tactics for any major intervention in the Baltic region, the south Caucasus, the Levant or North Africa. Strategic logic suggests that enlargement should cease and that the Alliance's mission should revert solely to the collective defence of NATO territory. But, politics is not logic, and NATO's fate is to become an obese and immobile collective security organisation, mired in the Balkans for a generation and pretender to a Euro-Atlantic security role it cannot fulfil.

Notes

1 The Conference on Security and Co-operation in Europe summit in Paris, 19–21 November 1990 produced the Charter of Paris for a New Europe. This document proclaimed that 'The era of confrontation and divisions of Europe has ended'. See www.osce.org/e/docs/summits/paris90e.htm, p. 2.
2 See James H. Wyllie, *European Security in the New Political Environment* London: Longman, 1997, ch. 2, for detailed consideration of the international organisations contributing to the security of Europe.
3 See 'The EU turns its attention from ploughshares to swords', *The Economist*, 20 November 1999, p. 51, for discussion of contrast between British and French views of EU defence force, and Dana Milbank and Steven Mufson, 'Blair reassures Bush on Europe defence force', *Washington Post*, 24 February 2001, p. A01 for illustration of British commitment to NATO.
4 See 'Achtung!', *The Economist*, 18 December 1999, p. 41, for analysis of German defence spending plans 2000–4.
5 See *The Alliance's STRATEGIC CONCEPT* (Brussels: NATO Office of Information and Press, 1991), p. 5, para. 16.
6 See 'The Alliance's strategic concept', North Atlantic Council, Washington DC, 23–24 April, 1999, Press Release NAC-S(99)65, www.nato.int/docu/pr/1999/p99-065e. htm.
7 See Hans J. Morgenthau, 'Alliances in theory and practice', in A. Wolfers (ed.), *Alliance Policy in the Cold War* (Baltimore, MD: Johns Hopkins University Press, 1959); George Liska, *Nations in Alliance: The Limits of Interdependence* (Baltimore, MD: Johns Hopkins University Press, 1962) and E. H. Fedder, 'The concept of alliance', *International Studies Quarterly*, 12 (1968), for discussions of the requirements for successful alliance.
8 See James Goldgeier, 'NATO expansion: the anatomy of a decision', *Washington Quarterly*, 21: 1 (Winter 1998), 94–5.

9 See Steve Crawshaw, 'Yeltsin calls for blanket security for all Europe', *Independent*, 12 May 1994, p. 7; Andrei Kozyrev, 'The lagging partnership', *Foreign Affairs*, 73: 3 (May/June 1994), 65; and Andrei Kozyrev, 'Partnership or cold peace', *Foreign Policy*, 39 (Summer 1995), 11–13, for illustration of Moscow's preference for collective security. See Dick Leonard, 'Eastward-ho for NATO expansion', *European Voice*, 19–25 July 2001, p. 9 for discussion of the probable eastward enlargement of NATO beyond the 1999 intake.

10 See E. H. Fedder, 'The concept of alliance', *International Studies Quarterly*, 12 (1968), 84 for a succinct and lucid exposition of the distinctions between collective defence and collective security.

11 For gloomy prognosis of NATO's prospects over longer-term see Fred C. Ikle, 'Why expanding NATO eastward is a deplorable idea', *International Herald Tribune*, 12 January 1995, p. 4; Michael Mandelbaum, 'Don't expand NATO', *Newsweek*, 27 December 1996, p. 17; and James H. Wyllie, 'NATO's bleak future', *PARAMETERS: US Army War College Quarterly*, 28: 4 (Winter 1998–99), 113–23.

12 See Andrew Gilligan, 'Russia, not bombs, brought end to war in Kosovo, says Jackson', *Sunday Telegraph*, 1 August 1999, p. 9.

13 Lawrence Freedman, *The Evolution of Nuclear Strategy* (London: Macmillan, 1983), p. 222. For further discussion, see Graham Evans and Jeffrey Newnham, *The Penguin Dictionary of International Relations* (London: Penguin, 1998), pp. 87–8.

14 See Allan Little, 'NATO, politicians "spiked our guns"', *Sunday Telegraph*, 5 March 2000, p. 13.

15 See Bradley Graham, 'Analysis: warnings of air war drawbacks', *Washington Post*, 27 April 2000, p. A1.

16 See Alan Philps, 'Israel to contain Hezbollah from the air', *Daily Telegraph*, 9 October 1999, p. 15; and Ralph Atkins and Avi Machlis, 'Israel bombs Syrian position in Lebanon', *Financial Times*, 2 July 2001.

17 See Marcus Warren, 'Russia mimics NATO Balkan tactics in Chechen campaign', *Daily Telegraph*, 25 September 1999, p. 16; and 'Russia's brutal power games', *The Economist*, 2 October 1999, p. 45.

18 See *The Alliance's Strategic Concept*, North Atlantic Council, Washington DC, 23–24 April 1999, Press Release NAC-S(99)65, www.nato.int/docu/pr/1999/p99-065e.htm, paras. 19, 21–3 and 40.

19 See Alan Philps and Graham Hutchings, 'Russians and Chinese form strategic axis', *Daily Telegraph*, 22 April 1997, p. 13; Ben Aris and David Rennie, 'Yeltsin presses for anti-NATO alliance with the Chinese', *Daily Telegraph*, 26 August 1999, p. 15; Marcus Warren and David Rennie, 'China and Russia hit back with new pact', *Daily Telegraph*, 16 July 2001, p. 4; and 'Remaking history', *The Economist*, 21 July 2001, p. 58.

20 See Stephen Blank, 'Russia's return to Mid-east diplomacy', *Orbis*, 40: 4 (1996); Michael Jansen, 'Primakov's progress', *Middle East International*, 7 November 1997, p. 6; Dean Godson, 'Soviet Union, er, I mean Russia', *Spectator*, 29 November 1997, pp. 12–13; and Ed Blanche, 'Russia steps up Mid-east arms drive', *Middle East*, July/August 2001, p. 19.

21 See Oskana Antonenko, 'Russia, NATO and European security after Kosovo', *Survival*, 41: 4 (Winter 1999–2000), 128–9 for discussion of Russian policy of 'multi-polarity'.

22 See Elizabeth Pond, 'Kosovo: catalyst for Europe', *Washington Quarterly*, 22: 4 (Autumn 1999), 82.

23 See Barry James, 'EU Plans reaction force in 4 Years', *International Herald Tribune*, 7 December 1999, p. 4.

24 See Tim Butcher and George Jones, 'Defence deal will help Europe tackle crisis', *Daily Telegraph*, 26 November 1999, p. 12.

25 For sceptical views, see Gerald Frost, 'Europe will shoot itself in the foot', *Daily Telegraph*, 1 December 1999, p. 28; William S. Cohen, 'On defence, Europe must turn words into action', *International Herald Tribune*, 7 December 1999, p. 9; 'In defence of Europe', *The Economist*, 26 February 2000, p. 23; and 'Defence budget restructuring: myth or reality?', *Strategic Survey 2000/2001* (Oxford: Oxford University Press for IISS, 2001), pp. 105–6.

26 See Michael Mandelbaum, 'Foreign policy as social work', *Foreign Affairs*, 75: 1 (Jan./Feb. 1996), 16–32 for discussion of the risks of ill-advised humanitarian intervention.

27 See Michael Akehurst, *A Modern Introduction to International Law* (London: Routledge, 1992), ch. 15, pp. 218–23; and Anthony Clark Arend and Robert J. Beck, *International law and the Use of Force* (London: Routledge, 1993), ch. 3, pp. 29–46, for discussion of the legal arguments about the use of military force in international conflict and support for the orthodox view that the UN charter constitutes both customary and statutory law governing the use of force between states.

28 Catherine Guicherd, 'International law and the war in Kosovo', *Survival*, 41: 2 (Summer 1999) 25.

29 See The North Atlantic Treaty, Washington DC, 4 April 1949, www.nato.int/docu/basictxt/treaty.tm.

30 See Mark Littman, *Kosovo: Law and Diplomacy* (London: Centre for Policy Studies, 1999), pp. 8–13.

31 See UN Security Council Resolution 1244, Press Release SC/6686, 10 June 1999, www.un.org/News/Press/docs/1999/19990610.SC6686.html for details of settlement; and see 'A just peace?', *Daily Telegraph*, 5 June 1999, p. 21 for critical editorial commentary on the political compromise.

32 See Christian Jennings, 'Kosovo stands divided by wealth', *Scotland on Sunday*, 28 November 1999, p. 21.

33 See W. F. Deedes, 'NATO's deadly legacy will cause years of suffering', *Daily Telegraph*, 13 September 1999, p. 12; and 'Sappers seek the deadly harvest of NATO's Kosovo cluster bombs', *Daily Telegraph*, 2 March 2000, p. 23.

34 See Misha Glenny, 'NATO fights mission impossible in Kosovo', *Sunday Telegraph*, 19 March 2000, p. 31; R. Jeffrey Smith, 'A year after the war, Kosovo killing goes on', *Washington Post*, 12 June 2000, p. A01; and 'The criminal crucible that is Kosovo', *The Economist*, 17 February 2002, p. 50.

35 See Allan Little, 'How Albright manoeuvred NATO into war', *Sunday Telegraph*, 27 February 2000, p. 29.

36 See Karl Vick, 'Africa has refugees, Kosovo gets money', *Washington Post*, 8 October 1999, p. A24; and Julius Strauss, 'UN squanders NATO's Kosovo victory', *Daily Telegraph*, 16 November 1999, p. 18.

37 See William Drozdiak, 'NATO poised to deploy troops in limited Macedonia mission', *Washington Post*, 14 July 2001, p. A14.

Further reading

Daalder, Ivo and Michael O'Hanlon, 'Unlearning the lessons of Kosovo', *Foreign Policy*, 116 (Autumn 1999), 128–40.

Dobriansky, Paula, 'Russian foreign policy: promise or peril?' *Washington Quarterly*, Vol. 23: 1 (Winter 2000), 135–44.

Levitin, Oleg , 'Inside Moscow's Kosovo muddle', *Survival*, 41: 3 (Autumn 1999), 102–23.

Wyllie, James H., 'European security: structures, challenges and risks', in David Gowland, Basil O'Neill and Richard Dunphy (eds), *The European Mosaic* (London: Longman, 2000), ch. 5, pp. 102–17.

3

European Union Intelligence Agency: a necessary institution for Common Intelligence Policy?

John M. Nomikos

What is intelligence?

There is no shortage of definitions of intelligence. Webster's dictionary defines it as 'the gathering of secret information, as for military purposes'. Jeffrey T. Richelson has defined it as 'the product resulting from the collection, evaluation, analysis, integration and interpretation of all available information which concerns one or more aspects of foreign nations or of areas of operation which is [sic] immediately or potentially significant for planning'.[1] In turn, Robert Bowie has defined it simply and elegantly as 'information designed for action'.[2]

While Richelson and Webster's definitions are too narrow, Bowie's may be too broad. Intelligence need not involve secret information exclusively. Nor does it, as Richelson's definition suggests, refer only to products as opposed to raw data. And though Bowie's definition underscores an essential aspect of intelligence, purposefulness, it does not distinguish intelligence from advertisement, propaganda or advocacy, all forms of information 'designed for action'.

Intelligence is best defined as information, collected, organised or analysed on behalf of actors or decision-makers. Such information may include technical data, trends, rumours, pictures or hardware. In books and manuals of intelligence, the basic intelligence cycle is usually depicted like this: [3]

$$\ldots \text{Collection} \rightarrow \ldots \text{Analysis} \rightarrow \ldots \text{Dissemination} \rightarrow \ldots$$

More often than not, the use to which the intelligence is to be put is missing from the intelligence cycle, as is the end-user himself. There are many elaborate models of the intelligence cycle in the literature. Jordan and Taylor describe such a cycle and include the user in their diagram – but only as an external mode whose involvement is only in setting requirements and receiving the finished reports.[4] Arthur S. Hulnick, in an article devoted to the consumer–user relationship, criticises the Jordan and Taylor diagram and proposes a much more elaborate scheme which does not exclude the user; but even he fails to follow up what happens to intelligence once delivered to the decision-maker.[5]

Limitations do apply: to be classed as intelligence, information must be collected, organised or analysed 'on behalf of' the consumers of that information. The 'or' in this sentence is critical. If the information is not collected for the decision-maker, then it must be organised or analysed for him. A pile of newspapers on a decision-maker's desk does not constitute intelligence. Even a set of clippings of those newspapers, organised by subject matter, is not intelligence. A subset of clips, selected expressly for the needs of the decision-maker, is intelligence. It is the particular organisation of the material for the decision-maker that may turn publicly available news into intelligence.[6]

Intelligence analysis

Similarly, information collected on behalf of a decision-maker but not organised or analysed for him, is also intelligence. Obviously, a National Security Agency (NSA) may retain raw data which have not been organised or analysed for the consumer but which fit the expressed needs of the consumer and are accessible on request. This, too, is intelligence. Intelligence analysis digests information and refines it for the purpose of assisting the policy-maker. Analysis implies not just the organisation of information but its examination as well. Analysis becomes estimates when it renders judgements about the implications of the findings. For example, intelligence analysis may point out that X has always been seen with Y whereas an estimate might, given evidence of X, predict the likely existence of Y.

Intelligence analysis and estimation must be done on behalf of the consumer, not the analyst, and should be as objective and relevant as possible. This threefold requirement is difficult to satisfy, yet key to the integrity of the product. Relevance, measured by the consumer's ability to assimilate and use the product, requires constant interaction between the analyst and the consumer. Objectivity, however, demands a certain distance and a willingness to consider all variables – not just the ones the analyst or his consumer has deemed most important in the past. However, in the real world, human nature intervenes to distort intelligence in several ways, such as politicisation and privatisation. Privatisation refers to the use of the intelligence process for personal or bureaucratic advantages, while politicisation is the skewing of intelligence for the purpose of influencing policy outcomes or vindicating policy choices. Whereas privatisation is found at all levels of the intelligence service, politicisation may be most evident at the top, where the ability to influence policy decisions is greatest. Although politicisation and privatisation are difficult to identify in practice, charges of one are usually accompanied by counter-charges of the other.

The intelligence process

Given our broad definition, the actors or decision-makers that intelligence serves can be anyone from a soldier or government official to a shopkeeper or child-carer. National intelligence involves the collection, organisation or analy-sis of information solely on behalf of national actors or decision-makers. A national intelligence service, in its most efficient form, will handle only that portion of the intelligence process that requires the security and secrecy such a service affords. Secrecy is necessary if the sources (national technical means, spies) or the policy areas (e.g. trade negotiations, defence policies) are sensitive. In the latter case, intelligence may include open source material. The national intelligence process involves everything from the establishment of collection requirements to the dissemination and assessment of collected information. An intelligence service is created to manage and appraise the process but not to assess it for policy purposes. Assessment is the responsibility of the consumer, in other words, the decision-maker. A functioning intelligence process then depends on both the intelligence officer/analyst and the consumer/decision-maker. The intelligence analyst ought to understand the needs, perspectives and working constraints of the latter, including the types of contingencies he faces,[7] and to apprise the decision-maker of constraints, changes, policy options, potential, etc. The consumer/decision-maker, in turn, comes to understand the limits of knowledge on which the intelligence is based, factoring them into a realistic assessment of the intelligence he has received.

Indeed, if a system functions correctly, it should be able to respond quickly and objectively to policy-maker needs and be able to anticipate future needs that policy-makers have not yet articulated. However, if the intelligence community does not take advantage of technological developments and reduce bureaucratic barriers, it will fail to meet its basic mission of providing policy-makers with timely, objective and useful intelligence.[8]

Background and reasons for a European Union Intelligence Agency

The end of the Cold War has created a world in which the relative stability between the two superpowers has disappeared. During the Cold War every action of a country was conducted in the light of the adversary relationship between the United States and the Soviet Union. Each European country, with a more or less developed intelligence agency of its own, participated in this superpower-led 'game' while also conducting espionage activities against its European partners, a practice which, although wound down in the post-Cold War era, is not altogether extinct now, by some accounts.[9] The world order is much more difficult to define nowadays, and new imperatives which have sprung to the fore since changes in Eastern Europe and Al Qaeda terrorism in the United States, as well as ensuing altercations in Afghanistan and Iraq which monopolised the headlines over the two years that followed the dawn of the new millennium, question the ability and mechanisms that the EU posesses in order to behave as an international actor.

The purpose of this chapter is therefore to examine the need for the European Union to have a fully fledged strategic intelligence agency – a suggested name could be the European Union Intelligence Agency (EUIA) – comparable, perhaps, to the Central Intelligence Agency (CIA) in the United States, and steps have already been undertaken, albeit tentatively, in this direction.

In the last two decades, the European Community has arguably become the dominant factor on the European scene, at least economically, if not politically, since the revival of the European Community after the years of eurosclerosis, through the Single European Act (SEA) signed in 1986, and the subsequent treaties. These newer treaties intensified and revitalised the depth of the integration process, and established the European Political Co-operation process, alongside the successive enlargements.[10] Perhaps more interestingly, the European Union has also started to become an actor of major importance outside the European continent, certainly economically, but also increasingly politically, interacting with other state actors such as the United States and non-state actors such as the United Nations.

The reasons for a European Union Intelligence Agency are given in the section that follows. Then a comparison is made between the CIA in the early years after the Second World War and an intelligence agency to be founded by the European Union. How an intelligence agency might fit in the overall European Union structure and what its shape and role might be are discussed in the following section. A conclusion will follow at the end of the analysis.

The cataclysmic changes that took place in Central and Eastern Europe inevitably changed the face of politics in Europe and in the Western world as a whole. The policies of the European Union and its member states towards the re-unification of Germany and the democratisation and market liberalisation of its eastern neighbours in Europe at a time of such change may well have been the most important that they had to formulate for many decades.[11] Nationalism has re-emerged in some of the countries of the former Eastern bloc and in the newly formed states of the former Soviet Union (several of which are facing simmering ethnic conflicts). The civil war in Yugoslavia is the first case of ethnic conflict leading to all-out war in Europe in the post-Cold War order. This civil war was arguably possible because neither the United States nor the former Soviet Union was there any longer to put pressure on the Yugoslavs to seek a peaceful solution and no other superpower stepped into the breach of providing the context of a broader power balance, which seemed to previously keep the lid on similar hotspots of instability.

During the Cold War, Yugoslavia was of strategic importance to both the superpowers, and thus neither one nor both of them would have interfered in the situation. Initially, the European Union was the only actor that had to deal with the situation in Yugoslavia and showed that it was ill-prepared for tasks of this magnitude. Other examples of current and potential conflicts can be traced in the on-going bloodshed in Chechnya, tensions between Slovaks and their Hungarian minority, Kaliningrad and many more.

Instabilities in the region of Eastern Europe and the Commonwealth of Independent States affect the members of the European Union. For instance, apart from the destruction and loss of life in the country itself, the crises in Yugoslavia caused an unprecedented refugee problem and huge economic burden on the EU. Many of the refugees from Yugoslavia fled to Western European countries, such as Germany, Greece, Italy and the Netherlands. These refugees from Eastern Europe and the problems associated with their rehabilitation have given a welcome excuse for the rise of neo-Nazi and other extreme right-wing movements in Germany, Austria, France and the United Kingdom, culminating in growing attacks on foreigners. By monitoring these and similar situations continuously, it might be possible for the European Union to take action soon. A more accurate analysis of the region could be achieved through an European Union Intelligence Agency.

Another area of instability on the periphery of (Western) Europe that could affect the European Union is the eastern Mediterranean, where the Arab–Israeli conflict has flared up again in recent years, and North Africa, where Muslim fundamentalism is re-emerging. Quite apart from the Community's economic interests as a whole suffering from this instability, particular southern member states such as Spain and France have to deal more directly with the effects. 'The strict interdependence existing between the European Union and countries such as Morocco, Algeria, Tunisia, Libya and Egypt, coupled with increasingly worrying demographic trends, create an obligation for Europe to work out a better and overall crisis management approach.'[12]

Last but not least, the increased need for co-operation among national intelligence agencies across the world, since the 11 September 2001, for the combating of terrorism, has renewed the need for European intelligence agencies to exchange intelligence in a more organised and regular manner and to work more closely together.

Institutional developments for intelligence co-operation in the 1990s

Although high-level support for increased intelligence co-operation in the European Union did not emerge until late 1990s, a significant amount of actual intelligence co-operation nonetheless occurred. There have been bilateral and multilateral intelligence exchanges, developments in the Western European Union, the Helios satellite project and intelligence sharing during military exercises and operations. While falling far short of a common intelligence policy, this co-operation has helped establish a baseline from which one could emerge, and co-operation has identified many of the problems that must be overcome.

To be effective, a European common intelligence policy under the umbrella of a European Union Intelligence Agency must be able to swiftly and accurately disseminate intelligence information to military forces. The ability to do so is crucial to the discussion of a European Intelligence Policy as well as the multinational corps agreed upon in Helsinki.[13] This capability could be achieved through the development of a European Command, Control, Communication, Computers, and Intelligence (C4I) capability. The European militaries however, have been unable as yet to develop an autonomous capability, instead relying on NATO and USC4I capabilities and infrastructure.

During the United Nations Protection Force (UNPROFOR) experience in Bosnia from 1992 to 1995, European militaries suffered from this C4I. The UNPROFOR experience shows how much the European militaries relied on NATO and US intelligence capabilities and infrastructure. The Combined Joint Task Force (CJTF) concept, agreed to at the 1996 NATO Summit in Berlin, permits a European-led force to use NATO intelligence and infrastructure assets when conducting military operations. The European Union has a long way to go in assembling a C4I capability.[14]

The Western European Union Intelligence Section and other initiatives

The Western European Union (WEU) has taken a leading role in developing and encouraging intelligence co-operation among European countries. Specifically, the WEU Intelligence Section and the WEU Satellite Centre (established in 1993 at Torrejon, Spain) have institutionalised to a certain extent European intelligence co-operation. These structures were incorporated along with the WEU into the European Union in 2000. WEU intelligence co-operation has focused primarily on imagery intelligence (IMINT) however, with a notable lack of emphasis on signals intelligence (SIGINT), human intelligence (HUMINT) and tactical intelligence co-operation. Although the WEU has provided a basis for future intelligence co-operation, these institutions will not serve as a satisfactory basis for a common intelligence policy.[15]

Although termed a 'WEU Satellite Centre', the facility neither owns nor operates any satellites. Instead, the WEU's Satellite Centre purchases commercial imagery and analyses it for the WEU council and individual WEU governments who request it. By 1998, approximately 40 per cent of the Centre's imagery came from France's SPOT 1 and 2 satellites, 20 per cent came from India's IRS-1C satellite, 17 per cent from Helios 1 (owned and operated by France, Spain and Italy) and 15 per cent from Russian imagery satellites. The Satellite Centre also orders imagery from ERS-1 and 2 (European Space Agency), Landsat 4 and 5 (USA) and Radarsat (Canada). The Satellite Centre has a budget of $11 million, which is approximately 37 per cent of the WEU budget, and has a staff of 68 persons.[16]

In addition to the above, the Schengen Agreement of 1990 on the abolition of border controls, coupled with the needs of Europol, provided for increased co-operation and information exchange in such areas as cross-border surveillance, cross-border hot pursuit, the use of communications monitoring equipment, the deployment of joint teams and so forth, in the context of criminal investigations, suspicion of drug-trafficking and terrorism. It becomes evident, therefore, that intelligence co-operation for the EU is not just a matter of external defence but also of internal security.

Indeed, the EU spent over three years, from 1997 to 2001, exploring new initiatives. First was the formulation of a new Convention on mutual assistance on criminal matters, building more drastically upon previous ones, which always came up against differing national legal systems and were of limited effect. Secondly, came a more radical EU–FBI joint telecommunications surveillance plan, an ambitious transatlantic venture for sharing intelligence through a global system. This restored some control over the use of new technologies such as the Internet and satellite-based communications and their security implications, and extended to the provision of a legal framework for the interception of all forms of telecommunications.[17] Predictably, this plan came under concerted attack with concerns voiced both within EU circles, as high up as the Commission,[18] for risking contravening the European Convention on Human Rights, and by many outside pressure groups and civil liberties campaigners.[19]

Comparison of the EU Intelligence Agency (EUIA) with the early years of the Central Intelligence Agency (CIA)

In the years before the Second World War, the United States kept a low profile in the international arena. The great powers at that time were European, mainly Britain and France. With the United States' entrance into the Second World War, it was forced to become an important actor in world affairs and, unlike post-First World War, emerged as one of two new superpowers in the aftermath of the second. The former great powers of Europe were too worn out, preoccupied with rebuilding and facing problems with their colonies. The Soviet Union came out of the war as the second major power. Not least because of their ideological differences, the two new powers became adversaries. Intelligence exchanges rained down upon the United States in a great torrent during the 1940s and early 1950s, culminating in the creation of the Central Intelligence Agency (CIA) in 1947 and the National Security Agency (NSA) in 1952. This occurred in part because the Second World War intelligence developments, such as those within the US Army (Military Intelligence Division), the US Navy (Office of Naval Intelligence) and in William Donovan's Co-ordinator of Information and Office of Strategic Service (OSS) organisations, provided the US government with the experienced and skilled personnel to make such post-war intelligence innovation possible.[20]

Until recently, the European Union has kept a relatively low profile in the world and European arena. With the sudden changes that have taken place it has been forced to play a more prominent role in Europe as a whole, and perhaps beyond, but even this has been predominantly in the form of financial and technical aid to Eastern Europe and humanitarian aid to the former Yugoslavia, rather than a credible political or security role. As with the United States in the post-Second World War era, the European Union has had little or no experience in dealing with these new problems. Post-1989, the Europeans expected that Europe would become a more peaceful and stable region, but the contrary has been the case.

Besides the threat of the Soviets and later the Chinese to democratic countries in different parts of the world, there was another reason for the founding of the CIA. The United States was not able to foresee the Japanese attack on Pearl Harbor in December 1941, even though considerable intelligence was available. 'The US Congress made public the full story of the Pearl Harbor tragedy, an almost perfect model of disastrous handling of crucial strategic intelligence.'[21] As a result the USA realised that an intelligence organisation was of vital importance for national security and that a co-ordinating central intelligence organisation would be able to perform the warning function better than the existing individual departmental agencies.

In July 1991, the European Union had to deal with a major crisis in Yugoslavia. Although initially their efforts seemed to have some success (the Brioni Agreement),[22] the crisis became a civil war and the European Union was unable to stop the fighting. One of the reasons for the failure of the European Union was the divided opinions and later actions of the individual members. In addition, the European Union did not realise how deep-rooted the conflict was between the different ethnic groups. Through continuous analysing of the situation, the European Union might have been able to realise sooner that a major conflict in Yugoslavia was inevitable and been able to defuse the conflict before it could explode. The Pearl Harbor experience for the United States could be compared with the Yugoslav experience for the European Union. Pearl Harbor was for the United States an important reason to found the CIA, and the Yugoslav crisis could be an important reason for the European Union to found the EUIA. It is not suggested of course that the solution of an EUIA is foolproof. The EU's conscientious attempts towards building a Common Foreign and Security Policy step by step during the 1990s did not render them better prepared for the Kosovo crisis. Indeed, despite the much longer – more than a decade – period at its disposal, the existence of the CIA did not prevent the US being totally unprepared for the terrorist attacks of the 11 September 2001 against the Pentagon and the twin towers of the World Trade Center in New York.[23] The CIA has failed in instances that, in hindsight, proved to be crucial,[24] so an organisation like the EUIA would not necessarily be a panacea, but could help pool resources and achieve better results in the EU's youngest areas of competence launched by the Treaty on European Union in Maastricht, the Common Foreign and Security Policy (CFSP) and Justice and Home Affairs (JHA).

The CIA is an intelligence organisation involved in both overt and covert actions and information gatherings. It is part of the executive branch and is independent, although it guides and receives intelligence from military and departmental intelligence organisations. The Director of the CIA reports directly to the President. An EUIA should not necessarily engage in covert actions; it might, however, eventually gather vital information through its own covert sources. Its most important task, as proposed here, would be the analysis of overtly gathered information and preparing it for use by the policy-makers.

The question of to whom the head of the EUIA will report will be discussed later. But, as with the CIA in the US political structure, the EUIA should be independent and not part of any other institution within the European Union. During its history of almost four decades, the CIA has gone through many changes in order to perfect its performance and develop into the intelligence organisation it is today.

Overcoming obstacles to the development of the EUIA

Some European intelligence co-operation developed during the 1990s, as mentioned above, but it fell far short of a common policy necessary for an effective Common Foreign and Security Policy (CFSP) and autonomous defence capability. An audit completed in 1999 by the WEU on defence capabilities stated that there was, as yet, no satisfactory sharing of strategic intelligence, either at the national or international level, that would enable joint European military staff to conduct in-depth analysis of a crisis situation.[25]

European intelligence co-operation to date has been hampered by emphasising national sovereignty over sharing intelligence. Where co-operation exists, it has been largely in imagery collection and analysis, using the WEU Satellite Centre. IMINT is a necessary capability, but an effective EUIA will also require co-operation in signals intelligence (SIGINT) and human intelligence (HUMINT), and will be able to integrate them in all-source intelligence products.[26]

Imagery co-operation to date, as illustrated by the WEU Satellite Centre, the Helios project and the small satellite procurement proposal, has been successful primarily because much of the technology is commercially based, which limits the need to share highly classified information. Security protocols have fostered an elaborate and cumbersome classification system for Helios imagery. The WEU Satellite Centre cannot receive signals from Helios directly and may only interpret the images. Even with increased European intelligence co-operation, 'with the multiplication of exchanges of information, potential risks will tend to increase, which may produce a reluctance to continue those exchanges'.[27]

Already at the turn of the century there were indications that security concerns might prevent the new Political Security Committee from performing its functions. Javier Solana, the EU high representative on foreign and security policy, and his staff, need access to intelligence to advise the Political Security Committee on security related matters. Nevertheless, European diplomats have voiced concern over the willingness of individual states to supply the new EU organs with highly sensitive intelligence data. The EU has yet to establish a satisfactory mechanism for sharing intelligence at the EU level.[28]

The second obstacle to intelligence co-operation is the fear of spoiling privileged relationships. Many NATO countries have individual intelligence-sharing agreements with the United States. The French, determined to reduce their dependence on US intelligence capabilities, are the driving force behind the drive for European autonomy. France developed the Helios system with Spain and Italy and has struggled to obtain German co-operation in the Helios 2 program, even though Italian and Spanish enthusiasm for continued participation in Helios 2 is waning. The French have also played an important role by developing a C4I system (command, control, communication, computers and intelligence capability) for use by a European-led Combined Joint Task Force (CJTF).[29] However France's enthusiasm for autonomy is not universally shared.

There is, for example, the UK–US intelligence co-operation. Although the British stress that this relationship has never been exclusive in one way or another, the US agencies themselves have felt a sort of ambivalence *vis-à-vis* the relationship that the UK services have with their European counterparts. Successive British governments, of whatever denomination, seek with as much fervour to reaffirm the 'special relationship' with the US, yet some British specialists feel that this special relationship might be an obstacle to wider European co-operation. Nevertheless, as long as decision-makers accept that the main issue is to analyse what Europeans agencies could achieve better by their own means, in a strictly complementary or in any case non-conflictual capacity in relation to NATO and the US, there appears not to be a serious impediment.[30]

The six European states which are NATO but not-EU members – Poland, Hungary, the Czech Republic, Turkey, Iceland and Norway – have also displayed alarm over attempts to move security policy out of NATO and into the EU. Turkey has even raised the possibility that if it remains excluded from EU security policy-makers, it might work within NATO to block the EU from using NATO assets. These six countries, along with other like-minded EU countries, may attempt to limit increased European security policy co-operation they deem threatening to existing relationships with the US through NATO.[31]

Institutional obstacles also stand in the way of increased intelligence co-operation. Intelligence organisations generally believe that no other organisation's analysis is as reliable as their own, which leads them to place more faith and confidence in their own work. These organisations also tend to view international relations as a zero-sum game, and may not agree with a co-operative approach to security and defence integration.[32]

Another institutional obstacle consists of the EU's and WEU's bureaucratic decision-making structures. As one critic notes, 'intelligence, as a profession that is concerned with the unknown, the surprising and the unwelcome, does not seem to lend itself easily either to the current pace of the CFSP or to its diplomatic nature, where all action must wait for a high-level inter-governmental decision and must never go beyond the scope of its language'.[33] Thus, the conservative nature of intelligence agencies coupled with the bureaucratic lethargy of the EU will also act to slow European intelligence co-operation.

The Treaty of Maastricht negotiated by the EU in 1991 helped set the agenda, establishing as EU objectives the implementation of a CFSP as well as the eventual framing of a common defence policy. There were no means established to implement a CFSP, however, nor did the Treaty of Maastricht make any specific mention of increasing intelligence co-operation within the CFSP framework.[34] The Gulf and Yugoslavian crises proved more of an impetus to a common European Union intelligence co-operation policy than Maastricht. Dependence on the US for intelligence during both crises convinced the Europeans that it needed improved intelligence collection capabilities, especially with regard to space-based assets.

The Treaty of Amsterdam, however, negotiated by EU member states in 1997, made several changes to the CFSP to enhance its effectiveness. First, the Treaty created the new office of High Representative for the CFSP (currently held by the former NATO Secretary-General Mr Javier) to 'assist the EU Council in matters coming within the scope of the CFSP, in particular through contributing to the formulation, preparation and implementation of policy decisions, and, when appropriate, acting on behalf of the Council at the Presidency's request, through conducting political dialogue with third countries'.[35]

Finally, following an Anglo-French initiative at St Malo, European Union leaders meeting in Helsinki, in December 1999, and at a follow-up meeting in Sintra, Portugal, in February 2000, agreed to major changes in European security and defence policy, many of which were initially suggested in Cologne. These new plans called for a 15 brigade multinational army corps of 50000–60000 troops supported by airpower and warships, to be combat-ready by 2003. Three additional bodies were also established to support EU defence policy: a Political and Security Committee composed of ambassadors with an advisory role to the EU Council of Ministers, a Military Committee of senior officers and a Multinational Planning Staff, which eventually, and in parallel, paved the way for the integration of the WEU.[36] While details of the intelligence support to be provided to the multinational force are not yet available, this level of support is likely to require significantly increased intelligence co-operation.

Tasks of the EUIA into the EU mechanism

The European Union is a unique international organisation. It is the only international organisation which contains supranational structures, meaning that, at least in traditional European Community affairs, 'the existence of governmental authorities is closer to the archetype of federation than any past international organisation, but not yet identical with it'.[37] The new willingness of the member states to work closely together in justice and home affairs and in foreign and security policy issues, albeit at an inter-governmental level, is not often seen in other international organisations. There are three main institutions in the European Union which are particularly important for the placement and the functioning of an EUIA.

The first one is the Council of Justice and Home Affairs, the Council of Foreign Ministers and that of the heads of state – the *European Council*. The Council is 'the principal decision-making body of the Community'.[38] The second one is the *European Commission,* which 'is responsible for formulating the specific policies of the EU, and its recommendations must ultimately be decided upon by the Council'.[39] The Commissioner for External Affairs is of particular importance to CFSP matters, but others also have valuable input in terms of home affairs, immigration and related matters. The third institution is the *European Parliament,* which 'is the sitting assembly of representatives from the member states'.[40] Since the Maastricht (1991) and Amsterdam (1997) treaties, the European Parliament has seen its co-decision powers increased in several areas of decision-making in the European Union, but its powers are still limited compared with parliaments in individual countries, particularly in foreign policy issues. As seen in chapter 5, many European parliament rulings on human rights violations for example, as in the case of Kurds in Turkey, are taken into advisement but not necessarily acted upon by the primary decision-making body, the Council.

How can the EUIA fit into this mechanism? Although the EU framework is far from the same as in the US political system, it is useful to use some of the insights the latter can offer.

As analysed earlier, the EUIA should be an independent institution like the CIA. As with the CIA it has to be answerable directly to a responsible person or institution. One scenario would indicate that the most likely candidate would be the European Commission and the President of the Commission. The latter is often given the same status as a head of state of a country, and yet can only represent the EU as a whole on a limited remit, in matters where a spectrum of strategies, from the maximum desirable to the minimum acceptable, have already been decided upon by the Council. The Commissioner in charge of external affairs would also be briefed by the EUIA on a daily basis. The Commission is a permanent body considered completely European, and not subject to national influences. According to this way of thinking, intelligence concerning security matters which are vital for Europe should be reported to the Commission on a regular basis. The Commission then could advise the Council in relation to pre-emptive, confidence-building, political or economic measures, which could be warranted, so that decisions can be made in good time, before the security threat acquires dangerous dimensions.[41]

An alternative scenario, more in touch with recent developments, would indicate that, since the Council of Ministers is the official decision-making body of the EU, it, and on its behalf, the High Representative for CFSP, should receive reports and analyses directly from the EUIA. This effectively already happens to some extent since the anti-terrorism intelligence co-ordination which accumulated in the year which followed 11 September 2001.[42] The problem is that, for example, a minister of foreign affairs, might have difficulties and conflicts in dealing with the foreign affairs of his own country and that of the EU at the same time, or that intelligence leakage of national importance, even to other EU partners alone, might compromise his or her country's security sensitivities. This clearly indicates that, unlike the CIA, an EUIA would have to have a clearly delineated area of competences, which provide the necessary data and analyses for the EU to be able to embark on common action, where appropriate, while steering clear of areas of exclusively national foreign policy and defence competence.

Although the European Parliament could be the one to approve the budget of the EUIA, as with most other EU operational budgets, it is difficult to envisage it overseeing the EUIA, unless, to draw a parallel with the United States, where the nearest equivalent, Congress, is responsible for the approval of the budget and the oversight of the CIA, the European Parliament in future also becomes a stronger institution, providing a bigger say in a more 'federal-looking' EU.[43]

With the introduction of the High Representative for the European Union's CFSP, the creation of the Rapid Reaction Force after St Malo, and the integration of the WEU, as an embryonic military pillar to the Union, the question is what the relationship between this new EU 'pillar', NATO and the EUIA will be like. One future solution would be a new Commissioner responsible for the defence portfolio to work alongside the Commissioners for External Affairs etc., to co-ordinate action determined by the European Council decision-makers and CFSP strategists and their different committees with EUIA input and the maintenance of relations with NATO. In a more integrated – if not federalised – EU this role could even potentially merge with that of the High Commissioner to avoid the multiple layers of operations, which traditionally hamper EU responsiveness and flexibility, and to streamline the process.

In the United States, the military establishment has its own intelligence agencies. It would be safe to assume that the military institution of the EU will have its own intelligence in as clear a way one day. One of the reasons for having its own agencies is that the military requires different intelligence information than the other departments. As in the United States, the EUIA would co-ordinate strategic intelligence, including that of the military. For a long-term prospect the EUIA should become an agency which recruits and trains its own personnel for the entire information gathering. It should not become an agency which hires only intelligence officers from the member states. This policy would make the EUIA a true European agency.

The story so far

Despite the problems outlined above, rapid developments have already taken place, albeit in a reactive rather than proactive way, in response to the impetus created by the events of the 11 September 2001, and the resulting international commitment towards a war on terrorism. The expression of support towards the United States after the bombing was unqualified by all EU heads of state. Indeed, a few weeks later the US administration was already embarking on a controversial war in Afghanistan in search of Al Qaeda and Osama Bin Laden. Even then EU foreign ministers swiftly brushed aside concerns, voiced mainly by smaller EU states, and supported the US action. At the same time, activity in different EU countries to stamp out terrorist 'nests', which were either related to recent events or were a more localised but long-standing, intensified and cross-border intelligence co-operation multiplied.[44] The Greek government shake-up of the main orchestrators of the '17 November' terrorist organisation and Spanish arrests of ETA and Al-Qaeda-related terrorists in Spain, were a result of heightened co-operation between the countries' own intelligence services, together with British, US and other European ones. Different countries took different steps towards tightening laws and regulations, such as conducting searches and spot-checks, the immunity of religious groups, immigration, police questioning and pre-sentencing holding times for suspects. Similarly, EU-wide, there was concerted effort to work together on this issue as much as possible. The EU redoubled its efforts, at various levels, to facilitate the exchange of intelligence and published a list of recognised terrorist organisations.[45] The EU Justice and Home Affairs Council of Ministers agreed on a long list of pre-emptive measures designed to anticipate attacks such as those in the US.[46] The list inevitably included tighter external border controls, more effective sharing of information between EU partners regarding third country nationals and early detection of suspicious activity, thus giving rise to increasing concerns over an even-more impenetrable 'fortress Europe'. The challenge which faces the European Union is clear: in the wake of international developments and its own increasing role as an international actor in global politics and matters of security, the European Union needs to develop, alongside its fledgling foreign policy and defence capability, a credible intelligence agency which respects the autonomy of the member states but can deliver in the areas of CFSP and JHA co-operation as these progress. At the same time, it needs to avoid becoming too introspective and insular, so that it does not shift the focus away from the long-desired '"areas of freedom, security and justice" to that of a mere integrated law enforcement zone'.[47]

Conclusion

In this research analysis it has been argued that the European Union should found an Intelligence Agency: the proposed European Union Intelligence Agency (EUIA). The general reason is that the international order has changed dramatically in the last few years and has not made the world more stable. The eastern and southern periphery of Europe are regions with much instability, but globally also there are no fewer threats, and the EU has become more active politically in the international arena. Crises, such as the one in Yugoslavia, regional or global terrorism and the effects of migration waves caused by wars, are having significant effects on the EU and its members. The lack of knowledge about other future conflicts in the region could be more costly than maintaining an intelligence structure as proposed in the research analysis.

A comparison has been made with the Central Intelligence Agency (CIA), the US strategic intelligence organisation. The Americans had little experience with intelligence prior to the Second World War, after which they suddenly found themselves in the position of superpower. This inexperience is also the case for the European Union, an emerging superpower. Perhaps that is where the similarity ends. To fit the EUIA into the EU mechanism presents many difficulties, because the divisions of power within the EU, in security and foreign policy matters, are not all that clear and indeed are in the process of remoulding with each new initiative, treaty and international development.

Without doubt, any future EUIA should become an independent institution. The EUIA should report directly to the European Commission and the European Council, although there are different ways in which this can happen as EU competence in the areas of CFSP and JHA increases. The EUIA should initially be small in size and just be a gathering point for information coming from the national intelligence organisations of the EU member-states. A model based on InterPol could be the basis for the EUIA, thereby respecting the sovereignty of the national intelligence services. In the distant future it could become an organisation with its own resources and minimally dependent on the individual intelligence services.

The main tasks of the EUIA would be information gathering from EU members' intelligence organisations and the independent analysis of this information. With this analysis the EUIA will advise the Commission and the Council on foreign relations and security issues. The method used would be overt for most of the information needed for thorough analysis. The EUIA could become a very useful instrument for policy and decision-makers of the European Union in the fields of foreign relations and military affairs, when the European Union establishes a self-standing military pillar. The Persian Gulf and Balkan crises have been sufficiently traumatic to convey the message that if the European Union is serious about achieving the objective of a common foreign, security and defence policy, there is an urgent requirement for a common European Union intelligence policy. This can only be achieved when the EUIA is independent and regarded as a true European institution.

In sum, the intelligence profession is at a watershed in its intellectual history. For nearly, a hundred years, the focus of intelligence operations had remained unchanged.[48] The categories of information required for country outlook assessment and the analysis of military capabilities and intentions were largely the same in 1909 and 1998. The events of 11 September in New York and the subsequent war on terrorism, brought to the fore more co-operation, across Europe and internationally, than we had ever seen before. Thus in the twenty-first century, intelligence work promises to be fundamentally different. If so, then an evolutionary approach toward the training of intelligence personnel and the development and organisation of collection methods and systems – even toward the process of analysis itself – will no longer suffice to assure timely and accurate intelligence about the threats ahead.

Notes

1 Jeffrey T. Richelson, 'The US intelligence community', *Dictionary of US Military Terms for Joint Usage*, Department of the Navy, Army, Air-Force, May 1995, USA, p. 2.
2 Ernest May, *Knowing One's Enemies* (Cambridge, MA: Harvard University Press, 1984), p. 3.
3 Amos Kovacs 'Using intelligence', *Intelligence and National Security*, 12: 4 (October 1997), 145–64.
4 Ames A. Jordan and William J. Taylor, *American National Security Policy and Process* (Baltimore, HD and London: Johns Hopkins University Press, 1981). In a similar vein, John A. Jenny, in his 'The need for system analysis', *US Intelligence Community, Center for International Security and Arms Control* (Stanford, CA: Stanford University Press, 1984), includes 'Action-policy-makers', in his diagram of the intelligence cycle on p. 7, but in the text explaining the diagram he, too, has very little to say about the use or the user except for 'if the policy maker is satisfied the process is finished', as though satisfaction and not effect is what is being sought.
5 Arthur S. Hulnick, 'The intelligence producer–policy consumer linkage: a theoretical approach', *Intelligence and National Security*, 2 (May 1986), 212–33.
6 Abram Shulsky, Deputy for Asia and Defense Strategy (Office of the Secretary of Defense) and Jennifer Sims, Professional Staff Member (Senate Select Committee on Intelligence), 'What is intelligence', *Working Group on Intelligence Reform*, Consortium for the Study of Intelligence, Washington DC, 1993.
7 *Ibid.*
8 'Intelligence requirements process', *Intelligence Community in the 21st Century*, Staff Study, Permanent Select Committee on Intelligence, House of Representatives, One Hundred Fourth Congress, Washington DC, March 1996, p. 10, Section III.
9 BBC News Online: World, 'Former intelligence officer claims Britain spies on EU', 4 January 1998, http://news.bbc.co.uk/1/low/world/43988.stm.
10 John M. Nomikos, 'The future of the US–European security relationship', *Peace And The Sciences Journal*, 26 (1995), International Institute for Peace, Vienna, Austria, 20–6.
11 Geoffrey Edwards and Simon Nuttalli, 'Common foreign and security policy', in Andrew Duff, John Pinder and Roy Pryce (eds), *Maastricht and Beyond – Building the European Union* (London: Routledge, 1994), p. 84.
12 Stefano Solvestri, 'European goals and interests', in Werner Weidenfeld and Josef Jannings (eds), *Global Responsibilities: Europe in Tomorrow's World*, (Germany: Berterlsmann Foundation, 1991), p. 80.
13 Walter L. Pforzheimer, 'Prospects for a European Common Intelligence Policy', Studies in Intelligence, Unclassified Document, Center for the Study of Intelligence, No. 9, CIA, USA, Summer 2000.
14 *Ibid.*
15 *Ibid.*
16 *Ibid.*
17 'EU: New Convention on mutual assistance in criminal matters' *Statewatch Bulletin*, 7: 4&5 (July–October 1997); see also: 'EU–FBI: EU–FBI telecommunications system moves two steps closer', *Statewatch Bulletin*, 9: 2 (March–April 1999).
18 The report by the Commission's working party can be found at: www.europa.eu.int/comm/dg15/en/media/dataprot/wpdocs/wp 18en.htm.

19 BBC News (www.bbc.co.uk), 'EU condemned over planned "snoop laws"', by Mark Ward, 16 May 2001.

20 Bradley F. Smith (1997), 'The American road to Central Intelligence Special Issue, Eternal Vigilance? 50 years of the Central Intelligence Agency', *Intelligence and National Security*, 12: 1 (January 1997), 1–20.

21 Ray S. Cline, *The Central Intelligence Agency Under Reagan, Bush, and Casey* (Washington, DC: Acropolis Books Ltd, 1981), p. 103.

22 On 7 July 1991 The European Union met with representatives of the Yugoslav government (Serbia, Slovenia, Croatia at the Brioni Islands). This resulted in the Brioni Declaration, which stated: (a) Yugoslavia parties will decide themselves about their fate; (b) The Yugoslav Presidency will have control over the Federal Army; (c) all parties will refrain from any unilateral acts, particularly involving violence.

23 M. Sandow-Quirk, 'A failure of intelligence', *Prometheus*, 20: 2 (1 June 2002), 131–42.

24 Jaap Donath (1993), 'A European Community Intelligence Organization', *Defense Intelligence Journal*, 2: 1 (1993), 15–33, Washington, DC.

25 Pforzheimer, 'Prospects for a European Common Intelligence Policy'.

26 *Ibid.*

27 *Ibid.*

28 *Ibid.*

29 *Ibid.*

30 Alessandro Politi, 'Why is a European Intelligence Policy necessary', 5–6, Chaillot Paper, No. 34, December 1998, WEU-Institute for Security Studies, Paris, France, pp. 5–6.

31 *Ibid.*

32 *Ibid.*

33 *Ibid.*

34 *Ibid.*

35 *Ibid.*

36 *Ibid.*

37 Robert Keohane and Stanley Hoffman, 'Institutional change in Europe in the 1980s', in Robert O. Keohane and Stanley Hoffmann (eds), *The New European Community: Decision-Making and Institutional Change* (Boulder, CO: Westview Press, 1992).

38 Timothy M. Devinney and William C. Hightower, *European Markets After 1992* (Lanham, MD: Lexington Books, 1991), p. 26.

39 *Ibid.*

40 *Ibid.*

41 See Jaap Donath, 'European Community Intelligence Organization'.

42 Giles Tremlett and Ian Black, 'EU plan to pool anti-terrorism intelligence', *Guardian Unlimited*, 2 March 2002.

43 Donath, 'European Community Intelligence Organization'.

44 Elizabeth Nash and Andrew Buncombe, 'Spanish police claim terrorist cell was planning suicide attacks in Europe', 27 September 2001, Independent.co.uk.

45 Stephen Castle, 'European Union lists terror groups', 29 December 2001, Independent.co.uk.

46 Ahto Lobjakas, 'EU Ministers agree to measures to preempt terrorist attacks, 20 September 2001, Eubusiness.com.

47 Monica den Boer and Jorg Monar, 'Keynote Article: 11 September and the Challenge

of Global Terrorism to the EU as a Security Actor', *Journal of Common Market Studies*, 40, Annual review (2002), 11–28.

47 'The strategic contribution of Intelligence', *In From the Cold*, Report of the Twentieth Century Fund Task Force on the 'Future of US Intelligence' (USA: Twentieth Century Fund, 1996), pp. 53–73.

Further reading

Dubois, D., 'The attacks of 11 September: EU–US cooperation against terrorism in the field of justice and home affairs', *European Foreign Affairs Review*, 7: 3 (2002), 317–35.

Duff, Andrew, John Pinder and Roy Pryce (eds), *Maastricht and Beyond – Building the European Union* (London: Routledge, 1994).

Herman, M. E., '11 September: legitimising intelligence?', *International Relations*, 16: 2 (August 2002), 227–41.

Weidenfeld, Werner and Josef Jannings (eds), *Global Responsibilities: Europe in Tomorrow's World* (Germany: Berterlsmann Foundation, 1991).

4

Recent developments in EU migration and asylum policies

Barbara Marshall

Migration into Europe is part of a growing world-wide population movement, which has its roots in the detailed knowledge of wide discrepancies in living standards in different parts of the world and the comparatively easy availability of transportation. Human rights violations, ethnic conflicts, natural disasters act as important 'push factors'. At the same time states are generally losing authority over key areas of political and especially macro-economic governance, which directly affect the living conditions of their electorates. Within rich countries the divide between rich and poor is growing, with an increasing number isolated from the benefits of the global economy and anxious over the reduced welfare budgets and the erosion of secured employment. A reaction against these developments is the new significance given to 'identity politics' with its rejection of 'global' forces and calls for a return to 'old', 'national' values, including national governments' promotion of 'national interests'. These have found a public voice in xenophobia and anti-immigrant attitudes.

National 'identity', which seems threatened by immigrants and their 'foreign' appearance, has shifted public opinion increasingly to the question of control. However, governments' control of immigration has always been only partial because there have been powerful economic interests working in favour of immigration. Sustained demand for cheap workers in a range of economic activities has acted as a powerful 'pull factor' for undocumented labour immigration.

In all EU member states migration and asylum have moved to the centre of the political debate. This has been characterised by confusion and contradictions. On the one hand demographic factors seem to indicate a need for more immigration. The UN survey, 'Replacement Migration: Is it A Solution to Declining and Aging Populations?'[1] forecasts a drastic decline in Europe's population and produces a number of models of the levels of annual immigration required in order to sustain Europe's present level of social benefits. A closer look at these predictions reveals, however, that this decline will only set in from 2010, and that the majority of EU countries will not be affected before 2020.

There are also significant differences between individual countries with the aging process in Germany, Italy and Belgium far more dramatic than in France, Portugal and Holland.[2] According to the EU Commission, working with Eurostat figures, there will only be a gradual slowing down of Europe's population until 2025, with a gradual decline of the labour force from 225 to 223 million.[3] A distinction also needs to be made between different kinds of immigration. At present European governments are particularly concerned about the decline of skilled labour. From the late 1990s Britain, Italy, Spain and even a country like Germany, which traditionally considered itself a country of non-immigration, passed new laws to permit residence of foreign workers.[4] At the same time a wider debate began in Germany about the merits of creating an area of controlled general immigration comparable with that of Canada.[5] However, this is in contrast to the large pool of unemployed within the Union, whose skills, it is argued, could be developed.[6] Above all, demographic and economic reasons in favour of immigration contrast with persistent difficulties in integrating immigrants, as the riots among seemingly well-adjusted ethnic communities in towns in northern England in the summer of 2001 indicated.

The European Union has for some time endeavoured to develop a common approach to migration policies, initially in the 1980s to compensate for the removal of internal borders in the process of creating the internal market. From the beginning the question of control over immigration was of central importance, and this narrowed on asylum seekers where governments are bound by international laws, such as the Geneva Convention. Their 'control' has shifted increasingly to devices preventing their arrival with a range of measures which resulted in the creation of 'Fortress Europe': the 'non-arrival' policies aimed at preventing foreigners without proper documentation access to Europe, such as visa requirements and the posting of immigration officers abroad; the shifting of responsibility for the processing of asylum requests to other countries, such as Eastern Europe where asylum systems were created; the build-up of a system of 'safe third countries' as a 'buffer' around the EU with the conclusion of re-admission agreements; the restrictive application of the Geneva Convention (persecution by non-state actors is not considered a valid reason for protection) with a multiplicity of protection statuses generating confusion and insecurities in the public about who is a 'genuine' refugee; deterrent measures such as detention and prevention of access to the labour market. This has been possible because of a steady decline in public support for asylum, which is explicable by a blurring of the distinction between immigrants and asylum seekers. The latter are increasingly criminalised as 'abusers' of the system and because of the growing involvement of criminals in the form of traffickers and drug pushers.

By the late 1990s particularly, the growth of irregular migration created the impetus for a new series of co-operative initiatives. While the number of asylum applicants coming to Europe declined from 479.762 in 1998 to 417.490 in 1999,[7] irregular migration increased. The US government estimates that up to 2 million people are smuggled annually world-wide,[8] of which about 500,000 arrive in Europe[9] with the help of traffickers for whom this trade in humans represents revenues of more than euro 5 billion per annum.[10] In response member states governments made a determined effort to co-operate more closely: 'cooperation among national agencies concerned with ... managing borders, immigration and asylum, and with the judicial and legal implications of rising cross-border movement became in the late 1990s the most active field for meetings convened under the Council of Ministers'.[11]

The realisation that anti-immigrant rhetoric is compelling governments to come up with a 'solution', but also economic needs seem to have contributed to a new consensus which is emerging both in the Commission and in the member states: Europe should open itself, albeit cautiously and in a controlled manner to more labour immigration. This would remove some of the incentive for the use of criminal traffickers by migrants and might reduce the pressure on the asylum system. However, the very flurry of activities reveals the extent to which this process has been fraught with difficulties. Migration and asylum have always been one of the policy areas in which there have been continued tensions between the Commission and the Council over the distribution of competences in the EC/EU. Moreover, national governments have been reluctant to pool their sovereignty or hand over decision-making to 'Europe' in this particularly sensitive policy area and fear that the Commission might force politically unpopular measures on them. At the same time there has not been sufficient trust in each others' procedures and motives to surrender control by accepting, for example, more qualified majority voting (QMV) as the basis for decision-making in the Council. In essence therefore the controversies surrounding migration and asylum have also been about the nature and limits of European integration.

Against the background of the emerging European migration and asylum policies from the early 1990s and the contributions by member states and European institutions to it, this chapter will focus on new developments in this policy area from the Amsterdam Council (June 1997) and, in particular, from the Council meeting at Tampere (October 1999). The latter has brought the Commission a great deal more competences in initiating policies to which it has responded with a wide array of Communications, Directives and Proposals both in the area of asylum and refugee policies and in the field of immigration. However, many of the more far-reaching proposals are unlikely to be approved by national governments. Indeed, successive Council resolutions seemed to reveal that their real priorities remained restrictions and control measures.

Commission and Council before the Tampere Conference

The Single European Act in its Article 8a stipulated the free movement of goods, capital, services and people, and there were immediate disputes about how this article was to be interpreted: to what extent were member states prepared to give up national sovereignty in favour of the Commission? A proposal by the

Commission in 1985, that it should take control, was rejected by the majority of member states. Decision-making remained firmly within the remit of national governments. Subsequently the Commission remained involved with a series of important initiatives and its objective has been to promote more comprehensive approaches to migration and asylum policies than those of the Council, which were dominated by negative concerns such as the control of numbers. In 1991 it published two proposals, one for immigration and one for asylum. In them it advocated a 'global approach' to these policy areas, which should go beyond measures relating only to borders and control. However, a number of national governments suspected that the Commission was again seeking to extend its powers. The Maastricht Conference therefore adopted the 'pillar structure' which left asylum and migration within the inter-governmental arena. Only visa policy came into Community competence under Article 100c.

In February 1994 the Commission published a further document in which it stressed again the necessity that migration should not only be seen in terms of control and security, but that the integration of already present immigrants was equally important for the well being of European societies.[12] However, there was little evidence that the Commission had made converts among national governments, which paid no more than lip service to these views. Two Commission proposals, presented in August 1995, for a 'Directive on the elimination of controls on persons crossing internal frontiers'[13] and for a 'Directive on the right of third-country nationals to travel in the Community'[14] were not accepted by member states, despite the provision authorising member states to reinstate controls 'in the event of a serious threat to public policy or public security'. One of the main obstacles has been that to allow the free crossing of internal borders would only produce the desired results if it was not limited to EU citizens but included all legal residents.[15] This was opposed particularly by Germany, which feared an increase in in-migration of third country nationals from other European states.

It was only at the Amsterdam Conference in June 1997 that the EU moved decisively in the direction of a common policy with the creation of the EU as an area of 'freedom, security and justice'. This brought a considerable increase in influence for the Commission with the transfer of some of the Pillar III matters into Union competence. On the basis of Articles 62 and 63 respectively, 'Amsterdam' prescribed the development by the Community of common norms and standards for the control of external borders, the issuing of short-term visas, co-operation in civil law matters and the safeguarding of the rights of third country nationals. In the area of immigration and asylum, uniform rules for the state with responsibility for the processing of asylum applications and minimum standards for the reception of asylum seekers should be established. Common standards for the recognition of refugee status and some form of temporary protection should be found. Further objectives were common measures against illegal immigration and the return of those migrants without legal status. A wider range of measures in the area of migration and asylum

were, however, exempt from the five-year time restraint (and their implementation seemingly removed into the distant future): the development of a
burden-sharing system for refugees; the establishment of common rules for
their entry and residence; the issuing of long-term visas, for family reunion and
for the free movement throughout the EU of third country nationals.

The array of objectives which 'Amsterdam' introduced appear impressive at
first sight. However, full implementation of these provisions will only come
about five years after 'Amsterdam' came into force, that is in the year 2004 at the
earliest. In the meantime decisions continue to be made in the Council on the
basis of unanimity. In other words, while common European policies were
accepted in principle, the Council rather than the Commission remained in the
driving seat of policy-making.

At the same time the 'Schengen *acquis*' with its comprehensive border crossing regime and control mechanisms came into the remit of the Community.
However, even this measure was fraught with difficulties, as the protracted
negotiations for a legal base of the 'Schengen Information System (SIS)' indicated. There was also renewed wrangling over the institutional arrangements.
Only shortly before the Amsterdam Treaty entered into force on 1 May 1999 did
governments agree to make the Council of Permanent Representatives
(COREPER) the co-ordinating body below the level of the Council and only in
September 1999 did the Commission set up the General Directorate for Justice
and Home Affairs.

Inter-governmental co-operation

These initiatives at the European level need to be seen against the background
of member states' interests and objectives. The slow and cumbersome development of intra-state co-operation and the mistrust and hesitations of member
states has often been described.[16] As noted above, their priority has been to keep
decision-making in this policy area under their control, as far as major issues of
national sovereignty were involved. No harmonisation of substantive policy
areas, such as agreement on the definition of a refugee[17] or the equalisation of
reception conditions, were achieved. There were two particularly controversial
issues among member states: border controls and 'burden-sharing'.

The policing of migration flows: border controls

Disputes over the control of internal and external borders in the EC/EU began
in earnest with the opening of the Iron Curtain, which brought for the European
Community the spectre of mass migration and a long land border in the east
which would be difficult to control. The signing of the Schengen
Implementation Convention due at the end of 1989 was postponed by six
months to June 1990 and was eventually achieved only because the German
Democratic Republic, in the inter-German negotiations at the beginning of

1990, gave the requisite guarantees to strengthen its eastern border.[18] It was not until 26 March 1995 that 'Schengen' came officially into force. Even then France required the extension of the 'initial phase of implementation into 1996';[19] the Dutch needed extra time to the end of 1995 to convert their airports;[20] and Italy and Greece were initially not admitted at all, due to the permeability of their borders. Controls have been intensified even between close neighbours such as Denmark and Sweden and between Sweden and the Baltic states.

There was open controversy between Germany and Austria over what, to the Germans, appeared to be the too loosely controlled Austrian borders. There were rumours that Germany would veto Austrian membership of Schengen.[21] Even after Austria and Italy joined in December 1997 and March 1998 respectively the land border between them continued to be controlled, and only controls on air passengers were lifted.[22]

Controls at the borders between Germany and its eastern neighbours have also been intensified.[23] The reinforcement of the borders between Poland and the Czech Republic with their eastern neighbours has been made a precondition for the widening of the European Union. These measures have been taken already, long before countries such as Poland or the Czech Republic actually were EU members, to a large extent in response to Germany's pressure. The Federal Republic of Germany also supported Belarus[24] in the period 1992–98 for the policing of its 650 km land border with Poland. It is clear that these countries are being used as a buffer by Germany to prevent potential through-migration at an early stage. Even an EU member such as Greece, in an attempt to catch up with the rest of Europe prior to membership of the Union's inner core, the Euro zone, established a special border police force, which co-ordinated the activities of the police, health and education services in order to stem the influx of migrants from Albania.[25] On 13 August 1999 the Greek Council of State endorsed the government's decision to recruit a further 1,230 border guards, bringing the total numbers of guards to 2,320.[26] Greece joined 'Schengen' on 1 January 2000.

The issue of border controls has remained of primary concern to EU member states. This was illustrated again by the conclusion of a co-operation agreement between the French and Belgian border police in March 2001,[27] by Britain's dispatch in the summer of 2001 of immigration officials to Prague airport to help screen out unwanted potential Roma asylum seekers[28] and Britain's efforts to persuade France to improve control over access to the Channel Tunnel by closing the Red Cross camp near Sangatte.[29] Spain's efforts to police the Gibraltar straights have become a major issue in national and EU politics.[30]

'Burden-sharing'

'Burden-sharing' of asylum seekers had been a long-standing objective of Germany which until the mid-1990s received more applications than the rest of the member states together.[31] However, there was never a chance that other countries would be prepared to shoulder the consequences of Germany's seemingly too generous asylum provisions. But it was the sharing of refugees from the former Yugoslavia which became one of the most divisive policy issues in the EC/EU throughout the 1990s. This was promoted notably by the refugee-receiving countries Germany, Austria and Sweden but staunchly opposed by other member states, notably the UK, France and the Netherlands, that is those countries geographically furthest removed from the emergency situation. A succession of international meetings made a range of proposals which were regularly turned down despite the fact that they included suggestions for the setting up of a European Fund for Refugees which could be utilised in cases of sudden emergencies.[32] But this lack of solidarity among member states in such an important policy area augured ill both for refugee protection and a further harmonisation of asylum and refugee policies at the European level. It was not surprising that, despite the worsening situation in Kosovo from the end of March 1999 and the growing number of people fleeing the area, the Commission's proposal for temporary protection was not even on the agenda of the JHA Council in May.

In line with the approach that any preparation for a possible refugee emergency would act as a 'pull factor', no emergency measures were in place once NATO's bombing campaign had begun on 24 March 1999. NATO and the EU claimed to be surprised by the scale of the expulsions of the population. But even when the humanitarian crisis had become obvious the EU Council decided not to adopt a common plan for reception quotas which had been put forward by Germany, Sweden and Denmark. As on previous occasions when 'burden-sharing' was on the agenda, the main opponents were the UK, France, the Netherlands, Spain and Finland. Instead, the EU promised aid to the refugees and to Kosovo's neighbours who had no choice but to shelter them. In the words of one leading German official, 'we are still far away from a common refugee policy in the EU'.[33] This view was confirmed by the Tampere Conference in October 1999 where the UK again refused to compromise on 'burden-sharing'.

Council and Commission: Tampere and after

From the late 1990s and beyond the Nice Treaty, successive Council Presidencies put forward proposals which aimed particularly at curtailing the rights of and the access to the EU of asylum seekers. For example, the Austrian Presidency in 1998 had suggested the modification of the Geneva Convention and the surrounding of Europe by concentric circles in which different measures of control would be enacted with the help of a 'carrot and stick' system for the participating states.[34] The French Presidency, in the summer of 2000 made four proposals, which further curtailed the access to the EU by migrants and asylum seekers (see p. 000). Against this background the decisions by the Council for Justice and Home Affairs meeting at Tampere in October 1999 appear in a positive light. The meeting had been called to review 'best practice' in the implementation of Amsterdam's area of 'rights and freedoms' and decided the further development of three policy areas: a common European asylum system which was to be based on the 'unrestricted and comprehensive application of the Geneva Convention'; the treatment of third country nationals and the more efficient management[35] of migration flows, which included the fight against irregular migration with tougher penalties for traffickers and closer co-operation of border control personnel. The Central European candidates, next up for EU membership were to accept the entire Schengen *aquis*. There was to be wide-ranging consultation with non-governmental organisations (NGOs) and refugee support groups prior to the publication of new draft legislation in the area of migration and asylum.[36]

The Commission was to publish one 'Scoreboard' report per Presidency on progress achieved, the first of which appeared in March 2000.[37] Although the Commission by April 2001 had to admit that both it and the Council 'had let the time-table slip' somewhat,[38] the Commission had in fact published a range of legislative proposals both in the area of asylum and refugee protection and of immigration policy generally, which together were considered the basis for a future EU migration and asylum policy.

Asylum and refugee policies

Three proposals in the area of asylum and refugee protection were particularly significant: the Commission's 'Draft directive for temporary protection and responsibility sharing'[39] of 24 May 2000, the 'Communication to the Council and the European Parliament: Towards a common asylum procedure and a uniform status, valid throughout the Union, for persons granted asylum'[40] of 22 November 2000 and the 'Proposal for a Council Regulation laying down the criteria and mechanisms for determining member states responsible for examining applications for asylum in one member state' (also termed 'Dublin II') of 27 July 2001.

The Directive setting out the norms for Temporary Protection was eventually agreed on 28 May 2001.[41] Although NGOs and refugee support groups voiced reservations[42] in the context of policy co-ordination within the EU, the directive signified progress. Furthermore, after a decade of disputes over the sharing of the 'burden' of refugees, a common Refugee Fund was set up on 28 September 2000, which for the first time introduced the acceptance by member states of the principle that states, which had to provide for a sudden influx of refugees, needed EU support. This was only achieved against the background of the Kosovo experience, where all member states had agreed on keeping refugees as far as possible in their regions of origin, that is future refugee flows would be small. It was also revealing that the Fund was pitifully small with Euro 216 million over five years. Moreover, 70 per cent of these funds are earmarked for voluntary repatriation and only 25 per cent for the reception and integration of refugees (with the remaining 5 per cent reserved for administration). It was also noteworthy that even this comparatively minor measure took more than nine months to negotiate and that agreement on the basis of unanimity was held up by the smaller states, 'eager to ensure their share of the cake even though their part of the responsibility of refugee reception in the EU is very small, if not negligible'.[43]

The significance of the Commission's position in the Communication on common asylum procedures lies in the maintenance of a protection-based, rights-centred asylum system against national governments' repeated claims that the Geneva Convention was no longer relevant in the present 'asylum crisis' (see below). The continued involvement of NGOs is guaranteed and the abandonment of controversial concepts such as 'safe country of origin' or 'safe third country' is advocated. Moreover, the document stresses the need for the granting of similar rights to refugees as to other categories of protected persons and of generous integration measures. But it also contains statements which, to refugee support groups such as ECRE (European Council on Refugees and Exiles) 'give cause for concern'.[44] For example, there is recognition in the document that immigration control measures may be negatively impacting on the right of asylum seekers to seek protection in the EU. Other points concern a possible limitation of a suspensive right of appeal; the consideration of policies to combat sudden mass influxes of refugees rather than facilitating access to EU territory (see p. 000); the acceptance of diverging interpretations of the Geneva Convention among member states[45] or the acceptance that other, shorter forms of protection might be substituted for the provisions of the Geneva Convention. These concerns intensified in 2002–3 with the tightening of anti-terrorism measures across the EU.

That the 1990 Dublin Convention, establishing the responsibility for the processing of asylum application among member states, came into force only in 1997 reflected again the reluctance of member states to co-operate in asylum matters. Under the Vienna Action Plan of December 1998 it was agreed to transfer the Dublin Convention into Community competence, which raised the shortcomings of the Convention to wider scrutiny. The Commission provided the background for the debate with two Working Papers, 'Revisiting the Dublin Convention: developing Community legislation for determining which Member State is responsible for considering an asylum application submitted in one of the member States'[46] of 21 March 2000, which was followed by a wide consultation with interested organizations,[47] and the 'Evaluation of the Dublin Convention'[48] of 13 June 2001. Among the many comments two critical points emerged: 'Dublin I' had proved ineffective, as in practice in 1998 and 1999 only 1.7 per cent of all asylum cases were actually transferred between member states.[49] More important from the perspective of refugee protection was the fact that 'Dublin I' had been implemented on the basis of differing asylum systems and diverging reception standards among member states. In the view of one refugee agency, 'Dublin I ' represented a 'protection lottery'.[50] In the light of these weighty criticisms it comes as a surprise to find that the new Proposal (Dublin II) continues the system of Dublin I more or less unchanged. As there is still no agreement on the harmonisation of substantive areas of asylum legislation the Commission concluded that 'it would not be realistic to envisage a system for determining the Member State responsible ... which diverges fundamentally from the Dublin Convention.'[51] However, the Commission is at pains to underline certain innovations which Dublin II will bring: new provisions outlining member states' responsibilities when allowing illegal residents to remain on its territory;[52] much shorter procedural deadlines to ensure asylum applications are processed rapidly; extending of deadlines to facilitate the transfer of asylum seekers; new provisions aiming at preserving the family unity of asylum seekers. Only the last promises an improvement from the perspective of asylum seekers; the rest attempt to 'toughen up' Dublin I. It is hard to see why these provisions should work better than Dublin I. Indeed for critical observers they raise the question 'whether they are merely intended to reassure public opinion that EU leaders are able to keep under control the problem of the "abuse of asylum"'.[53]

Immigration policy

The Tampere Conference had also called for a future approach to immigration 'in partnership' with the countries of origin, for the fair treatment of third country nationals already living in EU territory (that is with a focus on integration) and for the more efficient management of migration flows.[54] This was again the platform from which the Commission developed a number of initiatives. In 2000 it published a 'Communication on the Community Immigration Policy',[55] setting out its ideas for a new approach, particularly for a common policy on admission for economic reasons. In the field of legal immigration a draft directive on family reunification is under discussion in the Council[56] and a 'Draft Directive on the admission of Third Country Nationals (TCNs) for economic purposes'[57] has been published. Progress has been made on the establishment of a legal framework to ensure the fair treatment of TCNs legally resident in the EU, such as the legislation combating racism and discrimination[58] and the proposals for a directive concerning the status of long-term resident TCNs.[59] Agreement has also been reached on measures combating irregular migration. Thus the right to expel TCNs in this category has been recognised[60] and the harmonisation of financial penalties imposed on carriers transporting TCNs lacking the requisite documentation into member states (after the UK's demands for massive penalties were scaled down) has been adopted.[61]

The most comprehensive measure in this area so far has however been the 'Proposal for a Directive on the right to move and reside freely for EU nationals and members of their family'.[62] It goes further than the titles suggests and is designed to provide unified legislation for all EU citizens. It would replace most secondary legislation on almost all aspects of migration and would result in significant changes of the overall legal framework. It would apply to family members of migrant EU citizens, as well to those of non-migrants EU citizens, provided the Commission's proposals for family reunion were adopted, which is unlikely in the near future as the UK, Ireland and Denmark have opted out of this policy area and Germany has serious reservations about the Commission's 'generosity' when defining the maximum age of dependents entitled to join their families in the EU. One general shortcomings of the Proposal is that it does not address the issue of social security in the different member states. However, unequal social conditions in different member states will affect the adoption of EU-wide legislation. Governments of states with more generous provisions, such as Germany, are unlikely to consent, as a process of internal EU migration from less generous countries would commence to the detriment of its citizens.

The area covered by the Proposal is comprehensive.[63] The Directive would apply from 1 July 2003. Its very comprehensiveness will entail prolonged and controversial negotiations among member states.

The Commission's 'Communication to the Council and the European Parliament on an Open Method of Coordination for the Community Immigration Policy' of 11 July 2001[64] is equally ambitious. The overall objective is again the managed and orderly flow of people. In order to overcome member states' reluctance to co-operate an 'open procedure' for the evolving future immigration is advocated.

At the heart of this policy will be a common legislative framework, the basis of which has already been agreed by member states (Article 63 of the Treaty of Amsterdam). Modestly, the paper proposes a first phase as one of 'identification and development of common objectives'. The method should be implemented during an initial period of six years, that is the period on which a first evaluation of application of the 'Directive on the conditions of entry and residence of TCNs for the purposes of paid employment' must be made. Moreover, the principle of subsidiarity is considered particularly relevant to this policy area and should be preserved wherever possible, as is a need for solidarity among member states and the European institutions 'in facing the trans-national challenges presented by migration movements'.[65]

The open co-ordination method is intended to support and complement Community legislation whereas member states will remain in charge of implementation with regard to the number of migrants admitted over a particular time period, the establishment of horizontal assessment programmes and other measures which must be notified to the Commission. The latter suggests that the criteria for these assessment schemes could include the involvement of the social partners in the evaluation of economic needs or the comparison of recruitment procedures particularly in the countries of origin.

The Commission undertakes to table all relevant proposals by 2004 according to a time-table laid down in the 'Scoreboard'. It will also provide 'European Guidelines' in order to ensure the co-ordination of national policies, the

exchange of best practice and the evaluation of the impact of Community policies in third countries. The key element of open co-ordination is the adoption
by the Council of multi-annual guidelines, which should be accompanied by
specific time-tables for achieving goals which will then be translated into
national policies by setting specific targets. A first concrete step in the direction
of improved co-operation will be the availability of comparable statistics, which
'is of crucial importance for the effective monitoring and evaluation of common
immigration policy'. The available statistical material so far has varied greatly
between member states, with different priorities in the data collected. In the
Action Plan requested by the Council Conclusions of May 2001 this work will
constitute one of the key actions.[66]

The 'Communication' then makes detailed suggestions as to what the
European Guidelines could contain, within which national governments would
fix their national objectives. However, the fact that of the six guidelines in all,
four are devoted to the 'management of migration flows',[67] but only one for
'partnership with third countries'[68] and one for the' integration of third country
nationals'[69] reflects the priorities of the Commission. Member states are to
prepare annual 'Action Plans' in two parts: one to provide an overview of the
results of the actions carried out in the previous year and the other to make
proposals for the implementation of the migration guidelines at national,
regional and local levels in the year to come. Where relevant, reference to their
projection of labour demand for migrants as set out in the National Action
Plans for employment could be included.

The Commission is not only attempting to co-ordinate detailed national policies, 'in view of the multi-dimensional aspects of migration policy, the
European Parliament, the Economic and Social Committee and the Committee
of the Region should be involved' (p. 14). The Commission would also produce
an annual 'migration report'. These proposals were presented to the Laeken
Summit in December 2001.

While the Commission has thus been engaged in devising a comprehensive,
albeit complex migration 'package', the priority of member states has continued
to be the preoccupation with 'control' of asylum seekers and illegal immigration. Four proposals by the French Presidency in 2000,[70] were adopted by the
Transport and Telecoms Council at the end of June 2001 and by the JHA
(Justice and Home Affairs) Council in May 2001. These oblige member states to
impose 'appropriate sanctions', that is criminal penalties of a maximum of eight
years on any person who intentionally assists a TCN to enter or transit the territory of a member state. Stiff penalties for TCNs committing an offense and the
facilitation of their removal is envisaged in the other decisions.

One of the more revealing aspects of these decisions is the fact that the original French proposals emerged far harsher as a result of the negotiations between
member states – another example that, where migration policy is left to the
Council, decisions are reached at the lowest common denominator. In the
opinion of critical observers 'for migrants and asylum seekers the "area of

freedom, security and justice" consists largely of measures preventing their entry and removing them from the EU'.[71] Recent trends in European migration and asylum policies thus appear confused and ambiguous. There is institutional muddle, with different Councils now making decisions in this policy area and governments coming to 'political agreements' in migration matters,[72] by-passing national parliaments, with for EU policy-makers the perhaps not unwelcome result that NGOs find it increasingly hard to keep up with the newest developments and to provide the necessary scrutiny of policy and judicial co-operation.[73] Here is therefore another example of the general lack of accountability of EU policy-makers.

There is also ambiguity as to what the European objectives really are. On the one hand the Commission projects an impressive vision of an all-embracing European policy framework in which the Geneva Convention remains the cornerstone of refugee protection and which member states seemingly endorsed at Tampere and subsequent meetings. This contrasts with the absence of agreement on fundamental matters, such as the definition of a refugee or minimum standards for the reception of asylum seekers or the equalisation of social welfare provisions.

The wider vision of a European migration and asylum policy also comes up against the desire by all EU JHA Ministers to tighten controls, which have now found new support in the guise of the need to fight international terrorism. Furthermore, all governments face periodic elections and only European policies which can be presented as 'tough' to national electorates will be considered 'safe'. At best, future EU migration policies will therefore be hard on asylum seekers – the weakest element in the immigration area – while attempting to justify continued 'managed' immigration on the grounds of economic interests.

Notes

1 United Nations (UN), Secretariat, Population Division, Department of Economic and Social Affairs, 21: 3 (2000).
2 Feld, S. (2000), 'Active population growth and immigration hypotheses', *European Journal of Population*, 16: 1 (2000), 3–40.
3 COM 23 (2000).
4 *Business Week*, 23 October 2000.
5 *Die Zeit*, 23 May 2001.
6 *Ibid.*
7 ECRE, 'An overview of the proposals addressing migrant smuggling and trafficking in persons', Background paper, March 2001.
8 www.unhcr.ch.
9 *Observer*, 28 January 2001.
10 *Der Spiegel*, 30 April 2001.
11 Monica den Boer and William Wallace, 'Justice and home affairs: integration through incrementalism', in Helen Wallace and William Wallace (eds), *Policy-*

making in the European Union, 4th edn (Oxford: Oxford University Press, April 2000), pp. 493–519.

12 COM 23 final (1994).

13 COM 346 final CN95199 (1995).

14 COM final CNS950201, (1995) para 4.

15 European Parliament Opinion, 23 October 1996. *Official Journal* (*OJ*) C347, 18 November 1996. Note that schoolchildren, if part of group, are now allowed to cross internal frontiers without a special visa.

16 S. Collinson, *Europe and International Migration* (London: Pinter, 1996); A. Cruz, 'Schengen, ad hoc immigration group and other intergovernmental bodies', Briefing Paper 12, Churches Committee for Migrants in Europe, Brussels, 1993; D. Papademetriou, 'Coming together or pulling apart? The European Union's struggle with immigration and asylum', International Migration Policy Program, volume 5, Carnegie Endowment for International Peace, Washington DC, 1996.

17 Note the latest Commission effort in this area: 'Brussels draws up proposal for uniform definition of refugees', *Financial Times*, 13 September 2001.

18 A. Funk, *Migration News Sheet* (MNS), (Migration Policy Group, Brussels, 1994), p.25 also November 1993, p. 2.

19 *MNS*, January 1996, p. 2.

20 *MNS*, April 1995, p. 2.

21 *Süddeutsche Zeitung* (*SZ*), 26 June 1997.

22 Note, for example, the verdict by the ECJ (European Court of Justice) on 16 March 1999 that at the present level of European unity Articles 7a and 8a of the EC Treaty may not be interpreted as meaning that there is automatic abolition of border checks, *MNS*, April 1999, p. 1.

23 Poland and the Czech Republic have been encouraged to build up control mechanisms at the former's eastern borders and those between the Czech and Slovak Republics. Part of the DM 120 and DM 60 million which Germany paid respectively in the Readmission Agreements with these countries in 1993 and 1994 was diverted for this purpose.

24 With DM 6 million.

25 *Financial Times*, 8 December 1998.

26 *MNS*, September 1999, p. 3.

27 *MNS*, March 2001, p. 6.

28 *Guardian*, 28 August 2001.

29 *Guardian*, 30 August 2001; *Financial Times*, 5 September 2001.

30 *MNS*, several issues 2001.

31 P. Henshon and N. Malhan, 'Endeavours to export a migration crisis: policy making and Europeanisation in the German migration dilemma', *German Politics*, 4: 3 (1995).

32 For details see B. Marshall, 'Closer integration or re-nationalisation? Recent trends in EU migration and asylum policies: the case of Germany', *Journal of European Integration* (2000), p. 131 passim.

33 *MNS*, May 1999, p. 13.

34 Marshall, 'Closer integration or re-nationalisation?'.

35 Note that the term 'management' of migration has replaced the use of the harsher 'control' in the EU's official documents.

36 NGOs and refugee support groups have already produced a number of lucid publications, setting out their recommendations for the continuation of a humane

approach to refugee protection, based on established laws and procedures. The Academic Group on Immigration, made up of lawyers and academics, submitted recommendations to the Tampere Conference (AGIT, 1999). The European Sub-Committee of ILPA has worked out detailed proposals for the Commission on the content of future policies on asylum, third country nationals and family reunion (Immigration Law Practitioners' Association (ILPA), 1999).

37 'Scoreboard to review progress on the creation of an area of freedom, security and justice in the European Union', COM 167 (24 March 2000).

38 'Scoreboard' (May 2001), 4.

39 'Council Directive on Minimum Standards for giving temporary protection in the event of a mass influx of displaced persons and on measures promoting a balance of efforts among Member States in receiving such persons and bearing the consequences thereof', COM 303 final (2000).

40 COM 755 final (2000).

41 2001/55 EC (20 July 2001). *OJ* L212/12, 2001.

42 ECRE pointed to the lack of detail on procedure and the absence of a clause on *non-refoulement* (ECRE, 'Observations of the European Council on Refugees and Exiles on the European Commission's draft directive on temporary protection and responsibility sharing', London, January 2001). The United Nations High Commission for Refugees (UNHCR), by contrast, 'noted as a positive development the recognition that temporary protection is not an alternative to refugee status under the Geneva Convention' (*MNS*, July 2001, p. 10).

43 *MNS*, June 2001, p. 1.

44 ECRE, 'Summary Comments by the Council on Refugees and Exiles on the Communication ... Towards a Common asylum procedure', London, June 2001.

45 For Germany and France, for example, persecution has to be carried out by state agencies to qualify for asylum under the Geneva Convention.

46 Justice and Home Affairs, SEC (2000) 522.

47 Such as UNHCR, ILPA, Amnesty International, the Conference of Churches on migrants in Europe and ECRE.

48 SEC (2001) 756.

49 Danish Refugee Council (2000), The Dublin Convention. Study on its Implementation in the 15 Member States of the European Union. (www.drc.dk/dk/publikationer/rapporter/dublin/obser/index/php).

50 ECRE, Comments from the European Council on Refugees and Exiles on the European Commission Staff Working Paper 'Revisiting the Dublin Convention: developing Community legislation for determining which member States is responsible for considering an application for asylum submitted in one of the member States' (London, 30 June 2000).

51 Proposal, Para 5; ILPA, Explanatory Memorandum, Europe Group (2001), 4.

52 After six months presence in one country the processing of asylum applications of illegal immigrants becomes the responsibility of that country. This provision was welcomed by the UK because it will address the 'Sangatte' problem.

53 *MNS*, July 2001, p. 10.

54 SN 200/99 Presidency Conclusions of the Tampere European Council, 15–16 October 1999.

55 'Communication to the Council and the European Parliament on a Community Immigration Policy', Commission of the European Union COM 757 (2000).

56 COM 624 (2000), amended version of 10 October 2000.

57 COM 386 (2001). 'Conditions of entry and residence of third country nationals for the purposes of paid employment and self employed economic activities'.

58 Directive 2000/43, *OJ* L180 of 19 July 2000 and Directive 2000/78, *OJ* L303 of 2 December 2000.

59 COM 127 (2001).

60 Directive 2001/40 OJ L149 of 2 June 2001.

61 *OJ* C 269 of 20 September 2000.

62 COM 257 (23 May 2001).

63 Chapter I (Articles 1–4) sets out the purpose, scope and definitions, with a non-discrimination clause. Chapter II (Articles 5–6) sets out rules governing movement and residence for up to six months. Chapter III (Articles 5–13) governs the right of residence for periods over six months, including provisions on retention of rights in the event of death of the primary right-holder. Chapter IV (Articles 14–18) governs the right of permanent residence for EU nationals and their family members. Chapter V (Articles 19–24) contains provisions relevant to both residence and permanent residence, addressing the issues of territorial scope, family members' employment and self-employment, equal treatment, residence documents, checks by authorities, and procedural rules for persons who could purportedly be expelled on grounds *other than* public policy, security or health. Chapter VI (Articles 25–31) concerns restrictions on grounds of public policy, security or health. Chapter VII (Articles 32–39) contains general and final provisions.

64 COM 387 (11 July 2001).

65 Commission, 2001: 5.

66 7973/01 ASIM 10, adopted by the May 2001 JHA Council. The Commission has already published a staff Working Paper (SEC (2001) 602).

67 Every Guideline is followed by detailed further suggestions: Guideline 1 (p. 7) – Developing a comprehensive and coordinated approach to migration management at national level; 2 (p. 8) – Improving information available on legal possibilities for admission to the EU and on the consequences of using illegal channels; 3 (p. 9) – Reinforcing the fight against illegal immigration and trafficking by supporting the following measures ... 4 (p. 9) – Establishing a coherent and transparent policy and procedures for opening the labour market to third country nationals within the framework of the European employment strategy.

68 Guideline 5 (p. 10) – Integrating migration issues into relations with third countries, and in particular with countries of origin.

69 Guideline 6 – Ensuring the development of integration policies for third country nationals residing legally on the territories of the Member States.

70 These are: the Carrier Sanctions' Directive supplementing the provisions of Article 26 of the Schengen Convention (2001/51; *OJ* L187/45, 2001); the Directive and framework decision on 'facilitation' (10075/01) and the Directive on the mutual recognition of expulsion orders (2001/40; *OJ* L149/35, 2001).

71 Statewatch, 'Criminalising asylum: the EU adopts the French immigration proposals' (2001). www. statewatch.org/news/2001/aug/13asylum.htm.

72 The Agriculture Council adopted regulations updating Common Consular Instructions and the Common Manual on Border Controls on 24. 4. 2001. The Transport and Telecoms Council adopted the supplement to the provisions of the Schengen Convention.

73   ILPA, Explanatory Memorandum, Europe Group, Minutes 2, 7.

Further reading

Commission of the European Union (2001), Perceptions of the European Union. A
    Qualitative Study of the Public's Attitudes to and the Expectations of the EU in the 15
    Member States and in the 9 Candidate Countries. Survey, June.
ECRE (2001), 2000: Principled Implementation of the Tampere Conclusions?
Freeman, G. 'Modes of immigration politics in Liberal Democratic states', *International
    Migration Review*, 29 (1995), 4.
Harding, J. 'The Uninvited', *London Review of Books*, 3 February 2000.
Martin, S., 'Towards a Global Migration Regime', *Georgetown Journal of International
    Affairs*, 12: 1 (2002).
UN (United Nations), Secretariat, Population Division, Department of Economic and
    Social Affairs, 21 (2000), 3.
Wallace, H. and Wallace, W. (eds), *Policy-Making in the European Union*, (Oxford:
    Oxford University Press, 2000).

5

Enforcing human rights in Europe and beyond: international law and human rights in a changing world

Caroline Nolan

[handwritten: EU human rights declarations + ability to enforce them. UN & interm Crim court has that *(The Hague)]*

It is not so long ago since the study of international law was considered a 'luxury course'. A survey on the teaching of international law in US Law Schools in the 1950s presented the view that it was not perceived as a 'bread and butter subject' and they 'did not have time for it'. A Chief Justice speaking on the topic suggested that, 'I think it is safe to say that not one lawyer in five hundred, possibly not one lawyer in a thousand had ever a course in international law, not to mention being a master of the subject.'[1]

While the situation in relation to the teaching of international law (IL) has changed, it is not clear as to whether the view on the relevance of international law has improved, especially in the eyes of international relations (IR) scholars. While some scholars have suggested that the two disciplines, IL and IR, are 'so neatly complementary' that they could merge into a new joint discipline of 'the study of organised international co-operation',[2] others have written that the initiatives for inter-disciplinary collaboration between IL and IR has been limited.[3]

An IR perspective of the relationship between the two disciplines was clearly summed up in the 1950s by Professor Morgenthau[4] declaring that Legalism is one of the four intellectual errors of US post-war foreign policy – its companion errors being utopianism, sentimentalism and isolationism. He attacked the legalist–moralist approach as 'intoxicated with moral abstractions', and without regard for the continuous struggle for power in which all great nations are of necessity involved. Not alone in these thoughts, it is suggested that the legalist approach is naïve and, for the main part, irrelevant to understanding and explaining international affairs.

Defending the attack, the editorial comment in the *American Journal of International Law*[5] (AIJI) declared:

> Law is neither a frozen cake of doctrine designed only to protect interests in *status quo*, nor an artificial judicial proceeding, isolated from power processes, as Professor Morgenthau suggests; when understood with all its commitments and procedures,

law offers, as we have seen, a continuous formulation and reformulation of policies and constitutes an integral part of the world power process. Similarly, the moral goals of people – demands for values justified by standards of right and wrong – are not mere 'abstractions' without antecedents or consequences ... The moral perspectives of people, no less than naked force, are commonly regarded as among the effective sanctions of law. The whole United Nations project and a host of other contemporary activities and commitments bear compelling evidence of moral perspectives that today transcend the boundaries of nation states.

To the IL scholar these later comments seem prophetic in light of the changes that have occurred in the field of international human rights law in the last 50 years. In the eighteenth century and prior to the end of the Second World War the development of human rights was largely determined by the state itself, with some states establishing a Bill of Rights or incorporating human rights provisions into their Constitution, but there was little sense of states being bound by a core set of fundamental rights. However, since that time, significant developments have occurred with the advent of an International Bill of Human Rights in the form of the Universal Declaration of Human Rights, adopted in 1948, and a founding document in international human rights development. The instruments that make up this international Bill of Rights include the two subsequent Covenants that were adopted on the basis of that Declaration: the International Covenant on Civil and Political Rights (1966), and the International Covenant on Economic, Social and Cultural Rights (1966). Since then, an estimated 70 international instruments are now extant to protect a range of human rights from the right not to be tortured to specific conventions on the rights of the child. As an indicator of the acceptance by states of a core set of fundamental rights and their obligation to respect these rights, it is noted that by the end of 1998 140 states had formally ratified the International Covenant on Civil and Political Rights. Undoubtedly, there are regional differences and variations in the definition and priorities given to rights, and this is reflected in a range of instruments, such as the European Convention on Human Rights and Fundamental Freedoms (1950), the European Social Charter (1961), and more recent instruments to protect minority rights, such as the European Charter for Regional or Minority Languages (1992) and the European Framework Convention on the Protection of National Minorities (1994).[6] Traditionally, the Council of Europe in Strasbourg has been the 'home' of human rights development in Europe, but there are signs that the role and focus of the European Union on human rights are growing. For example, the new social chapter of the Treaty of Amsterdam raises a range of social issues requiring respect for human rights in the area of equality and non-discrimination in employment; and recognising the need to underpin these new developments, the Council of Ministers' meeting in Cologne, 1999, agreed to draft a Charter on Fundamental Rights with the stated object of making the overriding importance and relevance of human rights more visible in the European Union. Furthermore, a formal link between the European Convention on Human Rights and the European Union was established under the European Union Treaty,[7] and the European Charter of Fundamental Rights, proclaimed in Nice 2000, clarifies the relationship.[8]

While undoubtedly the developments in human rights on an international and European level have been dramatic, what does all this change signify? Arguably every state is in favour of human rights, as it would be difficult politically to sustain an anti-human rights policy. But this is quite a different proposition from stating that there is a commitment by states to provide for the adequate implementation, protection and enforcement of human rights. And, while most international instruments declare all rights to be equal, it is evident that rights are treated and respected in different ways. But how can we understand these changes and developments? Is the proliferation of international human rights instruments a new tradable currency in international relations and the invocation to human rights merely a political expedient to legitimise actions taken? Or will the European Union through its increased involvement in new policy areas bring a new dimension to human rights? Is it in a position to entrench human rights in decision-making through a 'carrot-led' codification approach, backed up by financial incentives? Are human rights moving in a context similar to that of the 'Green Movement', as it moved from being a sideline fringe issue to an integral part of policy planning and development? Is the current 'driver' of human rights in Europe a reaction to the moral outcry of events such as Bosnia–Hertzogonvia and/or a desire for greater economic stability, and/or a fear of race and religious tensions? Are we at the stage when we can speak of a pervading or new human rights culture?

How these issues are approached depends upon whether an IR or an IL perspective is adopted. These differing perspectives have been referred to as the 'two cultures' problem,[9] namely because each side is concerned with different questions leading to different answers.[10] This has been summed up in the view that IR is concerned with tackling and answering the questions, 'why is/how is?' whereas IL scholars are concerned with 'what is/what ought to be obligatory?'[11] This chapter does not set out to convince the reader that the international legal framework can explain international relations but it is concerned with examining where IL 'fits' in the world of politics and international affairs and explores areas where an IL perspective may help yield useful information and guidance towards how international and European actors may act.

The first section seeks to provide a brief explanation of IL processes and practice so as to provide a frame of reference in which to seek to understand new developments. It sets out:

- where international law can be found and how it is made;
- the different perspectives on international law along a continuum as to whether it is a body of law set in stone or a constantly changing problem-solving process.

This chapter will not turn you into an international lawyer – and you may be thankful for this – as it is not concerned with the history and legal jurisprudence

of international law, on which much is written,[12] but with examining the structures and processes that shape IL and the interplay between IL and IR. However,
it will provide some background information on how IL is formed and the
framework in which IL operates and a brief introduction to the debate and
discussions within IL on its future development. This information sets the
context in which to begin to examine and understand the tensions and interface
between IR and IL, with particular focus on recent developments in international and European human rights. An understanding of the dichotic nature of
IL is also necessary to explain the tensions that exist within IL itself.
Is it radical and dynamic in nature, pioneering change, or has it the more
commonly perceived role of codifying and underscoring decisions already
agreed among states? This dual role can be difficult to interpret. A frame of
reference is needed to understand when IL influence is strong and when it is
weak. How is it that sometimes IL seems to be the bulwark against our own
worst excesses whereas at other times it fails to protect against the most terrible
atrocities imaginable? Is it that, as Marcus Tullus Cicero put it, 'in the midst of
arms, law stands mute'. Just as there are various competing theories and stages
of development in IR, the history and development of IL has, and is, going
through similar phases of development with different theories as to how IL
evolves and changes. On the face of it the development of international human
rights has progressed considerably in the last 50 years.

The second section seeks to begin to develop a model through which it may
be possible to gauge the effect of IL on the behaviour of states and within states.
It set out to:

- examine the overlap between international law and international relations
  particularly in the area of co-operative and prohibitive regimes;
- understand how it is possible to 'weigh up' international law.

Many human rights instruments exist but what is their impact and effect in
controlling or influencing state actions and behaviour. It is possible that the IL
scholar would approach this subject by trying to define and clarify the rights
involved (what is) and examine the enforcement mechanisms available while
considering ways to strengthen them (what ought to be). This would include an
examination of the enforcement mechanisms currently used: the functions and
powers of the international courts, other judicial supervision, complaints procedures, monitoring and reporting mechanisms and with some attention to
foreign policy and corporate policy statements in these areas. However, it is
possible to suggest that the approach of the IR scholar might differ significantly,
perhaps even in reverse order, paying more attention to the foreign policy
commitments and the changing world order (why is), and having more concern
about politics and second guessing political expediency rather than be unduly
concerned about the legal courses of action available, especially as it is argued
that there is rarely a clear cut answer in many legal matters. After all, 'is not
international law honoured more in its breach than its observance'?

International human rights law has been decried as ineffective, and yet, at the same time, there are increasing efforts to introduce a 'rights-based approach' to help resolve tensions in our changing environment.

As we move to greater interdependence and live closer together in a rapidly changing world there is a sense that the changes required by new discoveries in technology, science, etc. have created their own imperative to adopt old rules and customs and devise new ways to manage and regulate our co-existence while conflict and political co-operation have also propelled us into a new world order. As recent commentators have stated, 'men find themselves working and thinking and feeling in relation to an environment which both in its world-wide extension and its intimate connection with all sides of human existence, is without precedent in the history of the world'.[13] There is a sense of being over-whelmed by this combination of events, and concern has been expressed that the slow machinations of the legal system are inappropriate to manage this envi-ronment. 'Never before has change come so rapidly, on such a global scale, and with such global visibility.'[14] This changing environment and, crucially, the speed of change and the range of new issues involved seems to suggest a need to devise new processes to respond to these situations.

The third section draws on two case studies, examples in an international and European context to begin to see how these processes interact in practise. Ironically, in many ways, it is the analytical skills and tools honed in the study of IR that will better equip the IR student to understand the rapidly changing developments in international human rights law, as a wide-angled lens is required to draw in the constituent parts.

The final section also seeks to draw some conclusions on the further develop-ments in international human rights law.

International law: structure and process

Part of the problem for the IR scholar in coming to deal with IL is that it is diffi-cult to find texts or information which are sympathetic to the scholar who is interested in an overview and passing knowledge of the subject, but who does not want the detail that most introductory texts present on sources of IL, juris-dictional and territorial issues, etc. Conversely, a casual perusal of the indexes of a number of textbooks on IR reveals only the most cursory reference to IL.

Where do you find international laws? How are they made? A simplified and somewhat traditional description of the basic structure of IL can be described as establishing the minimum rules of co-existence between states for their self-preservation. Some of the earliest agreements or laws concerned practical and basic issues around safe conduct, defence and security relations (state sover-eignty); international trade and freedom of the high seas (mutually beneficial reciprocal arrangements); and a decentralised enforcement system as each state had an interest in preserving the rules (self-reliance). The process by which these reciprocal/mutual interests were identified and clarified into 'law' has

been traditionally through reliance on (1) treaty, (2) custom, (3) general principles of law, and (4) legal opinion.[15] The practice has been that most weight has
been given to what has been laid down in treaty form – that is, has been
expressly agreed among the parties – and followed by reliance on customary
practice – that is, those practices built up over time as practices acceptable to the
parties concerned, the basic underlying principle being that states wished to
preserve their sovereignty and only came to arrangements with other states in
areas where it was conducive to all concerned.

International law went through a stage of development and growth with the
birth of the modern state system in the sixteenth and seventeenth centuries.
There have been several notable changes since then, which raise interesting
questions in relation to the future of IL. Can a system premised on a consensual/
mutual interest basis continue to operate when dealing with a significantly
larger number of states and diverse and competing interests that transcend
borders? As in the study of IR, states were also considered the main actors in IL
but in the important areas of human rights the individual is also a subject of
IL. For example, intervention into the territory of another state on human
rights/humanitarian grounds, presents a direct challenge to the principle of state
sovereignty and the presumed right of non-intervention in the territory of
another state. The concept of state sovereignty also seems out of place as a workable proposition when there is such growing fluidity around issues of location
and ownership. Can the system still rely on each state to preserve and take action
against breaches of IL within its jurisdiction or is there a need for more
'centralised' authority? Has this process begun? Almost all of the matters
referred to above seem to suggest that IL is ill-equipped to deal with a fast-
moving, global, interdependent international community. Yet, international
law and a rights-based approach is more talked about and called upon to resolve
and solve more of the international issues in the world today. For instance, the
setting up of a permanent international criminal court; interventions against
other states couched in IL terms; and the proliferation of covenants, conventions and declarations in new areas such as the right to development, economic,
social and cultural rights, developmental rights, etc. The key question for IR
scholars must be to what extent do states allow their decisions, choices and
actions to be modified or governed by the rules of IL? And when some new laws
come into force, such as the myriad of new framework conventions in matters
relating to the environment, as well as all of these human rights instruments,
how can we determine as to whether they are really setting down 'rules and laws'
which states must follow or setting out mere aspirations of expected state behaviour? Where do such rules fall on the continuum?

International law: a continuum?

The initial challenge facing an examination of the role and functioning of IL is
to address the conflicting views on the nature and character of IL and how it

operates? Is it a 'body of rules', constant and unaffected by the political arena in which it operates and appealing to objective legal principles? This view has support with those who believe that IL provides the rules that govern relations among states and are necessary for self-preservation. This view is predicated upon a natural law philosophy of international law.[16] As Judges Fitzmaurice and Spender in the South West Africa Cases wrote:[17]

> We are not unmindful of, nor are we insensitive to, various considerations of a non-judicial character, social, humanitarian and other ... but these are matters for the political rather than for the legal arena. They cannot be allowed to deflect us from our duty of reaching a conclusion strictly on the basis of what we believe to be the correct legal view.

From this perspective law provides stability. It is rational, clearly stated and consistent and brings order to an otherwise chaotic world. It is a set of rules given the status of laws and binding on states. The comparison is often made with domestic law within states and the sense that IL provides a similar framework of 'law and order' on the international stage. There are some notable differences, especially in the methods of law enforcement and the nature of the sanctions involved, but, nevertheless, the situations are considered comparable.

There is another view, a contrary argument, that it is not possible to separate IL from international politics, as:

> The authority which characterises law exists not in a vacuum, but exactly where it intersects with power. Law, far from being authority battling against power, is the interlocking of authority with power.[18]

The logical consequence following from adopting this latter approach is to see the operation of IL in a policy-oriented context.[19] In this setting, IL becomes a process which is cognisant of context, expectations, values, goals, etc., and it is a process directly involved in seeking to find solutions to problems. Viewed from this perspective law seems to lose some of its omnipotence and there is a sense that law might be more appropriately described as 'set on paper' rather than 'set in stone'. The consequences of accepting a policy-oriented approach to IL results in some changes to basic assumptions surrounding IL. The claim to appeal to an impartial set of rules in order to obtain the 'correct solution' is no longer possible. Instead, the working assumption is that IL reflects society, is man-made and gains its authority from appealing to norms and principles which can and do change over time.

However, this polarisation of IL as either being an unbounded fluid process or a solid set of rules can conceivably be also plotted along a continuum where some rules are given greater weight than others and some more likely to change. For example, in domestic law, one can conceive that the law not to commit murder will remain unchanged whereas the laws and definitions of proscribed and illegal drugs may change with new knowledge and information and changing values within a society. In other ways, the understanding of new technological information is challenging and influencing long-held customary laws on the use of the high seas and outer space.[20] Making an assessment of international rules and norms and monitoring these changes at the international level is quite a daunting task but decision-makers are not left to pure Machiavellian choices as there are some *guiding* legal principles, and 'customary' practice and precedents which provide the framework in which these issues are considered. While the system may not be as sophisticated as the domestic system it is possible to identify the process that develops and continues to develop over time, as common interests are identified, clarified and protected.

This is eloquently summed up by Professor Roslyn Higgins when she wrote:

> When ... decisions are made by authorised persons or organs, in appropriate forums, within the framework of certain established practices and norms, then what occurs is legal decision-making. In other words, international law is a continuing process of authoritative decisions.[21]

The issue then becomes one of seeking to understand where laws fall along this continuum and observing these changes in the system. It is hoped that greater understanding of these processes may lead to better answers relating to 'how and why' IL operates in international affairs.

International law–international relations: the overlap

The areas of overlap between IR and IL are primarily in the area of international co-operation, and this section will focus on the interaction between the language and process of regime theory, familiar to IR students, and the language and development of international human rights law.

IR regime theorists, such as Young, Keohane and others claim that self-interest is the main motivation to co-operate – when it is recognised that unilateral action cannot work as well as joint action. It is predicted that regimes are more likely to develop in situations where the result of co-operation will result in the reduction of transaction costs, for example trade agreements are better than trade wars. It is further suggested that even when the benefit is clear, the issue as to who pays, the form of action taken and the implementation process adopted are matters that affect the outcome. Several writers would appear to suggest that a minimalist approach to co-operation is often adopted as the course of action when coming to an arrangement.

These issues are also highly relevant in the area of IL. In the area of international human rights law there is a similar discourse that is couched in terms of 'negative' and 'positive' obligations on states. For instance, civil and political rights are generally referred to as being 'negative' in nature as they only require a preventive action by the state. For instance, the obligation on the state is *not to interfere* with the right to free speech, or *not to interfere* with privacy and family life, etc. In contrast, other rights, such as economic, social and cultural rights, are generally described as 'positive rights' requiring a proactive obligation by the state, such as *to provide* an adequate health service or provide primary educa-tion.[22] The specific characteristics and processes attributed to international prohibitive regimes, as espoused by Nadelmann,[23] and the observations made by such writers as Krasner,[24] Keohane and Nye,[25] Donnelly[26] and Young[27] on inter-national cooperation indicate that the same issues are being addressed, albeit in a different language.

The development of international human rights law to date falls loosely into the preventative action area. The nature of most of the human rights instru-ments has been to seek to set down a minimum acceptable standard of behaviour by states towards individuals living within their borders. These stan-dards have attracted some form of enforcement mechanism, such as the right to make an application under the European Convention on Human Rights, or a reporting mechanism to a committee of the United Nations, or have been enshrined into the constitutions of individual states. However, attempts to introduce more positive obligations on states have, for the main part, been couched in aspirational terms. Initially, therefore, it is intended to examine how prohibitive and co-operate regimes operate, with a view to adapting this model to see if it can usefully help in explaining current developments in international human rights law and also inform on current and future developments.

Prohibitive regimes, as the name suggests, aim to prohibit certain activity, whether in relation to piracy, drugs, crime or new forms of slavery associated with child labour, etc. Whereas regime analysis more generally focuses on areas of co-operation in society and suggests that there is more order, regularity of behaviour and general observance of custom and convention than the IR realist would cede. Regime theory neither suggests that there is uniform co-operation nor that all relations between states, or between states and non-state actors have the same weight. Instead it emphasises that attention must be paid to the *issues* surrounding an *area of interest* to discover where the balance lies. Accordingly the thrust of the concept of regime theory is to pay closer attention to the issue-area being examined in order to seek to predict the 'expected behaviour' and/or understand and explain the outcome. This suggests that there are some areas of activity that are more highly organised with clear rules or even codified regula-tion whereas other areas are more loosely framed. Regimes are also distinguished from once-off agreements as it is suggested that, 'Regimes form a network of rules, norms, principles and procedures rather than mere *ad hoc* substantive agreements.'[28] The perceived advantage of examining the regime process is that it provides a reasonable expectation as to the behaviour of actors in relation to a specific issue-area at a given time. The level of commitment to the arrangement depends on a number of factors, and states can choose not to abide by these rules but, arguably, the existence of the regime influences choices and decisions taken to varying degrees, depending on its real and perceived strength.

Ironically, just as the appeal of international law is often its claim to provide order and stability the appeal of regimes is in the flexibility provided to respond to changing events and information. The characteristics attributed to international prohibitive regimes seem particularly relevant to the human rights discussion. Nadelmann, writing on international prohibitive regimes, suggests the motivation involved in the creation of such a regime, rests on the satisfaction of material interests, but moral interests also play a dominant role[29] and goes on to state:

> International prohibitive regimes, like municipal criminal laws, emerge for a variety of reasons; to protect the interests of the state and other powerful members of society; to deter, suppress, and punish undesirable activities; to provide for order, security and justice among members of a community; and to give force and symbolic representation to the moral values, beliefs and prejudices of those who make the law.[30]

The five-stage process Nadelmann constructs in relation to how prohibitive regimes develop is also worth summarising at this stage. He suggests that at the initial stage the activity in question is in fact legitimate under certain circumstances, for example slavery, piracy, or more contemporary examples being perhaps the use of the death penalty, nuclear weapons, child soldiers, etc. However, at the next stage the activity is redefined as a problem or an evil. He suggests that it is quite often legal scholars, religious groups or other moral entrepreneurs who take up the cause. The third stage is when there is agitation for the suppression and criminalisation of the activity. At this stage the proponents include hegemonic influences as well as transnational entrepreneurs in the form of diplomatic efforts, education, economic inducements and organisational efforts, etc. If the efforts of the regime proponents are successful, then a fourth stage begins as the activity becomes the subject of criminal laws and police action and international institutions and conventions emerge to play a co-ordinating role. The fifth stage is marked by a reduction in the incidences of the proscribed activity. This process seems to suggest that by the time 'international law' becomes visible in the form of laws and conventions there is already a strong consensus in support of the actions taken and thus the 'law' rather than imposing rules actually has the support and backing of the actors concerned, and reflects the consent/consensus view on the matter. It is important to note that while this process has been explained as a linear progression there can be movements back and forth throughout the process. For instance, there was strong support to establish an international criminal court in the late 1940s with a General Assembly resolution requiring a drafting committee to work on a draft document; yet by the early 1950s the idea was shelved and it has taken almost 50 years for the aim to be realised.[31]

Now it is time to take this framework as a model and investigate whether applying this model can be a useful tool in understanding the influence of law and human rights on the decisions and future behaviour of European and international actors. To do this we will examine the regime network around different human rights issues and the players involved to see if it is possible to pick out some trends in this area.

Legal and process aspects of change in international and European human rights

In order to examine the processes described above two significant human rights developments are examined – the historic decision to establish an international criminal court, and current trends and new developments within the Council of Europe and the European Commission to institute human rights in the inter-related areas of economic, social and cultural rights including the rights of national minorities and language. The aim is to compare and contrast the influences surrounding regime developments and identify the components and indicators that influence the success or otherwise of the outcomes.

There is merit in adopting an approach that considers both the legal and non-legal/process aspects of the situation. The more legalistic way of examining exactly what has been decided is often a revealing starting point. It provides basic, but clear information on the scope of the right, the level at which the matter has been negotiated (e.g. UN, EU, Committee, etc.), and the form of the intended enforcement mechanisms. It may seem like stating the obvious but the question always needs to be asked – is the law clear on the matter? For instance, sometimes a careful reading of an international instrument will quite accurately reflect the 'ambiguity agreed' among the actors. In such cases a claim that the law is 'silent' and 'powerless' may reflect the actual situation that there is no agreed rule by which the states have agreed to be bound in the first place – rather than that the law has being flouted by states.[32]

Finding out what have been agreed and then supplementing the information with the IR perspectives on the process through which the decision was reached reveals key information on the likely effect and outcome of the human rights instrument. The decision to establish an international criminal court is an interesting study as it takes us from the beginning of the new era in human rights and provides a classic development process of an international human rights instrument, highlighting important issues around the make up of regime members, enforcement methods and the importance of the IR context at all times.

International criminal court

Perhaps one of the most significant developments in the history of international human rights law was the decision taken in Rome in July 1998 at the UN Diplomatic Conference to establish an international criminal court (ICC). The *process* which led to establishing the ICC bears an interesting resemblance to the international prohibitive regime process described by Nadelmann.

> Rome, 17 July [1998] – A major step in forging a missing link in the international legal order was taken this evening as a United Nations Diplomatic Conference decided to establish a permanent International Criminal Court with power to exercise its jurisdiction over persons for the most serious crimes of international concern. Those crimes are genocide, crimes against humanity, war crimes, as well as the crime of aggression, once an acceptable definition for the Court's jurisdiction over it is adopted.[33]

The Rome Statute to establish an International Criminal Court was adopted by an unrecorded vote of 120 countries in favour, seven against and 21 abstentions. Arguably the idea of establishing an international criminal court dates back to the Middle Ages,[34] but the main impetus to re-consider the issue came in 1948 when Resolution (260 B(III)) was adopted inviting the International Law Commission of the UN 'to study the desirability and possibility of establishing an international judicial organ for the trial of persons charged with genocide or other crimes over which jurisdiction will be conferred upon that organ by international conventions'.[35] The backdrop was the horror of the Second World War, and the International Military Tribunals of Nuremberg provided a procedural framework. While the issue was being discussed at the diplomatic–governmental level, there was strong moral backing and material interest to promote stability and order, and protection against increasingly deadly weapons. From a regime analysis perspective, the moral opprobrium and public outcry provided the motivation and support for states to act. But, why was no court established at that time? Quite quickly, by the time a draft was being considered in the General Assembly Meeting in Geneva in 1951 indecision and tensions surrounding the issues and even the very purpose of such a court. Within the Committee set up to proceed with drafting a convention, a minority proposed that the General Assembly be informed that 'the setting up of such a court now would involve very real dangers to the future development of international good feeling and co-operation'.[36] Many objections, concerns and fears were raised of frivolous or false charges being brought against states. In the end it seems that states' reluctance to trust an international court out-weighed their moral support for the proposal. And yet, 50 years later, the concept of an international criminal court has become a reality.[37] What has changed? Is it a reaction to the atrocities of Rwanda and the former Yugoslavia, just as there was a similar reaction to the events of the Second World War? While the establishment of the International Criminal Tribunals for the former Yugoslavia and Rwanda was welcomed, there is a sense that those Tribunals may have not achieved what they had set out to do and that they were hampered by procedural and jurisdictional disagreements over many issues, including the execution of warrants.[38] But what is the regime dynamic around the ICC? What was actually agreed? A legal commentary suggests that several provisions in the Treaty weaken and restrict the court's jurisdiction. There is an 'opt-out' clause allowing states to put themselves beyond the court's reach on war crimes[39] and the definition of some crimes has been narrowed.[40] The major concessions gained relate to the court's jurisdiction over crimes committed in *internal* armed conflicts, albeit the list of such crimes is shorter, and the right of an independent prosecutor to act and investigate cases, subject to pre-trial approval. This is not an exhaustive account of the new court but these issues are highlighted to demonstrate what has, *and has not*, been agreed.[41] Further, all prosecution investigations are dependent on state co-operation as the court will not have its own police force.[42] This information alone suggests that the ICC may not live up to some of the expectations raised. Concerns over this point were poignantly raised: 'we cannot and must not set up a wholly ineffective Court which is capable of making no more than empty gestures in the face of appalling atrocities being committed. That would be to do a great injustice to the victims of these crimes'.[43]

But then we also need to consider some of the process factors because it is suggested that even if there is poor law but strong political will then a liberal interpretation of the law can produce positive results. However, while most states supported the idea of an ICC, on the grounds of justice, there is a sense that some countries seemed to like the concept of the court – but not to be subject to its jurisdiction. It is significant that the USA was one of the seven[44] that voted against the Rome Statute and while the outgoing president Bill Clinton signed the treaty, the House of Representatives has had an active lobby against it.[45] So, what is the future for the ICC? Arguably the political backdrop in the 1990s of the conflicts in Bosnia–Herzegovina, and Rwanda created the impetus to renew efforts to push for such a court. The new factor, possibly stronger than in the 1940s is the increasing number of non-governmental organisations that have been able to mobilise effectively and on a transnational basis to advocate for the setting up of the ICC.[46] Undoubtedly, widespread media reporting also generated wider public awareness and concern that such atrocities would not go unpunished. The use of information technology also increased the networking capacity of many diverse organisations. It is possible to suggest that these factors were the added components that meant that the draft got to the table this time. The European Union also supported the ICC. From the position of knowing the legal limitations and recognising the regime factors involved it becomes easier to make an assessment of the influence of the ICC in the near future. The regime model helps to focus on the issues although it has its limitations in predicting the actual timing of events. However, the crucial point to note is that, just because a human rights issue has been codified or 'has become law', it is not an absolute indicator that it will be enforced or effect change. Nevertheless, it provides useful information. By recognising the context, and obtaining an understanding of what has, and what has not, been agreed, it sharpens our focus on the 'gaps' and areas where there are likely to be tensions among states. Thus, while the short-term success of the ICC is pessimistic, the very concept of establishing an ICC is radical and a new departure in IL. It may remain relatively inactive for several years but it is setting new markers in the nature of relations among states. It is setting up a new framework of thinking, new institutional support structures to provide universal protection against certain crimes and, in this sense, it is the sowing the seeds to generate a new dynamic for change in this area.

European human rights developments

It is interesting to contrast and compare the developments in relation to human rights on the international stage with the emerging trends developing around human rights within Europe. The development of rights within Europe had, for the most part, followed the lead set by the United Nations. However, in some areas of development there are signs of a very significant surge forward, focussing on developing new approaches to entrench human rights.

The World Conference on Human Rights in Vienna[47] in June 1993 reaffirmed the commitments of states to the purposes and principles contained in the international 'Bill of Rights' and chartered the progress that has been made in promoting human rights. It also set out a comprehensive Programme of Action referring to all human rights areas, with specific title headings on increased coordination on human rights, and on equality, dignity and tolerance. Shortly before that the Organisation for Security and Cooperation in Europe (OSCE) produced a Document at the Copenhagen Summit, with a chapter devoted to national minorities.[48]

Undoubtedly, it is confusing for IR scholars to hear of more instruments and laws being developed when the law in this area already appears to be clearly laid down. For instance, what is the point of developing rights around equality, dignity and tolerance when they seem to have been adequately codified within several important instruments,[49] including Article 1 of the Universal Declaration of Human Rights (UDHR) which proclaims, 'All human beings are born free and equal in dignity and rights' and within Article 14 of the European Convention on Human Rights (ECHR)?[50] It is not necessary to outline the history of atrocities on minorities and individuals to make the point that these instruments have not protected these rights. But, maybe when we pay close attention to what has actually been agreed in this complex area we will begin to understand why and the nature of the challenges ahead.

In general terms, it can be said that the European Convention on Human Rights has been the standard setter of human rights in Europe. It represented, in effect, an agreed and codified European 'bill of rights', with strong institutional and judicial enforcement mechanisms, and a host of various human rights committees within the Council of Europe and the European Union, pressure groups and NGOs working to enable the effective promotion, development and protection of the human rights set out in the Convention.[51] There is an innovative complaint mechanism[52] allowing any individual to petition the European Court of Human Rights should s/he believe that her/his rights have been violated under the Convention, and that domestic remedies have been exhausted. While states may have equivocated and delayed in relation to judgements made against them, no state has opted to withdraw from the Council of Europe.[53] But while the regime around these rights is strong there are other rights, such as economic, social and cultural rights, minority rights, etc., that have not enjoyed the same prominence. The development of human rights has been uneven and the indications are that some of the bigger challenges facing Europe at the beginning of the third millennium are connected with those rights that have either not been well defined or, although codified, have been without effective implementation mechanisms, for example the right to equality and

anti-discrimination measures on grounds of race, or religion, the right to participate in the democratic process, the right to active citizenship, the right to an
adequate standing of living as set out under economic social and cultural rights,
the right to self-determination, minority rights, and so on.

All of these questions impinge directly on political ideology. The issues
around equality and non-discrimination are closely linked to how minorities
are treated, what constitutes difference, and questions around policies of assim-
ilation and cultural diversity. These issues have been discussed and debated over
a long period of time, but, even within Europe, it has not been possible to reach
a consensus view on how to deal with these matters.[54] This becomes evident
when we view what had actually been agreed. For example, evidence of the
tensions around the definition of minorities is reflected in the fact that the
Universal Declaration of Human Rights (UDHR) makes no reference to
'minorities',[55] and even the more recent Framework Convention for the
Protection of National Minorities (1994) shies away from seeking to define what
constitutes a national minority. These tensions have led to the uneven development in the advancement of these rights.

The tensions also centre around the 'process' model in how the states chose
to deal with these rights. Is the balance still tilted more in favour of agreeing
prohibitive regimes? The system is more familiar with such an approach.
However, there is an interesting shift in emphasis in relation to these human
rights. When we recall that the EEC Treaty originally contained no specific
clauses on human rights and compare that with the rights-based language that
pervades EU documents now, it is clear that there have been some significant
changes. Undoubtedly the events of the early 1990s have been significant in
bringing some new rights to the fore while issues around enlargement have challenged the 'consensus' agreed in relation to other rights.

During the 1990s there has been a concerted effort at all levels to strengthen
and promote the range of rights in the area of minority protection and non-
discrimination. Examples include the Framework Convention on the Protection
on National Minorities (1994);[56] the complementary European Charter for
Regional or Minority Languages (1992);[57] amendments to strengthen the non-
discrimination provision of the European Convention on Human Rights;[58] the
non-discrimination provisions of the European Union,[59] the setting up of high-
level expert committees, the European Commission against Racism and
Intolerance (ECRI) under the Council of European and the European Union
Monitoring Committee (EUMC) under the European Union; as well as activities to strengthen the European Social Charter (1961)[60] and a host of other
declarations and recommendations and a high-level European regional conference in October 2000 in preparation for the World Conference against Racism,
Racial Discrimination, Xenophobia and Related Intolerance in September
2001.[61] The influence and impact of these provisions and activities is discussed
below. These instruments are mainly concerned with rights such as the rights of
members of minorities to: practise their religion, use their language and enjoy

their culture; to be taught or educated in their distinctive language; to parity of treatment and esteem; to freedom from incitement to hatred; to education in mutual tolerance; not to be treated as members of a distinct community against their will.

For example, under the European Convention of Human Rights the current right to non-discrimination, as set out in Article 14, is limited.[62] The structure of the right is negative in its formulation, for example the European Court has ruled that the role of the state is not to prevent private minority language education. The state has no duty to provide any special education rights to minorities.[63]

In contrast, the European Charter for Regional or Minority Languages and the Framework Convention for the Protection of National Minorities (Framework Convention) are couched in more open language. The Framework Convention is comprehensive and incorporates many of the language provisions contained in the Charter. The stated aim of the Framework Convention is to protect the ethnic, cultural linguistic and religious identity of each person belonging to a national minority. It is a legally binding document. However, the approach it takes is to encourage states to adopt programmes of activity at the national level and to embed them within their own national legislative systems.[64] The logic behind this is stated in the Explanatory Memorandum:

> In view of the range of different situations and problems to be resolved, a choice was made for a framework Convention which contains mostly programme-type provisions, setting out objectives which the parties undertake to pursue. These provisions, which will not be directly applicable, leave the state concerned a measure of discretion in the implementation of the objectives which they have undertaken to achieve, thus enabling them to take particular circumstances into account.

From a legalistic approach assessment these provisions set out good principles but leave much to the discretion of states. It is apparent that there are no 'best practice codes' developed as yet, and efforts are ongoing to find ways to address the complex issues. The vision and aspiration is clear but the process and the 'transaction cost' implications have yet to be determined. But this legislation allows for a pick-and-mix approach to the rights contained within it, suggesting a more facilitative carrot, rather than stick, approach. It will take time and effort to tease out the tensions. The fresh impetus given to these rights in the 1990s has inspired a language of rights and also a plethora of steering groups, committees, lobbying groups as well as increased public awareness of the issues. The pace of development is difficult to track but it is possible to say that these human rights issues are on the agenda and will shape the future of our societies. Human rights can instil emotive reactions and moral outrage, but the implementation of these rights has cost implications. The challenge that is emerging is whether the prohibitive/negative obligation process will be sufficient or appropriate to fully safeguard these rights and whether a more positive/cooperative regime is required?

In this respect the enforcement approach of the member states of the EU in relation to promoting and developing rights within the EU will be instructive. Human rights are moving to the inside track as evidenced by actions such as the adoption of the revised Social Charter, the European Union Charter of Fundamental Rights, the proposal put forward by the EU to be bound by the ECHR, the decision to publish an annual EU human rights report, the funding of human rights activity,[65] declarations of support of human rights developments at the UN and the Council of Europe and the requirement of new member states to fulfil a human rights statement to the effect that, 'membership requires that the candidate country has achieved stability of institutions guaranteeing democracy, the rule of law, human rights and respect for and protection of minorities'.[66]

The EU's remit is set to grow in the arena of social policy and human rights. While the language of some specific rights may not seem very different from, say, the European Convention on Human Rights provision on non-discrimination, the proposed implementation methods differ significantly. For example, Directives proposed in Article 13[67] of the Amsterdam treaty concerning non-discrimination in employment adopt a pro-active approach, factoring in the cost implications. The language is pro-active, and programmatic funding is proposed to combat discrimination, 2001–6.[68] This approach creates an environment in which the 'equality proofing' is carried out at the policy initiation stage seeking to entrench the right as an integral part. It will be interesting to monitor these developments. It is possible to envisage this type of approach being used in relation to other rights. However, the proviso would be that the areas would appear to be those where there is consensus and agreed action.

Conclusions

This chapter was concerned to expose the IR scholar to the differing perspectives of IL and move away from the stark account of IL as a set of rigid rules, oblivious to the needs of the real world. The emphasis was in presenting a view of IL and international human rights law that characterises law as being exactly at the point where it intersects with power and represents the interlocking of authority with power. From this viewpoint it was argued that law can serve a twofold purpose for the IR scholar, namely by providing a written account of the state of relations – power relations between states on given issues, flagging up contested areas, and producing draft strategies for change. Quite often it is possible for the non-IL scholar to get confused with the plethora of laws, conventions, UN resolutions and declarations without having a frame of reference for ordering or prioritising them. However, by actually investigating the law-making process, it becomes easier to observe the interaction of power, decision-making and authority, and to understand the content of the final document. This process is not perfect as timing is important and difficult to establish but it is argued that it can act as a marker for assessing the 'weight' to be given to a law.

The chapter was also concerned to point out what international law cannot do. It can regulate in areas where it is given authority but in the highly contested areas such as minority rights, peace and security, economic rights, it was argued that this authority has not been clarified and suggested that change would be slower in these areas.

However, applying this knowledge to the area of human rights it was possible to plot where certain human rights are located on the scale of development. It was argued that the proliferation of human rights instruments in the last 50 years had created a culture of human rights and that they have become part of the discourse of international actors. However, it was also suggested that the human rights implementation processes are changing. This is indicated by recent developments in Europe both in relation to the prominence of human rights, especially in the areas of economic, social and cultural rights, minority rights and non-discrimination and in the way that the Council of Europe and the European Union have adopted to promote and protect these rights.

Notes

1 Arthur T. Vanderbilt, Chief Justice, Supreme Court of New Jersey, reported in *American Journal of International Law*, 46 (1952), 140–3. A survey undertaken of the Association of American Law Schools revealed that, of 107 schools in the Association, only five required international law for an LLB degree. Of the schools, less than one-half (50) offered international law, even as an elective. The quality of the teaching was also examined and 30 per cent of the schools said that they would not be in a position to offer courses due to lack of properly trained personnel.

2 Kenneth Abbot, a law professor, in his lecture before the American Society of International Law in 1992 predicted this as a possible outcome between international law and the new approaches of International Relations. Discussed in R. Beck, A. C. Arend and R. D. Vanderlungt (eds), *International Rules, Approaches from International Law and International Relations* (Oxford, and New York: Oxford University Press, 1996), pp. 3–33.

3 R. Beck: 'International law and international relations: the prospects for inter-disciplinary collaboration', in Beck, Arend and Vanderlungt (eds), *International Rules*, pp. 3–33.

4 Myers McDougal, 'Law and power', Editorial Comment in *the American Journal of International Law* (AJIL) (1952), 102–14.

5 *Ibid.*, p. 105.

6 There are several other important bodies at European level, such as the Committee for the Prevention of Torture (CPT), etc.

7 Art 6.2 of the European Union Treaty.

8 The relationship being developed suggests that the European Convention on Human Rights sets out the minimum level of protection to be secured while making it clear that this does not prohibit the European Commission from setting a higher standard. This is being further developed under the Laeken Declaration of 15 December 2001,

which invites the Convention charged with preparing the institutional reforms of the Union to give thought to 'whether the Charter of Fundamental Rights should be included in the basic treaty and to whether the European Community should accede to the European Convention on Human Rights', Iglesias, Gil Carlos Rodriguez, President de la Cour de justice des Communautes europeennes, Audience solennelle de la Cour europeenne des Droit de l'Homme, 31 January 2002.

9 Beck, 'International law and international relations', p. 17.

10 An example is given of a joint workshop organised by the American Society of International Law (ASIL) and the Academic Council on the United Nations System (ACUNS) in 1992. It is said that the IL participants seemed either amused or annoyed by the IR colleagues' preoccupation with identifying independent and dependent variables whereas the IR participants could not identify with the lawyers' desire to characterise the substance of law without being concerned with it causal relationships to specific behaviours.

11 Beck, 'International law and international relations', p. 17.

12 For texts which discuss the nature of international law see: J. L. Brierly, *The Basis of International Obligation* (Oxford, 1958), H. L. Kelsen, *Principles of International Law* (New York: R. W. Tucker, 1966). For more general introductory texts to international law see: Michael Akehurst, *A Modern Introduction to International Law* (HarperCollins, 6th edn, 1993); I. Brownlie, *Principles of Public International Law* (Oxford: Oxford University Press, 6th edn, 2003); J. G. Merrills, *Anatomy of International Law* (2nd edn) 1981.

13 Graham Wallas, 'The great society: a psychological analysis' quoted in Mark D. Alleyne, *International Power and International Communication* (London: Macmillan, 1995), p. 6.

14 Our Global Neighbourhood, *The Report of The Commission on Global Governance* (Oxford: Oxford University Press, 1995), p. 7.

15 The following list is generally accepted as constituting the sources of international law. Article 38(1) of the Statute of the International Court of Justice provides: The Court, whose function is to decide in accordance with international law such disputes as are submitted to it, shall apply: (a) international conventions, whether general or particular, established rules expressly recognised by the contesting states; (b) international custom, as evidence of a general practice accepted as law; (c) the general principles of law recognised by civilised nations; (d) judicial decisions and the teachings of the most highly qualified publicists of the various nations, as subsidiary means for the determination of rules of law.
Taken from: Akehurst, *A Modern Introduction*, ch. 3, p. 23.

16 There is a long tradition of belief in a natural law system of international law. The philosophical tradition for this viewpoint was initially based on Roman and Roman Catholic Church teachings suggesting that the source of international law came from God. This was later developed to suggest that 'just principles' were derived from the interaction necessary for 'civilised living' – similar to the notion of the 'social contract' in domestic law. For a discussion on these issues see: Akehurst, *A Modern Introduction*, ch. 2.

17 South West Africa Cases, ICJ Reports (1962) quoted from Rosalyn Higgins, *Problems and Process, International Law and How We Use It* (Oxford: Clarendon Press, 1994), p. 4.

18 *Ibid.* This belief has its beginnings in the positive law tradition, in contrast to the

natural law tradition, as it argues that international law is man-made, where the actual behaviour of states is the basis of international law.

19 This policy-oriented approach has been dubbed the New Haven School and has been developed by Myres S. McDougal, Harold D. Lasswell and many others. For an account of the policy-oriented approach see: Lung-Chu Chen, *An Introduction to Contemporary International Law, A Policy-Oriented Perspective* (London: Yale University Press, 1989).

20 The international law of the sea has been renegotiated and the whole concept of the 'high seas' completely turned around in light of new information in the 1950s indicating the wealth of minerals available on the sea bed. Instead of leaving the 'high seas' as open territory to the more technically advanced nations, there was a successful 're-defining' of the high seas as part of the 'common heritage of mankind' thereby requiring that deep sea mining, to be regulated.

21 R. Higgins, 'Policy considerations and the international judicial process', *International and Comparative Law Quarterley*, 58 (1968) quoted in Problems and Process, p. 2. See note 8.

22 For example, the argument goes that the right to a fair trial does not require a resource implication for the state. Similarly a right not to be tortured requires the state to stop certain action (sometimes referred to as negative obligation), but this did not involve the state getting involved in any major resource costs. On the contrary, economic social and cultural rights all require the state to do something (a positive obligation) such as spend resources on health, education, housing, employment and/or social security. This argument does not stand up well to scrutiny. Ensuring a fair trial requires the provision of free legal aid, effective training of the police, judges and lawyers, instituting monitoring services and providing for Police Complaint Authorities, etc. Similarly the prevention of torture requires training, monitoring, inspections, complaints processes, tribunal investigations, etc. Arguably these distinctions between civil and political rights and those of social and cultural rights have more to do with political issues and positions and their historical development.

23 Ethan A. Nadelmann, 'Global prohibitive regimes: the evolution of norms in International Society', *International Organisations*, 44: 4 (1990), 479–526.

24 Stephen Krasner, 'Regimes and the limits of Realism: regimes as autonomous variables' and 'Structural Causes and Regimes consequences: regimes as intervening variables', *International Organisations*, 36: 2 (1982), 497–510.

25 Robert O. Keohane, and Joseph Nye, *Power and Interdependence* (Boston, MA: Little Brown, 1977).

26 Jack Donnelly: 'International human rights: a regimes analysis', *International Organisations*, 3: 40 (1986), 599–42.

27 Oran R. Young, *International Co-operation* (London: Cornell University Press, 1989).

28 Robert O. Keohane, 'The demand for International Regimes', *International Organisations*, 36: 2 (1982), 331.

29 Nadelmann, 'Global prohibitive regimes'.

30 *Ibid.*

31 George A. Finch, 'Editorial comment, draft statute for an international criminal court', *American Journal of International Law*, 46 (1952), 89.

32 A classic example is the right to self-determination, which has been claimed at

various times to justify certain actions. Despite the fact that it is included in the two main Covenants, The International Covenant on Civil and Political Rights and the International Covenant on Economic Social and Cultural Rights, the United Nations Human Rights Committee has recently held that the right is non-justifiable, in that the Human Rights Committee will not rule on any individual complaint about any alleged violation.

33 UN Diplomatic Conference Concludes in Rome with Decision to establish Permanent International Criminal Court, UN Information Office, Press Release, L/2889, 20 July 1998.

34 The wide acceptance of a concept of state sovereignty which excluded individuals as subjects of international law discouraged discussion of the subject during the period between the Napoleonic and World Wars, Quincy Wright, 'Proposals for an International Criminal Court', *American Journal of International Law*, 46 (1952), 61.

35 Finch, 'Editorial Comment', p. 89.

36 *Ibid.*, p. 90.

37 The Statute will come into effect after 60 signatures have ratified it. As of January 2002, 52 states had ratified the statute and it is anticipated that the International Criminal Court will come into effect before the end of the year 2002.

38 In a speech given in Washington on 1 April 1998, the President of the Tribunal, Judge Gabrielle Kirk McDonald, is reported as saying that, 'no matter how many suspected war criminals are tried and convicted for their role in the Balkan conflict, the efforts are a waste unless states co-operate with the tribunal. And, to ensure that international criminal justice has a future, we need active assistance beyond what States are required to do. Compliance must become the norm. States must execute our orders, states must arrest individuals, States must respond to our requests for facilities for convicted persons and for vulnerable witnesses. States must provide the resources that we require to be truly effective'. Valonda Bruinton, 'Former Yugoslavia Tribunal', *Voice of America*, 1 April 1998.

39 Human Rights Watch Text Analysis, International Criminal Court Treaty, 17 July 1998.

40 *Ibid.* Several of the definitions of crimes go back on existing international law. For example, it is well established that crimes against humanity have to be 'widespread and systematic'. The treaty also requires that, in addition, they must be committed as part of 'state, organisation, or group policy'. Further provisions state that the court cannot act unless the state of nationality of the accused, or the state where the crimes took place, has ratified the treaty. In practice, those two are very likely to be the same state: Pol Pot, Idi Amin, Pinochet, and many others committed atrocities on their own populations. This provision will dramatically reduce the number of cases that the court can act upon.

41 The court only gains jurisdiction to act – under the principle of complementarity – when the national system has failed to work, ensuring that the ICC will only operate in the most exceptional circumstances.

42 The treaty does require states to comply with the court's requests for co-operation. However, there are two major exceptions. First, as a result of US and French insistence, the state may withhold information or prevent an individual from giving evidence if, in the state's view, it would prejudice national security interests. The US proposal prevailed over one from the UK, which would have allowed the court to order a state to disclose information, if it was acting in bad faith. Second, a very vague

provision could allow states not to co-operate on the basis of inconsistency with their own 'fundamental national law', such as constitutional provisions.

43 Lionel Yee, Head of the Singapore delegation to the Preparatory Committee on the Establishment of an International Criminal Court, 'Finding the Right Balance', 5 The International Criminal Court Monitor, August 1997, quoted in Amnesty International Report: 'The International Criminal Court: making the right choices – Part III – ensuring effective state co-operation', AI Index, IOR 40/13/97, November 1997.

44 As the vote was unrecorded it is unclear which states voted against and different lists have appeared and include: China, Iraq, Israel, Turkey, Sudan, Iran, Libya, Qatar, Yemen.

45 Congressman Senator Jesse Helm has sought to have a radical act passed by Congress, the American Servicemembers Protection Act (ASPA), the impact of which would be to cut off aid to countries that support the ICC. While this act failed in its attempt to get through Congress in December 2001, it highlights the strong emotions extant. UK Ratified ICC Treaty as US considers anti-ICC legislation, Press Release, Coalition for International Criminal Court, 4 October 2001.

46 The international Coalition for an International Criminal Court (CICC) is a group of over 1,000 concerned non-governmental organisations that operates a very effective information sharing network as well as a lobbying role.

47 World Conference on Human Rights, Vienna 14–25 June 1993, General Assembly, GENERAL/A/CONF. 157/23, 12 July 1993.

48 The Document referred to such rights as the right to use one's mother tongue in public and to disseminate information in that language, the right to special educational, cultural and religious institutions. It also referred to positive obligations on states to 'create the conditions for the promotion of that identity'. This document is not legally binding.

49 Universal Declaration of Human Rights, 1948. The general principle of equality is also recognised in Article 7 of the Declaration and in Article 26 of the International Covenant on Civil and Political Rights (1966), Article 26, and in the European Convention on Human Rights, Article 14.

50 Article 14, 'The enjoyment of the rights and freedoms set forth in this Convention shall be secured without discrimination on the ground such as sex, race, colour, language, religion, political or other opinion, national or social origin, association with a minority, property, birth or other status'.

51 The main civil and political rights included the right to life, the right not to be tortured or subjected to inhuman or degrading treatment, the right to protection against slavery, the right not to be unlawfully arrested or detained, the right to a fair trail, the right to freedom of belief and expression, the right to free association, the right to privacy and family life, the right not to be discriminated against, the right to a remedy for breaches of these rights.

52 Article 25 of the Convention provides for the right of an individual to make a complaint. This is an innovative feature of European Convention on Human Rights as it means that an individual can make an application under the Convention.

53 Some states have complained about the jurisdiction of the court, especially after decisions made against them and threatened to withdraw from the Council of Europe.

54 A useful text on the historical developments and discussions on minorities is, P. Thornberry, *International Law and the Rights of Minorities* (Oxford: Clarendon Press, 1992).

55 *Ibid.*, chapter 13 The Omission of a 'minorities article' from the Universal Declaration of Human Rights. However, the UDHR does have an 'non-discrimination' clause.
56 It entered into force on 1 February 1998. It is the first multilateral instrument devoted to the protection of national minorities.
57 It entered into force on 1 March 1998. The Chapter proposes concrete measures by which language rights can be respected, particularly in the public sphere.
58 Protocol 12, a new article of the European Convention on Human Rights prohibiting all forms of discrimination was opened for signature in November 2000, having gone through a long legislative drafting process. It will come into effect when ten states have ratified it. Welcoming the adoption of the Protocol the then Council of Europe General Secretary Walter Schwimmer said that the Protocol was 'a sign of the times' and a 'major step in the fight against racism and intolerance ... we should not forget that the opening for signature takes place at a time of worrying political developments, Press Release, 'Twenty five states sign up to improve protection against discrimination', Rome, 4 November 2000.
59 Directive 2000/43/EC, relating to the implementation of the principle of equal treatment between persons irrespective of racial or ethnic origin, was adopted on 20 June 2000 by the Council of the European Union.
60 This Charter was revised in 1996.
61 For further information on developments in the area of minorities see website www.humanrights.coe.int.
62 One of the criticisms is that the protection only applies to the rights and freedoms set forth in the Convention. This means, for instance, that a case involving the right of access to civil service employment does not come within its remit and a state has no obligation to avoid discrimination, under Article 14 (case of *Glasenapp* vs. *FRG*, para. 53 (1986). For an interpretation of Article 14 read: D. J. Harris, M. O'Boyle and C. Warbrick, *Law of the European Convention on Human Rights* (London: Butterworths, 1995).
63 Belgian Linguistic case, No.2 (1968) 1EHRR. See also *ibid.*
64 The Framework Convention is monitored by an Advisory Committee, reporting to the Committee of Ministers.
65 For instance the EU had a number of programmes to fund human rights activity, it has arranged electoral observer missions to and has supported resolutions on a wide range of human rights matters: See EU Human Rights Report, 1999 for further details on all of the activities: http://ue.eu.int/pesc/human_rights/en/99/main5.htm.
66 Article 49 of the Treaty of the European Union.
67 Article 13 states, 'Without prejudice to the other provisions of this Treaty and within the limits of the powers conferred by it upon the Community, the Council, acting unanimously on a proposal from the Commission and after consulting the European Parliament, may take appropriate action to combat discrimination based on sex, racial or ethnic origin, religion or belief, disability, age or sexual orientation.'
68 The proposed Directives contain a General Framework Directive on Equality of Treatment in Employment, a Directive on Race and Equality of Treatment in employment, training, services, etc. and a third Directive to Combat Discrimination by providing funding to support legislation and good practice policy development.

Further reading

Alleyne, M. D., *International Power and International Communication* (Macmillan Press in association with St Anthony's College, Oxford, 1995).

Asbjorn, E., A. Rosas and T. Meron, 'Combating lawlessness in grey zone conflicts through minimum humanitarian standards', *American Journal of International Law*, 89 (1995).

Beritz, C. R., M. Cohen, T. Scanlan and A. J. Simmons (eds), *International Ethics* (Princeton, NJ: Princeton University Press, 1985, 4th edn, 1990).

Carey, J., 'The International Legal Order on Human Rights', in C. E. Black and R. Falk (eds), *The Future of the International Legal Order* (Princeton, NJ: Princeton University Press, 1972), pp. 268–90.

Carty, A., *The Decay of International Law: A Reappraisal of the Limits of Legal Imagination in International Affairs* (Manchester: Manchester University Press, 1986).

Cassese, A. and J. H. H. Weiler (eds), *Change and Stability in International Law-Making*, European University Institute, Series A, Law 9 (Berlin and New York: de Gruyter, 1988).

Crawford, J., *Democracy in International Law*, International Law Inaugural Lecture 5 March 1993 (Cambridge: Cambridge University Press).

Danilenko, G. M., *Law-Making in the International Community* (Dordrecht, Boston and London: Kluwer Academic Publishers, 1993).

Gray, A., 'Application of the Convention on the Prevention and Punishment of the Crime of Genocide (Bosnia and Herzegovina v. Yugoslavia) Admissibility and Jurisdiction', *International and Comparative Law Quarterly*, 46: 3 (July 1997).

Harris, D. J., M. O'Boyle and C. Warbrick, *Law of the European Convention on Human Rights* (London: Butterworths, 1995).

Hervey, Tamara, *European Social Law and Policy* (London and New York: Longman, 1998).

Roberts, A. and B. Kingsbury (eds), *United Nations, Divided World* (Oxford: Clarendon Press, 2nd edn, 1993).

Shihata, F. I., 'Democracy and development', *International and Comparative Law Quarterly*, 46: 3 (July 1997).

Steiner, Henry and Philip Alston, *International Human Rights in Context* (Oxford: Oxford University Press, 2nd edn, 2000).

Teubner, G. (ed.), *Global Law Without a State* (Aldershot, Brookfield USA, Singapore, Sydney: Dartmouth Publishing, 1997).

Winford, H., 'The history of intervention in international law', *The British Year Book of International Law*, 1992–93, 3rd year of issue.

Wright, Q., 'Proposals for an International Criminal Court', *American Journal of International Law*, 46 (1952).

Part II

Issues of economic development

Despite exploring small steps and policy competences in foreign political and security affairs, the European Union is recognisable worldwide as being, first and foremost, a powerful regional trading bloc. Indeed it has achieved its deepest levels of integration and most extensive progress on the economic front, both inside and outside its borders, and Part II attempts to reflect this by exploring the EU's economic position in the world today and contemporary areas of debate, in which it plays an active role, and which impact significantly in its economic relations with different parts of the world.

In Chapter 6, Luckhurst and Koutrakou provide a critical overview of EU institutional policy-making mechanisms and processes, highlighting the supranational and inter-governmental elements involved and the role these play in international economic relations. They then discuss the EU's position in the world economic system, in the context of the globalisation discourse, and attempt to demystify the dimensions and constraints that the globalisation process places upon the sovereign exercise by the EU, of control over its own fortunes and of choice over its web of economic relations on the world scene.

The EU institutions have become crucial in representing the EU's collective interests in the World Trade Organisation, the most identifiable driving force in what is perceived as the globalisation process, but also, to a lesser extent, in other international organisations and fora. The more successful the co-operation, indeed cohesion, between member states' opinions, the stronger, the more resolute and the more influential the EU's voice becomes internationally, on the Third World, on free trade, the environment and many more issues.

In Chapter 7, Koutrakou concentrates on the focus change in the EU's Third World policy, as exemplified by the 2000 Cotonou Partnership Agreement. This new agreement between the EU and the African, Caribbean and Pacific group appears to abandon the old aid and guaranteed non-reciprocal preferences for EU market entry schemes, opting instead for a rapid phasing out of these in favour of a less aid-dependent relationship, with the remaining advantages having many political and social conditions attached, and a definite move towards a relationship of free trade. This agreement bears all the hallmarks of a WTO-inspired scheme, yet it is also formulated in such a way so as to resist the worst of its pressures, resulting in an EU-led compromise which leaves all sides more or less uneasy about its future and, in many ways, is much too complex to implement. The chapter analyses the pros and cons of this shift in policy and airs the major voices of criticism and their origins.

The following two chapters examine aspects of economic co-operation between mainly the European Union and Eastern Europe.

At the beginning of the twenty-first century the EU is faced with the prospect of admitting up to 13 new member states within the next decade. Most of these applicant states have until recently been ruled by communist regimes, and ten years on they are still facing considerable economic, political and social problems. The alleviation of these difficulties demands dramatic changes in many areas of society, and in order for these changes to be successfully implemented new forms of political and legal organisation need to be created. While the EU and the rest of the world community has successfully encouraged realignments in economic and political spheres, it has been proved more difficult to create the necessary administrative structures and competences. This is proving to be one of the major stumbling-blocks for development.

Shifting patterns of political power and decision-making have created new forms of governance in Europe, which have been labelled multi-level governance by contemporary scholars. These political changes have placed greater responsibility on sub-central government politicians and administrators, many of whom have had little or no experience of international projects. In the applicant states, sub-central government and the bureaucracy mostly played a role that involved supporting decisions made at the central level. Established problem-solving procedures in both member state and applicant countries have created vastly different institutional restraints that can be difficult to overcome. In Chapter 8, Gooch examines co-operation between local authorities, and proposes that differences in administrative cultures between member and applicant states lie at the heart of many of the problems experienced in co-operative projects.

Staying with the eastern European example, O'Riordan and Jordan reassess environmentalism in Chapter 9, as it finds itself having become embedded in rules, organisations, political and legal structures, and ways of thinking and acting across the world. In many important respects, they argue, the environmental movement has served its purpose, been taken seriously and has become institutionalised. EU environmental policy, which celebrated 25 years of existence in 1998, provides a case in point. The trouble is that although sustainability is a very different concept from environmentalism, it as yet has no common currency or identifiable image. Environmentalism may well remain the politically acceptable and publicly identifiable buzz-word, but the real agenda nowadays is about sustainability.

The chapter examines the political conflicts and tensions within Europe which such a transition will inevitably provoke, and sets one agenda for environmental policy-making over the next decade. It then assesses how far this agenda is reflected in what is arguably the most fundamental historical development in Europe since the Second World War: the enlargement of the European Union into Central and Eastern Europe. If sustainability is to constitute more than a series of small changes to the status quo, then macro-scale geopolitical initiatives such as enlargement must be designed in a way which reconciles social, economic and environmental imperatives.

Negotiations over economic impact and competitiveness still dominate the bargaining between EU member states and their bargaining outside their borders. More and more non-state actors steadily become involved, if not in the actual decision-making processes, certainly in the prior consultations and preparations which shape them.

Based on a case study on the German and French nuclear industry, and interest representations in the process of the eastern enlargement of the EU, Saurugger addresses, in Chapter 10, the general question of the influence of non-state actors in the EU negotiation process. The complex interplay between national, Community and private actors contradicts strongly a purely inter-governmental view of the enlargement process. After the fall of the Berlin wall, the European Community was searching for a new role in Eastern Europe. One of its first actions was to launch programmes in order to ensure nuclear safety in Eastern Europe and the NIS. In managing these programmes, the Commission played an important role in organising the co-operation among Western European electricity producers and nuclear industries, especially considering that it had neither the competences nor know-how in this sector. Artificial networks were created which led to highly conflictual and hierarchi-cally unstable groups. In these groups competition between member states and different national nuclear industries as well as internal Commission conflicts offer an interesting study area in which the role of structures and hierarchies are analysed. At the national level, there is much evidence that national govern-ments still enjoy a great deal of leverage in shaping the social and economic conditions of their societies according to prevailing political preferences. At the European level, the need for the Commission to have external expertise allows interest groups to influence the policy-making process and to represent their interests directly in a much more pluralistic way.

Conflicts of economic and environmental interest are also encountered in the EU's Common Transport Policy, as Steve Dawe demonstrates in Chapter 11. The CTP and more recently the Trans-European networks, have traditionally been designed to underpin the functioning of a freer, faster Single Market. Several initiatives, like the Swiss and Austrian examples given in the chapter, are the product of long negotiations and periods of stand-offs between member states and the EU, or member states and neighbouring countries, as they can run contrary to other interests such as the handling of waves of immigration, the compromising of the environment and other issues which can have a more tangible economic impact and generate strong views.

This part of the book is rounded off by Chapter 12, where Fairbrass researches the behaviour of firms operating in the European market and internationally, in relation to European economic governance, and attempts to answer questions relating to their identity and interactions.

Studying neo-functionalist texts, she tries to identify signs of Europeanisation of firms which operate nationally and can operate in the EU market, particularly if they are to use this as a launching pad for international ventures, and exam-ines the impact of market structures, size of firm and national political economies on the lobbying behaviour of firms in Europe. The chapter is also concerned with Euro groups, and their role in European integration and economic policy-making. This again draws on the work of the neo-functional-ists who argued that Euro groups would play an important role in European integration. Since the work is consistently concerned with policy-making processes and the relationships between policy process actors, the work also refers to a body of literature which views the EU as a polity and draws effectively on public policy analysis/comparative politics.

6

EU economic governance in the present world system

Jonathan Luckhurst and Vassiliki N. Koutrakou

This chapter analyses the European Union's economic position in the context of the world economic system. It examines both key concepts and concrete policy directions advanced by EU institutions and policy-making élites to maximise economic outcomes within this world system. Alongside, it demonstrates the influence of the institutional structures and procedures that underpin EU economic policy-making.

In recent years policy debate in the advanced capitalist countries has often centred on the need for economic restructuring. The general consensus within policy-making circles, in most of these countries, has been that restructuring should take the form of greater market liberalisation and deregulation in order for national economies to flourish, or at least better resist negative outcomes, in what is often called the 'global economy' and 'era of globalisation'. These ideas, which have significantly influenced policy-making in the EU over the past decade, and the reasons behind these, will be analysed, in order to consider the effectiveness of EU policy responses.

The institutional design of EU economic governance

The EU's policy-making procedures often appear confusing, indeed almost Byzantine in their complexity. This impression is certainly encouraged by the complex nature of relations between member states; sub-state and increasingly transborder regions; the EU inter-governmental structures and institutions; and, *above* these, the EU supranational institutions, most notably the European Commission. These multiple tiers of bureaucracy, economic diplomacy and governance impact directly on the EU's economic policy-making. A number of different EU committees and institutions influence its economy and external economic relations. These include the main decision-making EU institutions that deal with foreign affairs, finance, trade and other related areas, such the Council of Ministers for Trade, Industry, Agriculture, or the European Council of Finance Ministers (ECOFIN) among others, and the European Parliament;

the diplomats and officials of the Council of Permanent Representatives (COREPER) who brief member states' ministers ahead of Council meetings and provide continuity in consultation between EU bodies and national governments; the bureaucrats of the European Commission who draft and, in the end, execute legislation; those who direct EU monetary policy at the European Central Bank (ECB), and those in the European Bank for Reconstruction and Development (EBRD) and the European Investment Bank (EIB) who fund development projects in regions like Eastern Europe and the Third World; the Committee of the Regions and the Economic and Social Committee which are key information-gathering and consultative bodies.[1] This brief list does not include the many other national, regional, sectoral etc. institutions and lobby groups which influence the EU's economic relations within the world economic system (for examples, see Table 6.1).

Table 6.1 *EU institutions and other organisations that influence external economic relations*

Supranational institutions	Nation-state institutions	European/international organisations
European Council	National parliaments	EU-level federations
European Parliament	and governments	such as: European
European Central Bank	Finance and economic	Trade Union Federation
European Court of Justice	ministries	[ETUC] and EU
European Commission, incl. representatives at WTO meetings and other international fora.	Trade and industry ministries, etc.	Employers' Federation
Consultative bodies	*Sub-state institutions*	*Local and national organisations*
European Economic and Social Committee	Regional and local councils, including	Employers organisations
Committee of the Regions	autonomous and	Trade unions
European Environment Agency	semi-autonomous assemblies, e.g.	Large companies and small businesses
COREPER, etc.	Scottish and Catalan parliaments	Consumer groups
		Farmers' organisations

Economic co-operation at the EU level has increased significantly during recent decades. Its origins date back to the founding of the European Coal and Steel Community in 1951 by France, Germany, Italy and the three Benelux countries. However things have advanced dramatically since then, especially after the Single European Act (SEA) of 1986, in which the European Economic Community (EEC) countries signed up to the creation of a Single Market and the deepening of the process towards greater economic union, furthered still with the Treaty of European Union, signed in Maastricht in 1992. The latter consolidated complete free trade within the then Community of 12 and paved the way for the Amsterdam Treaty of 1997 and the introduction of the European Central Bank, and a single currency (the euro), in 1999.[2] Despite some countries opting out – for a time at least – or being unable to join the new euro-zone at its inception, this sequence of events, coupled with continuing enlargement which had by now produced a European Union of 15 member states, led to an even greater realisation of the goal of a single, unified European economic bloc. Whilst such developments focused on internal (intra-Union) economic relations, there were consequences for external relations also, both in terms of the EU's interaction with other states and in terms of its policy structures for dealing with external economic pressures.

The greater size of the EU economy alone, when considered as a whole rather than a series of individual economies, combined with its prosperity, gives it a significantly different position in the world's political and economic system. The creation of a single currency zone certainly made politicians, economists and other analysts more aware of the EU as a single, powerful entity within the world system. Table 6.2, highlights this by comparing the original 11 (12 since 2001) 'euro-zone' countries, as a single economic bloc with its own currency, with the USA and Japan. It demonstrates that the EU economy, as it becomes increasingly unified, is challenging the supremacy of the US economy and the US dollar in world significance. For example, the EU's economy has in recent years managed to out-perform the US in some areas, such as exports and balance of trade, as shown in the table below.

Table 6.2 *Statistical comparison between the 11 euro-zone countries, the USA and Japan*

	Eurozone-11	USA	Japan
Population (1998)	292m	270m	127m
GDP (1998)	£4,041bn	£5,314bn	£2,329bn
Exports (1997)	£533bn	£424bn	£260bn
Trade surplus/deficit (3 Feb. 2000)	US$55.2bn	US$368.6bn	US$124.1bn
Stock market capitalisation (Oct. 1998)	£2,234bn	£6,776bn	£2,311bn
Inflation (April 1999–March 2000)*%	2.1	3.7	0.6
Unemployment rate (Feb. 2000)*%	9.5	4.5 (March)	4.9
Government debt, as % GDP (1997)	74.5	61.5	86.7

Sources: Eurostat (using exchange rate of 1 euro = £0.70) and **The Economist.*

The EU economy is second only to the United States in terms of Gross Domestic Product (GDP), and in terms of market-size the two are currently fairly equal. EU–US trade increased dramatically over the 1990s with the EU exhibiting a rapidly increasing trade surplus. Indicatively, between the years 1995 and 2000 EU exports of goods to the US rose by 125 per cent, while its imports from the US rose by 88 per cent.[3] Furthermore, the three economic powers are each other's greatest economic partners and, simultaneously, competitors, as the bulk of world trade passes between them. Consequent to attaining this position, the way in which the EU and its institutions deal with economic issues within the world system is vital to the world economy as a whole.

In terms of active policy involvement in the world economic system, the EU now sends its own representatives, as a full participant or observer, to meetings of the World Trade Organisation (WTO), Group of Eight (G8) most industrialised countries and other international institutions. When differences have emerged between the USA and EU countries over trade issues, such as the use of hormone feed in beef production, the EU's preferential terms for small-scale banana producers in the Caribbean and over genetically modified food exports from US agro-conglomerates, the EU and USA have sometimes behaved like two opposing economic 'superpowers' at WTO meetings. Their disputes have dominated recent WTO discussions. For example, at Seattle in 1999 – whilst the battles raged outside the conference halls between police and protesters – the US and the EU each attempted to encourage, even bully, smaller countries to support their negotiating positions vis-à-vis the other.[4] At such conferences the EU has certainly developed substantial negotiating power as a consequence of its united stance.

The ways in which the EU co-ordinates its policies in order to enhance its position in global-level negotiations, particularly the WTO meetings and rounds, contain supranational and inter-governmental elements.

In the EU's external trade relations, particularly with relation to WTO negotiations, there are areas which fall under the Common Commercial Policy and therefore under EU 'competence' and others which fall under the national one. On matters where there is mixed EU–national competence, the EU assumes the primary negotiating role.[5] Thus, in simple terms, where a common negotiating position is endorsed, for example, by the main decision-making body, the Council of Trade Ministers – a supranational body in its reach, despite employing intergovernmental methods in its decision-making – for bargaining at an international forum, this has supranational effect on the member states of the EU. In other words, they cannot differentiate their position from the common stance, once taken, on a specific issue, even if they have their own national representative at the international forum (in this case the WTO) where the negotiations are to take place. The baton of this negotiating position, which generally consists of a spectrum of positions in reality, ranging from the optimum, most desirable for the EU, outcome, to the least good, yet still acceptable, one, is then picked up by Commission – another supranational body – representatives who subsequently have the role of bargaining on behalf of the EU as a whole at the WTO – in which the EU has full participant status – along the limitations of the above spectrum of acceptable positions. Thus, put in basic terms, proposals for a particular stance at a WTO round are drafted by the Commission, are decided upon by the relevant Council of Ministers with input from the Parliament and then return to the Commission for the global haggling to begin. Naturally, in the process of arriving at the commonly agreed spectrum of negotiating positions, much inter-governmental-type bargaining and other consultation takes place. Meetings between national leaders, for instance during European Council meetings (comprising EU heads of state or government), or Councils of Ministers, Commission officials, together with input from COREPER, the European Economic and Social Committee, the European Environment Agency, and many other bodies, are used for consultation and co-ordination of member states' policy positions, wherever possible, prior to international level negotiations. Decision-making involves much bargaining, mutual concessions, favour-swaps and compromise, and is finally determined, depending on each issue, by voting procedures including unanimity, simple or qualified majority voting, etc.,[6] and involve usually the Council(s) of Ministers with portfolios closest to the area under scrutiny, and increasingly the European Parliament under the co-decision procedure.

Apart from the more formal procedures in place for the EU's official representation at the WTO, much informal, and more inter-governmental co-ordination of policy positions takes place on other occasions as well, as for example between those EU members which are also members of G8, that is Britain, France, Italy and Germany, prior to G8 summits where the EU as a whole has only observer status. It is known to happen increasingly in advance of certain United Nations conferences too, and in a variety of policy areas, including for instance the Kyoto Summit on the environment and climate change, which certainly impact on the world economy.

An example of direct *supranational* economic policy-making in the EU with less direct, nevertheless very significant, global repercussions, is the role played by the European Central Bank (ECB). This role is vital to the EU's capacity to deal with world economic pressures, and as such it impacts not only on member states, but also on European, non-euro-zone countries like the United Kingdom, and even on countries and regional trading blocs outside Western and Central Europe because of the integration of financial markets implied by globalisation. The ECB has the power to use interest rates to influence the euro's relative strength in relation to other currencies. This, coupled with its rules and restrictions on government borrowing and other levers of economic policy-making, places significant constraints on member states' economic policies, and displays a readiness and commitment by all to employ broadly common policy responses at times of economic prosperity and crisis alike.

This strong element of EU supranationalism in the financial and monetary aspects of economic policy-making, unsurprisingly influences developments at the global level because of the interdependence of share and stock markets in the developed world, and the rise and fall of currencies and interest rates. Furthermore, rises and falls in the value of the euro and the strength of the European economy greatly affect Foreign Direct Investment (FDI), and through this they affect trade and aid with Eastern Europe and the Commonwealth of

Independent States (CIS), the African, Caribbean and Pacific (ACP) countries, and other parts of the developing world, which rely substantially on EU trade and aid.

An example of the complexity in practice, as well as the potential benefits and pitfalls, of the institutional design of economic governance in the EU, when it half-heartedly tries to respond to global economic conditions, is the attempt to co-ordinate member states' employment policies. This became a high priority for policy-makers following the high levels of unemployment globally and, consequently, also across much of the Union during the 1990s. Employment policy became more prominent on the EU agenda with the SEA but even more so with the Social Chapter of the Maastricht Treaty, which envisaged commonly agreed broad regulations on health and safety at work, the setting of minimum wages and working hours, labour representation laws and other areas, while leaving the specifics of employment policy still in the competence of national governments. Following this, it was agreed that member states should develop a deliberate and co-ordinated policy response to the high levels of unemployment in the 1990s, and heads of government and employment ministers met in Luxembourg in November 1997 for an 'Extraordinary European Council on Employment'. This determined that member states would each formulate a National Action Plan (NAP) for combating unemployment and submit it to the European Commission for evaluation and consultation purposes. The Commission then set some general EU criteria for the NAPs, though each country had its own specific priorities and policies within this overall remit. Thus the NAPs, and the strategies developed as a result of the Luxembourg discussions, which became known as the 'Luxembourg process', represented a somewhat co-ordinated EU policy response to the unemployment issue which was both inter-governmental and supranational in character in response to serious instability in the world economic system at the time. Whilst this was partially effective, to the extent that some co-ordination was possible, this 'Luxembourg process' also highlighted some of the limitations on attempts at policy co-ordination between the member states. The European Commission, empowered by the Council of Ministers for employment, formulated some basic criteria for the NAPs, especially concerning guidelines for consultation, and it also re-affirmed the member states' declarations about the need for action at the EU level.[7] However, significantly, the actual policy programmes and implementation were devised by each government for their own national context. Furthermore, these programmes often differed greatly from country to country, for example the French NAP gave priority to a shortened working week (35 hours) whilst the British NAP focused on Blairite goals such as enhancing employability, with Gordon Brown's 'New Deal' as its centre-piece, thus producing a multitude of responses, often determined by national political interests, and variable effectiveness.

Even though different employment policy measures at national, or even at sub-national or regional levels are not necessarily a bad thing, and co-ordination does not have to mean homogeneity, what such examples illustrate is that there are often significant differences of opinion and strategy, which member states hold dear and which impede the European market functioning as one in the way that the United States' and Japan's markets do. Employment/unemployment policies within the EU impact also on immigration policies, which, despite the effort to harmonise, are still also very much inter-governmental, rather than supranational areas of policy-making, and beyond the common overarching guidelines display significant national variations. Another example is disagreement on issues such as the level of economic 'harmonisation' that should be attempted between member states following monetary union. Britain has fiercely criticised attempts by German politicians in particular – such as Oskar Lafontaine, the former Finance Minister, and Foreign Minister Joschka Fischer – to push for greater harmonisation of taxation and of other significant areas of economic policy-making. This demonstrates the divergence between German and British politicians on the issue of increased supranational powers for EU institutions, especially in politically sensitive areas of economic policy-making.

Whether the EU develops further in the direction of the German model, or whether it develops along more inter-governmental lines as British governments would prefer, will have a major impact on the nature of the EU's economic relations with the external world. If the EU does become more supranational in its economic governance, then it should be expected that the EU would increasingly operate as a single state-like entity within the world economic system.

EU economic policies and the world system

The above analysis highlights the significance of the EU's institutions and processes, both inter-governmental and supranational ones, in formulating EU policies and strategies within the world economic system. It is important to remember that the institutions themselves are no more neutral in their perceptions of the world system, due to their institutional character, than individuals, groups or states, since actors within the institutions bring their own policy biases or reflect their national ones. Indeed, such biases already exist within the structures of EU institutions, for example the ECB is controlled by central bankers who, unsurprisingly, adhere to liberal-capitalist ideology. Moreover, the actual statutes governing the ECB are themselves predicated on the theoretical assumptions of liberal capitalism and, to a large extent, neo-classical economic theory. An example of this is the assumption that central banks should prioritise price stability and the suppression of inflationary tendencies within the economy. Hence the ECB has a policy of keeping annual inflation within the euro-zone to below 2 per cent.

In order to understand why the EU responds with specific policies to pressures within the world economic system, it is therefore vital to understand the theoretical logic that leads policy-makers and institutions to follow these policies. Over the past decade EU policy-makers' perceptions of the world economic system have been increasingly influenced by the theory of globalisation. Although there is no commonly agreed definition of the term globalisation, with different analysts viewing it from their own – be it economic, political, social or cultural – angle and some proponents appearing more fundamentalist than others about the substance and the inevitability of its power and its impact, mostly everyone agrees as to the perceived trend of growing globalism in the several spheres which it is meant to encompass. According to Keohane and Nye, 'globalism is a state of the world involving networks of interdependence at multi-continental distances'.[8]

Globalisation and neo-liberal economic theory are encapsulated in the philosophy and practice of the World Trade Organisation, the successor of the General Agreement on Tariffs and Trade (GATT). Reinforcing the GATT before it, the WTO composes of and has been driven by, the most economically developed countries in the world – with China finally being admitted in 2001 – and has been instilled by their neo-liberalist/capitalist ideology, to which it in turn acts as guardian with respect to its member states or groups of states, while also trying to impose this ideology on the rest of the so-called Second and Third worlds. The WTO is therefore a conscious construct of the First World constituting a vehicle for globalisation and liberalisation in order to, ideally, achieve welfare for all. Some would doubtlessly argue that, rather than welfare for all, it is designed to push forward world market liberalisation, regardless of whether it provides benefits for everyone. Many globalisation theorists however, as well as policy-makers, consider it an entity which has fast become more than the sum of its parts. As such, they perceive it to be a driving force which, in turn, drives its creators and imposes enormous pressures on those, inside and out, who do not follow the rules.[9]

The popularity of globalisation theory is based partly on the perceived decline of alternative theoretical models, especially those of a more socialist or statist bent. It has also gained support as a consequence of different pieces of anecdotal evidence, such as the increased size and significance of international financial and other cross-border markets, faster and better technologies and communications, as well as the continuing growth and influence of large multinational corporations (MNCs) which exert significant power within the world economic system.[10] Such evidence appears to support the globalisers' claims with regard to the declining influence of national governments in the face of increasingly powerful global market forces.

Even though there are actually a range of issues that bring into question some of the key assumptions of globalisation theory, the 'Third Wayist' agendas in, most predominantly, the United States, Germany and the United Kingdom – as advocated by former US President Bill Clinton, German Chancellor Gerhard Schröder and British Prime Minister Tony Blair – have embraced the fundamental principles and rhetoric of liberal globalisation discourse. This has significantly increased its influence on EU economic policy-makers, as many EU politicians and institutional actors have been persuaded by at least some of the arguments in favour of this interpretation of globalisation theory. This has involved the implicit acceptance of key political-economic tenets of neo-liberalism, such as economic policies of privatisation and deregulation. Likewise, many left-wing politicians and policy analysts across Europe, east and west, have abandoned their former support for either state-socialist or Keynesian-style economic intervention. Whilst some have turned to 'green politics', many erstwhile advocates of socialism and state welfarism have come out in favour of deregulation and private-sector-oriented economic policies, once associated with the 'bête-noire' of the European left, Margaret Thatcher, and her allies on the neo-liberal right.

Whilst Blair and his political allies espouse the benefits of globalisation for the wealthy as well as the developing countries, the evidence is not nearly so compelling. In fact the world remains deeply divided between the wealthiest countries and those which are significantly poorer, the latter forming a majority in numerical and population terms. Billions of people in the developing and under-developed countries are very much excluded from the perceived benefits of a globalising world order.[11] Instead, a core–periphery model of economic relations characterises the economic relations between the wealthiest countries, including the EU and the rest.

Here it is useful to state some of the evidence which undermines the liberal–globalists' assertions about the present world system. This will facilitate a more accurate assessment of the EU's politico-economic relations within the world system. Paul Hirst and Grahame Thompson, in their book entitled, *Globalization in Question*, have provided an analysis of contemporary patterns of economic relations which undermines many myths of globalisation theory.[12] Like several other academics and political economists such as Neil Fligstein, David Held, Noam Chomsky or Allen J. Scott, Hirst and Thompson have identified, like Kenneth Ohmae before them, a 'triad' of blocs at the core of the core–periphery model, consisting of the USA (plus the North Atlantic Free Trade Area or NAFTA), Japan (plus the 'Tiger' economies of the Pacific Rim) and the EU. These three blocs together dominate the world economic system as its key political and economic actors.

If globalisation really did constitute a true new system of world economic interaction which transcended the core–periphery model of rich and poor states, or even one which was moving away from such a two-tier system, then statistical evidence should provide some support for this. A system of genuinely global economic interaction should demonstrate signs of greater integration of the 'periphery' states. However the evidence, to the contrary, shows little sign of greater integration of the majority of the periphery countries. Neil Fligstein uses statistics from the United Nations (UN), the GATT – now WTO – and the Organisation for Economic Co-operation and Development (OECD) to demonstrate that between 1953 and 1995 a fairly constant level of world trade, fluctuating between 60 and 70 per cent, was controlled by the wealthy 'core' countries.[13] Table 6.3, shows that a similar pattern of core–periphery disparity is evident in world distribution of foreign direct investment (FDI) during the 1980s (investments which enter a country from foreign sources).[14] This decade was indicative of the pattern over the past 50 years, and these figures demonstrate that the rapid expansion of FDI during the 1980s did not end the massive disparity in inward investment between the wealthy and poor states. As Held *et al.* note, post-1945 FDI flows between the wealthy countries, which constitute the OECD, have grown faster than those to developing countries, therefore FDI stocks continue to be significantly concentrated in the former.[15] This evidence certainly contradicts any claims from advocates of 'liberal globalism' that the poorest countries of the world are benefiting as much as the wealthy 'triad' groups of countries from the contemporary structure of the world economic system.

Table 6.3 *Investment flows and populations, 1981–91*

	Population (millions)		(%)	Investment flows 1980–91(%)
Total world	3,292,195		100	
(A) USA and Canada	275,865		14	75
EC and EFTA	357,767	=	14	75
Japan	123,460			
(B) Ten most important developing countries, in terms of flows*	1,519,380	=	29	165
A + B (approx.)			43	91.1

Source: P. Hirst and G. Thompson, *Globalization in Question* (Cambridge: Polity Press, 1996), p. 68.
Note: *Singapore, Mexico, China, Brazil, Malaysia, Hong Kong (now in China), Argentina, Thailand, Egypt, Taiwan.

Another important aspect of globalisation theory is the assumption that recent systemic change makes it much more difficult, if not impossible, for governments to actively use policy-making to direct their economies. It has always been the case that world economic pressures significantly impact on national economies, especially those with greater openness to international trade. However it is not true that EU states have substantially less power to influence their domestic economies, or the economy of the EU as a whole, as a consequence of recent changes in the world economy that are impervious to the actions of policy-makers, which is how globalisation is often portrayed, almost as if it were some elemental force. Rather it is important to stress that it is government policies which have changed the world system, especially those policies of governments within the triad blocs of North America, East Asia and the EU. This is much more than a semantic argument, as it is vitally important to note that the most powerful governments, especially in the USA, the EU and Japan, have chosen to guide the world economic system towards much greater international market and financial openness. This has been achieved in recent years, in particular, by utilising the WTO, the G8 and other organs of 'core-state' power. The implication is that policy-makers are still directing the world economic system, not vice versa. Therefore the EU, as a key member of the triad, has the potential to encourage a more egalitarian distribution of global wealth, as well as a more environmentally friendly system of world economic production. The 'Kyoto Accord' on industrial pollution emissions and climate controls, however unsuccessful, is indicative of the types of policies that the EU could be instrumental in encouraging other countries to agree to impose on world industrial production.

Hirst and Thompson have done much to bring into question the simple version of globalisation theory and liberal globalism. For example, their analysis of MNCs demonstrates that they are more closely tied to national, home-based territories and geographic clusters of states than globalisation theorists claim.[16] They have similarly questioned the assumption that trade is more liberalised today than ever before. They point to the pre-1914 'Gold Standard' period as a contradiction of this view, by pointing out that the ratio of trade and capital flows to GDP was higher in this period than during the 1980s.[17] Held similarly uses International Monetary Fund (IMF) statistics to show that the growth of trade between 1950 and 1973 was 5.8 per cent per annum, whilst in the years 1973–96 it was only 4.1 per cent per annum. World economic output grew at 3.9 per cent and 3.3 per cent per annum, respectively, during these two periods.[18] This corroborates Hirst and Thompson's claim that the late twentieth century did not witness an inexorable increase in the 'globalisation' of world trade. Kleinknecht and Ter Wengel also demonstrate the close proximity in levels of exports and imports of goods, as a percentage of gross national product (GNP), in countries such as France, Germany, the UK and the USA, in a comparison of national figures for 1913 with 1994.[19]

Therefore statistical evidence for key trading states does not support the notion that a dramatically new system of more globalised trade exists. Fligstein puts the case for relative historical continuity more simply, stating that in late 1995 international trade as a percentage of world economic activity stood at about 14.7 per cent, very close to the 14 per cent level it reached in 1913, its previous peak.[20] All this evidence is important when considering the EU's position within the world economic system, and the possible scope for future policy-making. Rather than implying that the EU and its member states must resign themselves to their economic fates, the evidence suggests that the present world system is not so unique, and that neo-liberal-style 'laissez-faire' economic strategies are not that much more imperative now than they were in the past, when Western Europe managed to flourish in the post-war era with more interventionist national economic strategies.[21]

More recently, whilst political rhetoric and important policy developments, such as the rules governing the ECB, have highlighted the influence of neo-liberal and liberal–globalist ideas in the EU, the overall politico-economic direction of its institutions and policy-making has not been so clear-cut. There are still many areas where national government and EU institutional interven-tion occur, despite the preponderance of anti-interventionist sentiment in influential economic policy-making circles. The Common Agricultural Policy (CAP) is one major example of this kind of intervention, designed to protect and sustain EU agricultural production. Thus, rather than simply having opened up the EU's economy to global competition, recent economic policies have involved a process both of increasing the EU's exposure to global market forces, whilst simultaneously protecting member states from some negative consequences of greater world economic interdependence and interaction.[22] The EU is not alone in this. East Asian regionalism of the ASEAN–AFTA type (Association of South-East Asian Nations and ASEAN Free Trade Area) can be seen as a step towards globalisation, because of its leakage of power away from nation-states and towards broader structures, but it can also be seen as a defence against further fragmentation and protectionist efforts by international competitors, and a re-empowerment of member nations through a controlled joining of forces. Similarly NAFTA, an agreement between the US, Canada and Mexico, can be seen as a response to so-called 'Fortress Europe'. In other words, 'Europeanisation has acted both as a conduit for global forces and as a shield against them, opening member-states up to international markets and compe-tition at the same time that they protect them through monetary integration and the single market'.[23]

It is useful here to cast a glance back to the NAPs, and world economic circumstances in the late 1990s, especially issues raised by the world economic crisis of that period. This series of problems began in East Asia, in Thailand, then spread across a number of countries in the developing world. It also affected more industrialised regions. It was arguably the monetary policy inter-ventions of Alan Greenspan, the chairman of the US Federal Reserve, combined with the buoyancy of Western stock markets, especially the US's Dow Jones Industrial and Nasdaq technology-sector indexes, which helped prevent these economic disturbances in less wealthy countries from sending the wealthy capi-talist countries into recession.

There were some key policy differences between Western policy-makers about how to deal with the world situation. The EU's agenda for tackling unem-ployment, which coalesced around the NAPs initiative, was just a part of this global policy debate. Not surprisingly, the US government chose to avoid any policies that hinted at Keynesian interventionism. The closest the Clinton administration came to anything approaching this was the 'work-fare' and welfare-to-work schemes, which tended towards punitive measures to cajole Americans into accepting any kind of employment before becoming eligible for welfare benefits. Such programmes did nothing to actually create new jobs, either in the private or public sector. The EU was much more interventionist, with the NAPs a key part of its response to the general sense of economic malaise. Whilst member states acted very differently within the NAPs framework, even the least-statist country, the UK, had more significant state programmes as part of its employment strategy within the NAPs framework than would have been acceptable to the US government. This included a small 'public sector works' element, in the Environmental Task Force scheme but also included significant government targets on raising employment levels, especially amongst young adults, which the British government invested directly in, by subsidising employers' costs under the aegis of its employment scheme, paying a part of young employees' wages to employers who joined the programme.[24] As noted earlier, the French government introduced even more ambitious elements into its NAP, especially the measure to introduce a statutory limit of 35 hours to the working week. The NAPs of these two member states are representative of the range of policies employed across the EU within the NAPs framework, and demonstrate that member governments of the Union took a much more interventionist approach than the US government to tackling employment issues created by the world economic problems of the 1990s.[25]

In contrast, the Clinton administration and US Congress did little in the way of direct state intervention. Instead they preferred to leave the fate of the US economy largely to Greenspan's monetary policies and the 'feel-good' factor that persisted in the stock exchanges, especially the Nasdaq – which at the time seemed to have lost its sense of economic reality, with investors choosing to ignore the asset value of technology companies in favour of their over-inflated share prices. The consequences of this, and of the failure of Greenspan and the Clinton government to inject some sense of reality into the markets, came afterwards, with the dramatic falls in stock-market prices in 2000–1, especially the 'bursting' of the tech-sector 'bubble'.

Contrasting the policies of the EU and the US in dealing with the economic problems at the end of the 1990s offers an insight into the dangers faced by the EU in its position as 'second fiddle' to the USA, in world economic, political and even strategic matters. Whilst each was able to follow its own policy-making agenda in certain areas of internal economic policy, the global economic circumstances at the time affected both. It was in the context of international attempts at policy co-ordination that the US domestic agenda asserted itself at the expense of EU policy. US political conservatism limited the EU's scope for encouraging significant change within the world economic system, in order to try to alleviate some of the problems. For example, during the global economic disturbances of 1998, British finance minister Gordon Brown tried to encourage greater policy co-ordination between the leading economic powers. He believed that greater transparency of international financial institutions and dealings would help to stabilise the world economy. The then German finance minister, Oskar Lafontaine, believed that more significant reforms were necessary. He supported measures to foster much greater economic growth in developing and under-developed countries, including the cancellation of poor countries' financial debts to Western countries and institutions. Whilst the US government showed some interest in Brown's more limited proposals during 1998, when the world economy began to recover from the shocks of that year, even these lost US support.

Lafontaine and others have also advocated the introduction of the so-called 'Tobin tax', first suggested by the economist James Tobin. This involves the levying of a tax on all international financial transactions, the proceeds of which would be redistributed to the world's poorer countries via an international fund institution. Aside from this, the other main aim of this tax would be to reduce the amount of short-term international economic transactions, especially those of a highly speculative nature. These have tended to increase financial and economic disruption during times of world economic uncertainty, as investors pull out of countries which they perceive as being more susceptible to short-term economic threats. The Tobin tax would counter such speculation by making highly speculative, short-termist international investments less attractive due to the levy imposition. The French government of Lionel Jospin emphasised its continued support for this measure. Indeed, Jospin and the German Chancellor Gerhard Schröder stated, in a joint declaration, that they planned to set up a joint working group to study 'how to control the financial markets better', and that '[the German and French governments] are agreed that [they] must discuss all the instruments that would make globalisation economically efficient but also control it socially'.[26] However the USA continued to oppose such reforms, preferring the present structure of the world's financial and economic system.

With their combined scope for world-wide influence, the USA, the EU and Japan certainly have the power to push for new policy mechanisms to deal with international structural deficiencies when they arise. These could include measures such as preferential trade deals to protect the export potential of under-developed regions of the world; also the encouragement of inward FDI in developing countries, through various pro-active policies and incentive programmes from wealthy states; and the provision of extensive trade credits to countries such as Brazil, Indonesia and Russia in times of economic crisis. However the trend of recent decades has been to increase the exposure of national economies, including those of less developed countries, to the vagaries of laissez-faire capitalism. The US's victory at the WTO against the EU's subsidy for small-scale banana producers is evidence of the unwillingness of its political establishment to allow any form of international 'redistributive' economics to get in the way of corporate capitalism and profits. Subsequently, particularly after Johannesburg, the administration of George W. Bush signalled its even greater opposition to any interventionist measures which might impinge on US corporate profits, by reneging on the Clinton government's previous support for the Kyoto climate agreements. The fact that the EU is still supporting these measures, and has put diplomatic pressure on the USA to re-commit to the environmental agreements, demonstrates, as in its confrontations with the USA at the WTO, that the Union now feels capable of asserting itself through diplomacy even over major economic policy differences with the USA.

Whilst the key strategic relationship for the EU, including in economic terms, continues to be with the USA, future EU policy will have to focus on other relations as well. Already however, and despite previous, actual or threatened, small-scale trade wars with Japan, and a fair number of disputes at the WTO, the EU's links with South-East Asia are painstakingly cultivated through various channels, most notably the ASEM (ASEAN–EU Meetings) process. Despite its increased relationship with Latin America since the Spanish and Portuguese accession in 1986, the United States remain the major economic partner for that area. Eastern European and former Soviet markets, whether future membership plans are involved or not, are another major target area. Development issues, such as poor countries' economic restructuring, generally towards a more marketised model of economic production, continue to bring new challenges to EU policy-makers. For example, if the Kyoto agreements are not implemented, as looks likely in the short term, there could be significant environmental, social and economic implications, especially as a consequence of greatly increased industrial production and pollution in countries such as China, Indonesia and India. Once again, the EU's longer-term response to the Bush government's initial opposition to the Kyoto agreements will be vitally important to the future of the world environment and the future pattern of world economic development.

The EU is key to drawing the USA back into negotiations over international environmental controls, with its diplomatic leverage, as the USA's main strategic ally, decisive to this end. Even the world's most powerful country, and even with some tacit support by Japan, could feel isolated in the face of serious and sustained criticism from the rest of the world, including its closest allies. Such criticisms would likely encourage the growing environmental lobby in the USA to campaign harder against Bush's opposition to international climate control measures. Another factor which could change Bush's scepticism towards Kyoto, to remain with this example, and his apparent willingness in the early months of his administration to 'go it alone' (for example, reneging on the 1972 Anti-Ballistic Missile (ABM) treaty with the former Soviet Union, as well as his scepticism in relation with international environmental concerns) is the aftermath of the 11 September attacks on New York and Washington DC. Recent events have encouraged the Bush administration to reconnect, to some extent, with the world via international diplomacy, and generally encouraged them to place greater priority on US external relations. If this attitude lasts beyond the present state of crisis and the conflict in Afghanistan, then there might be more chance of future co-operation, between the USA and the EU in particular, in areas of international economic policy co-ordination. This would be especially useful in countering future world recessionary pressures and economic instability. Nevertheless, it should be remembered that the scope for such action will most likely remain limited, as the Bush administration is even less inclined to allow government interference in world markets than the Clinton regime during the late 1990s.

Conclusion

This chapter highlights the institutional design of EU's economic governance in its external economic relations and its importance, given the key position which the EU now occupies within the world economic system. The first part of this analysis argues that the EU's economic governance is currently caught between two prevailing institutional models, inter-governmentalism and supranationalism. The future of EU governance in general, and specifically its economic governance, will be decisively influenced by the extent to which these models are utilised in EU institutional structures and procedures. If the EU takes on more supranational powers over its member states' external relations (extra-EU), then the Union will increasingly act, and be perceived, as a more state-like entity within the world system. This could give the Union greater leverage in negotiations with external states and other economic actors, however it would also constrain individual member states if they wished to follow their own agendas in certain policy areas. At present, the degree of inter-governmentalism, which is still in operation in negotiations and even in decision-making affecting some policy areas, and the introduction of more flexibility in further integration apparent since the Nice Treaty,[27] in conjunction with the strengthening of selected supranational mechanisms, such as the establishment of a new Directorate General in the European Commission specifically dealing with foreign trade,[28] demonstrates a dual approach by EU policy-makers to co-ordinating policy positions in external economic relations, and dispatching coherent EU delegations at international fora, such as the WTO.

Whilst these differences in governance structures will influence the EU's response to future developments within the world economic system, it is also vital to note the likely impact of member states' policies on future EU policy-making with relation to the world economic system. We have already analysed the political differences in important areas of economic policy, often, though not always, with Britain on one side and France and Germany on the other. Further enlargement is likely to cause more divisions as well as alliances in the course of policy-making bargaining processes. The extent to which the EU follows either of these policy paths will be decisive for the future of EU economic policy-making, both internally and in external relations.

There are certain problems and issues in the world economic system that the EU will need to deal with, regardless of its institutional structures and procedures and its general politico-economic direction. The nature of its responses to these developments will be highly significant for the world system. The EU and the other triad blocs each have significant economic power within the present world system. Consequently, policy-makers within these countries have the capacity to advocate new institutional mechanisms to enhance world economic stability, and to better co-ordinate efforts to counter specific threats to the world economy. The EU, as the second most powerful economic force within the world system (after the USA), clearly has scope to push for such measures, especially with support from other countries and world regions. The extent to which the EU states can agree on policy goals, as well as the Union's capacity to make alliances with other states, will affect the level of influence it can exert on the USA to this end.

The development of institutional mechanisms for co-operation between the EU's own member states, in many policy areas, not just economics, could certainly act as a kind of blueprint for future attempts at better international co-ordination in countering world economic problems. Whilst these would most likely not extend to the level of partnership achieved between EU states, the lessons of greater international co-operation within the EU certainly demonstrate the potential benefits of such interstate links. Post-Second World War international institutions such as the World Bank, International Monetary Fund and even the United Nations also provide institutional foundations upon which co-ordination of international economic policy might be further enhanced. However the EU will almost certainly find itself having to contend with US political opposition, since US policy-makers will continue to support the principle of international free trade with minimal regulatory interference.

Notes

1 John Peterson and Michael Shackleton, *The Institutions of the European Union* (Oxford: Oxford University Press, 2002).
2 For a history of European economic integration, see: Malcolm Levitt and Christopher Lord, *The Political Economy of Monetary Union* (Basingstoke: Macmillan, 2000). Also: F. McDonald and S. Dearden, *European Economic Integration* (Harlow: Longman, 1998, and later editions).
3 Terrence R. Guay, *The United States and the European Union* (Sheffield: Sheffield University Press, 1999).
4 David A. Sanger, 'A grand trade bargain', *Foreign Affairs*, 80: 1 (Jan./Feb. 2001), 65–75.
5 H. Wallace and W. Wallace, *Policy-Making in the European Union* (Oxford: Oxford University Press, 2000).
6 For the latest agreements on decision-making procedures and quotas, and details on relevant and related administrative reform, see the 'Treaty of Nice', 2001/C 80/01, *Official Journal of the European Communities*, 10 March 2001.
7 Commission of the European Communities, DG V '1998 Joint Employment Report', Office for Official Publications of the European Communities, Luxembourg, 1998.
8 R. O. Keohane and J. S. Nye, 'Globalisation: What's new? What's not? (And so what?)', *Foreign Policy* (Spring 2000), 105.
9 Björn Hetnne, András Inotai and Osvaldo Sunkel (eds), *Globalism and the New Regionalism* (Basingstoke: Macmillan, 1999).
10 For a case study of TNCs' role in the Philippines, see: Karen T. Fisher, and Peter B.

Urich, 'TNCs: aid agents for the new millennium?', *Development in Practice*, 11: 1 (February 2001), 7–19.

11 See, for example, Linda Main, 'The global information infrastructure: empowerment or imperialism?', *Third World Quarterly*, 22: 1 (2001), 83–97.

12 P. Hirst and G. Thompson, *Globalization in Question* (Cambridge: Polity Press, 1996).

13 N. Fligstein, 'Is globalization the cause of the crises of welfare states?', EUI Working Paper SPS, No. 98/5., European University Institute, Florence, September 1998, pp. 12–13.

14 Original sources used by Hirst and Thompson: *World Population Prospects, 1990* (UN, 1991); *China Statistical Yearbook, 1991; Statistical Yearbook of the Republic of China,* 1991; *TNCs and integrated international production* (UN, 1993).

15 D. Held, A. McGrew, D. Goldblatt and J. Perraton, *Global Transformations* (Cambridge: Polity Press, 1999), p. 248.

16 Hirst and Thompson, *Globalization in Question*, pp. 91–4.

17 *Ibid.*, pp. 26–9.

18 Held *et al.*, *Global Transformations*, pp. 163–4.

19 A. Kleinknecht and J. Ter Wengel, 'The myth of economic globalisation', *Cambridge Journal of Economics*, 22: 5 (September, 1998), 638. The original source is: A. Maddison, *Dynamic Forces in Capitalist Development* (Oxford: Oxford University Press, 1991).

20 Fligstein, 'Is globalization the cause of the crises of welfare states?', p. 9.

21 See also: Sandro Sideri, 'Globalisation's dilemma: economic blocs or global economic apartheid?', *The European Journal of Development Research*, 11: 2 (December 1999), 141–75.

22 V. N. Koutrakou and J. Luckhurst, 'The globalization versus liberalization paradox and the European Union', Special Strategic Paper No. 81, RIEAS Athens, 2000.

23 D. Smith, D. Solinger and S. Topik (eds), *States and Sovereignty in the Global Economy* (London and New York: Routledge, 1999), p. 172.

24 Commission of the European Communities, DG V, '1998 Joint Employment Report', Part I, 33.

25 Commission of the European Communities, DG V, '1998 Joint Employment Report', Part I, 42.

26 'Germany and France target money markets', *Guardian*, 6 September 2001.

27 D. N. Chryssochoou, *Treorizing European Integration* (London: Sage, 2001).

28 David Allen and Michael Smith, 'External policy development', in Geoffrey Edwards and Georg Wiessala, 'The European Union: Annual Review of the EU 1999/2000', *Journal of Common Market Studies* (Oxford: Blackwell Publishers, 2000), p. 105.

Further reading

The Economist, 'Financial/economic indicators', 29 April–5 May 2000, London.

7

New directions in the EU's Third World policy: from aid to trade under the watchful eye of the WTO

Vassiliki N. Koutrakou

The co-operation agreement between the European Union and the African–Caribbean–Pacific group of countries (EU–ACP) signed in Cotonou, Benin, in June 2000, saw the beginning of a new 20-year chapter in the history of trade and aid relations between the two entities. It was also described as a 'quantum leap', irrevocably redefining this long-standing relationship at the dawn of the twenty-first century. Aside from the enthusiastic rhetoric, it is not surprising that the new parameters and directions heralded by this agreement were a product of long and intensive negotiations, unrelenting international pressures and bitter compromise. This chapter examines this major change of focus in the EU's traditional Third World policy, the dynamics behind it and the concerns hidden behind the optimism, as well as the voices of hope and criticism with respect to the prospects of the Cotonou Agreement.

A look back in history

In mapping the path to Cotonou, it is contextually relevant to reflect briefly on the beginnings of the journey which takes one back to the creation of the European Economic Community (EEC) in 1957, a mostly economic milestone in European history with less immediate political and security dimensions at the time, alongside a decolonisation process in progress, which particularly affected the African continent, opening up a whole can of benign and malignant worms in economic, political and military terms.

With economy and trade uppermost in the EEC's collective mind, and an anxiety to maintain close relations with former – or about to become former – colonies, and to defend on-going business interests, evident particularly in France but also in the other former colonial powers among the original six EEC members, the EEC's founding treaty, the Treaty of Rome, already introduced and institutionalised aid and trade links between the new Community and its member states' Overseas Countries and Territories (OCTs), many of which were already en route to becoming independent. A year later, 1958, the European

Development Fund (EDF) was created, on top of the Community's general budget, and in 1963 the first of two Yaoundé Conventions was signed by the EEC and 18 newly independent African countries plus Madagascar. These conventions established a system of aid which included short-term financial aid, longer-term developmental financial and technical assistance, preferential trade agreements, grants and loans. The pattern of a convention 'renewing the vows' of this new relationship occurring at regular, approximately five-yearly, intervals continued with four Lomé Conventions, from 1975 to 2000, each of which increased both in numbers of participants, and in sophistication in terms of instruments of financial aid. The EEC turned to the European Community (EC) and then to the European Union and its membership gradually increased from six to 15. In turn, the former OCTs increased in numbers at every stage, to 77, with each new EC member bringing along its own special relationships with its former colonies (as with Britain's entry in 1973 which extended the Lomé protocol to parts of the Commonwealth) to be included in the European Community's Third World Aid policy, thus creating a new group of partners under this scheme which transcended Africa, and assumed the name ACP group of countries. The aid mechanisms also became more diverse and complex, comprising programmable and non-programmable aid, wide-ranging and more specific measures to treat problems in narrow geographical regions or whole countries or groups of countries, responding to general or sectoral needs, long-term issues or temporal and seasonal crises. Aside from the aid for combating poverty, disease and social problems, these agreements envisaged financial grants for construction, irrigation, transport and other projects, low-interest or no-interest loans, stabilisation packages for commodities ranging from mineral resources to agricultural produce like cocoa, which can be prone to price instability, and, most importantly perhaps, complex preferential trade instruments negotiated between the EU and individual ACP countries or, on occasion, group to group pacts.

Although the power differential was overwhelming at these early stages, with the emphasis on aid rather than trade and with the European Community having a free-hand at agenda-setting and more or less able to impose any terms they chose to a group of countries with, to differing degrees, bad organisation, unstable political systems, unresolved external and internal security issues, often appalling economic problems and next to no cohesion or even co-operation between them, it is still possible to claim that there was interdependence between the two groups. The Third World obviously needed help from anyone who was able to give it, and this powerful new economic group emerging in Europe, the constituent members of which were, arguably, partly responsible for the volatile hybrid-politico-economic state, which some of these countries found themselves in, in the vacuum of the post-decolonisation era, was a very welcome source of aid and continuing investment. European Community countries too had, nevertheless, not only rising and shocking awareness and prominence of Third World issues in public opinion back home and internationally to contend with, but also much economic interest and unfinished business with the former colonies to respond to. Mining resources, favourable tax havens, cheap labour, the potential creation of new markets for European products, flexible business conditions offered by 'grateful' governments, increasing prosperity in the EU itself, bringing with it increasing sophistication of western tastes for exotic fruits, vegetables, artefacts, etc. available all-year round, necessitated a stable and safe framework of continuing and organised links. Both sides therefore entered these agreements with clear expectations for mutual benefits.

Key points of the Yaoundé–Lomé system

One can identify several key points in the old EU Third World aid policy as expressed in the Yaoundé–Lomé system, which also define its best characteristics as well as the main focus of criticisms against it.

The Lomé Conventions comprised a system of preferential access to the EC/EU market, which allowed them to export nearly all goods – apart from agricultural goods where they posed a threat to the Common Agricultural Policy (CAP) – at almost zero duty. This measure was non-reciprocal, which meant that the ACP countries could freely export into Europe while they could still protect their own, more fragile markets, by not having to afford the same courtesy to European products entering them. This measure provided welcome relief to fledgling export industries in the ACPs, but also bred criticism. Specifically, even though it may have been naive to expect the EC/EU to act without the regard for self-interest and self-preservation of a rational actor, the organisation was frequently accused of scoring relatively easy points with a pretentious policy, while at the same time maintaining its hard protectionist line in trade areas where conceivable competition to EU products – as in agriculture, mentioned above – was at stake (as with the Multi-Fibre Agreement which instigated preferential trade in textiles with boundaries-brakes, preventing the volume imported in the European market increasing to levels which threatened home production). Furthermore, it was recognised that the effectiveness of co-operation was further undermined because insufficient consideration was given to the institutional and policy framework of the ACP countries themselves, which meant that the benefits which could have been reaped by the non-reciprocal nature of market-access were scarcely exploited. For example, the increase in exports by the ACP to the EU over the 1987–98 decade was so small in numerical terms, it was considered negligible.[1]

The Lomé Conventions also included a variety of financial grant and loan-giving schemes which, volume wise, made the EC/EU the largest donor of developmental aid to the Third World. The major benefit of this aid, from the perspective of many ACP countries, was that it was for the most part unconditional, unlike the stringent, often debilitating, conditions which were attached to aid from other countries, or institutions like the International Monetary

Fund and the World Bank or IBRD (International Bank for Reconstruction and Development). This was, however, also the source of some of its most important drawbacks. First, despite the undertaken commitment to implement these conventions within a framework of 'dialogue' which saw officials going through the motions, actual understanding and interactive communication was insufficient and ineffective. The EU does not possess the resources to send people on the ground to work closely with locals in the carrying out of projects, given that its own member states fiercely argue over the slightest increase in the main EC/EU budget and associated funds like the EDF. Therefore, despite increasing its co-operative links with other international and non-governmental organisations operating in different regions, in order to optimise efficiency and the use of human-power, overall supervision, evaluation and control were often less than satisfactory. In addition, considering the fact that many of the ACP countries in question have been facing severe political and military instability, including wars, civil wars, coups d'état, etc., it is not surprising that much aid ended up in the wrong hands, and was often said to have been used to bolster dictatorial regimes or to buy weapons. Administratively speaking, there was also a mismatch between the partners, with faults on both sides. The central EC/EU bureaucracy was often accused of procedures too slow and cumbersome in the dispensation of aid, while many of the APC administrative structures at national and local level were, in cases, too embryonic or too corrupt to make the intended use of the given aid, or liaise effectively with the donors, resulting in more wastage of resources.

Perhaps more severely, the EC/EU was sometimes criticised of being nearly as guilty, through its specific trade measures, its foreign direct investment (FDI) and its other financial packages, as the IMF, the IBRD and other donors of encouraging and perpetuating the old colonial dependency instilled in Third World countries, inherently enticing them towards specialising in single, or limited range, crop production regimes (like bananas), or producing types of commodities irrelevant to indigenous populations and designed for 'western' markets (from specialised industrial materials to coffee), while discouraging, contrary to the expressed policy aims, diversification, which might reduce exports and therefore those countries' ability to pay off assorted international loans, and would better serve indigenous populations and restore to them a status of relative food-sufficiency. Although this criticism was targeted at the EC/EU much less than other aid and loan giving bodies, because of its more flexible approach and lack of conditionality, it was nevertheless a consideration.

After over 35 years of Yaoundé and Lomé, many million ECUs (European Currency Units), and several evaluation reports, the results of the policy were, at best, mixed. Despite the incalculable benefits of poverty and disease having been alleviated in many places and some qualified success stories in longer-term development too, the ACP countries had hardly yet graduated into self-standing economies, nor were they on a very tangible course to throw off their dependency chains in the foreseeable future. Malawi for instance, hailed as a relative success story in EU–ACP co-operation, was not prevented however from suffer-ing continuing vulnerability to drought, like Zambia and Angola alongside it, and falling back into near humanitarian disaster status by early 2002 after three years of failed crops. EU market shares gained by ACPs were in their majority (around 60 per cent) concentrating on no more than ten products and, what is more, these very market shares even were declining while in the same period countries outside the ACP were increasing their shares of the EU market, so the picture showed clearly that whomever the blame lay with, 'most ACP countries failed to take advantage of 25 years of Lomé preferences'.[2]

The world in 2000 and the World Trade Organisation

By 1995, the mid-way point of the fourth ten-year Lomé, and despite the small reforms which had been added and implemented with every renewed conven-tion to keep up with the demands of the times, not only were the weaknesses of this policy becoming all too apparent but international circumstances had radi-cally changed and demanded reform.[3]

As mentioned above, progress was sluggish and many ACPs had come to expect and rely permanently on the handouts and their guaranteed preferential trade agreements. Although they pressed for the continuation of the status quo, continuing along the same route would therefore be, if anything, inhibiting further motivation to reform, innovate and go forward, as many were clearly reluctant to cease operating along their traditional economic patterns even where there was the developed infrastructure and the scope to realistically aspire to do so.

At the same time, regional economic agreements had formed in some of the more dynamic parts of the ACP, such as ECOWAS (Economic Co-operation of Western African States) and SADC (Southern African Economic Community). Despite the disparities and conflicting interests between their members and, consequently, their limited success, they taught certain African states how joining voices and capabilities, did not only achieve results domestically, but also made their needs better heard internationally, and improved their bargain-ing position. The power differential between EU and ACP was shifting, if only slightly, with more group-to-group agreements, and both the agenda and the agenda-setting arrangements showed signs of needing to be rethought.[4]

The European Community's (European Union since 1991) priorities were changing too by the late 1990s. The Mediterranean enlargement of the 1980s strengthened the Community's focus on its Mediterranean policy and began to internalise, to an extent, Spain's and Portugal's traditional trade links with Central and South America. The 1990s were marked by the dissolution of communist regimes in Eastern Europe and the Soviet Union itself. Economic and political reform came at a high price, Germany was reunited and several Eastern European countries signed association agreements with the EU with a view to accession. During the pre-Cotonou era, therefore, the EU turned its

attention markedly and redirected many of its trade and aid flows towards its
neighbours of Central and Eastern Europe (CEE).[5] Between 1987 and 1998, EU
direct aid to the CEE and the newly independent states of the Commonwealth of
Independent States (CIS) which succeeded the Soviet Union increased tenfold.

At the same time, financial pressures on the EU deriving from the 1991
Maastricht Treaty, which heralded the countdown towards the completion of
the Monetary Union by the end of the decade, and the start of a Common
Foreign and Security Policy and co-operation in Justice and Home Affairs, with
all their associated costs, coupled by the expense of the Iraq–Kuwait and
Yugoslavia campaigns, made member states resist budget increases more tena-
ciously than ever. The arguable successes of the Lomé thus far and the 'donor
fatigue' deriving from the mixed results accompanied by the niggling criticisms
regularly hurled at the EU despite best efforts, contributed to the ACP cause
seemingly slipping lower in the list of the EU's priorities. In 1996, the European
Commission started a Green Paper consultation process on 'Relations Between
the EU and the ACP countries on the Eve of the 21st Century'.[6]

The 1990s also saw the intensification of the globalisation phenomenon and
its chief expression in the growing integration of international financial markets
and the liberalisation of trade, championed by the rising role of the GATT
(General Agreement on Tariffs and Trade) turned World Trade Organisation
(WTO). Free trade, as promoted by the WTO, has its basis in neo-liberal
economic theory, which promotes the removal of barriers, which hinder the
flow of international capital, goods and services through world markets.
According to this, the abolition of all barriers and restrictions and the liberalisation of trade enhance competition, nations are able to concentrate on the
production and exportation of commodities in which they enjoy comparative
advantage over their competitors and enjoy the benefits of importing those
goods which other nations could produce at a lower marginal cost. This should
ensure maximisation of welfare for all involved, and the opening of new markets
and trading opportunities. Neo-liberalism can arguably be considered a
symptom of globalisation, and of the increasing interdependence and co-operation which bring it on. At the same time, however, it can be seen as a policy and
an ideology, which acts as a vehicle for the perpetuation and advancement of
globalisation, by making sure that those very constituent, or enabling notions,
interdependence and co-operation, are free-flowing and uninhibited by protectionist measures, unlike the interdependence and co-operation one finds in
agreements such as Lomé, which find expression in special, exclusive agreements, which can stem globalisation and act as barriers to it. Governmental or
supranational intervention, therefore – such as subsidies, support of infant
industries and preferential agreements, of the type, in other words, that all WTO
signatory countries and the EU denounce yet quietly continue to operate, both
domestically and in their relations with their economic partners, to give themselves a comparative advantage – are an anathema to globalisation and WTO
policy.

Over the 1990s, the WTO saw an avalanche of complaints by its members against one another, for breach of free-trading regulations and anti-competitive behaviour.[7] As the bulk of world trade passes mainly between three poles of economic activity, the EU, the USA and Japan with the 'Tiger economies', more or less marginalising the rest of the planet, the launch-pads and at once the targets of most complaints were naturally these three poles of the so-called 'Triad', and particularly the USA and the EU. The disputes naturally did not only concern domestic measures displaying protectionism, such as subsidies for agriculture, which can be found both in the US and the EU, or industrial patents, etc., but also exclusive agreements forged by the poles with groups outside the poles themselves. Perhaps the most notorious case of the late 1990s was the 'banana dispute' in which a disgruntled US, with sizeable business interests in South American banana production, brought a case and threatened a trade war against the EU for allowing preferential access to Caribbean bananas at much lower market entry prices than the South American ones, thus artificially rendering the latter uncompetitive in the EU market.

Pressures by the WTO in recent years to reform its own agricultural, and to a lesser extent, industrial policies and abolish all forms of restrictions to trade, have been expressed through strained compromises and contrived resolutions to the above and countless more disputes, after acrimonious settlements and fierce confrontations at WTO meetings.[8] The earlier rows of the GATT's Uruguay Round mainly over the EU's CAP, were, if anything, intensified by the time of the Seattle meeting in 1999, over a whole range of issues, mainly centring on free trade versus sustainable development, particularly affecting environmental issues and issues to do with the Third World, whose points of view were largely excluded from the talks. Even though the WTO had granted the EU a waiver in relation to some of its protectionistic practices where these were justified by its Third World aid policy, by Seattle things came to a head.

These above pressures from all directions led to the compromise deal which became the Cotonou 'Partnership Agreement' between the EU and the ACP.

The Cotonou 'Partnership Agreement'

The new deal is a much more conditional aid-to-trade 20-year transitional package with different tiers and different speeds, which combines trade, politics and development, with a starting budget of 25 billion euros, and is based on five so-called 'pillars': a comprehensive political dimension, new participatory approaches, a strengthened focus on poverty reduction, a new framework for economic and trade co-operation and the reform of financial co-operation.[9]

The political dialogue, which the first pillar promotes, effectively gives the EU the power to exert pressure on regimes and demand political progress alongside any help given towards economic progress. Human rights, democratic principles and the rule of law make their appearance as conditions for the smooth running of the proposed dialogue and resulting co-operation, with suspension of EU aid suggested in the case of violations. Peace-building measures and conflict resolution also figure in situations where the recipient countries are at war with each other or are facing civil wars. Quite how this dialogue is supposed to take place and to what extent its outcome will be decisive as far as the granting of aid is concerned remain unclear, particularly considering the fact that the lack of democratic rule in several ACP countries is a given and that conflict is rife. Although the incentive to democratise and respect human rights cannot, obviously, be a bad thing, what is clear is that the institutional and regulatory framework has been put in place to be used as and when more leniency or toughness is warranted, in other words at the EU's discretion – quite possibly with the advisement of what is increasingly termed as 'the international community'.

The second pillar consists of innovative provisions to promote the participation of non-state actors and the involvement of 'civil society', the private sector, economic and trade unions and local governments in the formulation of policy and access to resources. The EU, partly because of the aforementioned lack of own resources and personnel to oversee financed projects on the ground, has for some time had to rely on co-operation with non-governmental actors and other international agencies, women's associations, environmental movements, etc., sometimes on an *ad hoc* or informal basis, taking particular care not to be drawn in to specific political agendas. Such structured co-operation can only be a positive new departure. Through this pillar many of these actors, as well as non-state actors within recipient countries, are now expected to be consulted and involved more formally in the process, where appropriate, before implementation of the project, from the drawing board to the field, in the hope of a better informed, more responsible and therefore more efficient operation. Although the EU cannot expect the level of local governance and organisation which exists within its own borders – and even there the degree of evolution and potency of local authorities varies enormously – it is determined to involve more indigenous actors than just the national governments in the process, in the expectation that the real needs will become clearer and the operations more transparent. Some ACP countries have a credible private sector, and some have trade unions, and there has been some liberalisation and decentralisation trends in others, but for many expectations of a multitude of actors, representing different interest groups in a balanced way, positioned around a negotiating table and hammering out solutions in a modern pluralist manner, can safely be said to be slightly unrealistic. Non-state actors within most ACP countries are not only few, but they also lack information on initiatives and EU funding mechanisms, and they often lack legitimacy, depending upon the good will of the national governments for inclusion. The phrase 'where appropriate', specifically included in the PA, effectively maintains the status quo, as it is logistically difficult for the EU to identify and evaluate such actors, and press for their inclusion, unless they have previously been singled out and promoted by their own governments. This makes the 'civil society' participation a goal difficult to fulfil. Furthermore, even though co-operation at all levels seems to be encouraged by the agreement, the new approach returns to a country-by-country focus, and it is unclear how much regional integration outfits between ACP countries (like ECOWAS, SADC mentioned above and others) will be in a position to play a negotiating role.

The pillar on poverty reduction and eventual eradication is clearly nothing new, but has an added urgency which stems from frustration with continued poverty, despite the significant amounts of past aid, and the pressure from the WTO for Third World countries to transcend aid dependence and graduate to full trading actors. Target setting, a higher onus on national and local authorities in recipient countries and an integrated approach which involves, on the ground, a multi-pronged strategy, looking at political, economic, cultural, social, gender, environmental and institutional interactions, coupled with the involvement of the United Nations and a global strategy to combat poverty and tackle underdevelopment, are tied in to try and tackle the issue holistically. One need only remember the criticism of the EU as causing as much damage with its Common Agricultural Policy for specialisation – rather than diversification – of production in certain countries of the Third World as benefit to them through aid and preferential agreements.

This pillar, together with the fourth one on a new trade plan, which will reinforce any effects gained by trade co-operation and development, are perhaps the backbone of what the Cotonou Agreement's developmental aid-to-trade transition is in actual terms. This is also where the different tiers and speeds enter the equation. According to the fourth pillar, the WTO's waiver to GATT Article 1, allowing the EU to continue with its aid policy through preferences to the Third World, contravening the rules of free trade, is renewed conditionally until 2007, to allow most ACP countries to get up to speed for participating independently in world trade. During this time, however, the old Lomé-style preferential agreements will have to be phased out and be replaced by reciprocal economic partnership agreements (EPAs), some early in the period, some later (39 identified as lesser developed countries (LDCs)), which will gradually bring down the barriers to trade. The EU also undertook the commitment not to ask for a further waiver beyond 2008; however how many of the ACP will be full international players by 2008, how many are still likely to be in transitional part-Lomé and part-free trade type arrangements and how many will be hopelessly behind and needing the full 20-year scope of Cotonou, if not beyond, is totally unclear.

The final pillar is as much about tidying up the EU's own procedures for dispensing aid as it is about the efficient and effective use of aid by recipients. The former ensures that aid is now channelled through one envelope for all non-reimbursable aid, and one for risk capital and loans, particularly with a view to supporting private enterprise, thus simplifying and hopefully speeding up administration and bureaucracy at the Brussels end. The latter means that aid allocation is, as of 2000, based on an assessment of each country's needs and will be performance-related, with no automatic renewal but with a possibility to regularly adjust resources through a system of continuous 'rolling program-ming'. This proposition promises less wastage by poor performers and reward to good ones, which makes for better use of the available resources. Nevertheless, particularly in the new 'divide-and-rule'-type reality of the differ-ent tier and speed groups among the ACPs, it gives considerable discretionary powers to the EU in allocating resources, and affords it blind trust for suffi-ciently taking into consideration special circumstances and appropriately measuring performance.

Speculation on prospects

The Cotonou Agreement provides a comprehensive framework of co-operation measures between the EU and the ACP, renewing and furthering the traditional interdependence between the two groupings. It contains generous amounts of aid but also strict conditions attached to its dispensation. It is ambitious yet is a result of extensive compromise between the European Union and its Third World partners under the watchful eye of the World Trade Organisation. Both sides made concessions, although the EU gained the most. As the stronger party, it raised the stakes, and although the ACP initially adopted a defensive position, wanting to keep the status quo, they later compromised rather than lose their special, but seemingly eroding, trade relations with the EU.[10] After the enthusi-astic fanfares which welcomed the signing of the agreement, it is unsurprising to discover that behind the scenes each side felt it had needed to concede enough to make it reasonably unhappy with the final outcome, despite the brave front put on for official purposes.

The WTO, by its nature unhappy about tolerating the perpetuation of prefer-ences and pressing for free trade world-wide, if possible here and now, was quite unhappy that the EU and the ACP had stood their ground staunchly enough to secure a 20-year stay of the liberalisation of their trade, even if they had become committed to fairly drastic steps in this direction along the way. However criti-cisms of the WTO were growing at all levels over this period and the WTO had to heed the warnings. Analysts saw world trade and wealth in recent years flow increasingly among the three poles of the Triad, globalisation perceptibly marginalising any 'Second' or 'Third' world, more than ever before. In addition, concerns by NGOs about the richer becoming richer and the poorer becoming poorer, growing global unrest and protest movements – notably the Anti-Globalisation Movement among others – against specific or generic traits of globalisation, capitalism and free trade and the policies of the World Trade Organisation, gradually made their voices hard to ignore, and became stronger at each WTO meeting. Pressures by governments too led to the decision to formally include Third World representatives in WTO meetings, since the November 2001 WTO meeting in Doha, and a more flexible approach in the WTO's reception of the EU–ACP Cotonou Agreement.[11]

Under the WTO's pressure, the EU was forced, at Cotonou, to reform many of its procedures and to accept that its preferential trade arrangements, under the guise of benevolent aid giving, would have to be curbed and wound down, and that the windows of exclusivity in trade which it traditionally enjoyed with many former colonies would be short-lived. Still, the EU salvaged enough discretionary powers over the running of the scheme to give it useful operating control. Besides, the conditionality of the aid and its regulated nature, through the envisaged performance-related packages, makes good economic sense and stands to ensure higher returns per expenditure package than before, which will be good for the public relations' image of the Union too. Nevertheless, the mechanisms put in place, purporting to make bureaucracy and administration simpler in theory, appear far from likely to achieve this. The financial packages may have been bunched into two envelopes, but the bodies involved in the drawing up of specific policy measures, the maintenance of the dialogue and the implementation of projects have effectively multiplied, if one takes into account, apart from the national government representatives of the ACPs, the numerous sub-state and regional actors, the NGOs and the United Nations and its agencies. Co-ordinating these actors and making for cost-efficient and mean- ingful consultation will heavily test the EU's organisational skills and may indeed increase the times between decisions, periodic evaluations and dispensa- tion of aid packages, which were already found to be lengthy.[12]

It is of no surprise that most voices of concern originate from Third World countries, as well as non-governmental organisations and pressure groups which operate in them or on their behalf.[13] The pervasive fear is that Cotonou is forcing a host of disparate countries into the straitjacket of 'Western'-imposed free world trade, at a pace much faster than most can cope with and with ques- tionable repercussions. The major criticism is not of trade but the type of free trade the WTO presses for and the EU is forced to endorse, more or less reluc- tantly, and impose. Put differently, this viewpoint sees liberalisation as based too much on an arrogant and dogmatic declaration of opinion of a 'one size fits all' policy rather than the examination of the evidence and an assessment of the likely impact of this policy on developing countries.[14] The WTO principle of non-discrimination, whereby a country should not discriminate between its own and foreign products or services, means that governments of developing countries cannot take measures to combat poverty if those measures interfere with trade. An example is Ghana where the necessity – as identified in IMF and World Bank directives – to use all available resources to pay off foreign debts and be competitive has led to favouring uniform crops good for international trade but useless for domestic consumption, or new and unfamiliar crops prone to failure, threatening food security, while people have to pay extortionately high prices for small amounts of clean drinking water and basic sanitation. Naturally Cotonou shields at least some ACP countries as much as possible from having to face the harsh reality of 'cut-throat' free trade immediately, but will the remaining years of the WTO waiver, or even the 20-year final and irrevoca- ble deadline of the EU–ACP Partnership Agreement be enough to prepare these countries, some currently in desperate poverty and squalor, to be thrust into the fully competitive 'First-World' global markets? Just over 30 out of the 77 ACPs should have replaced their old agreements with the EU with EPAs by 2005, and this should put them on the road to smoothly and gradually integrating into the world economy. If they decide they are not in a position to do so they will most likely be transferred to a Lomé-style system which will be much less generous than the old one. The rest (LDCs) will have longer to comply with this route, but, for some, the mere notion appears akin to science fiction considering that many 'Western' countries, like the United Kingdom, adopted free trade long after they had become leading industrial powers.[15] Furthermore, many argue that the playing field is far from level, as free theory might dictate, but slanted in favour of the developed countries. The developed world wants free movement of capital, goods and services, but not of labour, for which the barriers are erected higher than ever. Many developing countries are dominated and bullied by multinational companies (MNCs), bending their tax, social and environmental policies to accommodate their needs for fear of displeasing them and losing the investment they so heavily rely on. Major foodstuffs' and textiles' producers like the United States, the European Union and Canada may preach free trade but subsidise their own products, pushing prices down and making it difficult for Third World farmers to get decent prices for their own produce, or impose import tariffs where imported products may compete with domestic production, thus making market penetration difficult.[16] Again, Cotonou may provide a short-term buffer zone timewise, but this time period is minute when set against the monumental transformation which is being expected of many of the ACPs, considering the odds stacked against them.

Conclusion

If it goes according to plan, The EU–ACP Partnership Agreement signed in Cotonou could be the beginning of the end of Third World dependency, and a boost to healthy interdependence and co-operation in the context of globalised trade. It has the potential to strengthen the relationship between the Third World and Europe, reduce wastage of resources and upgrade and open up new markets. It could encourage democratisation and resolution, or at least containment, of conflicts, and better economic and social conditions. Although its make-up does reflect the EU's position both as the ACP countries' leading international trading partner and the world's largest provider of official developmental assistance, by reaffirming its superior negotiating position, it also encourages the strengthening of dialogue and interaction between different sub-state and non-state players, as well as regional co-operation between states, which can be positive steps towards economic growth and the empowerment of whole – as yet disadvantaged – regions. The tying in of social, political and other parameters to economic support may appear limiting on the face of it, but if successful it is bound to contribute towards more effective and sustainable development. The big question is whether the implementation of the agreement can yield the results envisaged in the text. Without seeming unduly pessimistic, one is perplexed by the over-ambitious nature of the agreement, and the vagueness which pervades it in terms of goals and procedures. As outlined above, there are serious concerns about the continuing subordinate role of the ACP in the decision-making following the consultation process, in the increased conditionality of aid, in the manner in which all the different layers of actors are to be mobilised, in the time-frame put forward and its sketchy nature and in the feasibility of transformation of the majority of ACPs as they currently stand into world players on the international trade arena.

With three years down, the next seventeen years will doubtlessly see much transformation on the world stage, on all sides, and much change on all sides will indeed need to take place if some of the goals of Cotonou are to be realised.

Notes

1 www.news.bbc.co.uk, 23 July 2000.
2 K. Whiteman, 'Africa, the ACP, and Europe: lessons of 25 years', *Development Policy Review*, 16: 1 (March 1998), 34.
3 G. Forwood 'The road to Cotonou: negotiating a successor to Lomé', *Journal of Common Market Studies*, 39: 3 (2001), 424.
4 R. Gibb, 'Post-Lomé: the European Union and the south', *Third World Quarterly*, 21: 3 (2000), 457–81.
5 G. R. Olsen, 'Western Europe's Relations with Africa since the end of the Cold War', *Journal of Modern African Studies*, 35: 2 (1997), 299–319.
6 http://ehosttvgw12.epnet.com (on 1996 Green Paper). See also: Marjorie Lister, 'The European Union's Green Paper on relations with the African, Caribbean, and Pacific countries', *Oxford Development Studies*, 26: 3 (Oct. 1998), 375–90.
7 www.wto.org.
8 Sarah Hogg, 'Supporters of free trade need to seize initiative', *Independent*, 19 June 2000.
9 The EU–ACP Partnership Agreement, Cotonou 2000, *EU Courier*.
10 http:losp.topcities.com (see particularly: *Guyana Chronicle*, 7 January 2001).
11 Guy de Jonquières, 'Move to bring more poor countries to trade round', *Financial Times*, 4 February 2002.
12 'Europe on a mission', *Guardian*, 6 July 2001. (www.guardian.co.uk).
13 See for instance: www.oneworld.org; www.greenpeace.org; www.worldsocialforum.org; www.tradejusticemovement.org.uk; www.ethicaltrade.org; www.oxfam.org.uk; www.christianaid.org.uk, and many more.
14 D. Green and M. Griffith, 'Globalisation and its discontents', *International Affairs*, 78: 1 (Jan. 2002), 59.
15 B. R. Scott, 'The great divide in the global village', *Foreign Affairs*, 80: 1 (Jan./Feb. 2001), 175.
16 G. Younge, 'Penalising the poor: the west wants the free movement of capital, but not of labour: It is illogical and immoral', *Guardian*, 19 March 2001.

Further reading

Grilli, E., *The European Community and the Developing Countries* (Cambridge: Cambridge University Press, 1993).

Lister, M. *The European Union and the South: Relations with Developing Countries* (London: Routledge, 1997).

Lister, M., *European Union Development Policy* (Basingstoke: Macmillan, 1998).

McQueen, Matthew, 'Lomé versus free trade agreements: the dilemma facing ACP countries', *World Economy*, 21: 4 (1998), 421–44.

Mehmet, O. *Westernising the Third World* (London: Routledge, 1995).

Micklethwait, J. and A. Wooldridge, 'The globalisation backlash', *Foreign Policy* (Sept./Oct. 2001), 16–26.

Mohan, G. et al., *Structural Adjustment: Theory, Practice, and Impacts* (London: Routledge, 2000).

Nilson, L., 'Trading relations: is the roadmap from Lomé to Cotonou correct?', *Applied Economics*, 34: 4 (10 March 2002), 439–52.

Olsen, G. R., 'European public opinion: Aid to Africa', *Journal of Modern African Studies*, 39: 4 (2001), 645–647.

Page, Sheila, and Adrian Hewitt, 'The New European trade preferences: does "Everything but Arms" (EBA) help the poor?', *Development Policy Review*, 20: 1 (March 2002), 91–102.

Rodrik, D. 'Trading in illusions', *Foreign Policy* (March/April 2001), 54–62.

Srinivasan, T. N., *Developing Countries and the Multilateral Trading System*, (Boulder, CO: Westview Press, 1998).

Thomas, Janet, *The Battle in Seattle* (Golden, CO: Fulcrum Publishing, 2000).

UNIDO, 'Gearing up for a new Development Agenda', United Nations Industrial Development Organisation, Vienna, 2001.

Van Reisen, Mirjam, *The North–South Policy of the EU* (Utrecht: International Books, 1999).

8

Transboundary co-operation and regional networks in Sweden and the Baltic States: integration on the new European frontier at the turn of the century

Geoffrey D. Gooch

A contemporary trend in Europe is the shift of political power in what at first sight seems to be two opposite directions; from the national state to the European Union and from the national central state level to regions. On closer examination, however, it can be seen that these two tendencies are often inter-connected, and they can be seen as forming different parts of a circle of redistribution of political power in which the EU plays a vital role. The first shift of power from nation states to the EU will not be discussed here. Instead, the ways in which the decentralisation of political power is connected to the development of new regional political networks in the Baltic region will be explored. In order to do so, domestic and international forms of co-operation in a county in the central part of Sweden will be analysed. Two central aspects of regional co-operation will be examined. The first is the domestic co-operation between municipalities in the Swedish county itself. The second is the co-operation between Swedish municipalities and municipalities in the Baltic States.

One of the most important trends in Swedish regional and local administration during the last decades has been decentralisation[1] and there seem to be a number of driving forces behind the trend towards the devolution of central political power to sub-central governmental levels in Sweden. These include a belief in the greater efficiency of regional and local political and administrative units, ambitions to increase and revitalise democracy, and the needs of central governments, with dwindling budgets and increasing costs, to pass on the responsibility for the implementation of policies to other, lower levels. Decentralisation usually creates positive connotations in Sweden and is seen to be synonymous with increased political participation, better possibilities to influence decision-making, greater local autonomy, more effective organisations and benefits for democracy. It is therefore seen as a necessary realignment of power from large central institutions to institutions at a lower administrative level. The move towards decentralisation can of course also be seen in many other European countries, and especially in countries such as France, Italy, Portugal, Great Britain and Denmark.[2]

This recent interest in decentralisation in Sweden has often been connected with regionalism. A number of factors have influenced this renewed interest in regions. First, Sweden's economic development during the 1990s has not been especially strong. At the beginning of the 1970s Sweden held a fourth place among the worlds' nations as far as GNP was concerned. By 1997 the country had slipped down to eighteenth place. From 1979 to 1989 Sweden's economic growth was 2.1 per cent a year; during the 1990s it decreased to 0.7 per cent a year. These negative trends have led to a renewed interest in the conditions that affect long-term economic growth. Secondly, Sweden's entry into the European Union on 1 January 1995 contributed to an increase in the importance of regions for the economy. Significant parts of the EU's different programmes, and a large percentage of its budget, are aimed at improving regional activities and development. The free movement of goods, services, investments and labour have led to a decline in the importance of national boundaries as far as trade is concerned,[3] and regional economies are expected to play an increased role in the future.[4] The seven Regional Objectives that existed up until January 2000 have now been replaced with only three. The system for allocating regional aid was revised at the Agenda 2000 summit in Berlin in March 1999, and a total budget of 213 billion euros was set for the years 2000–6. The new Objective 1 status is only granted to the Union's poorest regions; Objective 2 status is granted to areas which are in need of assistance but which do not have such serious problems as Objective 1 regions. Objective 3 is aimed at projects that stimulate employment and equal opportunities, and is not geographically based. Parts of north and central Sweden are eligible for the new Objective 1 support, and parts of 17 Swedish counties can receive funding under the new Objective 2.

At the same time as changes have been occurring in Sweden, much more radical transitions have been taking place in the Baltic States. The problems caused by the collapse of the Baltic economies at the beginning of the 1990s were to a large extent the result of the sudden loss of the Soviet market. They were and are the most acute of the problems being faced by the Baltic States and Russia today. After the denial of nationalism during the Soviet period, the rise of ethnic conflicts and nationalism in the 1990s have also created problems, within Latvia and Estonia, between these countries and the West and especially between Latvia and Russia. Together with these difficulties the Baltic States and Russia are experiencing problems caused by the lack of experience and competence of many of the authorities that are expected to formulate and implement policies. After the fall of Communism the Baltic Sea has ceased to be a barrier that divides east from west. Hierarchical and authoritarian forms of government have gone out of fashion in most parts of the Baltic States, and attempts are being made to replace these with efficient and democratic forms of politics and administration. This is not an easy task and the problems facing the Baltic region are extremely complex. Inter-regional co-operation in the area is therefore faced with the problems of countries with radically different political and administrative traditions and cultures, each trying to solve different sets of problems, often by different means.

Regional and local authorities in Sweden

In Sweden there are three political and administrative levels, central government, county and local authorities. All of these can be referred to as 'normative regions', which are administratively or politically created, as opposed to 'functional regions', which are based on geographical resources.[5] All of these three levels are represented by directly elected political institutions, and each have the right to finance their activities through taxes and fees. Central authorities have traditionally been strong in Sweden and have used a number of tools to steer and regulate regional and local activities. The first are the classic tools of administration – budgets, regulations and directives. The second set of tools utilises strategies to develop methods and competence. By this is meant that central government tries to influence regional authorities through educational programmes, seminars and by encouraging regional authorities to seek the advice of central groups of experts. The third form of influence is through various forms of evaluation and judgement that can be used to steer sub-central government in a specific direction.[6] Nordic regional policy has however changed from its earlier centrally steered model to a model in which regions can to a greater and greater extent formulate their own goals within certain frameworks. At the same time they are left to manage more and more on their own resources. During recent years important decisions concerning market and industrial issues as well as regional planning have been delegated from the central to the regional levels. This new-found regional independence has led to an increased sense of self-confidence, especially in regions with good economic development. In the Nordic countries regional support from the central authorities has decreased, and in some countries, such as Denmark, it has been replaced by the support provided by the EU. In Sweden, however, central government is still responsible for the distribution of regional support. [7]

Regional policy

The main ambition of regional policy in Sweden, according to official goals, is to create sustainable development, justice and freedom of choice among living conditions in different parts of the country.[8] The most important aim is however to unify regions so that these can contribute to Sweden's development. According to the government sustainable development should be achieved through the utilisation of existing resources in the different regions. Equity also plays an important part in the government's aims; regional policy should help to create an even distribution of welfare throughout the country, inhabitants should enjoy similar living standards, and regional policy should help inhabitants to live and work in different parts of the country.[9] In order to achieve these aims it is felt that municipalities and County Councils should co-operate in organised ways. This is considered to be especially important in decision-making processes and when conflicts arise between different municipalities. The number of projects in which Swedish municipalities co-operate is steadily increasing but it is difficult to determine the exact number. In 1998 the Federation of Swedish Municipalities (*Kommunförbundet*) conducted a survey and received information concerning 210 existing projects involving organised municipal co-operation. The actual number is most probably far higher. Of these projects 65 dealt with business, industry and tourism; 60 with 'general' issues; 45 with communications; 30 with education; and ten with the labour market.[10] There are also at least 150 registered companies with more than one kommun as owner.[11] In 1996 Sweden's County Governors (landshövdingar) were given the task of developing plans for co-operation within their counties with the aim of increasing economic growth and employment. The so-called 'growth-agreements' are primarily concerned with the ways in which trade and industry can be developed within the counties, and how state funding should be distributed to various projects. Among other things money is channelled into the development of business initiatives, the establishment of new businesses, networks of students and researchers that can help to develop new knowledge-based industries, regional 'invention-workshops', ways to improve co-operation between the various official actors who distribute state funding to the labour market, etc. Ways to strengthen the companies that work internationally and to lock foreign companies in to the regions are also supported, as are the development of 'clusters' of companies with specific competencies. The Department of Trade and Industry will later use these 'agreements' to formulate national aims and goals for development. The county of Östergötland presented its plan to Mr Rosengren, the Minister of Trade and Industry in Linköping on 15 February 2000. According to the Minister, the plan was one of the best three in Sweden, although he did comment on the lack of co-ordination between and exploitation of environmental, technological and developmental issues. Twelve organisations in the County have supported the formulation of the plan, including employer and employee organisations. The plan consists of strategies for improving the potential for trade and industry, stimulating the development of small and medium-sized industries and the creation of industrial clusters, improving IT infrastructure and raising educational levels. The agreement will be implemented between 2000 and 2002 and will cost about 3,400 million euro a year. The county will finance this initiative by utilising existing tax incomes.

The Baltic States

The Baltic States lie by the Baltic Sea, in the western part of the East-European Plain. The countries are mostly flat and a large proportion of the countryside consists of lowlands. They are predominantly rural countries and large tracts of land are relatively unspoilt. This is partly a result of the dominant farming methods of the last 50 years that concentrated on creating large-scale collective farms that left other areas intact. During the post-war period when agriculture was collectivised, large areas of marginal agricultural land were abandoned and left fallow. It is also partly a result of the way in which substantial areas of land were designated by the state as nature reserves and military areas. Many coastal areas were restricted areas, as the authorities sought to prevent the inhabitants of the state from fleeing over the Baltic Sea to Sweden and other countries. Together with the areas that are still intensively used, and those that are extensively used, these abandoned areas present a mosaic-like landscape, exhibiting varying degrees of human impact.[12]

Among the countries of former Eastern Europe the Baltic States hold a special position. They were integrated directly into the Soviet Union as Soviet Republics in the 1940s, while other countries of Eastern Europe were dominated by Communist systems but not directly a part of the USSR. After the break-up of the Soviet Union most of former Soviet republics became members of the new Confederation of Independent States – the CIS. The three Baltic States Estonia, Latvia and Lithuania did not. Despite a number of similarities between the three Baltic States they cannot however be bundled together as a block. Differences in history, population, economies, linguistics and culture are significant, and it is often easier for these countries to co-operate with other non-Baltic countries than with each other. Russian was the common language used in communication between the three countries during the Soviet period. Resentment against the Soviet occupation has however left many people in the Baltic States reluctant to use Russian, and therefore without a common language. The issue of language and ethnic groups is in fact one of the major problems that Estonia and Latvia faces today. As Glenny[13] has pointed out, during the Communist regime ethnic conflicts were not admitted, as nationalism was seen to be something that only belonged to Capitalist society. Ethnic conflicts did exist however, such as those between ethnic Germans and Vietnamese workers in East Germany, and the anti-Semitism that was found in several East European countries.[14] During the 1990s nationalistic sentiments have become apparent in many of the former Eastern European countries.[15] Latvia is the country with the largest minority population, followed by Estonia. The population of Latvia was, in 1997, 2,479,870, of which 1,371,569 (55.3 per cent) were classed as Latvians and 805,684 (32.5 per cent) as Russians.[16] The remaining 12.2 per cent consisted of Belorussians (4 per cent), Ukrainians (2.9 per cent), Poles (2.2 per cent), Lithuanians (1.3 per cent), Jews (0.4 per cent), Gypsies (0.3 per cent), Estonians (0.1 per cent), Germans (0.1 per cent) and other nationalities (0.9 per cent). These figures demonstrate the radical demographic changes that have occurred in Latvia during the last 65 years; in 1935, 77 per cent of the population of Latvia were Latvians and 8.8 per cent Russians. The result of the influx of Russians and other nationalities during the Soviet occupation are even more notable in the capital city of Riga, where only 38.5 per cent of the city's population were Latvian at the beginning of 1997.[17] Following the break-up of the Soviet Empire at the end of the 1980s and independence for the Russian Federation in 1992, protection of the Russian community outside of Russia became an important question on the political agenda for the new Russian Federation. The countries of the former Soviet Union found themselves with significant ethnic Russian populations and about 60 million former Soviet citizens suddenly found themselves 'abroad'. Of these, about 25 million were Russians and approximately 35 million belonged to other nationalities.[18] This means that about 17 per cent of the total Russian population of the former USSR came to live in the 'near abroad';[19] of these, almost 500,000 were in Estonia and 800,000 in Latvia. While it may not be technically correct to equate the USSR with Russians, the sentiments of most Soviet citizens were that the Soviet nation never existed, and that the Soviet state was seen as an extension of the Russian nation.[20] The ways in which the struggle for independence of these countries from the USSR had assumed an identity, centred around culture, language and nationalism, led to the emergence at the beginning of the 1990s of social and political conflicts based on ethnic identity. The ethnic conflicts of the early 1990s resulted in, and were aggravated by, the disputes over citizenship rights in the two countries, in which ethnic Russians were seen by themselves, and by Russia, as discriminated against. During the first years of independence, Estonia succeeded in creating relatively harmonious relations with its ethnic Russian population, despite the conflict between the new national government in Tallinn and the predominantly ethnic Russian city of Narva on the Russian border. In Latvia, however, the situation was aggravated by the prolonged conflict over citizenship rights, and the lack of political influence of the ethnic Russia population.[21] It should be noted, however, that relations between ethnic Latvians and ethnic Russians are not only based on conflict. The move to independence in Latvia could not have succeeded without the neutrality or support of non-Latvians, as ethnic Latvians constituted only 52 per cent of the republic's population in 1989.[22] Also, inter-group relations are not uncommon; in 1988, for example, one third of marriages in Latvia were between Latvians and non-Latvians.[23] In Latvia, ethnic minorities now account for nearly 44 per cent of the population, and of these, 685,000 people do not have Latvian citizenship; a significant proportion of these are former citizens of the USSR who have no citizenship at all.[24]

The situation in Estonia and Latvia is therefore complicated by the fact that, while the vast majority of the new political elite are ethnic Estonians and Latvians, and Estonian and Latvian are now the official languages of the countries, there are at the same time some parts of the countries, and many areas in the main cities, where Estonian and Latvian is hardly heard at all.[25] The demands made upon language proficiency in Estonian and Latvia as a prerequisite for work in the bureaucracy have also led to a rapid decrease in the number of non-Estonians and non-Latvians working as civil servants and an influx of new, mostly young and inexperienced administrators. This often means that ethnic Russians are now dependent on decisions taken by civil servants who may be unaware of their problems at best and directly opposed to their presence in these countries at worst.[26] Although the demands on the use of Latvian in all official situations has now been modified this still constitutes a major problem for large parts of the populations.

Regional co-operation in Sweden and the Baltic States

It has been pointed out that one of the major aims of regional development in Sweden is to achieve sustainable development. Although many Swedish authorities and organisations stress economic and social aspects of sustainability in their own development, when it comes to co-operation with the Baltic States environmental aspects are often at the fore. Sweden is however a country with relatively few major environmental problems. For most of the Baltic States and Eastern Europe, not to mention Russia and the other CIS countries, environmental sustainability is a luxury that must often take second place to more pressing issues, such as unemployment, social unrest and criminality. While the governments of the applicant states may stress the need to adopt to EU environmental standards, this is not necessarily a major concern for the majorities of the populations of these countries.[27]

A major recent initiative in environmental politics in Sweden is Agenda 21, which was incorporated into the political agenda during the first half of the 1990s. Although Agenda 21 as formulated in Rio considers economic, social, as well as ecological aspects of sustainability, ecological elements have come to dominate the Swedish Agenda 21 objectives. This is partly perhaps because the Swedish government sees sustainability as an area in which it can 'be an international force and an example to other countries' competitiveness'. Governmental support for ecological sustainability is also to a considerable extent based on the way in which it is seen as able to 'contribute to generating employment opportunities, growth and greater competitiveness'.[28] Growth, competitiveness and the creation of new jobs are seen as products of the move to a sustainable society, and a 'sound economy' is seen as 'essential to ecologically sustainable development'. In 'A Sustainable Sweden' the Swedish government describes sustainable development as the means by which 'those living today should be able to meet their needs without jeopardising the ability of future generations to meet theirs'.[29] In 1992 the Swedish government formulated *A Swedish Action Plan for the 21st Century*,[30] and ten sectors were identified as pivotal for environmental protection at the national level. At the same time the prominence of initiatives at the local level was emphasised.[31]

Swedish strategy for achieving sustainable development is therefore to a large extent based on governmental initiatives and efforts.[32] Policies formulated at governmental and local authority levels are seen as crucial, together with the contributions of market forces. By 1995, about 50 per cent of the municipalities had employed a specific Agenda 21 co-ordinator, and all 289 had by 1998 initiated formulation of their Local Agenda (LA) 21 directives. In approximately two-thirds of the municipalities, LA 21 has been organised as a direct responsibility of the municipality boards. Although citizen participation has been an official goal in all of these incentives,[33] and despite the official emphasis on a bottom-up approach, it has been difficult to achieve satisfactory levels of citizen participation.[34] Only a small proportion of the Swedish population is at present engaged in LA 21. According to the Statistics Sweden (SCB), the percentage in 1997 amounted to no more than 3 per cent of the population on average.[35]

A number of the projects that started in the 1990s have had the ambition to develop co-operation between municipalities in Sweden and between Swedish and Baltic municipalities in the fields of environment, democracy and development. Two recent initiatives are ÖSTSAM (East Sweden) and co-operation within the SWEBALTCOP programme (Eastern and Southern Sweden Baltic Sea Co-operation Programme). The first is domestic and has as its goal the development of the region and of a regional identity. The second is international and aimed at stimulating Swedish–Baltic co-operation. In 1996, as a major part of their efforts to co-ordinate regional development, all the political parties in the county's municipalities, together with politicians in the county council in the county of Östergötland decided on a voluntary basis to create ÖSTSAM. ÖSTSAM is an (ideella) organisation with the ambition of creating the necessary conditions for regional development. It is also hoped that ÖSTSAM will also be able to function as a legitimate representative for the region. At the same time as ÖSTSAM was created, the old municipal federation (*Östergötlands Kommunförbund*) was dissolved. The areas in which ÖSTSAM aims to be most active are traffic and transport, IT, marketing, trade, industry and tourism, education, environment and health, culture, international co-operation and research and development. ÖSTSAM is also the local co-ordinator of the SWEBALTCOP initiative. This programme was initiated under Article 10 of the European Regional Development Fund (ERDF) of the EU. Its purpose is to support cross-border co-operation between local and regional authorities with the aim of facilitating closer integration between the EU and the transition countries of the Baltic region. The elected local and regional levels of 12 Swedish counties, among them the county of Östergötland (the East Sweden Area), govern the programme administration. SWEBALTCOP objectives include supporting the economic and political transition of local and regional authorities in the Baltic States, preparing them for membership of the EU, protecting the environment, encouraging cross-border co-operation, stimulating co-operation between local and regional authorities and developing political and professional networks around the Baltic Sea. The three main priorities of the programme are the environment, economic development, and modernisation of local and regional government administration. In February 2000 SWEBALT-COP financed 30 large projects with on average about 260000 euro each. There were also 29 smaller projects with about 3500 euro each. Some of the Swedish municipalities are too small to manage working with the Baltic States by themselves and new forms of co-operation have therefore developed between Swedish municipalities.

Although economic issues are crucial for both the Swedish and Baltic participants it is important to remember that economic processes cannot be treated as separate issues apart from other aspects of development.[36] This means that environmental issues for example, cannot be dissociated from economic development, and the development of democracy and economic welfare in the Baltic States is also dependent on the creation of a well-functioning administration. In an ideal situation the administration would be able to guarantee the legal rights of citizens, to be able to objectively process cases, and also to follow political decisions. Unfortunately many of the countries of the former Eastern Europe lack the administrative capacity necessary for the successful implementation of new policies,[37] a fact which has also been noted in the European Union Agenda 2000 report. This lack of satisfactory administrative structures that is to be found in most Baltic municipalities creates major problems, in all forms of Swedish–Baltic co-operation. The European Commission has noted that the Baltic States especially have problems with the administrative structures necessary to successfully implement environmental and legal issues. It should be remembered that as former Soviet republics the Baltic States have been forced to build upon a legacy of centrally steered administrations, and governmental structures and legal authorities that were often seen primarily as ways of guaranteeing political control. The experiences of the last 50 years have created administrations in which civil servants are not sufficiently experienced in independent decision-making and implementation. These administrations need to develop the necessary competence for the new forms of work. This is a major hinderance for the implementation of policies in these countries, and the competence of the civil service needs to be raised considerably and ways need to be found to initiate improvements of the administrative structures.

In this respect Sweden and Swedish municipalities can play a major role, as the Swedish administrative culture with its emphasis on service to citizens is in many ways unique.[38] When considering the implementation of projects in the Baltic States it is necessary to note that the ways in which administrations function is the result of a considerable number of factors. These factors include traditions, resources, levels of competence, and there are also near relationships between the norms of political systems and the ways in which these political systems organise administrative structures.[39] These norms are a part of the political culture of a country, and while political culture may be difficult to measure precisely, it is still apparent that different countries each have specific ways of making political decisions and implementing them.[40] When two different political and administrative cultures attempt to work together the importance of formal and informal institutions becomes acute. Bureaucratic norms and standard operating procedures differ radically between different organisations. This is more important than the political landscape of the municipalities, and administrative cultures play a greater role than political loyalties.

The issue of norms and political culture also raises the question of mentality, and how to change the ways in which people think. In the Baltic States this may prove to be the hardest problem to solve, for as Nordlöf-Lagerkrantz and Lagerkrantz[41] have pointed out, the heritage of the Soviet era is strong and this is an issue that it is not possible to make laws about.

Despite these problems the co-operation between Swedish and Baltic municipalities is in fact creating new transboundary networks of actors consisting of groups of organisations and/or people who have a common interest in a policy's development and implementation. The new networks often consist of politicians and administrative officials from both high and low levels of an administration together with, in some cases, pressure groups and representatives of private businesses. These contacts are usually most successful when they involve a number of the main political and administrative leaders in the participating municipalities, as this demonstrates the importance of the project as the role of political leadership is still pivotal in many parts of the Baltic States. In theory these networks can be quite large,[42] but they may only consist of a few key people. One of the issues that complicate the possibilities of co-operation between municipalities is the relative size and resources of the potential partners. This aspect is important, as it is likely that municipalities that are of about the same size will find it easier to establish successful contacts. If one of the municipalities has access to greater resources in the form of funding, competence, access to information, etc., then the co-operation may become one-sided, and one of the partners may be able to dictate the conditions for the co-operation. This is obviously a problem in Swedish–Baltic co-operation. As regards the cities of Motala in Sweden and Daugavpils in Latvia, for example, which are twin cities, Motala has more than ten times the economic resources of Daugavpils and less than one-third the number of inhabitants. This puts it in a potentially strong position that it may or may not utilise. In this respect it is also important how dependent the municipality is on outside factors. A municipality's dependency on the outside world determines its room for strategic action, and therefore the demands that it can make on other partners in any negotiations.[43] The breakdown of trade with the Soviet Union and later Russia has left many Baltic towns and cities dependent on a limited number of newly developed contacts with Western industries and therefore in a weak negotiating position. This is however often weighed up by the good will of the Western partners. Another aspect that is important to take into account is the geographic distance between the potential partners. In a recent survey of municipal politicians in the county of Östergötland it was shown that most of the politicians only considered co-operation with other nearby municipalities to be feasible.[44] In order for municipalities to develop networks with distant partners there must therefore be substantial incentives. In the case of Swedish–Baltic co-operation the SWEBALTCOP programme provides this incentive in the form of economic support to the participating Swedish municipalities.

To a certain extent the problems associated with the implementation of regional development networks in Sweden and the Baltic States is a problem of both goals and methods. Project methodologies are often based on seminars, and the aim of these seminars is to provide forums for the exchange of information and experience between the project participants. Swedish civil servants and politicians generally attempt to adopt a bottom-up approach that is radically different from the top-down authoritative methods of the Communist era that still exist in many parts of the Baltic States. Despite these ambitions communication is often one-way, with the Baltic participants taking a passive role. Two different traditions therefore meet in this co-operation. First, a traditional way of looking at an administration as a hierarchical, technically competent organisation that is able to rationally solve problems, an approach with some similarities to Max Weber's (1864–1920) view that an effective, efficient and predictable administration was a prerequisite for functional public service.[45] Ex-Communist versions of hierarchical administrative structures are common in post-Soviet countries, and even if their main aims have changed since the fall of Communism, in many authorities their organisational methods and structures have not. Pitched against this model is the Swedish network model based on consensus seeking and discussion.

Differences in approaches and goals can be illustrated through Figure 8.1. The vertical axis of the diagram represents the aims of the participants, the horizontal axis the preferred means of achieving these aims. Together these form four possible strategies, A, B, C or D. Point A represents a chosen strategy that emphasises collective solutions and the formulation of a collective vision. It is in many ways typical of the Swedish political culture and trust in this strategy has played a major role in the education of workers through, for example, evening classes, in which they were trained in organisational methods and democratic thinking. Point B represents a technocratic formulation of a vision. Perhaps the European Union can serve as an example of this strategy. Point C demonstrates collective, practical solutions. User co-operatives that organise child-care centres are an example of this way of working. Point D represents technocratic solutions to practical problems. Examples of this strategy might be the creation of a buy-and-sell system of municipal organisation or the building of a district-heating system.

Obviously there are considerable differences between the points, and it is these differences that must be addressed in the implementation of cross-border municipal projects. It is a question of reaching agreement on the standard operating procedures of a project, for as Hill has noted 'the policy-making process will be influenced by constitutions, rules, political structures and standard operating procedures'.[46] Swedish municipalities often approach co-operation from point A. There is a preference for collective action and for the formulation of visions. Baltic participants, on the other hand, often start out from point D. They are used to technocratic ways of working and are looking for practical solutions to practical problems. In order for the participants in a project to successfully work together there has to be some kind of consensus on goals and

Figure 8.1 *Aims and means of achieving them*

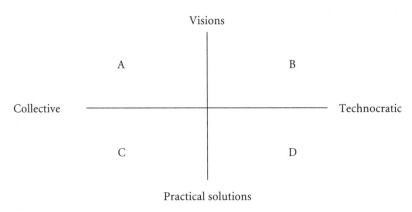

methods. The question is: who will change? In Sweden administrations have power, power that comes from the knowledge that they possess concerning the nature of the work, awareness of the difficulties that exist and the comparative advantages of information compared with politicians.[47] If the administration also has control over the indicators, methods of evaluation and translation of information, and if the administration at the same time formulates the evaluation of a process then it also has considerable possibilities to steer the ways in which the results are understood.[48] These conditions often lead to an excess of confidence in their own standard operating procedures on the part of the Swedish participants, which may lead to conflicts with their Baltic partners. If the Swedish participants cannot succeed in maintaining the interest of their Baltic partners in their strategies then there are three main alternatives. A municipality can adopt a 'consensus seeking' or 'imposing' approach in its relations with other municipalities.[49] If the Swedish representatives choose consensus seeking then they can move their strategy from point A to point D, the creation of simple agreements concerning teacher exchanges, health workers, etc. The second alternative is that the strategy could be reformulated to point B. This would involve an emphasis on working together with the political, administrative and technical elites of the Baltic partners in order to formulate a vision. In this alternative it is not certain that open seminars would be the most efficient way of working. The third strategy would be to move to point C. This alternative stresses collective solutions to practical problems and could involve grass-root projects aimed at involving schools, housing neighbourhoods, NGOs, etc. in practical work on environmental and developmental issues. There are of course other alternatives. The Swedish municipality can choose an 'imposing' strategy and continue with strategy A even if this does not seem to be the optimal at the moment, while at the same time attempting to move the Baltic participants from point D towards point A.

In effect the two conflicting typologies of methods presented in the figure also represent rational and incremental models of policy implementation. The two alternatives in the top part of the diagram can be seen as rational implementation models in which a finalised plan or vision is seen as one of the first steps in the implementation process. According to this model information on alternative solutions needs to be collected and an evaluation made of the possible alternatives. The officials responsible for implementation should then follow these directives. The two alternatives in the lower part of the model represent a more incremental way of policy implementation, in which each problem can be addressed as necessary. According to these models some decisions can be left to the 'street-level bureaucrats' who implement the solutions, and policy is the result of an on-going process that can be discovered first in the implementing stages.[50] There are two arguments that can be used against co-operation based on the use of rational decision-making models in the Baltic States at the present time. One is that there was a tradition of formulating grand plans in the former Soviet Union, which then might or might not be adhered to. A tradition of formulating plans, which are then not adhered to is not conducive with efficient implementation. The second problem is that rational implementation demands considerable resources, a reasonably predictable future scenario and an absence of major conflicts between different interests. None of these can be said to exist at the moment in most parts of the Baltic States. The alternative is the incrementalist model that allows policy to be flexibly formulated during the implementation process. The main argument against the incremental model is that it is more difficult to achieve the major changes that are necessary through piece-meal processes.

To sum up, one of the main problems facing co-operative projects between member and applicant states, together with a lack of funds to cover the costs of the work of the applicant participants, is that of intercultural differences in administrative cultures and communication. Low levels of background knowledge of each country's history, politics and culture often intensify these problems as does lack of experience of international co-operative projects on the part of sub-central governments. The different administrative cultures and experience of the participating municipalities create problems and a deeper knowledge of the administrative capacities of each partner therefore needs to be obtained. Ways to increase the knowledge base of both member state and applicant country participants, together with ways to develop intercultural competence and build administrative capacity are therefore vital if co-operation is to survive the rough road ahead.

Notes

1 SOU (Swedish government), Regional frihet och ststlig ansvar – en principiell diskussion, Inrikesdepartementet, Stockholm (1998).
2 *Ibid.*, p. 69.

3 G. Hallin and A. Malmberg, *Attraktion, konkurrens och regional dynamik i Europe* (Stockholm, Institute för regionalforskning, 1996).
4 P. Krugman, *Geografi och handel* (Stockholm: SNS Förlag, 1996).
5 Hallin and Malmberg, *Attraktion*.
6 L. Ramfelt, *Nordiska strategier för regional utveckling – finns de?* (Sweden: Holstebro, 1997).
7 J. Mönnesland, *Regional Policy in the Nordic Countries – Background and Tendencies* (Sweden: Holstebro, 1997).
8 SOU, Regionalpolitik för hela Sverige, Stockholm, Närings-och Handels-departementet (1997), p. 188.
9 *Ibid.*
10 S.-G. Johansson, 'Regionerna ett elitprojeckt', *Kommunaktuellt* (Stockholm, 1997), pp. 14–15.
11 S.-G. Johansson, 'Vad händer med demokratin när kommunerna samarbetar?', *Kommunaktuellt* (Stockholm, 1999), pp. 14–15.
12 J. Priednieks, *et al.* National Biodiversity Action Plan for Latvia (Riga: World Bank, Global Environmental Facility, WWF Baltic Programme, 1995).
13 M. Glenny, *The Rebirth of History* (London: Penguin, 1993).
14 *Ibid.*
15 G. Schöpflin, *Politics in Eastern Europe* (Oxford: Blackwell, 1993).
16 Latvia, C. S. B. o., *Statistical Yearbook of Latvia* (Riga: Central Statistical Bureau of Latvia, 1997).
17 *Ibid.*
18 R. Sakwa, *Russian Politics and Society* (London: Routledge, 1996).
19 *Ibid.*
20 I. Bremmer, 'Post-Soviet nationalities theory: past, present, and future', in I. Bremmer and R. Taras, *New States, New Politics: Building the Post-Soviet Nations* (Cambridge: Cambridge University Press, 1997).
21 N. Melvin, *Russians Beyond Russia: The Politics of National Identity* (London: Royal Institute of International Affairs, 1995).
22 Muiznieks, N., 'New states, new politics: building the post-Soviet nations', in I. Bremmer, *Roy Taras* (Cambridge: Cambridge University Press, 1997).
23 Melvin, *Russians Beyond Russia*.
24 European Communities, 'Agenda 2000: Commission opinion on Estonia's application for membership of the European Union', Office for Official Publications of the European Communities, Luxembourg, 1997.
25 Dawisha, K. and B. Parrott (eds), *The Consolidation of Democracy in East-Central Europe* (Cambridge: Cambridge University Press, 1997).
26 Melvin, *Russians Beyond Russia*.
27 Gooch, G. D. 'Environmental beliefs and attitudes in Sweden and the Baltic States', *Environment and Behavior*, 27: 4 (1995), 513–39.
28 SOU, 'A sustainable Sweden', Stockholm, Environment M.O.T. (1996), p. 2.
29 *Ibid.*, p. 1.
30 SOU 104 (1992).
31 Prop. 93/94: 11, p. 13.
32 Svedin, U. A., H. a. Orniäs *et al.* 'Decay and revitalisation in two Swedish communities', in T. O'Riordan, *Sustainability, Locality and democracy in Europe* (London: Earthscan, 2000).

33 SOU 105 (1997), pp. 174–5.
34 Gooch, G. D., *Environmental Risk, Sustainability, and Empowerment: A Case Study of Interpersonal Interaction, Environmental Communication, and Local Agenda 21*; *Sustainability, Risk and Nature: The Political Ecology of Water in Advanced Societies* (Oxford: Oxford University Press, 1999).
35 SOU 105 (1997), p. 35.
36 B. Hettne, *Internationella relationer* (Lund: Studentlitteratur, 1996).
37 B. Toresson, *Med Berlinmuren i backspegeln – på obanad väg mot framtiden*, (Stockholm: PM Bäckström Förlag, 1995).
38 B. Werneström and M. Höög, *Östeuropaproject med stats- och EU-stöd*, (Stockholm: Norstedts juridik AB, 1996).
39 J. Blondel, *Comparative Government* (London: Prentice Hall, 1995).
40 O. Petersson, *Hur styrs Europa? Den politiska maktutövning i Europas stater*, (Göteborg: Fritzes förlag AB, 1995).
41 U. Nordlöf-Lagerkrantz and J. Lagerkrantz, *Östeuropa* (Stockholm: C.E. Fritzes AB, 1993).
42 O. Petersson, *Kommunalpolitik* (Stockholm: Nordstedts Juridik AB, 1998), p. 227.
43 J. Pierre, *Den Lokala Staten* (1994), p. 51.
44 Hallström, 1999.
45 D. Held, *Models of Democracy* (Polity Press, 1987).
46 M. Hill, *The Policy Process in the Modern State* (London: Prentice Hall, 1997), p. 123.
47 B. Rothstein (ed.), *Politik som organisation* (Stockholm: SNS Förlag, 1997), p. 11.
48 L. Lundquist, *Förvaltning, stat och samhälle* (Lund: Studentlitteratur, 1992), pp. 95–100.
49 M. Hill, *The Policy Process in the Modern State*, p. 125.
50 *Ibid.*, p. 148.

Further reading

Bremmer, I. and R. Taras, *New States, New Politics: Building the Post-Soviet Nations* (Cambridge: Cambridge University Press, 1997).
Gustafsson, Q., UKommunal självstyre (Stockholm: SNS Förlag, 1999).
Jones, B. and M. Keating, *The European Union and the Regions* (Oxford: Clarendon Press, 1995).
Krugman, P., *Geografi och handel* (Stockholm: SNS Förlag, 1996).
O'Riordan, T., *Sustainability, Locality and democracy in Europe* (London: Earthscan, 2000).
Swedish Government, Regional näringspolitik, 1999 www.sb.gov.se.

9

An ever-more sustainable union? Integrating economy, society and environment in a rapidly enlarging Europe

Andrew Jordan and Timothy O'Riordan

Environmental conflict and co-operation in an enlarging Europe

Since the 1960s, environmentalism has become embedded in rules, organisations, political and legal structures and ways of thinking and acting across the world. In a word it has become 'institutionalised'. There is no better example of environmentalism's achievements than the EU. At its founding in 1957, the EEC had no environmental policy, no environmental bureaucracy and no environmental pressure groups. At first, environmental rules emerged slowly because of the need to secure the support of every single state in the Council of Ministers (CoM). Given the absence of a specific Treaty base, those supporting a greater role for the EEC learned to operate 'terra incognito', that is until the environment was formally entrenched in the Treaty by the Single European Act (SEA).[1] For various reasons, the member states chose to turn a blind eye and EU environmental policy continued to expand. Since 1957, the EEC has grown from six to 15 member states, without any obvious relaxation in environmental standards.[2] Far from it, the environmental *acquis communautaire* – the corpus of principles, policies, laws, treaties and practices adopted by the Union – has grown spectacularly and now encompasses nearly 500 legal measures and six action programmes.

In many important respects, environmental policy should be regarded as one of the great success stories of the EU as it struggles to create 'an ever closer union among the peoples of Europe'.[3] Although implementation remains patchy, EU environmental policy has its own identifiable institutional status, which is important in the political battles in Brussels. And, unlike many other areas of EU competence, the environment has always attracted relatively high levels of popular support among European citizens, who otherwise feel deeply concerned about the remoteness and secrecy of EU institutions.

Environmentalism may well remain the politically acceptable and publicly identifiable buzz phrase, but the real agenda nowadays among environmental policy-makers is 'sustainability'. Sustainability covers the intricate relationships between maintaining life support processes, caring for nature and exercising social justice in the removal of vulnerability amongst peoples and ecosystems. Sustainability is a 'process' of human development that satisfies the needs of current generations without compromising the ability of future generations to meet theirs.[4] The trouble is that although sustainability is a very different concept to environmentalism,[5] it as yet has no common currency or identifiable image outside environmental policy communities.

The EU provides a pertinent case study of the practical difficulties associated with making the transition from environmentalism to sustainable development in a geographical region which exhibits very high levels of environmental and economic interdependence. In the 1980s, the EU accelerated long-established plans to achieve a single, highly integrated European market. At the same time, it also developed many new environmental policy measures to address the environmental interconnections between the member states. These include transfers of pollution and waste across borders, and the important natural habitats that straddle political borders. However, we will show that, while the EU has a very well-developed system of environmental regulation,[6] environmental protection priorities tend to be compromised when the really big 'history making' decisions are made in relation to the future economic and social strategy of European integration. A good example was the Internal Market initiative in the late 1980s,[7] but there are, as we shall show, many others. If it is to mean anything, the sustainability transition should be about finding new ways to bring these two processes of co-operation – the first driven primarily by economic priorities, the second by environmental concerns – into harmony with one another for the benefit of future generations.

In this chapter we examine some of the political conflicts that the sustainability transition is provoking in Europe. Then we assess how far sustainability is reflected in what is arguably *the* most fundamental political and economic development in the EU since its founding in 1957: the imminent enlargement into Central and Eastern Europe. We argue that enlargement is first and foremost a lagged response to the political, military and economic challenges generated by the sudden collapse of the Soviet Union in the late 1980s. So far, the EU has been slow to recognise and respond to the potentially huge environmental repercussions of such a venture, that is to think and act 'sustainably'. There is, for example, precious little evidence that enlargement is being considered synoptically either by the Commission or the member states. If the EU is really serious about achieving an ever-more sustainable union among the peoples of Europe, then the big, history-making decisions on macro-scale geopolitical issues (such as the internal market, economic competitiveness – now being addressed via the 'Lisbon process' – and enlargement) will have to be designed in ways that fully reconcile social, economic and environmental imperatives.

From environmentalism to sustainability

In many important respects, the environmental movement has served its purpose. Over the past quarter of a century, environmentalism has become embedded in rules, organisations, political and legal structures and ways of thinking and acting across the world.[8] In a word it has become institutionalised in political systems such as the EU.[9] Environmentalism may well remain the politically acceptable and publicly identifiable buzz phrase, but the real agenda nowadays in most national policy systems is about sustainability. There are almost as many definitions of sustainable development as there are writers who contemplate it.[10] The Commission believes that sustainability offer the EU 'a positive long-term vision of a society that is more prosperous and more just, and which promises a cleaner, safer, healthier environment.'[11]

The trouble is that, though sustainable development (or 'sustainability') is very different to environmentalism, as yet it has no common currency or identifiable image outside environmental policy communities, departments and agencies. However, since the Amsterdam Treaty, the EU has been under a legal requirement to implement sustainable development by integrating environmental considerations into *all* policy areas. How well is it achieving this task? There are a number of admittedly crude 'policy indicators' against which we can assess this shift:

1 The development of broad *sustainability strategies* to integrate social, economic and environmental objectives, backed up by *local action*.
2 *The scope for environmental policy integration* (EPI), that is the integration of environmental protection requirements into the design of policies in other sectors (e.g. agriculture, energy, etc.).
3 *The compilation of environmental and social indicators* of quality of life and ecological tolerance as a basis for legitimising action, and evaluating the sustainability transition.

Sustainability strategies

Sustainability was first mentioned in the Maastricht Treaty,[12] but the EU did not actually begin to prepare an EU Strategy for Sustainable Development until 1999, when the Helsinki European Council invited the Commission to prepare a Communication on sustainable development. There was, of course, the 1992 Fifth Environmental Action Plan (entitled 'Towards Sustainability') produced by Directorate General (DG) Environment, but it did not really bind the other EU institutions together in a joint enterprise. Its successor, the Sixth Programme, is notably more focused in its approach,[13] but it is still regarded as the Commission's statement on sustainability, rather than the EU's. In its 'global assessment' of the Fifth Programme, the Commission concluded that 'practical progress towards sustainable development has been rather limited, mainly because there was no clear recognition of the commitment from Member States and stakeholders, and no clear ownership by other sectors of the programme'.[14] The key test of the EU's long-term commitment to implementing sustainable development is how well it engenders that spirit of joint ownership and responsibility. An important start was made by the Commission, which recently proposed an EU 'Strategy for Sustainable Development'.[15] This strategy will have to be regularly revised and reviewed by the CoM, otherwise sustainable development will always be regarded as the Commission's – and only the Commission's – responsibility.

In the meantime, one has to look to the local level for evidence of significant institutional change. Agenda 21 (the blueprint for sustainable development agreed at the Rio 'Earth Summit' in 1992) included a chapter on the role of local government in implementing sustainability. By the end of 1996, local authorities the world over were supposed to have asked their local communities how they wanted to move, or were preparing to move, towards sustainable development, by creating their own Local Agenda 21 (LA 21)[16] strategy. Some local authorities undertook exhaustive reviews and implemented far-reaching strategies, while others did nothing.[17] But both national and international efforts are noticeably active in the LA 21 area. LA 21 has been able to capture the imagination, to promote action amongst community groups and people that would not otherwise have been stimulated, or involved, and given local action and ingenuity a place on the international stage.

LA 21 could be the grass-root catalyst for serious institutional innovation in the areas discussed above. It is by far the most appropriate forum for initiatives such as job trading, credit unions, civic action and educational awareness raising. Examples of best practice are beginning to emerge[18] and illustrate the potential for real innovation at the local level. The United Nations recently examined the work done to implement LA 21 measures in various parts of Europe. Only 1800 municipalities have responded so far, so there is still a long, long way to go. Discussion and analysis has still to be translated into implementable strategies and actions 'on the ground'.

Environmental policy integration

Integration can be achieved by *concentrating* environmental responsibilities in one distinct ministry, or *extending* them across all government departments; it can involve creating new (or reorganising old) institutional *structures* or adapting the *processes* and *procedures* by which they operate. In practice most countries of the EU have chosen a mix of these. Most states have created large environment ministries – the BMU (Bundesministerium für Umwelt) in Germany is the most notable example, the UK's DETR (Department of the Environment, Transport and the Regions) another.[19] Building new ministries and agencies is publicly visible and politically attractive, but it does not always address unsustainable development at root or deal with situations where sectoral policies are clearly running in opposition to each other. New institutional machinery (inter-departmental committees and environmentally biased cabinet groups) must also be developed to share ideas, resolve conflicts and ensure that sectoral policies pull in the same direction.

A large obstacle to sustainability lies in the lack of encouragement from the top, namely the prime minister or president, the unwillingness of the main economic departments (finance, industry, employment, energy, transport) to address sustainable development within the main framework of economics policy and the relative political weakness of environment ministries.[20] From this perspective, it is hardly surprising, but not helpful, that responsibility for sustainable development rests with environment ministries, who seek to co-ordinate but have no effective power to integrate.

Environmental Policy Integration (EPI) is doubly difficult to achieve in the EU, which is an immature and highly sectorised political and administrative system. EPI is, however, now beginning to appear as a focused European ideal and is in fact a legal requirement of the 1999 Amsterdam Treaty (Article 6). Until then, DG Environment had been the only forceful advocate of EPI, whereas other DGs essentially continued with 'business as usual'. A review of the implementation of the Fifth Environmental Action Programme summed up the situation as follows: 'insufficient awareness of the need and a lack of willingness to adequately integrate environmental and sustainable development considerations into the development of other policy actions [means that] ... sustainable development essentially continues to be seen as the business of those who deal with the environment'.[21] The European Council finally responded to Article 6 in 1998 by initiating the 'Cardiff process' of reporting. This process involves different sectoral formations of the European Council (for example trade, agriculture, energy, etc.) preparing summaries of how they are implementing EPI in their respective policy fields and identifying indicators of performance (see below). However, the progress made to date has been extremely slow and patchy, chiefly because of the deep divisions between policy areas and the lack of concerted pressure from heads of state.[22] Several member states do have their own, national mechanisms to 'green' policy-making, but these are poorly integrated with EU policy-making.[23]

Sustainability indicators

The Organisation for Economic Co-operation and Development (OECD) is pioneering an approach to sustainability indicators, and this is having an influence on the way the sustainability transition is audited. In this early stage in the evolution most of the indicators are either economic or ecological in character. The social dimension, notably in the all-important area of empowerment, is notably missing. The key point about sustainability indicators is that they link in the three strands of sustainability, they promote the cause of, and can be used to measure the progress towards, EPI, and they are designed to be community created. However, the indicators developed by various sectoral formations of the Council to audit the Cardiff process have been rightly criticised for being overly cautious, narrowly drawn and opaque.[24]

At the local level, however, there have been significant advances in the development of sustainability indicators. Due largely to the impetus of Agenda 21, indicators are now being developed which incorporate a stronger ethical and equity dimension. This can partly be explained by the involvement of local people and stakeholder groups in their development, who bring with them a demand for measures that are meaningful to their lives. Until there is a distinct move in this direction at all levels, the role of such indicators will primarily evaluate environmental change rather than sustainable development in its more rounded form.

To conclude, having experienced 25 years of almost constant growth, EU environmental policy has reached watershed.[25] In the past, DG Environment advanced the environmental *acquis* by denying that it was in anyway involved in an open-ended political project. This strategy of 'integration by stealth'[26] succeeded admirably in implanting environmental policy in the EU, but it is ill suited to the new challenges that the sustainability transition is bringing. Remember, sustainability is about deliberate, long-term planning, not 'muddling through'. It is about integrating policies across sectors, rather than adopting a strongly sectoral perspective. And it is about building environmental protection requirements in at the beginning of policy-making, rather than tackling the after affects when policies have already been decided. In the next section we assess how far the plans for enlargement correspond to this new, more sustainable model of policy-making.

Enlargement: boon or burden for the environment?

The EU's long-term geo-political strategy is to broaden its membership to include countries from the former Eastern bloc. The primary motivations are, of course, political and economic, not environmental. Politically, enlargement is an attempt to address the security concerns that emerged around the time of German unification. It is also economically driven by the desire to open up new markets for European goods and services. In principle enlargement, which could conceivably, after the Irish ratification of the Nice Treaty and the 'green light' given by the Copenhagen Council of December 2003, lead to an organisation with 30 or so members by 2010, will have enormous environmental implications for both the existing members and the new entrants. However enlargement has also forced the EU to grapple seriously with 'big' political issues such as the budget, Common Agricultural Policy (CAP) reform and cohesion funding, which have been put off for years to maintain good interstate relations. The EU has chosen to set itself a very tight timetable: the first wave of entrants, six in total (Cyprus, the Czech republic, Hungary, Poland, Estonia and Slovenia), is due to be completed by 2004. A second wave of up to ten more states (including Romania, Bulgaria and Latvia), would then begin to join soon after. Admitting so many poorer member states will have a dramatic impact on the way the EU distributes regional assistance, on the central budget (which every member state pays into), on the CAP and on the procedures for agreeing environmental rules.

For our purposes, the key question is how far are sustainability principles informing these discussions? In pursuing enlargement, is the EU seeking new forms of co-operation with third parties that respect the interdependence of environment and economic systems, or is the logic of political and economic union trumping environmental arguments? The most notable difference between the forthcoming enlargement and previous ones is that the EU will be dealing with many low-income states at the same time. The fact that all the likely candidates have such weak environmental protection systems and low standards of living arguably makes the enlargement eastwards the most difficult and complex environmental challenge the EU has ever faced. Average GDP in the current member states stands at around 13,000 GBP per annum, but in Poland it is less than a third of that level. Poland, though, is one of the more advanced candidates, far richer than the Romanians and the Bulgarians in the second wave who are less than half as well off as even the Poles. To put the challenge in an historical perspective, when Spain, Greece and Portugal joined the EU their average GNP per person was half the average of the existing member states. In the Central and Eastern European Countries (CEECs) the average GNP per person is less than one-third of the average in the present member states. The EU's long-term political strategy is to broaden its membership by including countries from the former Eastern Bloc. Such an expansion has enormous sustainability implications for both the existing members and the new entrants.

The main decisions relating to the EU's policy on enlargement were taken at the December 1995 Madrid European Council by EU Heads of States, although there has been an implicit assumption that enlargement is 'a good thing' ever since German unification in 1989. The 1995 European Council nonetheless established that it should respect the basic uniformity of the *acquis communautaire*. Enlargement should not proceed on an 'à la carte' basis with each new entrant choosing at will from the current corpus of laws. In principle there could be flexibility with states moving at different speeds, but always in the same direction. As far as the new entrants are concerned, accession should depend on acceptance of the critical mass of the 'acquis'. Assistance with economic and technical measures would be granted in special circumstances to those that needed it, but only in ways which preserved as far as possible the coherence of the single market.

In July 1997, the Commission finally presented its ideas about the process of enlargement to the European Parliament in a document entitled 'Agenda 2000'. Running to more than 2,000 pages, it details the changes that will have to be made to the existing decision-making procedures and policies of the Union, particularly the much criticised CAP and the various structural funds which transfer aid from the richer north of the Union to the poorer countries to the south and west. In 1997, these funds totalled some £60 billion per annum and are politically and economically vital to recipient countries. Due to considerable uncertainty about the political and legal complexion of a new Europe, there have been intense disagreements over many important institutional matters such as representation in the CoM. Contrary to popular opinion, small states are currently over-represented in the CoM, and a way needs to be found to achieve a better balance between voting power and population. Without greater majority voting, maximalists such as France fear decision-making will grind to a halt if unanimity is retained among a group of 20 or 30 states. Such questions are extremely important because they will affect the delicate balance of power between small and large states and, by implication, between environmental leaders and laggards in an enlarged union. The fate of the cohesion funds (the part of the EU budget allocated to improving basic infrastructure in the poorest parts of the EU) is another live political issue. Agenda 2000 recommends pegging social spending, which means all states will have to accept reductions if costs are to be contained. The problem is that three of the current recipients, Spain, Portugal and Greece, refuse to accept that they will not be poor after the next round of enlargements. The largest of these so-called 'cohesion' countries, Spain, has threatened to veto the whole enlargement process unless its current budget is substantially expanded. There is an obvious danger that environmental priorities will be squeezed out by states' concern to protect their economic self-interest.

DG Environment succeeded in placing the environment on the agenda for the pre-accession talks, but it is highly unlikely that any of the new entrants will be able to conform to the EU's current environmental requirements in the short term. Indeed, the difficult task of determining appropriate transition periods has hardly begun. Bringing these countries' water and air quality up to current standards will require a huge investment in infrastructure. The new entrants' own budgets will not be able to bear the sort of sums currently under discussion, and current members will doubtless resist any major largesse. The enormous challenge of cleaning up highly polluted environments in the Czech Republic, Hungary and the Baltic States makes the successes achieved over the last 25 years look rather more modest. Either the current member states agree to finance the necessary improvements or there will have to be wholesale derogations and implementation deficits which could eventually undermine the integrity of EU environmental law. The fear within DG Environment is that if the new member states are granted derogations it will be harder to deny the existing cohesion states special treatment, at which point the whole *acquis communautaire* could begin to unravel.

So far, detailed talks with the six candidate countries, which are in the first wave of entrants (Cyprus, Hungary, Poland, the Czech Republic, Slovenia and Estonia), and those following immediately behind, have centred on fairly malleable issues such as research, education, rules for small businesses, culture, etc. Progress has been brisk, not least because the cost implications are relatively manageable. Detailed discussions on the environment, budgetary matters and agriculture, however, pose more serious political problems and are being put off until later. The environment is particularly problematic. Much work needs to be done in the six candidate countries to align their national environmental policies with the environmental *acquis*. In a Communication published in May 1998, the Commission explained that '[n]one of the candidate countries... will be able to achieve full compliance with the environmental *acquis* in the short to medium term'. Policy-makers are still grappling to overcome this apparent impasse. One solution might be to grant the CEECs transitional periods (the 1995 entrants were granted a four-year period of adjustment, which will end in December 1998), but this could threaten the internal coherence of the environmental *acquis* and disrupt the functioning of the internal market. It would also reduce the Commission's ability to raise the standards of laggard states, which has arguably been one of the most significant achievements of EU environmental policy to date.

The other is to mobilise massive new resources to assist the CEECs to implement the environmental *acquis* as quickly as possible. The main difficulty here is the size of the sums required. The Commission's Communication put the total cost at between ECU 100 bn. and 300 bn. for the eleven candidate countries – a sum which equates to 3–5 per cent of their GDP for the next 20 years.

The EU has decided to tackle this apparent *impasse* by proceeding along two tracks simultaneously:

• *Progressive institutional alignment:* In 1998, the CEECs were asked to submit detailed plans by March 1999 showing how they will implement the full canon of EU environmental law. These plans will eventually form part of the accession agreements, which each country will have to sign to gain full membership. The preparatory process currently involves regular rounds of meetings between national officials to discuss the transposition of the 500 or so items, which currently constitute the environmental *acquis*.
• *New and additional finance:* Cleaning up the highly polluted environments of the CEECs and putting in place adequate environmental policies represent an unprecedented challenge for EU environmental policy. The new members' finances are already limited and overstretched, therefore unless proper environmental assessment procedures are in place, environmental groups warn that the new money will simply fund 'concrete pouring' projects, such as roads, airports and power stations, which undermine attempts to protect the environment.

Enlargement also poses a longer-term threat to the existing dynamics of EU environmental policy. It is widely recognised that enlargement demands an overhaul of the complicated and unwieldy procedures for arriving at decisions in the EU. The unspoken fear is that the new entrants will form a coalition with existing EU states with poor environmental records, either to block ambitious policy proposals within the Commission or to prevent their adoption in the Environment CoM. To date, the nexus between DG Environment and the Environment Council has driven up environmental standards in the EU. If enlargement upsets the current balance between leaders and laggards in environmental standards, the EU's ability to maintain this progress could be severely curtailed.

Sustainability: a framework for making 'history-making' decisions?

Environmental groups feel that the debate about enlargement has not yet fully acknowledged the scale of the sustainability challenges. In fact, the EU appears to have operated just as it always does, making the geopolitical decision to enlarge without first explaining how it will be reconciled with its current policy commitments, most notably in relation to sustainability. Enlargement (like the internal market) was presented as a 'good thing' – an inevitability almost – and the detailed cost–benefit analysis as well as the messy negotiations over precisely how it would be achieved were deferred until a later date.

History tells us that when the EU makes important 'history-making' decisions, environmental considerations tend to get pushed aside by weightier matters, such as achieving material wealth, creating jobs and tackling inflation. A good example was the internal market initiative of the 1980s, which aimed at removing the remaining impediments to the free flow of goods and services, capital and labour among member states by 1992. According to Albert Weale and Andrea Williams (1993), there were political, intellectual and organisational reasons why the environment got such short shrift. DG Environment was elbowed aside by the trade and industry Directorates in the Commission, and too poorly represented on key panels such as the Cecchini committee. That committee actually did not publish its report on the environmental implications of the internal market until a full four years after DG III (Internal market) had submitted its influential Internal Market White Paper to the 1985 Milan European Council, and over two years after the signing of the SEA. It is significant that there are currently no plans to undertake a similar environmental assessment of enlargement, which seems now to be a foregone conclusion.

It is worth remembering that the Single Market program had very similar goals to the current enlargement, namely bringing sceptical states such as Britain more into the fold, extending and improving internal markets to facilitate economic growth and to allow European businesses to compete in world markets. These were geopolitical considerations against which environmental arguments could not hope to compete. In the end, environmental arguments fell on deaf ears because there was 'simply too much weight pushing in the opposite direction'.[27] EU environmental policy was then left to adapt to the internal market process in the same way that it will have to adapt to enlargement. DG Environment openly admits that transposing the existing body of environmental legislation into the legal systems of the new entrants will be a huge problem, and that implementing it will be more complicated still. But these issues were not openly and thoroughly discussed when the critical decision to enlarge was first made.

Environment did not, therefore, feature highly in the last big history-making decision made by the EU – the internal market. Then again, environmental policy in the mid 1980s was neither as politically, nor as legally, established as it is today. But nearly 20 years later, environment (or sustainable development) is still struggling to make headway in the discussions about enlargement. In fact, there is almost an air of inevitability surrounding the process of enlarging the EU, which is primarily being pursued for economic and political purposes, not sustainability. What is missing, environmentalists say, is a vision of Europe in 20 or 30 years' time, which accords with the basic principles of sustainable development. There is certainly precious little evidence of sustainability playing a major part in plans for a unified economic and political system within the *current* borders of the Union. The impression given is that developing sustainability policy is DG Environment's responsibility while the other DGs press ahead with plans to maximise economic growth, liberalise trade and promote greater transport. It is revealing that the Environment Council only recently (June 1999) ordered a sustainability strategy for the EU to give the integration process a stronger environmental steer. Of course by then, the big 'history-making' decision about enlargement had already effectively been taken. And yet this decision will have huge spillover effects on such issues as agricultural reform, regional funding and institutional reform, which will determine the future shape of the EU far into the new millennium.

Conclusion

The EU has openly embraced sustainable development as a framework for guiding the future development of the EU. The 1999 Amsterdam Treaty made it a fundamental goal of European political integration.[28] Efforts are being made to 'green the EU' by integrating environmental considerations into sectoral policies. In all these respects, the EU is typical of a much wider transformation in environmental thinking, which has seen environmentalism transform itself from its late twentieth-century, guilt-inducing and separate identity into a much more diffuse social and political transformation, termed sustainability.

However, the institutions that have given the world 'development' have not been significantly dented by environmentalism. Rather, an important theme behind the development of the environmental *acquis* is how easily environmentalism is incorporated into those institutions by a process of accommodation and legitimisation. True, there are laws and regulations, agencies and watchdog groups probing and barking. They have served to create a culture of environmental sensitivity in governments, boardrooms and classrooms. But the fundamental ethos of 'development' holds sway.

Sustainability is now an overriding legal goal of EU integration. The big question is whether it can hold its own against the powerful economic forces pressing for enlargement. So far, it looks like environmental protection and sustainability are still being thought of as 'add ons' rather than as providing the 'positive long-term vision' offered by the Commission in its sustainability strategy. One only has to think back to the start of the 2000 'Lisbon process', which sets a new strategic goal for the EU of becoming 'the most competitive and dynamic knowledge-based economy in the world capable of *sustainable economic growth*' (emphasis added). As initially conceived, Lisbon did not explicitly mention sustainable development. An environmental dimension was not added to the Lisbon strategy until 2001, when the Swedish Presidency initiated a long-term review of progress in delivering social, economic *and* environmental objectives, based on Commission synthesis reports and headline indicators. So, although the political profile of sustainability has risen significantly in the last ten years, it does not function in the all-embracing, long-term manner that environmentalists would like it to.

Notes

The research reported in this chapter was generously funded by the ESRC, under its 'Programme on Environmental Decision-Making' (M535255117), which is managed by the CSERGE at the UEA in Norwich.

1   A. J. Jordan (ed.), *Environmental Policy in the EU* (London: Earthscan, 2002); A. J. Jordan, *The Europeanisation of British Environmental Policy* (London: Palgrave, 2002).
2   A. J. Jordan, 'The construction of a multi-level environmental governance system', *Environment and Planning C (Government and Policy)*, 17: 1 (1999) 1–18; Jordan (ed.), *Environmental Policy*.
3   A. Weale, 'Environmental rules and rule-making in the EU', in Jordan (ed.), *Environmental Policy*.
4   COM 264 final (2001).
5   A. J. Jordan, 'Environmental policy: protection and regulation', in N. Smelser and P. Baltes (eds), *International Encyclopaedia of the Social and Behavioural Sciences* (26 volumes) (Oxford: Elsevier, 2001); Jordan (ed.), *Environmental Policy*.
6   Jordan (ed.), *Environmental Policy*.
7   Jordan, *Europeanisation of British Environmental Policy*.
8   Jordan, 'Environmental policy'.
9   T. O'Riordan *et al.*, 'Institutions for political action', in S. Rayner and E. Malone (eds), *Human Choice and Climate Change*, Volume I (Columbus, OH: Battelle Press, 1998).
10 D. Pearce *et al. Blueprint for a Green Economy* (London: Earthscan, 1989).
11 COM 264 final (2001) (emphasis in original).
12 Jordan (ed.), *Environmental Policy*; Jordan, *Europeanisation of British Environmental Policy*.
13 COM 31 (2001).
14 COM 543 (1999).
15 COM 264 (2001).
16 ICLEI (International Council for Local Environmental Initiatives), 'Local Agenda 21 Survey', Toronto, Canada, 1997.
17 T. O'Riordan and H. Voisey (eds), *Sustainable Development in the EU* (London: Frank Cass, 1999).

18 ICLEI, 'Local Agenda 21'.
19 A. Weale *et al.* 'Environmental administration in six European states', *Public Administration*, 74 (1996), 255–74.
20 O'Riordan and Voisey, *Sustainable Development.*
21 COM 453 (1994).
22 B. Görlach *et al. From Vienna to Helsinki: The Process of Integration of Environmental Concerns in All Policies of the EU* (Germany: Wuppertal Institute, 2000); M. Ferguson *et al.* (ed.), 'The effectiveness of the EU Council integration strategies', Report to the UK DETR, London, IEEP, 2000.
23 A. J. Jordan and A. Lenschow, '"Greening" the EU: What can be learned from the leaders of EU environmental policy', *European Environment*, 10: 3 (2000), 109–20.
24 Ferguson *et al.* (eds), *Effectiveness of the EU Council Integration Strategies.*
25 Jordan (ed.), *Environmental Policy.*
26 A. Weale, 'European environmental policy by stealth?', in Jordan (ed.), *Environmental Policy in the EU.*
27 A. Weale and A. Williams, 'Between economy and ecology? The single market and the integration of environmental policy', *Environmental Politics*, 1: 4 (1993), 45–64.
28 A. J. Jordan, 'Step change or stasis? EC environmental policy after the Amsterdam Summit', *Environmental Politics*, 7: 1 (1998), 227–36.

10

Co-operation or competition? Nuclear energy and the Ostpolitik of the European Union

Sabine S. Saurugger

A study on German and French nuclear industry interest representations in the process of the *Ostpolitik* of the EU,[1] provides the grounds for asking a general question on the forms of non-state actors' participation in the policy-making processes. Since 1989, the European Community has been searching for a new role in Eastern Europe, launching programmes in, among other areas, nuclear safety. In managing these programmes, the European Commission played a novel but important role in organising the co-operation among Western European electricity producers and nuclear industries. Artificial networks were created, which led to highly conflictual and hierarchical unstable groups. In these groups competition between member states and different national nuclear industries as well as internal Commission conflicts offer a highly interesting study area, in which the role of structures and hierarchies can be analysed.

In concentrating on the questions of which factors influence the different forms of interest intermediation of non-state actors in the policy-making processes, this chapter argues that domestic and European political structures mediate the way interests are represented in policy-making processes taking place at the European level.

This chapter will be divided into three sections. In the first section, the hypothesis that guide this particular study of interest group activities will be presented. In the second section, the chapter will discuss the Community system as a resource for interest group activities, before entering, in the third section, into a more detailed presentation of the competitive situation inside the Commission, which offers and restricts means of access at the same time.

Interest group studies: overly Euro-centric?

Research on the representation of interests at the European level has mush-roomed since the 1980s. Whilst scholars working on this subject before the signature of the Single European Act (SEA) in 1986 were essentially part of the neo-functionalist school of thought and considered that interest groups were the driving force behind the European integration, the enlargement of powers of the European institutions by the SEA and the developments of interest groups' activities at the European level have increased the interest of researchers working in the field of private interest representation. For neo-functionalists, interest groups are a central factor of integration, and lead inevitably to a reformulation and reconstruction of societal and sectoral interests. This transformation of interests would result in the formation of specific transnational patterns of interest representation, which would influence the allegiances and identities of the actors, and furthermore their political representation. At the end, this integration process would lead to the creation of a distinct European identity and particular modes of European interest representation. Whilst the theoretical approaches in this field seem to have diversified, the main conclusions appear to have stayed the same: through the interaction of different economic and political interest groups at the European level, a European political arena, and thus an autonomous European interest representation will be created.

This chapter argues, however, that a great number of these analyses are overly Euro-centric, and neglect the fact that the actors are deeply rooted in their national political systems. The study of French and German actors in the nuclear industry in the policy-making taking place during the Union's *Ostpolitik* shows that representation of interest is not only dependent on opportunity structures offered at the European level, but is also largely influenced by particular structures existing at the national level. Their role, however, varies due to the mediation role of structures, both on the national and on the European levels. This means that country-specific modes of political exchange interact with EU-level specific opportunity structures, which permit or block access to interest representation which runs contrary to an often cited hypothesis that the activities of interest groups at the European level would lead to an autonomous form of European interest representation.[2] In defining a legitimate order and, therefore, different ways to exercise political power, these structures mediate the activities of actors and allow interest groups to intervene at various decision-making levels.

The relationship between interest groups and national authorities as well as the Commission services can be characterised as more or less tight networks. Networks can be defined as a result of more or less stable co-operation in a complex environment between actors who know and recognise each other, negotiate, exchange resources and might share norms and interests.[3] In this respect, networks represent structures that mediate actor's activities, and in a more constructivist approach, their ideas and values.

At the European level, the creation of networks in the particular case of nuclear safety in Eastern Europe is a means for both the Commission and the interest groups to increase their legitimacy: the Commission because of its lack of competencies in this field, the nuclear industry because the image of nuclear energy is deteriorating, in particular in Western Europe. At the domestic level, these networks were historically constructed and serve the purpose of political as well as interest representation.[4]

The central actors of this study are interest groups. For the present purposes, interest groups are defined in a broad way as entities which seek to represent the interests of particular sections of society in order to influence policy processes.[5] This definition allows us to take into account not only interest organisations, such as unions or federations, but also firms and industries which represent their interests at national and European levels. The study will concentrate on the nature of the relationship between European/state actors and interest groups, and the impact of these relations on the Union's *Ostpolitik*. For this reason, it is necessary not only to analyse the strategies of interest groups, but also the context in which these strategies are built.

The Community system as resource

The accident which took place at the Chernobyl nuclear power plant in April 1986 was the first in a long series of events which showed that the conditions of nuclear power plants in Central and Eastern Europe, as well as in the Commonwealth of Independent States (CIS), were quite preoccupying. In most of the cases, the conditions of these plants did not satisfy the requirements of international safety standards and practices.

In the Central and Eastern European region, 20 reactors are of interest: six in Bulgaria, four in each of Hungary, the Czech Republic and Slovakia and two in Lithuania. A certain number of countries depend to a high degree on nuclear electricity production (Bulgaria 40 per cent and Lithuania 85 per cent). Production is, on the one hand, necessary for the security of supply, but, on the other, for export, which is of considerable importance for these countries' economies. Given the preoccupying situation of nuclear power plants in Central and Eastern Europe, which deteriorated even more after a serious accident at the Kozloduy power station in Bulgaria in 1991, European, international and governmental institutions were compelled to react.

The decision to transfer the management of the financial programmes to the European Community, and more precisely to the European Commission, was taken by the governments of the G-7 during its Paris Summit in 1989. However, whilst some researchers[6] view the reaction of the European Community subsequently to transfer the responsibility to manage the nuclear safety programmes to the Commission as a logical answer to a given problem, a detailed analysis shows a much more complex situation. A game takes place in which different actors (Commission services, private actors and national governments) search for resources and supplementary powers.

Agenda-setting powers through national authorities?

In 1989 at the G-7 Summit in Paris, the participating governments transferred the responsibility of the management of financial funds, granted in the framework of various bi- and multilateral programmes in Central Europe, to the Commission. The first programme concerned the economic restructuring of the two Central European countries, which were the most advanced in their economic transition: Hungary and Poland. The PHARE programme (Poland–Hungary Assistance for Economic reconstruction) was very soon extended to other Central and Eastern European Countries (CEEC). A similar programme was created for the Commonwealth of Independent States in 1992: the programme Technical Assistance for the Commonwealth of Interdependent States (TACIS). In 1990, the governments of the EC member states asked the Commission to take appropriate measures in order to improve the nuclear safety of Central and Eastern European power plants. The Commission used mainly the PHARE and TACIS programmes in order to support various industrial projects and to assure the independence of the CEECs' nuclear safety authorities.

However, it was only in July 1992 at the Munich G-7 Summit that assistance priorities for the Central and Eastern European Countries as well as for the CEI in the context of nuclear safety were decided in the framework of a precise Action Plan. This strategic document classified the Eastern reactors, built according to the Soviet model, into two categories: upgradeable reactors, which might be modernised under certain circumstances, and non-upgradeable reactors, which had to be shut down as soon as possible. The Action Plan foresaw the improvement of the existing reactors, through financial support, and the improvement of the organisation and control of safety; a distinction was thus made between the responsibilities of the different actors dealing with safety requirements and the competencies of the local safety authorities. While the first issue concerns in particular the competencies of technical safety organisations, the operators, the nuclear industry, as well as the international financial institutions, the second issue deals with the nuclear safety authorities in the European Community.

One might conclude that the subject of nuclear safety was put on the agenda by the governments of the EC member states. However, keeping it there would be too simple. The nuclear industry, as well as the operators of nuclear power plants were confronted with a difficult situation after the Chernobyl accident in 1986. The French firms EDF, Framatome and COGEMA realised that the critiques became more and more important, even though the French society has shown only little interest in these matters compared with the German population. In Germany, Chernobyl was the reason for an impressive protest movement, which had domestic implications. In 1990, during the negotiations of German reunification, the German operators decided not to modernise the Eastern German reactors in Greifswald and Stendal, built according to Soviet model; the financial cost was considered too high. As a consequence, the nuclear power plants were decommissioned. This situation in France and in Germany increased the awareness of nuclear operators and industries. In particular EDF, on the French side, Siemens, Bayernwerk and RWE, on the German side, had numerous contacts with their respective governments regarding the subject of nuclear safety and nuclear energy in Eastern Europe and invited them to put the problem on the agenda.[7] The role of the agenda-setter of interest groups is thus channelled through national administrations, which have exclusive competence in the sector of nuclear safety.

The situation presents a paradox. Despite the fact that nuclear power was part of the Community's founding treaties, the Commission lacks the technical and legal competencies in the field of nuclear safety. However, member states required the Commission to develop strategies in the field of nuclear safety regarding Eastern Europe, while at the same time responsibility for this sector was to remain with national governments. At the beginning of the 1990s therefore, confronted with a lack of information on the condition of the nuclear reactors in Eastern Europe, the Commission was obliged to seek expertise from the nuclear industry.

The creation of consortia

Since 1989, the Commission, and in particular Directorate General Energy (DG XVII),[8] responsible for energy policy, has established very close contacts with European industry on the subject of nuclear energy. Two reports were drawn-up by DG XVII, which underlined the necessity to co-operate with the European industry in order to assure a higher level of nuclear safety in Eastern Europe and the continuity of nuclear energy in Central and Eastern Europe.[9] DG VXII is particularly close to the nuclear industry and is confronted with the same challenges for this reason. The loss of importance of the nuclear sector in Europe concerns this DG as much as it concerns the European nuclear industry. The industry faces heavy competition from the USA and, in the case of nuclear safety in the East, from British and US consulting firms, which, according to one official are considered as 'not qualified at all'.[10]

On this basis, the Commission invited the operators of nuclear power plants to establish the first consortium in 1990. TPEG (Twinning Programme Engineering Group) counts amongst its members the French electricity producer EDF, the German RWE, the Belgian and Italian firms TRACTEBEL and ENEL, as well as Spanish, British and Swedish operators. TPEG played a very important role in the programming of projects. In the sectors of nuclear waste treatment and nuclear fuel, two other consortia were created (Cassiopée and EFCC (European Fuel Cycle Consortium)).

The creation of the consortia aimed at permitting the operators of Western European nuclear power plants to co-operate and not to enter into competition with regard to the very fragile Eastern European market. The German Minister of Finance warned the nuclear industry: 'If there is once more a similar catastrophe to Chernobyl, nuclear energy has no more place in Europe which would have terrible consequences for the European nuclear industry'.[11] This discourse must also be considered in a very specific context. French–German co-operation has been reinforced since the end of the 1980s and has witnessed the establishment of RISK-AUDIT – a Franco-German nuclear safety expert group – (GRS[12] and IPSN[13]) or the common project for the construction of a new nuclear reactor (European Pressurised Water Reactor – EPR) of the French Framatome and the German Siemens which prepared a industrial merger, decided in 2000. This Franco-German '*rapprochement*' was observed with suspicion by their southern European partners. The weak position of the Italian and Spanish nuclear industries compared with that of the Germans and French, and a significant degree of criticism was expressed in the Council of Ministers by the Italian and Spanish government representatives, as well as through informal contacts with the Commission.[14]

The creation of the consortia of operators of the nuclear industry were soon followed by another consortia, recognised as particularly important by the Commission, but also this time by another service, the Directorate General for environment and nuclear safety (DG XI).[15] One official clearly stated: 'We are in charge of nuclear safety, and not, as is DG XVII, of the promotion of nuclear energy. It is nuclear safety which is in jeopardy in Eastern Europe, but DG XVII does not want to understand'.[16] The consortium CONCERT (Concertation on European Regulatory Tasks) established in March 1991 includes the European Nuclear Safety Authorities. The group RAMG (Regulatory Assistance Management Group), a part of CONCERT, supports the Central and Eastern European nuclear safety authorities. Finally, the consortium TSOG (Technical Safety Organisation Group) assists the Commission by bringing its technical support to the nuclear safety authorities in Central and Eastern Europe and the CEI.

The consortia thus established at the beginning of the 1990 had to provide reports on the condition of the nuclear power plants in Eastern Europe and the CEI. On this basis, the Commission took decisions on the programmes of financial support in the framework of PHARE and TACIS. On the one hand, the establishment of the consortia prevented the competition between firms of different nationalities and allowed the Commission not to be permanently confronted with the preferences of member states' governments for a particular firm. On the other hand, the consortia did allow the firms to be taken seriously and to rebuild their reputations in a sector which is in a crisis in Western Europe. At the same time, the absence of open conflict and competition among nuclear industries seems to have created and reinforced the Commission's credibility and legitimacy.

In this context, the total absence of Eurogroups, such as Foratom and Eurelectric/Unipede, must be noted. Eurelectric/Unipede was confronted with the problem of liberalisation of the electricity market, and seemed only slightly interested in the nuclear sector in Eastern Europe. Only in 1998, a working group was established by Unipede/Eurelectric to deal with this question.[17] The internal structure of Foratom, consisting in national fora of West European nuclear industries, has very little representation amongst its members. Nuclear industries and nuclear operators do not identify themselves with Foratom and prefer to act individually.[18]

As suggest S. Mazey and J. J. Richardson, one can state that the weakness of Eurogroups, in particular in the nuclear sector, is the reason that the actors approach the Commission and the Council individually.[19] By the notion 'weakness', we must understand more than only financial weaknesses, but also the incapacity to overcome internal differences among their members, a situation which has deteriorated since the liberalisation of the electricity market.

National differences?

The setting-up of the consortia shows the existing equilibrium between French and German actors in all the consortia of the nuclear industry, authorities of nuclear safety and technical organisations. In the field of nuclear operators, however, EDF seems to be the big winner. Very few German operators are part of the consortia. This is due to a difference in structure of the German and French electricity market. Whilst engineering is a strong component of European Development Fund (EDF) which can offer expertise in this sector, the German electricity sector has strong commercial competencies, which have been of little use in the Eastern European nuclear electricity market until now. To this particularly, one must add the German situation in the nuclear sector, which is more than dubious. Regarding the relations between private actors and national administration, a parallel concerning the relationships these actors have established with Commission services can be observed. Whilst EDF has particularly close relations with the French government, given its status as monopolistic and public enterprise in the electricity sector in France, one can observe that it has the same contacts with the European Commission. Even more so, as EDF[20] regularly sends a certain number of experts to the Commission, where they obtain the status of 'detached national experts'.[21] Contrary to France, the German operators and nuclear industries keep permanent contact with the German ministries, without, however, attaining the same degree of closeness. Consequently, the German interest representatives are not in the same situation as the French to become detached national experts. One could echo S. Mazey and J. J. Richardson's statement that the 'procedural ambition of many Commission officials to seek a stable and regular relationship with the affected interests might be seen as presenting a particular advantage to those lobbyists used to that type of policy style at the national level'.[22]

Another Commission strategy could be observed: in order to allow the participation of interest groups in the political process, it presents high policy matters as technical issues. This strategy allows, as the analysis has shown, even closer association between the competent private actors, without neglecting the control of the information produced.

However, the Commission is not a unified actor: the strategies and practices of the Commission services are diverse and sometimes contradictory and the consortia found themselves in a situation of competition among different Director Generals. This constraint for the Commission in its search for power was met by another: the publication of an independent report by West European nuclear safety authorities directly transferred to the Council without presenting it to the Commission.

Constraints in the search for power?

The complex power game inside the Commission

Between 1989 and 1999[23] three Directorate Generals shared the small competencies that the Commission has in the field of nuclear safety: Directorate General Energy (DG XVII), DG Environment, Nuclear Safety and Civil Protection (DG XI) and DG External Relations (DG I/IA). DG II, Finances, is the fourth actor which joined the group of three on questions of financial and economic viability of projects. This division of competencies allows the analysis of the relations between interest groups and European institutions in more detail.[24] The structure of the relationship between different Commission services influences the practices of private actors and forces them to adapt to new patterns and changing situations. At the beginning of the Community's *Ostpolitik* in 1989, nuclear energy was managed by DG XVII, nuclear safety by DG XI (radiation safety). Both, DG XI and DG XVII, wished to deal with the nuclear issue in Central and Eastern Europe from a technical point of view. However, the mobilisation of politicians was very high and the College of Commissioners, in particular under pressure from Jacques Delors, decided that the question was of a purely political nature and that DG I should be in charge of this problem. In particular, after the creation of the PHARE and TACIS programmes whose management was attributed to DG I, shortly after divided into DG I and DG IA, there was no doubt left about the centre of competence on this issue.

But this concentration on the political side had consequences for the relationship between nuclear sector interest groups and the Commission. The nuclear issue of Central and Eastern Europe was reconsidered from the point of view of nuclear safety and no longer under 'nuclear energy' as a whole. This approach has considerably weakened DG XVII in the power game, re-enforced the position of DG XI, without however according it new competencies, and created a pole of power inside DG IA. Inter-service consultations are chaired by DG IA; it decides on the distribution of financial programmes, without, however, forgetting to ask 'technical' services for agreement, and has become the main access point for interest groups. The main reports are drafted by DG IA[25] and it is the assistant Director General or the Director General himself who is contacted by interest groups, and who contacts the candidate countries or other European institutions on this subject. In this respect, the Commission's strategic document regarding the enlargement process published in 1997,

Agenda 2000, occupies a central place, not only concerning agriculture, but also regarding the issue of nuclear safety. One of the officials judged severely the importance that DG IA gives to this document: 'Agenda 2000 is the Bible in the nuclear safety sector, and DG IA repeats this all the time. Nevertheless, it is not the Council which has published this document.'[26]

The activities of interest groups in this sector are affected by this situation as their relationship with DG XVII was characterised by mutual understanding. The actual situation seems to be much more difficult for private actors *vis-à-vis* a DG whose leaders are slightly sceptical *vis-à-vis* the nuclear sector. The inter- est group's search from legitimisation, in following a 'responsible' attitude in Eastern Europe, seems to be put in jeopardy.[27] The situation in this sector is even more complicated as no coherent approach exists *vis-à-vis* the problem of defective nuclear power plants in Central and Eastern Europe. Each country is treated differently, due to their particular political situation. There exists in particular a difference between the approach to nuclear operators and to nuclear safety authorities who produce simultaneously reports for DG IA. An assess- ment study of nuclear power plants in Central and Eastern Europe presented by a group of independent national experts strongly criticised the lack of differen- tiation between technical support organisations and regulation authorities in the member states of the EU, whose activities should serve as an example for the establishment of independent regulation authorities in Central and Eastern Europe.[28]

Constraints coming from interest groups

However, the Commission's quest for power was not unanimously accepted by all actors in the nuclear sector. At the beginning of 1999, a European group of nuclear safety operators, WENRA (West European Nuclear Regulators), was created under the leadership of the director of the French nuclear safety author- ity, André-Claude Lacoste. This group, independent of any Commission created consortia, released a report on the condition of nuclear power plants, without elaborating on any general criteria which the candidate countries should to follow in order to accede to the EU. It is important to recognise this document, which was first presented to the Council before being transferred to the Commission, as a warning for the Commission in its search for more compe- tencies. According to public authorities and nuclear regulators, the Commission must not elaborate on criteria for accession in the field of nuclear safety. The Directorate Generals XVII and XI, in collaboration with DG IA have attempted exactly this, as the chapter has shown earlier. The central term used by actors in this field is 'safety culture', which must be shared with their Central and Eastern European colleagues. The officials interviewed never mentioned nuclear safety 'criteria', but rather a 'culture of nuclear safety'.[29] However, paradoxically, the content of the paper approaches clearly DG IA's position, as it requests the immediate closure of certain nuclear power plants considered very dangerous. This concerns in particular the Czech power plant Bohunice, the Bulgarian

Kozloduy and the Lithuanian Ignalina. The report, rewritten later in 1999, was first met with severe opposition from the operators and nuclear industries' side, in particular from French and German interest groups.[30]

In this context, two elements must be underlined. The first concerns the relationship between public authorities and nuclear safety regulators. The fact that WENRA was established independently from the Commission and without informing it, as well as presenting the report first to the Council, shows at what point Commission activities are perceived as danger for national competence in the field of nuclear safety.

Secondly, and paradoxically, the reaction of nuclear operators and industries whose actions in the field of nuclear safety were indirectly criticised by the report, shows to what extent the interests of these actors seem to be jeopardised. On the one hand, they are opposed to a communitarisation of the nuclear sector, in putting forward the argument that the nuclear safety criteria differ from one country to another, and that the influence of anti-nuclear member states such as Austria would even more diminish the nuclear activities in Europe. On the other hand, the nuclear industry and operators have realised that the Commission represented the main actor in the nuclear sector regarding Eastern Europe, due to the politicisation of the question at the beginning of the establishment of the Community's *Ostpolitik*. Their activities in co-operation with the Commission show to what extent their legitimacy depends on the recognition of the Commission.

Conclusion

The analysis has shown that the political exchange between interest groups, Commission services and member states' governments takes place in multiple policy networks. Although no particular 'autonomous European interest representation' can be observed in our analysis, it shows that the strategies and practices of the actors were influenced by the structures and relations among them, at both the national and European levels. A double legitimation takes place: first, the reinforcement of the legitimacy of the Commission's actions in this field, even though national governments and regulatory authorities oppose them regularly and, second, improvement of the image of actors working in the field of nuclear safety vis-à-vis the European societies. The co-operation between the Commission and interest groups in the nuclear sector leads to a definition of the problem and makes the 'match of the problem and the policy'[31] possible.

The argument that the process of policy-making at the European level is characterised not only by the interaction of a number of national actors, both public and private, but also by the complexity of the negotiation process and the weak formalisation of decision-making procedures was followed by a question: which factors influence the strategies of and the relationships between the abovementioned actors during the development of the Union's *Ostpolitik*? It has been clearly proven that it is not sufficient to take only the actors' 'objective interests' into account in assessing their strategies. In order to analyse their actions, one must consider the structures within which they act. Thus, structures at national and European levels influence actors' behaviour. In defining a legitimate order, and, therefore, different ways to exercise political power, these structures mediate the activities of actors and allow for both the Commission and the interest groups to intervene at various decision-making levels. Although this study concentrated on the strategies and the influence of interest groups, the important role of the Commission as an actor was evident. The Commission played a central role, both in creating structures and as an actor in shaping the policy processes. Therefore, not only its role as mediator should be underlined, but also its attempts to gain power during the establishment of the *Ostpolitik* and the enlargement process as a whole.

The Commission has used its agenda-setting competences and has invited the interest groups in the area of nuclear energy and safety to produce expertise. The European system constituted a resource for industrial actors in this context. Although the Commission has only insignificant competences in the field of nuclear power, it was able to offer, in co-operation with private actors, the necessary expertise to allow the elaboration of solutions for the condition of nuclear power plants in Central and Eastern Europe.

However, instead of establishing stable networks, its activities met three obstacles. First, the divergent attitudes of the different national nuclear actors, due to the different political organisations in which these industries, operators and nuclear safety authorities interact. Secondly, the share between competences inside the Commission between DG IA, DG XI and DG XVII, which were mutually opposed and which made the networks even more instable, must be underlined. Finally, a certain amount of opposition from member states, which were opposed to the Commission's desire to increase its competences in this domain. Whilst both interest groups and different Commission services were influential in the modalities of the Union's *Ostpolitik*, there is nonetheless substantial evidence that national governments still enjoy a great deal of leverage in shaping the social and economic conditions of their societies according to prevailing political preferences.

Notes

1 As the research period, on which this chapter is based, lasts from 1989 to 1999, the term 'European Union (EU)' will be used when considering the entire period or, more specifically, the period after 1993. Before the ratification of the Maastricht Treaty the notion 'European Community (EC)' will be used.

2 S. Mazey and J. J. Richardson (eds), *Lobbying in the European Community* (Oxford: Oxford University Press, 1993).

3 In accordance with P. Le Galès and M. Thatcher (eds), *Les réseaux en politique publique* (Paris: L'Harmattan, 1995), p. 14. For a detailed and theoretical discussion of the policy network approach, which is used as a metaphor in this chapter see

D. Marsh and R. A. W. Rhodes (eds), *Policy Networks in British Government* (Oxford: Oxford University Press, 1992). See also J. J. Richardson, 'Approches de la décision politique nationale et européenne fondées sur l'acteur: communautés de politique publique, réseaux par questions et communautés épistemiques', in P. Le Galès and M. Thatcher (eds), *Les réseaux en politique publique* (Paris: L'Harmattan, 1995); H. Kassim, 'Policy networks, networks and European policy making: a sceptical view', *West European Politics*, 17: 4 (1994) 15–27; M. Thatcher, 'The development of policy networks analysis: from modest origins to overarching frameworks', *Journal of Theoretical Politics*, 10: 4 (1998); M. Thatcher, 'Les réseaux de politique publique: bilan d'un sceptique', in Le Galès and Thatcher (eds), *Les réseaux*; D. Marsh (ed.), *Comparing Policy Networks* (Buckingham: Open University Press, 1998), pp. 13–14; David Marsh and Martin Smith, 'Understanding policy networks: towards a dialectical approach', *Political Studies*, 48 (2000), 4–21; Colin Hay and David Richards, 'The tangled webs of Westminster and Whitehall: the discourse, strategy and practice of networking within the British core executive', *Public Administration*, 78: 1 (2000), 1–28.

4 For a very detailed study of the French and German nuclear networks see W. Rüdig, 'Outcomes of nuclear technology policy: do varying political styles make a difference?', *Journal of Public Policy*, 7: 4 (1988) 389–430; M. T. Hatch, *Energy Policy in Western Europe* (Lexington, KY: University Press of Kentucky, 1986).

5 M. J. Smith, *Pressure, Power and Policy Process: State Autonomy and Policy Networks in Britain and the US* (Pittsburgh, PA: The University of Pittsburgh Press, 1993); W. P. Grant, *Pressure Groups, Politics and Democracy in Britain* (London, Philip Allan, 1989); M. Offerlé, *Sociologie des groupes d'intérêt* (Paris: Montchrestien, 1998).

6 In particular M. J. Haaland, *Energy Policy in the European Union* (London: Routledge, 1997).

7 Interview, French Ministry of Foreign Affairs, 10 November 1998.

8 As the research period of this study ends in 1999, Directorate Generals are referred to by Latin numbers, according to the pre-1999 reform system.

9 Interview, Commission, DG IA, 20 June 1999.

10 Interview, Commission, DG IA, 20 June 1999; 28 July 1999. DG IV concluded that consortia in the sector of nuclear energy do not inhibit competition in the market.

11 *Frankfurter Allgemeine Zeitung*, 8 July 1992.

12 Gesellschaft für Reaktorsicherheit.

13 Institut de protection et de sûreté nucléaire.

14 Interview, European Commission, DG IA, 20 May 1999, 20 June 1999.

15 Interview, European Commission, DG IA, 9 December 1998.

16 Interview, European Commission, DG XI, 9 December 1998.

17 Interview, Unipede/Eurelectric, 26 November 1998.

18 Interview, Siemens, 6 July 1999, Framatome, 10 August 1999; EDF 4 August 1999.

19 Mazey and Richardson (eds), *Lobbying in the European Community*, p. 8; A. McLaughlin and J. Grant, 'The rationality of lobbying in Europe: why are Eurogroups so numerous and so weak? Some evidence from the car industry', in Mazey and Richardson (eds), *Lobbying*. See also M. Olson, *The Logic of Collective Action* (Cambridge, MA: Harvard University Press, 1965).

20 But also other French nuclear industries.

21 This practice is widespread at the European level, and concerns not only French actors.

22 Mazey and Richardson (eds), *Lobbying in the European Community*, p. 9.
23 See note 9.
24 See for example L. Cram, *Policy-Making in the EU: Conceptual Lenses and the Integration Process* (London: Routledge, 1997); T. Christiansen, 'Tensions of European governance: politicised bureaucracy and multiple accountability in the European Commission', *Journal of European Public Policy*, 4: 1 (1997), 73–90.
25 COM 635 final (1993) *Communication de la Commission sur la sûreté nucléaire dans le contexte de l'électricité en Europe centrale et orientale et dans la Communauté des Etats indépendants*; *Stratégie de court à moyen terme pour les programmes de sûreté nucléaire PHARE et TACIS – Document de la Commission pour les comités de gestion PHARE et TACIS*; June 1996; COM final (2000) *Agenda 2000*; COM 134 final (1998) *Communication de la Commission concernant les actions dans le domaine nucléaire en faveur des pays candidats d'Europe centrale et orientale et des nouveaux Etats indépendants.*
26 Interview, European Commission, DG XVII, 28 July 1999. One has nevertheless to underline that the nuclear issue appears under the chapter 'Energy' in Agenda 2000 and not under 'Nuclear Safety'.
27 Regarding this argument, see also A. G. Jordan and J. J. Richardson, *Government and Pressure Groups in Britain* (Oxford: Clarendon Press, 1987).
28 M. R. Hayns, E. Hicken and P. Tanguy, 'Nuclear Safety Assessment Study', October 1996.
29 Interviews, Siemens, 6 July 1999, EDF 4 August 1998; Framatome, 10 August 1999; RWE, 27 January 1999, Bayernwerk, 2 February 1998; Preussenelektra, 9 November 1999; Foratom, 26 July 1999; Eurelectric, 26 November 1998; Permanent Representation of France, 9 December 1998.
30 Interviews, Siemens, 12 July 1999, Framatome, 10 August 1999; EDF, 4 August 1999
31 Jordan and Richardson, *Government and Pressure Groups in Britain*, p. 93.

Further reading

Avery, G. and F. Cameron, *The Enlargement of the European Union* (Sheffield: Sheffield Academic Press, 1998).
Greenwood, J. and M. Aspinwall (eds), *Collective Action in the European Union: Interests and the New Politics of Associability* (London: Routledge, 1998).
Hatch, M. T., 'Corporation, pluralism and post-industrial politics: nuclear energy policy in West Germany', *West European Politics*, 14:1 (1991), 73–97.
Howlett, D. A., *Euratom and Nuclear Safeguards*, (Basingstoke, Macmillan, 1990).
Landau, A. and R. Whitman, *The Enlargement of the European Union: Issues and Strategies* (London: Routledge, 1999).
Mayhew, A. *Recreating Europe: The European Union's Policy towards Central and Eastern Europe* (Cambridge: Cambridge University Press, 1998).
Müller, H., *How Western European Nuclear Policy is Made: Deciding on the Atom* (Basingstoke: Macmillan, 1991).
O'Neil, P. H., 'Atoms and democracy: political transition and the role of nuclear energy', *Democratization*, 6: 3 (1999), 171–89.
Scheinman, L., *The International Atomic Energy Agency and World Nuclear Order* (Washington, DC: Resources for the Future, 1987).

11

Cross-border transport: the EU policy agenda

Steve Dawe

This chapter begins with a historical account of EU transport policy. A brief case study of the Austrian experience of cross-border transport follows. The chapter concludes with some reflections on the implications of this history for Eastern Enlargement.

The idea of a Common Transport Policy (CTP) for the European Community is to be found in the original Treaty of Rome (Title IV and Articles 3e and 74–84). This owes its origins to the Treaty of Paris,[1] as Gwilliam notes:

> It adopted provisions previously contained in the Treaty of Paris aimed at the elimination of conscious national discrimination as an initial step, looked to the progressive approximation of national transport policies as an intermediate requirement, and saw the application to the transport sector of the general rules of the free internal market as the ultimate end.[2]

A French attempt had been made within the Council of Europe to establish a High Authority for transport, comparable with that of the European Coal and Steel Community (ECSC). This was approved by the Parliamentary Assembly but not passed on by the governing Committee of Ministers to member states.[3] Article 74 of the Treaty of Rome requires member states to seek Community objectives through a common transport policy. Article 84 confined the Policy to road, rail and waterways but gave the Council of Ministers powers to act on marine shipping and air transport if unanimity was obtainable. This seemed intended to imply that transport was equivalent to external economic relations and agricultural policy, but the progress was slow. This was despite the precedent of liberalised road transport within the Benelux Union.[4] As Ermenger comments, the Treaty articles concerned provide little substance.[5] Weidenfeld suggests that 'a fundamental harmonisation was ... never seriously intended'.[6] In fact, the 1961 Schaus Memorandum and the subsequent Action Programme of 1962 referring to European transport policies are principles, guidelines, discussions and not a fully developed policy capable of implementation.[7] Ross suggests that: 'major modal interests were scarcely motivated to work for the abolition of a policy environment which sheltered them from exposure to outside competition'.[8]

Carlo degli Abbati examined the slow development of the CTP, and singled out the Council of Ministers for its unwillingness to use its powers.[9] This brief account of the period 1958–87 is derived particularly from Erdmenger and Whitelegg.[10]

Major policy developments in the Common Transport Policy 1958–85

A preliminary basis for the CTP was prepared by a Council Decision establishing Transport Committee rules in September 1958.[11] From June 1960 to December 1970, nearly all transport-related Decisions, Directives, Regulations, Resolutions – and a 1965 Council Agreement on transborder transport issues – were concerned with ending discriminatory practices and fostering harmonisation through common rules.[12] Notable exceptions included the first Council Decision considering investigation of infrastructure costs, leading to the formation of a Transport Infrastructure Committee in 1978, and some initiatives on social issues.[13] Up until the 1950s, rail accounted for over half of all haulage and transport-related employment. This was to sink to less than one-fifth by the 1990s. The overall rail network also declined 20 per cent.[14]

The CTP was one victim of the French 'empty-chair' policy, during 1965–66. In pursuit of an implementation of the Common Agricultural Policy (CAP), French ministers ceased attending the Council of Ministers, undermining Community decision-making from the end of June 1965 until the so-called 'Luxembourg compromise' of February 1966. Meetings of the Council of Transport Ministers were delayed, beginning again on 19–20 October 1966, with the CTP only getting an effective re-launch in December 1967.[15]

In 1972, the EC extended its exclusive prior concern with road, railway and inland waterway harmonisation issues to include international coach and bus services.[16] The contemporary notion of a CTP, consolidating various initiatives, seems to be primarily based upon a communication from the Commission to the Council of October 1973. This was essentially a successor to the 1962 Action Programme.[17] Nevertheless, limited progress was still recorded for the period up to 1973.[18] The Council of Transport Ministers' meeting in November 1973 ran aground on differences between the six original member states and the three newcomers.[19]

The Council, in 1978, established the Transport Infrastructure Committee. This had the effect of obliging member states to inform the Commission of transport infrastructure initiatives of Community interest.[20]

During the late 1970s, the Community began to diversify its transport policies to include sea and air transport; it had already addressed inland waterway and navigation issues.[21] The Commission had developed the view, expressed in a 1979 document, that the CTP could not secure identified Treaty of Rome objectives unless full consideration was given to infrastructure.[22] The European

Investment Bank (EIB) avers that: 'from the early days of the Community the creation of European Transport, telecommunication, and energy networks has been one of the priorities of the EIB, since its main tasks include supporting balanced regional development and European integration'.[23]

A Council Decision in 1981 opened negotiations with Austria on a variety of transport issues;[24] A Council Regulation in 1982, giving 10 million ECU to transport infrastructure development and research including Channel Tunnel studies, was the result of European Parliament (EP) pressure.[25] A Directive of July 1982 extended freedom from quotas and licensing to Combined Transport; during 1980 to 1984 the Community attempted to promote Combined Transport, stimulated in part by the desire to shift goods on to rail for journeys through countries with restrictions on road haulage like Austria and Switzerland.[26] The EP produced material on transport across the Alps on three occasions over 1973–81. The EP was alarmed by the Austrian transit tax introduced in 1978 and by the Swiss 28 tonnes limit for heavy vehicles negotiating alpine passes, which led to new agreements with both of these countries.[27]

The most important EP initiative during this period was to take action against the Council for failure to develop the CTP, from 1978.[28] On the 9 March 1982, the EP requested information on the progress of the CTP and passed a resolution outlining principles for the Policy's further development. Although this resulted in a wide variety of Commission documentation,[29] the Parliament was not satisfied, taking the Council to the European Court of Justice (ECJ) in 1983. Eventually, in May 1985, the Court of Justice decided that the Council had infringed the Treaty of Rome by: 'failing to ensure freedom to provide services in the sphere of international transport and to lay down the conditions under which non-resident carriers may operate transport services in a member state'.[30]

This was despite an acknowledged 170 Community measures on transport issues.[31] At first sight, the Court's criticism may seem peripheral to transport policy. However, failure to satisfy this pre-condition meant that a CTP could not be created from diverse national transport policies. Transport policy was seen at this time as a matter of eliminating forms of discrimination and correcting market 'distortions'.[32]

The Common Transport Policy and the Single Market

The Commission's 1988 transport action programme was ambitious and within a year was downsized to seven projects, including Channel Tunnel Rail Link (CTRL) and improvement of the Brenner route.[33] A general view of the CTP as a failure is shared by many academics and EU officials.[34] In 1986, the Commission had drawn up an ambitious medium-term transport infrastructure policy incorporating ports and airports, road and rail access to the Channel Tunnel and access routes to the Brenner Pass in Austria.[35] The Commission also made clear its support for the use of private capital for public infrastructure.[36]

Nevertheless, the Channel Tunnel project was able to obtain an EIB loan of £1 billion at this time.[37]

After the publication of the Single Market White paper, transport ministers agreed two objectives in November 1985. Firstly, a free transport market without qualitative restrictions; secondly, liberalisation within the transport sector to remove remaining distortions of competition, both to be achieved by 1992.[38] As Bayliss points out, the SEM effectively bound the then 12 Community member states to seven EFTA (European Free Trade Association) countries.[39] It therefore had profound implications for Europe-wide cross-border transport. The movement of freight by road depends critically upon the level of use of roads by other users. The 168.5 million cars in Europe in 1994 are forecast to become 205 million by 2005.[40]

The Coming of Trans-European Networks

At this point, reference to the continuing CTP[41] ceases because the proposed Trans-European Transport Networks (TENS) were developed in a process largely independent from the CTP. In 1989, the Commission began looking once again at potentially important links within the Community, later building some of these concerns into the Maastricht Treaty.[42] In June 1992, the Commission adopted a proposal for a Council Decision which would create a Trans-European Road Network, supported by the Council of Ministers on 15 March 1993.[43] The overall road network imagined is 56,000 km of motorways – involving upgrading not just new build. The rail network envisaged is 70,000 km of which 23,000 km are designated for High Speed Rail.[44]

Vickerman credits the European Round Table of Industrialists (ERT) with pushing the TENS forward and of benefiting in part from Commission failure to adequately define the CTP.[45] He also noted, in the same discussion, how quickly the focus of the TENs moved from new build to optimising use of existing infrastructure. Ross observes that the agenda-setting impact of the European industry leaders might have resulted from leverage acquired over governments swayed by a comparative decline in competitiveness.[46]

Eventually, the TENS were to include: roads, rail links, combined transport, inland waterways, a trans-European airport network, sea ports, a European maritime transport traffic management system, an air traffic management network and a comprehensive information and management system for the networks as a whole.[47] In addition, energy, environment and information networks were also proposed and agreed.[48] Ross notes the importance of the term 'Trans-European' rather than 'Trans-Community' since it was envisaged that the Networks would link the EU to its neighbours.[49]

The ERT encouraged the various industrial sectors to talk more to each other and to take an interest in national development plans. This culminated in the 1993 discussions of transport ministers in which priorities identified over a long period were amalgamated into the TENs plans.[50]

Despite the early Community interest in issues later featuring in the TENs, officials concede a definite role for the ERT, in spearheading them, at least, in the words of one senior official, 'at the very beginning – launching this idea of TENs'.[51] Similarly, the then Director of the European Federation for Transport and Environment (T&E) believed the ERT was responsible for developing and setting the TENS agenda.[52] Charlie Kronick, then Greenpeace Climate campaigner, believed that the ERT could be identified as having originated the TENs and considered it to be dominated by motor industry and fossil fuel interests.[53] A Directorate General (DG) XI official suggested that the ERT 'had a major role in promoting and highlighting what they saw as missing links in the European transport network.[54] Similarly, Johnson has commented on the 'mid-1980s push' for the TENS notably by Mr Agnelli.[55]

Turner sees the TENs as being conceived from integration imperatives and as part of an 'emerging network economy' in which production is internationalised and cross-border relations become crucial. He believes the TENs are a 'powerful force' for a process of 'informal integration', meaning integration emerging out of practical considerations and serving diverse roles.[56] Transport infrastructure within Europe at the end of the 1980s was reaching saturation levels of usage, due continuous growth over about 20 years of 2 per cent per annum in freight traffic and 3 per cent for passenger traffic, accompanied by declining infrastructure investment.[57] Missing links, environmental problems and the need for trans-European transport networks consequently featured strongly in a Green Paper and White Paper on transport, produced by the Commission in 1991 and 1992, respectively.[58]

The 1989 Strasbourg summit called for an action plan to speed up the development of trans-European infrastructure networks. This led very quickly to the 1990 Action Plan which incorporated a number of guidelines on the development of trans-European networks: dealing with volume of trade through better infrastructure; interoperability and interconnection, meaning compatibility of technology and services; a dimension effect, referring to the need to see a European aspect in proposed infrastructure development; quality improvements; a cohesion effect, integrating the Community. A precedent had been set for trans-European information networks since the Community had permitted the France Telkecom-Deutsche Telecom joint venture to create a private advanced telecommunications network for transnational corporations.[59]

DG VII responsible for transport produced a report on road networks as part of the TENs in 1993.[60] The common belief in DG VII seemed to be that new motorway construction, a substantial feature of the Trans-European Transport Networks once the 14 priority projects are complete, will relieve congestion and thereby pollution. However, when one senior DG VII official was pressed on how this philosophy had not worked in the case of the M25 around London, he conceded that traffic management measures, road-pricing and looking at mobility, accessibility and modal change would all be necessary if new motorways were to cut congestion and pollution.[61] In fact, another official admitted that – as at September 1997 – 'We have not analysed the effects of new infra-structure in the periphery.'[62]

It is clear that the Commission had hastily put the earliest master plans for the TENs through the European Parliament under Article 75 of the Single European Act, just before the ratification of the Maastricht Treaty, as a 'temporary measure to allow for progress'. In other words, initial consultation with the Committee of Regions and subjecting the TENs to the new Co-Decision proce-dure would be avoided.[63] Subsequent awkwardness in the Parliament concerning the TENs may stem in part from this attempt by the Commission to avoid Co-Decision.

At the European Council held in Brussels in late 1993, a White paper on 'Growth, Competitiveness and Employment'[64] was presented, incorporating 26 infrastructure projects of which nine were high-speed rail projects representing two-thirds of projected costs.[65] The Commission presented guidelines for the development of the TENs to both the EP and the Council on 7 April 1994.[66] A month before, the Council of European Transport Ministers meeting in Crete had agreed 14 priority corridors later to be reflected in 14 priority projects in the TENs programme.[67] These fourteen projects were accepted, upon recommen-dation by the Christophersen group, at the Essen European Council of December 1994: nine were high-speed rail projects.[68] The Essen Council also provided more money for the transport infrastructure part of the TENS.[69] However, it did so by passing responsibility adroitly back to member states: to increase funds available for the TENs.[70] The Commission later added 21 further transport projects in February 1995.[71] Considerable discussion then ensued on the adoption of a financial regulation for the TENs. The EP Committee on Transport and Tourism attracted praise from environmental groups for the inclusion of new clauses on cost–benefit analysis, corridor assessment and strategic environmental assessment.[72]

Austria: a case study in cross-border transport

This section is about the international politics of transport in Central Europe. To provide what can only be a brief illustration of this topic, we are going to look at Austria and the EU policy agenda; Austria's relationship with its neigh-bours concerning transport issues; the Transit Agreement and Austria's Accession to the EU; the Brenner Base Tunnel, a priority Trans-European Transport Network; and finally implications for Eastern enlargement.

Austria and the EU policy agenda

Austria has transport and environment concerns in regard to the Alps. This arises partly from restrictive Swiss policies which divert transit traffic through Austria. Austria also faces the burden of being a major route from Eastern Europe, where road traffic levels are growing faster than in Western Europe.

Prior to Austria's membership of the EU, the commercial carriage of goods in Austria using vehicles registered in other states was subject to approval under the Austrian Goods Carriage Law of 1952. Approval granted by the Ministry of Public Economy and Transport and conditioned by bilateral and multilateral arrangements and reciprocity was accompanied by multilateral agreements concluded under the auspices of the European Conference of Ministers of Transport and later the EU under the Transit Agreement (described below). Bilateral agreements had been concluded with virtually all states in Europe with special arrangements for some.[73] The trade relationships of Germany with Italy and Eastern Europe and of Italy with the whole of northern Europe create pressures upon Central Europe's limited number of north–south transit routes.[74]

An interview with Austrian Environment Minister Martin Bartenstein in early 1995 offers an Austrian government view. Asked about difficulties in securing agreement on the traffic protocol of the Alpine Convention, Bartenstein observed that the original minimal demand of the Austrian government had been for no new Alpine road crossings. However, other states were pursuing the construction of new roads right up to the borders of Austria. The Austrian government had offered that the Alpine Convention should contain a list of criteria for such plans but this was not agreed. Both the regional government in the Tyrol and the Federal government were unwilling to back down over the traffic protocol.[75] Austria's position after the collapse of discussions on the Protocol was that informal talks should be held between the EU, Germany, Italy and the regions affected by transit, with a further report to the Standing Committee of the Alpine Convention in October 1995. Meetings were to follow during 1996. Outside these discussions, the Bavarian Environment Minister was saying road building projects would not be 'thwarted' or abandoned and was fulminating against 'the exaggerated national interest and disloyal behaviour of Austria'.[76] Point 7 of a June 1080 resolution of the Austrian National Council, instructing the Austrian government on conduct of negotiations with the EU, stipulated that the transit issue should be dealt with separately from membership and be resolved before negotiations. This was not achieved.[77] Negotiations in March 1994 did, however, conclude most matters.[78]

The Transit Agreement and Accession

The Transit Agreement (The Agreement between the Republic of Austria and the European Economic Community on the transit of goods by road and rail) was concluded in 1992, coming into effect from 1 January 1993 for a period of 12 years.[79] The Agreement is divided into five 'Titles'. Title I offers the 'Aims, scope and definitions' of the Agreement. This is preceded by a preamble which places heavy emphasis upon Austrian environmental concerns, for example: 'Whereas the problems caused by trans-Alpine transit traffic call for a lasting solution which safeguards the quality of life of local residents, protects the environment and guarantees international trade.' Transit traffic is defined as 'traffic through Austrian territory from a departure point to a destination, both of which lie outside Austria'. Title II (Articles 4–11 inclusive) is concerned with rail transport and combined transport.[80] Title III on Road Transport (Articles 12–16 inclusive) is primarily concerned with environmental impact issues such as how traffic-related emissions may be reduced. Title IV (Article 17 only) is concerned with checking for maintenance of standards. Title V (Articles 18–25), 'General and final provisions', covers matters like non-discrimination, dispute resolution, the setting up of a Transit Committee and details concerning the entry into force of the Agreement.

The Brenner Base Tunnel

The Brenner region of Austria is the subject of political sensitivity regionally and nationally throughout Austria. A 1993 interview with the Deputy regional premier of the Tyrol, Hans Tanzer, outlined the reasoning in favour of a new tunnel. Tanzer asserted that it was not possible to have more traffic above ground and that the only expansion option for the future was underground. The interviewer, Peter Sonnberger, pointed out that opposition movements have grown up wherever the proposed tunnel's emergence points above ground would be sited.

An interview with Jurgen Erdmenger of DG VII conducted in 1996 offers some insights. He suggested that if the principle that national governments continue to determine transport infrastructure upon their own territory is retained, then the Brenner Base Tunnel idea was of no interest to Austria but of great interest to the EU. The national interest criterion was a crucial principle behind the selection of the priority and future trans-European transport projects.[81] The Brenner route is one of the major transit routes through Austria.[82] Rail transit on the Brenner Route doubled from 1988 to 1991: from 4.6 million metric tons to 9.1 million.[83] As part of the Transit Agreement the Austrians agreed to a variety of upgrades in the Brenner area. In the long term, a new tunnel was to be constructed.[84] The proposed Brenner Base Tunnel is a 55 km rail tunnel in the Brenner Pass which is part of a 409 km stretch of high-speed rail line connecting Munich, Innsbruck and Verona. This is the result primarily of upgrading existing lines. Given the topography, the route involves a total of 256 km of new tunnels, to be completed by 2010.[85] The route was amongst the top priority projects confirmed at the Corfu European Council summit, 24–25 June 1994.[86] Described as having 'open financial plans', the Brenner Base Tunnel was defined as being a joint high-speed rail and combined transport project. At that time, 20,000 million ECU were believed to be needed for the project, which was believed to have the potential to reduce road traffic through the region because of increases in rail speeds. A European Commission official dealing with transport matters in Austria said that achieving a public–private partnership for a huge railway project crossing mountainous territory would be difficult to achieve. From her experience, the member states involved were all saying, in the Autumn of 1997, that the Brenner Tunnel could only proceed on the basis of a public–private partnership.[87]

The reasoning for Austrian interest in the Tunnel option is made clear in a substantial press release from the Federal Ministry of Public Economy and Transport.[88] From 1970 to the present, the annual volume of freight moved by road has multiplied seven-fold, from 3 to 22 million tonnes. The release also cites a report of the European Conference of Ministers of Transport predicting a 51 per cent increase in goods traffic for 1990–2010.[89] Significantly, the predicted increase in east–west transit traffic through Austria for 1987–2010 was 170 per cent.

A senior Austrian official was cautiously optimistic about the availability of private finance for infrastructure in Austria.[90] Wolfgang Rau, of the *Verkehrsclub Österreich*, was however dismissive about the availability of private finance.

On 12 June 1994, Austrians voted in a referendum to join the EU. It is noteworthy that on 9 June 1994, Wolfgang Roth, Vice-President of the EIB, promised that the Bank would contribute 35–40 per cent of the construction costs of the Brenner Base Tunnel. However, two years later, Claes de Neergaard, Vice President of the EIB responsible for Austria, was forced to admit that expectations concerning the project were unrealistic and that, 'It is much too early to talk about finance.'[91] This was a year after he had given a more confident assessment, pointing out that a total of 17.2 billion ATS in funds were agreed or in preparation.[92]

Germany and Italy tried to resist Austria concerning transit issues. At first, Austria had been proposing to stop all road construction over the Alps, and – when defeated on this – pressed for full cost–benefit analysis and strategic environmental assessment. The Austrian government clearly thought this would prevent road building, but the Italian government and that of Bavaria retreated a little by indicating they would settle for the construction of projects already agreed. The German government was less amenable, having a general transport plan agreed in the Bundestag which it expected the Austrian government to accept in full.[93] The Austrian government declined to do so.

The EU had anticipated problems by concluding a bi-lateral agreement with Austria in 1992, to last until 2004.[94] This was partly the result of campaigning efforts by people resident in affected areas.[95] This effort had the eventual effect of controlling the number of heavy goods vehicles in transit through an 'ecopoint' system of transit licenses, monitored by a Transit Committee.[96] However, Viktor Klima, as Minister of Transport, permitted the Transit Agreement to proceed with 164,000 more journeys identified as having taken place than official Austrian statistics of the time. (The EU had been pressing for an even larger total figure of 1,600,000.) This had the effect of building traffic growth into the Agreement, although the political presentation of the Agreement was that it would limit both heavy goods vehicles and pollution. On the latter, the Austrian government had agreed to emissions of nitrogen oxide

44 per cent higher than that permitted in both the EU and Austria.[97]

Transport department head, Günther Hanreich, had been defending his superior Minister Klima against charges of excessive concessions in January 1994. He and Klima had been travelling all over Europe to explain the importance of a transit agreement. Interviewing Hanreich, a journalist could not get any response to her challenge that the agreement with the EU did nothing about the entry of vehicles into Austria from Eastern Europe. Hanreich predicted no further compromise on the eco-point system.[98]

The EU had suggested the eco-points system rather than one based upon the number of transit trips and threatened to pull out of the negotiations if agreement was not speedily obtained.[99] An Austrian Socialist MEP on the European Parliament's Transport Committee, commenting in November 1995, observed that the system of redistribution of eco-points built into the hurried final version of the Transit Agreement had the effect of penalising: 'countries that use their eco-points economically and whose trucks are less detrimental to the environment'.[100]

Austria's case for special treatment was strengthened by a Swiss referendum of 20 February 1994 blocking any increase in transit routes through Switzerland.[101] In joining the EU, Austria accepted a long-term increase in lorry weights from 38 to 40 tonnes and a reduction in taxes upon lorries from 70,000 ATS a year to 17,000 ATS a year. All import–export limitations would be cancelled and an unrestricted number of bilateral lorry journeys would be possible as a result of a loophole concerning 'combined export and import transit traffic'.[102]

Clearly, the Swiss government will observe very closely the circumstances of Austria in relation to transit policies. The EU has an incentive to single out Austria for special treatment in this policy area if it means the accession of Switzerland to the EU.

It is noteworthy that the Austrian National Environmental plan has no reference to placing general restraints on vehicles from outside the EU which may not meet emissions standards whilst travelling through Austria. Given the substantial increases in such traffic, this is a serious omission, as a senior government official conceded.[103] Research suggests the 1990 modal split for goods traded with Eastern Europe – 70 per cent by rail, 30 per cent by road – would reverse by 2010.[104]

Austria has continued to resist EU pressures to conform to the transit regime originally agreed in 1998. Environment Minister, Martin Bartenstein, placed considerable stress upon the significance of road transport being predicted to account for 80 per cent of goods traffic by 2010.[105] Neil Kinnock prefaced a September 1998 gathering of EU transport ministers by predicting agreement if Austria agreed to a modest toll reduction, In January 1998, the EU had secured Swiss agreement to end the ban on lorries over 28 tonnes entering Switzerland: the ban would be replaced by heavy charges. Austria, however, indicated it would block the deal unless it was allowed to retain equivalent charges upon heavy goods vehicles using the Brenner Pass.

Austrian Transport Minister Einem was of the opinion that agreement would be easier after the German general election of 27 September 1998 and a Swiss referendum on transit issues to be held on the same day.[106] The EU was insisting that all seven bilateral accords sought by Switzerland must be agreed as a package, the result of negotiations since 1994. Since it incorporates an increase in the 28 tonne limit to 40 tonnes, the deal is controversial.[107]

The TENs continued to experience financial difficulties up to June 1998, with the Cardiff summit of Heads of State and of Government to be presented with a proposal to double the TENs budget. By this stage, three projects were due to be completed by 2000 but several were in serious doubt, including the Brenner Base Tunnel.[108] In February 2000, the ECJ has indicated that tolls currently in place on the Brenner motorway contravene the Directive concerning the carriage of goods by road. The case will now result in a decision by the judges of the European Court of Justice at some future date.[109]

Looking East towards enlargement

Discussions at ministerial level between EU transport ministers and transport ministers of applicant states are in progress, as part of the so-called 'Structured Dialogue,' and pre-Accession negotiations.[110] One result of this is a proposal for a Council decision on the carriage of goods by road involving the EU, Hungary, Bulgaria and Romania. This places considerable emphasis on the promotion of combined transport, presumably partly in deference to Austrian sensitivity on this matter.[111] It is clear that Accession negotiations in general are dominated by the desire of the countries in Transition to have transitional periods for the application of various parts of the *Acquis*. By 16 March 2000, Hungary alone had requested 35 such transitional periods. However, up to the same date, key applicant states Hungary, Poland, Slovenia, Estonia and the Czech Republic had not asked for any derogations from EU rules, meaning permanent exemptions in a specified area.[112]

Since trade has resulted in a 50 per cent increase in movements between Western and Eastern Europe 1990–2000, there is general concern in Austria about the impact upon the Vienna area in particular.[113] This is not exclusively a concern about physical trade. There may also be concern about greater movement of people into Austria being facilitated by more road transport in particular. The exclusion of Central and Eastern European states from some discussions concerning the future development of common asylum policies may contribute to such anxieties.[114] Dramatic increases in private car use in Eastern Europe may also impact on neighbouring countries like Austria.[115]

The main observation which can be made about this account is that transport and its relationship to the environment and to people has considerable potential to create conflictual situations. These seem most likely to surface at the borders between the 'EU-15' and prospective entrant states.

Notes

1 It is worth noting that the European Conference of Ministers of Transport was formed in Brussels on 17 October 1953, out of the European members of what is now the Organisation of Economic Co-operation and Development. This occurred just after the Treaty of Paris came into force, providing 'institutionalized inter-governmental co-operation' in inland transport. This early initiative did not, however, provide any impetus to the CTP. (Carlo degli Abbati, *Transport and European Integration*, Commission of the European Communities, Brussels, 1987, p. 25).

2 K. W. Gwilliam, 'The Common Transport Policy', in A. M. El-Agraa (ed.), *Economics of the European Community* (London: Philip Allan, 1990), p. 230.

3 Abbati, *Transport*, p. 27 and John F. L. Ross, *Linking Europe* (London: Praeger, 1998), pp. 40–1.

4 Abbati, *Transport*, p. 32.

5 Jurgen Erdmenger, *The European Community Transport Policy: Towards a Common Transport Policy* (Aldershot: Gower, 1983), pp. 11–12. Dr Erdmenger was working in the Directorate General for Transport, Commission of the European Communities, at the time of this work's publication and was still working in this Directorate up to September 1997. See also: John Whitelegg, *Transport Policy in the EEC* (London: Routledge, 1988), p. 6. (The Treaties establishing the European Economic Community and the European Atomic Energy Authority were signed on 25 March 1957.) (Abbati, *Transport*, p. 31). Vickerman also agrees with Erdmenger, for example R. W. Vickerman, 'New Transport infrastructures and economic inte-gration in Europe', Channel Tunnel Research Unit, University of Kent at Canterbury, paper prepared for World Conference on Transportation Research, Yokohama, Japan, July 1989, p. 1.

6 Werner Weidenfeld, 'The transport policy of the European Community to date', in Kenneth Button (ed.), *Transport Policy – Ways into Europe's Future* (Gutersloh: Bertelsmann, 1994), p. 14.

7 Whitelegg, *Transport Policy*, pp. 9–11. Lambert Schaus was the first European Transport Commissioner. Carlo degli Abbati does not seem to agree with this perception, regarding these documents as signifying 'a remarkably comprehensive transport policy plan'. Abbati, *Transport*, p. 53.

8 Ross, *Linking Europe*, p. 44.

9 Abbati, *Transport*, pp. 45–8.

10 Erdmenger, *European Community Transport Policy*, as above, and Whitelegg, *Transport Policy*.

11 Council Decision, 15 September 1958, setting up rules of the Transport Committee established by Article 83 of the Treaty of Rome, *Official Journal* (*OJ*) 25, 27 November 1958, p. 509. These rules were subsequently amended, as were many of the Directives, Decisions and Regulations listed below. In order to maintain brevity, reference to these amendments is not made here.

12 Examples include: the first Council Directive in the area of transport on common rules for international transport, *OJ* 70, 6 August 1962, p. 720; Council Decision of 13 May 1965, which is concerned with the harmonisation of some provisions affect-ing competition in transport by rail, road and inland waterway, *OJ* 88, 24 May 1965, p. 1500; Council Regulation No. 1017/68 of 19 July 1968, applying rules of compe-

tition to transport by rail, road and inland waterway, *OJ* L 175, 23 July 1968.

13 Council Decision, 22 June 1964 – Survey of infrastructure costs, *OJ* 29, June 1964, p. 1598. (Initiatives in this area lead to the formation of the Transport Infrastructure Committee.) Also, for example, Council Regulation No. 1161/69, 26 June 1969, 'Obligations inherent in the concept of a public service (in transport by rail, road and inland waterway)', *OJ* L 156, 28 June 1969, p. 1. See also Whitelegg, *Transport Policy*, p. 13.

14 Ross, *Linking Europe*, pp. 68–9.

15 Abbati, *Transport*, pp. 60–1.

16 Council Regulation No. 516/72, 28 February 1972, 'Common rules for shuttle services by coach and bus (between member states)', *OJ* L 67, 20 March 1972, p. 13; Council Regulation No. 517/72, 28 February 1972, 'Common rules for regular and special services by coach and bus (between member states)', *OJ* L 67, 20 March 1972, p. 19.

17 Communication from the Commission to the Council, 'Development of the common transport policy', 25 October 1973. (*Bulletin of the European Communities*, Supplement 16/73). See also: Whitelegg, *Transport Policy*, pp. 14–15.

18 Whitelegg, *Transport Policy*, p. 15.

19 Abbati, *Transport*, p. 66.

20 Whitelegg, *Transport Policy*, p. 21.

21 Examples include: Council Recommendation, 21 December 1978, 'Training certification and watch-keeping for seafarers', *OJ* L 33, 8 February 1979; Council Directive, 20 December 1979, 'Subsonic aircraft (limitations on noise emissions)', *OJ* L 18, 24 January 1980, p. 26.

22 European Commission, 'A transport network for Europe: outline of a policy' (*Bulletin* 8/79) and quoted in Whitelegg, *Transport Policy*, p. 20.

23 'The EIB and Trans-European Networks', *EIB Information*, No. 86, November 1995, p. 1.

24 Council Decision, 15 December 1981, Austria (*Bulletin* EC 7–8/1981, point 2.1.58). This was a follow-up to a Communication from the Commission to the Council, which incorporated Community assistance to Austria – a non-member state – for motorway construction (COM, 11 April 1980, COM(80)86).

25 Council Regulation, 30 December 1982, 'Financial support (in the field of transport infrastructure)', *OJ* L 376, 31 December 1982.

26 Whitelegg, *Transport Policy*, p. 155.

27 Committee Report No. 85/73, 'Transport infrastructure across the Alps' (Resolution recorded in *OJ* C 49, 28 June 1973), p. 12; Committee Report No. 500/75, 'Traffic Through Austria and Switzerland' (Resolution recorded in *OJ* C 100, 3 May 1976), p. 12; Committee Report No. 1, 186/1981. Erdmenger, *European Community Transport Policy*, p. 1 points out that the concentration of Community population in the central areas of the Community had produced a general trend in traffic flow north–south/south–north through non-member states in the Alps and across the Channel to Britain. This may well have contributed to pressures for transport initiatives on these routes. See also: Whitelegg, *Transport Policy*, pp. 26–7.

28 Committee Report No. 1, 420/1982, 'Proceedings against the Council (of the European Communities for) failure to act (in the field of transport policy)', (Resolution recorded in *OJ* C 267, 11 October 1982), p. 62.

29 In March 1981, the Council transformed some Commission proposals into a

Resolution with ten key points for a transport programme 1981–83 (Whitelegg, *Transport Policy*, p. 15); The ten key points included the implementation of measures in the area of transport infrastructure and resolving problems in intra-Community transit via third countries but did not address a wider transport agenda of 36 issues advanced by the Commission (Erdmenger, *European Community Transport Policy*), p. 23.

30 Erdmenger, *European Community Transport Policy*, p. 23; Whitelegg, *Transport Policy*, pp. 15–16.

31 Abbati, *Transport*, p. 79. He also notes, however, a further 40 plus measures lying dormant in the Council of Ministers for periods sometimes exceeding ten years (p. 221).

32 Whitelegg, *Transport Policy*, offers a considerable amount of material on French and German transport policies in particular.

33 Ross, *Linking Europe*, p. 53.

34 John F. L. Ross, 'When co-operation divides: Oresund, the Channel Tunnel and the new politics of European Transport', *Journal of European Public Policy*, 2: 1 (1995) 116.

35 Ninety million ECU were allocated by Council Regulation on 22 December 1986 to selected transport projects, including approach roads to the Channel Tunnel and a new Brenner Tunnel under the Austrian Alps. (Commission of the European Communities, 'Twentieth General Report on the activities of the European Communities 1986', Brussels 1987, p. 267).

36 European Commission, 'Medium term transport infrastructure policy', COM 340 final (1986). Also see: Whitelegg, *Transport Policy*, pp. 24–6.

37 Whitelegg, *Transport Policy*, p. 166.

38 Ross, *Linking Europe*, p. 52.

39 Brian Bayliss, 'Industry, industrial location and the role of transport in a Single European market', in Jacob Polak and Arnold Heertje (eds), *European Transport Economics* (Oxford: Blackwell, 1993), p. 266.

40 Ross, *Linking Europe*, p. 9.

41 See for example, *OJ*, Debates in the European Parliament, 1996/97 Session, report of proceedings 5–6 June 1996, Brussels, on the Common Transport Policy Action programme 1995–2000.

42 Ross, *Linking Europe*, p. 121.

43 Commission of the European Communities, Directorate General on Transport, Motorway Working Group, *Trans-European Networks: towards a master Plan for the Road Network and Road Traffic* (Brussels, 1993), pp. 2–3.

44 Ross, *Linking Europe*, p. 192.

45 Brief interview with this researcher, 2 July 1998.

46 Ross, *Linking Europe*, p. 224.

47 European Commission, Directorate General for Transport, *The Trans-European Transport Network* (Brussels, November 1994), pp. 8–9. By August 1995, the surface transport plans alone could be considered to consist of 140 road schemes, 11 rail projects, 57 combined transport projects and 26 inland waterway links. See also Chris Bowers, *Ten Questions on TENs: A Look at the European Union's Proposals for Trans-European Transport Networks from an Environmental Perspective* (Brussels: European Federation for Transport and Environment, 1995), p. 3.

48 European Commission, *Trans-European Networks*, Report of The Group of Personal

Representatives of the Heads of State or Government – the Christophersen group (Brussels, 1995). Ross, 'When Co-operation decides', p. 121, notes that transport is responsible for about 30 per cent of EU energy use. However, the linkage between transport policy and the EU's advocacy of greenhouse gas emission reduction remains weak, not least in the failure to agree a Carbon Tax.

49 Ross, *Linking Europe*, p. 122.

50 Interview with Caroline Walcott of the ERT, 3 September 1997.

51 Interviews with senior official specialising in Trans-European Networks, DG VII, European Commission, Brussels, and with Junior official, DG VII, 4 September 1997.

52 Interview with Gijs Kuneman, Director, European Federation for Transport and Environment, 1 September 1997.

53 Interview with Charlie Kronick, Greenpeace Transport Campaigner, London, 20 October 1995.

54 Interview with senior official, DG XI, European Commission, Brussels, 2 September 1997.

55 Debra Johnson, presentation, Trans-European Networks conference, organised by University Association for Contemporary European Studies, London, 16 June 1995, (hereinafter referred to as TENS conference).

56 Colin Turner, presentation, TENS Conference.

57 High Level Group, 'European high-speed rail network', *High-Speed Europe* (Brussels: European Commission, 1995), p. 16.

58 COM 46 (1992), 'Green Paper on the impact of transport on the environment: a community strategy for sustainable mobility', 20 February 1992; COM 494 (1992), 'The future development of the Common Transport Policy: a global approach to the construction of a Community framework for Sustainable Development', 2 December 1992.

59 Colin Turner, *Trans-European Networks: The Infrastructure for the Internal Market* (London: University of North London Press, 1994), pp. 5–6 and 9; European Commission, 'Towards trans-European networks for a Community Action Programme', White Paper, COM 585 (Brussels, 1995).

60 Commission of the European Communities, *Trans-European Networks*.

61 Interview with senior official in DG VII, 4 September 1997.

62 Interview with junior official in DG VII, 4 September 1997.

63 Bowers, *Ten Questions*, p. 5.

64 European Commission, 'Growth, competitiveness and employment', White Paper, COM 700 (Brussels, 1993).

65 Olivier Hoedeman, 'TEN in trouble, Concrete Action: news on European transport projects and actions to resist them', *Concrete Action, Journal of Nature and Youth*, 3 (Oslo, December 1994), Olivier Hoedeman, 'TEN Time-Bomb', *Concrete Action* 2 (July/August, 1994).

66 COM(94)106 Final. The European Conference of Ministers of Transport, looking primarily at Germany, France and the Netherlands, had produced a study of the economics of high-speed trains which would have informed the involved transport ministers. European Conference of Ministers of Transport, *High-Speed Trains* (Report of the 87th Round Table on transport economics, held in Paris 16–17 May 1991 and published in Paris, 1992).

67 *High-Speed Europe*, p. 73.

68 This account is taken from *High-Speed Europe*, p. 36. It is worth remembering that the 14 priority projects advocated by Christophersen were in part a distillation from extant national transport plans such as the 1992 French outline plan; the Swiss Rail 2000 System and New Alpine Rail Links project; the Austrian Neue Bahn system; the Channel Tunnel and its rail link.

69 *Concrete Action, Journal of Nature and Youth*, 4 (Oslo, February/March 1995).

70 Robert McDonald, 'TENS cost hundreds of billions', *European Trends* (Economic Intelligence Unit, first quarter, 1995), p. 12.

71 European Commission, 'Guidelines for the development of the Trans-European Network – 21 New Transport Infrastructure projects', *Transport Europe* (March, 1995).

72 Press Release and notice of press conference on the environmental impact of the TENs, both 16 May 1995, issued on behalf of: World Wide Fund for Nature, European Federation for Transport and Environment, Birdlife International, Friends of the Earth, Greenpeace, ASEED Europe (Action for Solidarity, Equality, Environment and Development).

73 Wilfried Puwein, 'The regulation of across-border road goods transport', *Monatsberichte* (monthly report) 10/94 of the Institute for Economic Research, 1994, pp. 579–80 Weixler suggests that the multiplicity of agreements made control of transit traffic 'almost impossible'. Helmut Weixler, 'At the end of Europe's exhaust pipe', *Profil* (news magazine), Vienna, 13 November 1995.

74 Puwein, 'Regulation of across-border road goods transport', p. 585.

75 CIPRA (Commission Internationale pour la Protection des Alpes). Interview with Environment Minister, Martin Bartenstein, *Die Alpenkonvetion*, 1 (Spring 1995, Vienna).

76 This account is taken from the journal *Die Alpenkonvetion*, 2 and 3 (1995) and 4 (1995–96), produced by CIPRA ÖSTERREICH.

77 Weixler, 'At the end of Europe's exhaust pipe'.

78 Höll, Otmar and Helmut Kramer, 'Globalization, normalization and Europeanization of a small(er) state's foreign policy: the case of Austria', paper prepared for the 25th European Consortium on Political Research Joint Session of Workshops, Workshop: 'Small states in the transforming European system', Bern, 27 February–3 March 1997, p. 10.

79 Transit Agreement. References to this Agreement are to the official Austrian Government translation as supplied by the Austrian Federal Ministry for Public Economy and Transport, dated 29 December 1992.

80 'New traffic routes in Tyrol are not politically acceptable' (Interview with Hans Tanzer, Deputy Regional Premier of the Tyrol with Peter Sonnberger, *Verkehr und Umwelt* (Transport and Environment) (Vienna, July–August, 1993 edition).

81 Austrian Society for Traffic Policy, 'Jurgen Erdmenger and Trans-European Networks' (Society for Traffic Policy, INFO no. 80, 7 February 1996, no location for publication).

82 The others are Tauern: Munich–Salzburg–Villach; Pyhrn–Schober Pass route: Regensburg–Graz; the Danube route: Nuremberg–Vienna. This list excludes Eastern European access to Austria which tends to pass through Vienna and its environs.

83 Austrian Society for Traffic Policy, 'Rail transit on the Brenner has doubled' (undated, Vienna).

84 Transit Agreement, Annex II.

85 Transit Agreement, Annex V.

86 *High-Speed Europe*, pp. 129–131. There is an additional corridor Venice–Vienna which involves a similar 22 km base tunnel at Semmering and a projected new 400 km line Vienna, Graz to Taravisio in Italy. This chapter concentrates for reasons of brevity upon the Brenner Base Tunnel.

87 Interview with a Commission auxiliary responsible for transport matters in Germany and Austria, DG VII, Unit A3 (Brussels, 4 September 1997).

88 Federal Ministry of Public Economy and Transport, Republic of Austria, Press Release, 'Austria's position in the negotiations for entry to the EU with regard to the Transit agreement' (January–February 1994).

89 'Austrian Federal Railways invests in infrastructure', *News from Austria*, 8/96, 19 April 1996.

90 Interview with Senior Ministerial Advisor, 19 April 1996.

91 EU Online – *Grüne Zeitschrift für Grosse Informationssprünge,* 'Stellen wir den EU einen Baum auf', No. 2, September 1996, 'Vienna – Environment Transit: brought to a standstill', p. 14.

92 'European Investment bank supports Austria's railway infrastructure', *News from Austria*, No. 22/95, 24 November 1995.

93 Interview with Matthias Schickhofer, Greenpeace Austria, Vienna, 10 April 1996.

94 John Palmer, 'European Union reaches Russian border', *Guardian*, 2 March 1994. (Transport Minister Streicher signed the Agreement in October 1991 although Austrian requirements had not been met.)

95 Puwein, 'Regulation of across-border road goods transport', p. 582.

96 Eco-points were calculated in the following manner for heavy goods vehicles over 7.5 tonnes in weight: the level of Nitrous Oxide emission per kilometre per hour (agreed to be 15.8g NOx/kWh) was multiplied by the number of transit journeys for such vehicles in 1991. The resulting figure was to represent the total number of eco-points for 1991, providing a base line. From then onwards, 'the initial value equivalent to the total number of ecopoints for 1991' was to be reduced each year. 1991 was considered to represent 100 per cent with a 1992 figure of 96.1 per cent, 1993, 87.9 per cent, continuing until a figure of 40 per cent by 2003. In other words, a 60 per cent emission reduction was to be achieved. Percentages given for 2002 and 2003 were qualified by the consideration that the 15.8g figure would itself have been reduced in practice by the availability of heavy goods vehicles with only a 5g emission figure by these years. (This description follows the official translation of the Agreement between the Republic of Austria and the European Economic Community on the transit of goods by road and rail of 29 December 1992, provided by the Austrian Federal Ministry of Public Economy and Transport, referring to Article 15 and Annex VIII.) In addition, it was agreed to freeze permitted traffic movements at the 1991 level: 1,264,000 for EU-origin goods vehicles and 211,100 for Austrian. These figures were revised upwards by the Transit Committee on 14 July 1994. Ecopoints issued by the Ministry of Public Economy and Transport were initially distributed according to the number of transit trips made by carriers of the states involved in transit in 1991. Ecopoints are primarily distributed to carriers on the basis of trips undertaken in the past.

97 The figure of 15.8g/kWh originates from earlier limits prevailing in the EU, as found by Fritz Gurgiser of the Transit Forum. Gurgiser was very sceptical about

levels of emissions as officially stated since he believed the emissions were measured in workshops contracted to lorry manufacturers and he claimed to have
personally seen rigged documentation (Weixler, 'At the end of Europe's exhaust
pipe').

98 Lisalotte Palme interviewing Günther Hanreich – 'No exchange possible' –
Transport department head Günther Hanreich and the way he sees the transit negotiations in Brussels. *Profil*, Vienna, 17 January 1994.

99 Weixler, 'At the end of Europe's exhaust pipe'. The EU and Austria both used a limit
of 9g/kWh for emissions of nitrogen oxide. The Agreement used 15.8g/kWh. The
Agreement was estimated to need seven years of operation, up to 1998, for the eco-
points allocated to meet the environmental limits for these emissions prevailing in
Austria before it entered the EU.

100 Quoted in Weixler, 'At the end of Europe's exhaust pipe'.

101 Francisco Grannelli, 'The European Union's enlargement negotiations with Austria,
Finland, Norway and Sweden', *Journal of Common Market Studies*, 33: 1 (March
1995), 131–2.

102 Karl Brandner, 'Transit treaty threatens trailers', *Concrete Action*, 3 (Oslo,
February–March 1995), p. 13.

103 Interview with Senior Ministerial Advisor, Vienna, 19 April 1996.

104 Puwein, 'Regulation of across-border road goods transport', p. 586.

105 M. Bartenstein, 'Collective commitment to sustainable traffic development should
not remain a one day wonder', 14 November 1997 (article downloaded from
Austrian government's web site).

106 'Road Tolls could solve Alp traffic row – Austria' (downloaded from *Reuters* news
service, 16 September 1998); 'EU's Kinnock says has solution to Brenner Pass row'
(downloaded from Reuters news service, 15 September 1998). On the threat of legal
action being maintained: 'European Federation for Transport and Environment –
T&E Bulletin. Brussels', *European Federation for Transport and Environment*, 70
(July 1998).

107 Marcus Kabel, 'Swiss truck fee vote could make or break EU ties' (Reuters press
service, 24 September 1998).

108 *T & E Bulletin*, 69 (June 1998).

109 Press and Information Division, European Court of Justice, Press Release 10/2000,
15 February 2000, Case C–205/98, *Commission* v *Austria*. 'Advocate General Saggio
suggests that the Court should declare that the tolls levied on the Brenner Motorway
are contrary to the Directive concerning the carriage of goods by road.'
(http://curia.eu.int/en/cp/aff/cp0010en.htm).

110 Michael Alexander Rupp, 'The pre-accession strategy and governmental structures
of the Visegrad countries', Karen Henderson (ed.), *Back to Europe: Central and
Eastern Europe and the European Union*. (London: UCL Press, 1999), p. 94.

111 Proposal for a Council Decision concerning the conclusion of the Agreement
between the European Community and the Republic of Hungary establishing
certain conditions for the carriage of goods by road and the promotion of
Combined Transport. Document 599PC0665(02), 31 January 2000.
http://europa.eu.int/eur-lex/en/com/dat/1999/en_599PC0665_02.html.

112 Breffni O'Rourke, 'Enlargement negotiations adhere to tough criteria', *Central
Europe Online*: www.centraleurope.com/features.php3?id= 143299.

113 David Banister, Dominic Stead, Peter Steen, Jonas Akerman, Karl Dreborg, Peter

Nijkamp and Ruggero Scheicher-Tappeser, *European Transport Policy and Sustainable Mobility* (London: Spon, 2000), p. 64.

114 Sandra Lavenex, 'Migration and the EU's new eastern border: between realism and liberalism, *Journal of European Public Policy*, 8: 1 (2001), 24–5.

115 Andrew Francis, 'Environmental issues in CEEC transformation: environment as a challenge to enlargement', in Mike Mannin (ed.), *Pushing Back the Boundaries: The European Union and Central and Eastern Europe* (Manchester: Manchester University Press, 1999), pp. 160–1.

Further reading

Bischot, Günter and Pelinka, Anton (eds), *Austria in the New Europe* (London: Transaction Publishers, 1993).

Coccossis, H. and Nijkamp, P. (eds) (*Overcoming Isolation: Information and Transportation Networks in Development Strategies for Peripheral Areas* (Berlin, 1995).

12

The Europeanisation of firms and the role of Euro-groups in European integration

Jenny Fairbrass

For over 40 years, scholars of the European Union have puzzled over the respective roles of, and interaction between, state and non-state actors in the integration or policy-making process. Some of the earliest writers, for example the neo-functionalists,[1] anticipated that the combined activities of supranational policy-makers and transnational interests groups would play a central role in EU integration. When, in the 1960s, actual events in the EU failed to bear out these predictions, other International Relations approaches (i.e. intergovernmentalism), gained prominence. This perspective makes powerful claims for the persistence or resilience of the nation state in EU policy-making,[2] relegating the Commission and interest groups to a minor role. However, even this framework has come to be criticised and later rejected by some scholars. Consequently, more recently, alternative accounts have come to the fore (e.g. multi-level governance). Some of these more recent attempts[3] to characterise the EU, re-affirm the significance of the interaction between (sub)national and supranational actors in creating an EU polity.

This chapter responds to the issues raised by the various approaches referred to above by continuing to explore the interaction between the various policy actors and their respective roles in EU policy-making. It examines the 'Europeanisation' of firms, measured here in terms of the firms' *direct interaction* with EU level policy-makers or in their use of Euro-groups as channels to the EU level of governance. The chapter also explores the role of Euro-groups and tests to what extent the widely held view of Euro-groups as 'weak' and 'ineffective' is supported by the evidence collected. The chapter presents selected empirical evidence drawn from a survey of business actors (that is, firms) and their connections with national and EU level policy-makers, and the part played by intermediaries such as national and European trade associations.

The chapter unfolds as follows: first, there is a survey of the literature concerned with the political activities of individual firms and trade associations; second, empirical data are presented, exposing the activities of UK and French firms in three industries and their collective groupings; third, the chapter draws some conclusions about the reported behaviour of the organisations.

Earlier empirical studies: firms and Euro groups in the EU

It would seem that individual firms have become increasingly willing (or find it advantageous) to have direct contact with EU-level policy-makers rather than relying on traditional intermediaries such as the national government or collective groupings such as trade associations. Coen[4] notes the emergence of 'direct EU lobbying' in the 1990s as a relatively new practice for many firms (in the 1970s/1980s firms had tended to lobby via national governments and European federations). Green Cowles[5] discerns four phases of development (see Table 12.1) in the political behaviour of (large) firms during the period from the 1960s to the 1990s, in which the establishment of 'European-level big business organisations' has made it possible for large firms to by-pass long established as well as national industry associations in influencing EU legislation and programmes ... [so that] European and national industry associations – long recognised as the voice of industry – must now co-ordinate or compete with large companies not only for influence in EU industrial and regulatory policy, but also for membership and dues.

The impression conveyed by these writers is one of (growing) impotency of collective groupings in the EU arena, despite their growing numbers[6] and the ascendancy of individual firms. These findings have been confirmed elsewhere. Other scholars,[7] who have focused on the role and activities of trade associations, particularly, the European groupings have also found them to be 'weak' and 'ineffectual'.

Table 12.1   *Four phases in the development of the collective action of big business*

Phase and decade of origin	Dominant incentive	Dominant format	Commission role	Examples of organisations
1. 1960s	Selective Social	Informal group of individuals	Yes	Groupes des Presidents
2. 1960s, 1970s	Collective Political	Transformed Eurofederations	Mixed	Pharmaceutical, Information Technology
3. 1980s	Collective Political	Direct Large Firm Associations	Mixed	ERT, EU Committee
4. 1990	Collective Political	Direct Large Firm Associations	Minimal	ENER-G8, ICRT

Source: Cowles Green, 1998, 114.

Until recently the most common form of collective action at the European level was the European Federation, formed from a collection of national trade associations. These usually, because of their highly federated structure, tend to be slow and cumbersome, and often are unable to reconcile internal, nationally founded differences.[8] Crucially, Grant[9] argues that the weakness of the European Federations is likely to leave the multi-national enterprises (MNE's) increasingly exasperated, and more likely therefore to engage in 'direct representation' or to establish direct membership organisations. As a response, increasingly, European groups that permit direct membership by businesses.[10]

The internal, organisational structure of the federated groups of itself may hinder the group's ability to reach meaningful policy choices.[11] The consultation process may have to be lengthy as more than 15 national associations may have to be consulted. They may not be able to resolve national differences. Moreover the fact that the European federations are felt to be ineffective may in turn result in further weakness when firms, and particularly, large firms, choose to undertake direct action on their own account.[12] That is to say, 'perceived weakness' may breed further 'weakness'.

The European Commission's perceptions of European groups are likely to be vital. When the Commission believes the Euro group to be weak, it may resort to consultation with national associations and individual firms. In so doing, may further undermine the Euro-group.[13] There is a danger that the Commission may develop quasi-clientelistic' relationships with a limited number of groups: those that can keep up with the pace of Commission proposals. Often it is only national trade associations and MNE's, rather than the Euro-groups,[14] for reasons of structure and internal decision-making procedures as already referred to above, that are able to keep abreast of EU decision-making.

There is, however, some evidence to suggest that the Commission does prefer to consult with Euro-groups, as it lacks resources (staffing and expertise), and consultation is difficult.[15] In terms of benefits the European Commission may derive, there is the advantage of appearing to be 'even-handed'.[16] In addition, the European Commission may need the assistance of Euro-groups, in terms of their ability to supply technical information and advice, to assist with implementation, and perhaps, most importantly, to act as an 'international referee'. The Euro-group could reconcile or smooth over national differences, before proposals reach the desk of the European Commission administrators and policy-makers. The Commission would almost certainly prefer to be relieved of such an irksome task. Accordingly, it has clearly encouraged the establishment of Euro-groups.[17]

The main causes of (actual or perceived) weakness of European groups may derive from their lack of finance and personnel, adequately skilled or trained personnel. Moreover, it has been argued[18] that national associations, who feed into the European Federations may deliberately keep them 'on short supplies' of funding and staffing, as the former have their own agenda to satisfy (national associations have to justify the subscription fees they charge and have a vested interest in their own survival). In any case, the national associations may also want to play a 'national card'[19] and risk having to relinquish their policy objectives in reaching a diluted common European position.

For those firms wanting to influence EU policy, there are a number of routes open to them:[20] via the national government, via a Euro-group, or by direct contact. Grant argues that the 'national' channel is still used because it allows pressure groups to pursue views divergent from their European counterparts, or where the group agrees with the Euro-group the case can be reinforced. The national route may also have proved to be resilient because, as Greenwood and Ronit[21] observe, in many cases the member state continues to be the main implementation agent of EU policy. It is a 'tried and tested' route for industry; it is openly available to business concerns of all sizes including small organisations. In addition, where conflict does arise between the different national interests it may be more beneficial to act on a national basis. In some cases, to win an argument in Brussels it is necessary to have national government support (i.e. the Council of Ministers in the final decision-maker).

However, drawing on Olson, McLaughlin and Jordan[22] argue that there are serious doubts about the merit of any collective action, let alone the dubious benefit of joining a weak and disunited European group. They support Olson's contention that there is merit in being a 'free rider'. There is no need for firms to join a group, as they can still derive benefit from collective gains without incurring the 'costs' of membership. One of the consequences for firms of adopting a 'free rider' strategy is that an under-mobilisation of firms is likely to arise and there will be little growth in the number of Euro-groups.[23]

As a counter argument, it should be noted that there are several potential rewards of collective action.[24] Larger firms, who dominate the Euro-groups, may find that any unilateral approaches to the European Commission may be rebuffed in the name of even-handedness; whist a collective advance to the European Commission may be carried out disguised behind the policy position of the group. McLaughlin *et al.*[25] go so far as to suggest that such collective action may be indispensable even for large companies, and note that there has been an increase in the level of domination of Euro-groups by the large firms.[26]

One of the benefits[27] of belonging to a group is the availability of 'early warnings'. Other benefits[28] may include a relatively low investment with high returns, in terms of developing a symbiotic power-dependence relationship with the European Commission; the chance to influence the collective strategies of the group as a member; the status of group membership; social contact; a 'listening post' and 'early warning' for regulatory changes; and personal career development for staff of firms seconded to the Euro-group.[29]

The main advantage of Euro-group membership may lie in the need and ability of the firm and national trade associations to operate more than one channel of lobbying. Sargent[30] refers to the choice between individual and collective action. She suggests that individual-level action may be preferred when the issue is only of concern to the one organisation, the implementation phase has begun, the organisation agrees with neither the national government nor the Euro-group or when the organisation is deliberately trying to influence the national government. Collective action, she argues, might be more appropriate when policy is likely to have a negative impact on the firm, to add weight to the individual position or when the organisation is trying to encourage support from 'sister' organisations. In other words, one method may be employed in order to compensate for the deficiencies of another.[31] Sargent finds that rarely do the associations use all channels simultaneously, but that where an issue was of greater weight, then more channels would be exploited and greater significance would be attached to the direct channel. She also finds that the majority of the groups researched placed equal emphasis on the national government and the Euro-group route.[32] She does point out that independent action by large firms, for example those with their own Brussels office, can supplement and aid the work of the Euro-group. Grant[33] also emphasises the value of the Euro-group as an additional route (to supplement the national or direct route).

More recently Bennett[34] has conducted some important empirical work on the subject of trade associations in Britain, and their favoured lobbying routes with respect to the EU. In terms of the routes available to the groups for EU lobbying he employed a four-way categorisation: the direct route, the national route, the European route and the 'Brussels Strategy',[35] amended to a three way analysis.[36] His chief findings[37] were that firms employed multiple routes. He found that the 'national route' was the most important one for all categories of association; that firms would exploit meetings with UK Ministers, officials and agencies to channel their views to the EU. Only the 'Federations' did not regard this as their main channel. Overall, the second most important route was the European route (via the European association); this was the most widely used, and for the Federations this was the most important conduit. The third ranked route was the 'Brussels Strategy', that is having a Brussels office. The 'Brussels Strategy' was not widely utilised except by the 'Corporate trade associations' and the 'Federations'.[38]

Bennett further (statistically) analyses the relationship between choice of lobbying route, size of firm, nature of sector and type of business association in a more recent text.[39] He analysis examines the extent to which firms employ direct lobbying. Bennett concludes,[40] that the most important factor that determines direct lobbying is the size of the firm: that is direct lobbying is really only an option for large firms. However, he qualifies this by stating that the extent to which large firms use direct lobbying is affected by other factors: the nature of their industrial sector, the extent of its organisation, the sector's size and weight and the type of business association to which the firm belongs within the sector. From his data and statistical analysis, Bennett concludes that direct lobbying is more likely where the associations contain large firms, the sector is concentrated and the association is relatively small.

Empirical evidence: Europeanisation of firms and the role of Euro-groups

The data presented below are drawn from a postal survey (with about a 30 per cent response rate) of approximately 250 firms, 70 trade associations and 50 elite interviews, over a period spanning from 1995 to 1999. The firms surveyed were registered in the UK and France in one of three industrials sectors: telecommunications, energy (gas and electricity) and insurance. Interviews were conducted with all categories of policy actor: individual firms, national trade associations, European associations, national central government policy-makers and administrators, European Commission staff and MEPs.

Membership of trade associations

About 80 per cent of the firms reported being members of a national association, compared with about 30 per cent belonging to a Euro-group. Around 47 per cent of the national associations were members of a Euro-group (see Tables 12.2, 12.3 and 12.4 for details).

Table 12.2   *Firms' membership of national trade associations*

Valid	Frequency	%	Valid %	Cumulative %
Yes	69	80.2	80.2	80.2
No	14	16.3	16.3	96.5
No data	3	3.5	3.5	100.0
Total	86	100.0	100.0	

Source: Postal questionnaires.

Table 12.3   *Firms' membership of European trade associations*

Valid	Frequency	%	Valid %	Cumulative %
Yes	26	30.2	30.2	80.2
No	57	66.3	66.3	96.5
No data	3	3.5	3.5	100.0
Total	86	100.0	100.0	

Source: Postal questionnaires.

Table 12.4   *Membership of Euro-groups*

Valid	Frequency	%	Valid %	Cumulative %
Yes	9	47.4	47.4	47.4
No	6	31.6	31.6	78.9
Is a Euro-group	4	21.1	21.1	100.0
Total	19	100.0	100.0	

Source: Postal questionnaires.

As far as the behaviour of the firms is concerned, these data indicate a greater reliance on national associations than Euro-groups (and this is borne out by the interviews conducted), although some Euro-groups do not permit direct membership by firms in any case.

Preferred EU contact routes

Among the firms the most commonly reported route for making contact with the EU was via the national association (about 26 per cent of the firms). However, direct contact was reported as the second most frequent mode of behaviour (about 16 per cent). Five per cent or fewer of the firms reported using a public relations firm, the Euro-group or the national government (see Figure 12.1). In contrast, about 47 per cent of the trade associations chose to make direct contact with EU policy-makers, although 42 per cent reported using a Euro-group to act as an intermediary (see Table 12.5).

Table 12.5   *Use of Euro-group for EU contact – by national associations*

Valid	Frequency	%	Valid %	Cumulative %
Yes	8	42.1	42.1	12.8
No	3	15.8	15.8	25.6
Is a Euro-group	4	21.1	21.1	45.3
No data	4	21.1	21.1	66.3
Total	19	100.0	100.0	100.0

Source: Postal questionnaires.

Figure 12.1   *Preferred EU contact routes among firms*

EU lobbying route (1st)

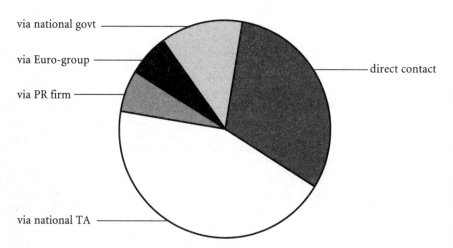

Source: Postal questionnaires.

Frequency of contact with national and EU policy-makers
For both individual firms and the national trade associations there is a more frequent pattern of contact with national government officials than EU-level policy-makers (see Tables 12.6, 12.7, 12.8 and 12.9). This suggests a bond between firms and associations and national decision-makers, and a limited degree of 'Europeanisation'.

Table 12.6 *Frequency of contact with national government – among firms*

Valid	Frequency	%	Valid %	Cumulative %
Never	11	12.8	12.8	12.8
Daily/weekly	11	12.8	12.8	25.6
Monthly	17	19.8	19.8	45.3
Annually	18	20.9	20.9	66.3
No data	29	33.7	33.7	100.0
Total	86	100.0	100.0	

Source: Postal questionnaires.

Table 12.7 *Frequency of contact with the Commission – among firms*

Valid	Frequency	%	Valid %	Cumulative %
Never	34	39.5	39.5	39.5
Daily/weekly	5	5.8	5.8	45.3
Monthly	6	7.0	7.0	52.3
Annually or less frequently	40	46.5	46.5	98.8
No data	1	1.2	1.2	100.0
Total	86	100.0	100.0	

Source: Postal questionnaires.

Table 12.8 *Frequency of contact with national government – among trade associations*

Valid	Frequency	%	Valid %	Cumulative %
Daily/weekly	10	52.6	52.6	52.6
Monthly	5	26.3	26.3	78.9
Annually	2	10.5	10.5	89.5
No data	2	10.5	10.5	100.0
Total	19	100.0	100.0	

Source: Postal questionnaires.

Table 12.9   *Frequency of contact with the Commission – among trade associations*

Valid	Frequency	%	Valid %	Cumulative %
Never	1	5.3	5.3	5.3
Daily/weekly	7	36.8	36.8	42.1
Monthly	6	31.6	31.6	73.7
Annually	3	15.8	15.8	89.5
No data	2	10.5	10.5	100.0
Total	19	100.0	100.0	

Source: Postal questionnaires.

Interview data: Euro-groups assessed

Telecommunications Euro-groups

In this domain there are a number of Euro-groups, the most notable of which are the Association of European Telecommunication Network Operators (ETNO) and ECTEL, representing the telecoms operators and telecoms manufacturers respectively. ETNO was described by national operators as 'useful' since it facilitated the exchange of information and views among the various national associations. A leading member of staff of BT's Government Relations department in Brussels[41] commented that BT had, 'put a lot of effort into ETNO because of its influence with the Commission ... for example, for 'damage limitation' ... as other members of ETNO are hostile to [market] liberalisation'.

This perception of ETNO was confirmed by the Commission itself, ETNO (and ECTEL) 'are viewed as insiders', although on occasions because of internal conflict they may not be able to produce papers. Under those circumstances, the Commission[42] 'may need to turn to individual companies'. ETNO's activities are supplemented by *ad hoc* and other informal arrangements. One Commission staff member noted that such *ad hoc* coalitions tend to be 'issue specific'.

Nevertheless, ETNO was thought[43] to be 'in need of reform ... it lack[ed] empowerment ... [was] too slow'. The decision-making process within ETNO involves consultation with all national association members. Invariably the policy position reached was of the lowest common denominator variety. In consequence, ETNO was restructured in 1997, with a view to increasing its strength. One of the European Commission respondents interviewed attested[44] to the improvement in ETNO's performance following reorganisation: 'now (1996/97) [he finds] ETNO is much more effective and cohesive. Before it was "loose" with much internal conflict. Now there is a more general acceptance of market liberalisation.'

ECTEL was established in 1986, earlier than ETNO (1991). This was largely a response to the evolution of market liberalisation that occurred at a different pace in the market for services compared with the market for products. The composition of ECTEL (it includes EU and non-EU members) does give rise to some of the internal differences. For example, some difficulties have arisen from the varying national technical standards in the different member states. ECTEL's constitution does not permit membership directly by individual firms. This may also contribute to its limited effectiveness. The European Commission itself has recommended that ECTEL review its membership policy to allow individual direct corporate members.

As in ETNO, so too in ECTEL, the major European firms take a leading role. The large firms tend to be the most actively involved, as they can afford to devote funding and personnel to the Euro-group. The European Commission is aware that ECTEL is dominated by the 'big firms', and that the views of the smaller firms may not be well represented. From the European Commission's point of view both ETNO and ECTEL are treated as 'indicators' of industry views. Commission respondents were aware that internal policy differences in ECTEL and ETNO had led to a failure to produce policy papers. Under such circumstances the European Commission would turn to individual firms,[45] and in so doing may have inadvertently itself undermined the Euro-group.

Energy Euro-groups

There is a range of opinions about the effectiveness of energy Euro-groups. Evidence available suggests that both Eurogas and Eurelectric experience internal conflict, although the differences within the former are reported to be more pronounced than the latter. In common with the telecommunications sector, energy Euro-groups suffered from internal discord over the issue of EU market liberalisation (the SEM programme). Whilst Eurogas felt that it was important to seek a common position, as this would be more persuasive with the EU, this would often be a 'lowest common denominator' position. However, the group was unable to achieve this, the main problem being the disparate nature of the European national market conditions. On the subject of disunity within the European gas industry, a senior member of staff of Eurogas stated,[46] 'before 1990 [there was] almost unanimous opposition to gas liberalisation – there was solid opposition to change – except British Gas. [Therefore, Eurogas had] an opinion forming role. [It] has to try to co-ordinate views . . . bring industry together.'

The evidence from firms surveyed suggests that one of the members of Eurogas was often isolated and opposed to the majority of the membership. The majority were opposed to the gas market liberalisation proposal, whilst the major UK member was enthusiastically in favour. For that reason, the UK firm believed that it was vital to be active in Eurogas, as part of a defensive strategy. In participating actively in the Euro-group, the UK firm had provided a high-ranking official to take up a senior role in the association. This again bears witness to the large firms' strategy of attempting to control the activities of the Euro-groups. The UK firm's overall assessment of the Euro-group was that it was 'ineffective' and 'old-fashioned'.

In contrast, Eurelectric was perceived to contain a more coherent membership, which finds common positions easier to reach. As a consequence

Eurelectric produces a greater volume of briefing papers than does Eurogas.[47] Clearly, the charge that some Euro-groups are ineffective, as a consequence of their internal national differences is borne out by the energy sector. MEPs interviewed found both Eurogas and Eurelectric to be 'effective' if measured in terms of their ability to produce briefing papers. In common with the views expressed by national government officials and European Commission staff, the MEPs questioned attested to the value of being fully informed about the internal differences within the Euro-groups. Clearly, it is much more likely that policy is going to be workable if policy-makers are fully aware of the range of views about any given issue.

The Insurance Euro-group

The Comité Européen d'Assurances (CEA) represents the insurance industry at a European level. Like many other Euro-groups, the CEA consists not only of EU national associations, but also includes non-EU national groups. Such a breadth of membership can cause organisational and policy coherence problems. Unanimity may be difficult among the EU member associations, but problems are potentially magnified when the membership extends to national associations from non-EU states, owing to the possibility of an increased diversity within the group.

In an attempt to strengthen the CEA as a lobbying organisation, in the early 1990s, it considered altering its structure to admit direct corporate members. This change was inspired, according to the CEA respondent, by witnessing the improved performance of European Chemical Industry Federation (CEFIC) as a result of allowing direct corporate members. The CEA had[48] recognised that, 'the next step is to have large companies as direct members ... although it is a taboo subject with members [as this may result in the marginalisation of national associations]'.

This point highlights the rivalry between national and European groups for the same 'constituency', a contest that can render the Euro-group weak and ineffective. The CEA is aware that some of the national groups have the opinion that they can 'do better' than the CEA in conducting business with the European Commission.

The Commission often requests information and technical advice from the CEA. According to one Commission official,[49] 'there is an "adult relationship" between the Commission and the CEA. [We] need each other. [We] are both looking for information in what is a highly technical area.'

The CEA will attempt to put forward a policy paper, and offer a 'serious and credible' position. Generally the policy papers do not exhibit divided views. To arrive at common policy positions, the CEA normally utilises its committee structure. As with other Euro-groups this internal consultation process can be protracted.

Broadly across the insurance sector, there are conflicting views about the value of the CEA. Some UK industry respondents expressed the opinion that the

CEA does not impress the European Commission, because of the CEA's efforts to achieve unanimity that often result in 'lowest common denominator decisions'. Although the respondents did admit that the CEA is 'recognised' by the European Commission, they also argued that it would be in a stronger position if it did not try to hide its internal differences: such openness would be more helpful to the European Commission.

When questioning European Commission staff about the role of the CEA, it was commented that[50] the CEA seemed to be 'well organised' and could be relied upon to produce promptly policy papers. The European Commission official described their relationship with the CEA as 'satisfactory', and attested to having a 'high opinion' of the CEA, particularly in light of its difficulties in dealing with wide-ranging national differences among its members. The European Commission staff are aware that the CEA papers may 'hide cracks', and that it would be essential for the European Commission to discover the nature of the concealed differences. The European Commission attested that it has less contact with national associations than with the Euro-group.

One insurance firm staff member[51] did however observe that he had witnessed an increasing harmony within the CEA as more members had begun to accept the EU's moves towards market liberalisation and de-regulation. Nevertheless, several UK industry interviewees stated that they preferred to access the EU via the Association of British Insurers (ABI), as an additional channel to the CEA. In addition, some of the national associations may well be perceived as being more fruitful as EU lobbying conduits, since they appear to be, or are, better organised than the Euro-group.[52] They may be capable of clearer and quicker policy responses.

There was approval for the CEA's earlier attempts to become more effective. Changes to amend the structure and organisation of the CEA, which dated from 1992, were felt to have made it a more useful lobbying group. One national association employee, working in the section responsible for European issues, did conclude[53] that, 'the CEA is now much more effective than 5 or 6 years ago – it has better relations with the Commission. The Commission is receptive [to the CEA] because it wants help with implementation [of law].'

It was generally accepted that the CEA does have a good relationship with the European Commission,[54] and particularly DG XV. For example, it was argued that the CEA had been notably successful when negotiating the directives concerning 'block exemptions', and the CEA had operated as an 'umbrella', through which the national associations had funnelled information on national market conditions. However, some doubts were expressed about the CEA's merits as a source of information about the EU. One national industry respondent stated that sometimes the CEA would be able to 'tip the wink' about forthcoming EU developments, but that sometimes the national government officials were a better and quicker source of information.

In contrast to the relationship between the CEA and the Commission, the relationship between the CEA and the Parliament appears to be less well developed. One MEP interviewed who sits on an EP committee responsible for insurance issues has had no contact with the CEA, and is much more likely to hear from the ABI. This is, in part, explained by the fact that the MEP interviewed was a British MEP. There appear to be nationally based patterns of contact between MEPs and lobbying groups. The same MEP had had no approaches from the Fédération Française de Sociétés d'Assurances (FFSA), which is one of the French national associations in the field of insurance.

Non-sectoral patterns

Commission respondents attested that it was not unusual to find policy differences between the national trade associations and the European group, and that often the Euro-groups were forced to produce 'bland' statements in order to reconcile internal differences. Several of these respondents reported discernible changes within the Euro-groups from the 1960s/1970s, when the Euro groups were 'local, friendly, amateur' and mainly Belgian staffed bodies, to the 1990s, by which time they had become much more 'professional, sharp and focused'. However, several of the Commission respondents interviewed did describe the Euro-groups as being still 'too big, too slow' and 'relatively weak'. One Commission official described[55] Euro-groups in the following terms, they are 'too big, too slow ... [they have a] slow reaction time ... [they have a] lengthy consultation process [and produce] fuzzy measures'.

A number of Commission respondents did comment that they preferred to work with Euro-groups, despite the efforts of national associations to be heard. Nevertheless, one Commission official did comment[56] that whilst:

> the Commission prefers to listen to Euro-groups rather than national ones, there are too many [of the national groups]. Even so, some national organisations will still try lobby [the Commission], especially when they think the European group doesn't represent them very well or there are disputes within the European trade association.

It was also commented that Euro-group staffing levels were an important issue. One Commission official commented[57] that:

> of six or seven European trade associations [with which the respondent had contact] about two or three were good. They had a secretariat in Brussels, ten or fifteen staff and could offer position papers. The others with fewer staff can't cope. They rarely make substantial contributions [to the debate] – don't produce – are not taken seriously [by the Commission].

Conclusions

The evidence reveals that firms have engaged in direct contact with EU level policy-makers, as well as channelling their interests to the EU via intermediaries. In other words there is some evidence of Europeanisation of the firms, as defined for the purposes of this study. However, firms persist in relying more heavily on the national trade association as their most commonly used route for interacting with EU-level policy-makers. There is evidence that the firms place little store by the Euro-groups. This suggests, that contrary to neo-functionalist predictions, the transnational groups (that is, Euro-groups still play a relatively minor role in EU policy-making in contrast to national associations.

The survey confirms the findings of earlier research that the Euro-groups are relatively weak. Many of the causes identified by the earlier research persist: internal structures hinder quick and effective decision-making and the internal divergence of views mitigates against producing anything other than lowest-common-denominator decisions and results in 'bland' position papers on the part of the Euro-groups. Consequently, firms, national associations and the EU policy-makers compound this impotency (weakness) by by-passing the Euro-groups and establishing direct relations.

The evidence collected here suggests that firms do not make an either/or choice between direct contact and using an intermediary. The data indicate that firms utilise more than one route to channel their views to the EU. The various conduits can be used to supplement each other. If a collective organisation such as national trade association or a Euro-group cannot provide the most advantageous connection, then the firms seek alternatives such as direct contact or the national government.

In summary, what does the data reveal about the various theoretical approaches referred to at the outset? There is limited support for neo-functionalist ideas. Domestic actors have transferred some of their expectations, political activities and loyalties to the new regional centre[58] but they have not done so in a way that jeopardises or relinquishes their connections with their national governments. Sensibly they have widened their options, using whichever intermediary or policy-making target seems to be most fruitful. Similarly, there is evidence to support the MLG contention that (sub)national actors have established direct relations with supranational policy-makers, by-passing the national level of governance. Perhaps, the theory that is least well supported by these data is the intergovernmental approach. The data do suggest that EU policy-making is not solely or even predominantly about what member states want: supranational and subnational actors do have a role in policy-making. In the final analysis, there has been some Europeanisation of firms, and Euro-groups do seem to be quite impotent. However, the relationships are dynamic and there is every possibility that they will change further as the EU continues to develop as a polity.

Notes

1 E. Haas, *The Uniting of Europe* (Stanford, CA: Stanford University Press, 1958).
2 A. Moravcsik, *The Choice for Europe* (Ithaca, NY: Cornell University Press, 1998).
3 G. Marks, L. Hooghe, and K. Blank, 'European integration from the 1980s: state v multi-level governance', *Journal of Common Market Studies*, 34: 3 (1996) 341–78.

4 D. Coen, 'The European business interest and the nation state: large firm lobbying in the European Union and member states', *Journal of Public Policy*, 18: 1 (1998), 75–100.

5 M. Cowles, 'The changing architecture of big business', in J. Greenwood and M. Aspinwall, *Collective Action in the European Union* (London: Routledge, 1998), p. 109.

6 S. Mazey and J. J. Richardson (eds), *Lobbying in the European Community*, (Oxford: Oxford University Press, 1993).

7 *Ibid.* p. 8. W. Grant, in Mazey and Richardson (eds), *Lobbying in the European Community*, pp. 30–1. A. McLaughlin, and G. Jordon in Mazey and Richardson (eds), *Lobbying in the European Community*, pp. 131–3. A. McLaughlin, G. Jordan and W. Maloney, 'Corporate lobbying in the European Community', *Journal of Common Market Studies*, 31: 2 (1993), 191–2. J. Greenwood and K. Ronit, 'Interest groups in the European community: newly emerging dynamics and forms', *West European Politics*, 17: 1 (1994), 31. J. Greenwood and L. Cram, 'European level business collective action: the study agenda ahead', *Journal of Common Market Studies*, 34: 3 (1996), 451.

8 *Ibid.*

9 Grant, *Lobbying in the European Community*, pp. 34–5.

10 Greenwood and Cram, 'European level business collective action', p. 451.

11 McLaughlin, Jordon and Maloney, 'Corporate lobbying in the European Community', p. 192.

12 *Ibid.* p. 191.

13 J. Knight, S. Mazey and J. J. Richardson, 'Groups and the process of European integration: the work of the Federation of Stock Exchanges in the European Community', in Mazey and Richardson (eds), *Lobbying in the European Community*, p. 162.

14 Mazey and Richardson (eds), *Lobbying in the European Community*, p. 22.

15 McLaughlin and Jordon, in Mazey and Richardson (eds), *Lobbying in the European Community*, p. 122.

16 *Ibid.*, p. 202.

17 A. McLaughlin and J. Greenwood, 'The management of interest representation in the European Union', *Journal of Common Market Studies*, 33: 1 (1995), 150.

18 McLaughlin, Jordan and Maloney, 'Corporate lobbying in the European Community', p. 191.

19 Mazey and Richardson (eds), *Lobbying in the European Community*, p. 23. McLaughlin, and Jordon in Mazey and Richardson (eds), *Lobbying in the European Community*, p. 122.

20 W. Grant and J. Sargent, *Business and Politics in Britain* (Basingstoke: Macmillan, 1987), p. 94.

21 Greenwood and Ronit, 'Interest groups in the European Community', p. 42.

22 McLaughlin and Jordon in Mazey and Richardson (eds), *Lobbying in the European Community*.

23 *Ibid.*, pp. 123–4.

24 *Ibid.*, 201–4.

25 McLaughlin, Jordon and Maloney, 'Corporate lobbying in the European Community'.

26 *Ibid.*, p. 191.

27 McLaughlin and Jordon in Mazey and Richardson (eds), *Lobbying in the European Community*, p. 132.
28 Greenwood and Ronit, 'Interest groups in the European Community', p. 43.
29 *Ibid.*
30 J. Sargent in Grant and Sargent, *Business and Politics in Britain*.
31 *Ibid.*, pp. 229–32.
32 *Ibid.*, p. 228.
33 Grant in Mazey and Richardson (eds), *Lobbying in the European Community*, p. 29.
34 R. J. Bennett, 'Influence in Brussels: exploring the choice of direct representation', *Political Studies*, 47: 2 (1999) 240–57. R. J. Bennett, 'The impact of European economic integration on business associations: the UK case', *West European Politics*, 20: 3 (1997), 61–90.
35 *Ibid.*, 1997, pp. 66–9.
36 Bennett, 'Influence in Brussels', pp. 241–2.
37 Bennett, 'The impact of European economic integration', pp. 61–90.
38 *Ibid.*, pp. 74–6.
39 Bennett, 'Influence in Brussels', pp. 240–57.
40 *Ibid.*, pp. 254–7.
41 BT, Interview with Author, Brussels, 16 April 1997.
42 European Commission, DG XIII, Interview with Author, Brussels, 17 June 1997.
43 BT, Interview with Author, Brussels, 16 April 1997.
44 European Commission, DG XIII, Interview with Author, Brussels, 18 June 1997.
45 European Commission, DG XIII, Interview with Author, Brussels, 17 June 1997.
46 Eurogas, Interview with Author, Brussels, 21 November 1997.
47 European Commission, DG XVII, Interview with Author, Brussels, 17 April 1997.
48 CEA, Interview with Author, Paris, 31 July 1997.
49 European Commission, DG XV, Interview with Author, Brussels, 17 April 1997.
50 *Ibid.*
51 Royal Insurance, Interview with Author, London, 24 June 1996.
52 ABI, Interview with Author, London, 17 January 1996.
53 ABI, Interview with Author, London, 17 October 1997.
54 *Ibid.*
55 European Commission, DG XVII, Interview with Author, Brussels, 17 April 1997.
56 European Commission, DG XIII, Interview with Author, Brussels, 30 July 1997.
57 *Ibid.*
58 Haas, *Uniting of Europe*, p. 16.

Further reading

Moravcsik, A., *The Choice for Europe* (Ithaca NY: Cornell University Press, 1998).

Part III

The high technology factor

Technology has been increasingly pervasive in every aspect of economic, social and even political life in the developed world since the era of industrialisation, and one might indeed argue, much earlier than this, since humans first started manipulating the crops they grew and the ways in which they grew them. Early on in the twentieth century, the effect was still mainly indirect and affecting predominantly economic performance. Since the Second World War however, and in particular since the 1980s, developments in high technology have gone hand in hand with economic, miltary and political power too, gaining a more visible position in international relations. High technologies occupy whole new industrial sectors; like electronics dominate the electrical, and telecommunications' sectors are enabling manufacturing processes from textiles and heavy machinery manufacturing to chemicals and pharmaceuticals, and from the banking and other service sectors to aeronautics and transport. Since the 1980s competitiveness in high technologies has itself become the object of policy-making because of its crucial part in the economic competitiveness of any one nation or regional group, but globalisation and cross-border ventures and take-overs soon put paid to any attempts at protectionism as a way of securing a competitive advantage. Equally importantly, high technologies have been increasingly underpinning changes in political and social life, increasing the opportunity and immediacy of awareness and participation through advances in communications, the media and the notion of the 'global village', and this same opportunity and awareness has enabled the questioning of some of these very technologies, and thus made them central to varied debates, such as the continuing debates over atomic energy and biotechnologies.

It is such issues which we bring to the fore in Part III, for once as valid topics of debate in themselves, rather than peripheral, alongside more traditional areas of international relations.

In Chapter 13, Hazel Dawe examines the Euratom treaty, in conjunction with political developments in attitudes to nuclear power, and tries to ascertain how these have affected the practical application of the Euratom treaty in the light of two case studies.

The case study on Austria looks at the potential for conflict between Austria's Nuclear Prohibition law and its membership of the European Atomic Community. It examines how the Commission and the Austrian government view the current application of the main purpose of the Euratom Treaty, the speedy development of a strong nuclear industry.

The case study on the French nuclear tests on Mururoa examines the actual operation of the treaty provisions for the health and safety of workers and resident populations. It looks at the attitude of the Commission towards its powers and how they are delineated with member states' own prerogatives.

The conclusion attempts to assess the current state of the efficacy or otherwise of the Treaty in the current political climate.

With continuing globalisation of commerce, and societal moves towards a more information-based economy, the role of advanced telecommunications and information technology networks and services in European competitiveness is becoming increasingly vital. Telecoms is one of the few technological fields in which Europe can be said to outperform Japan and come close to the USA, and this is the field studied in Chapter 14 by Nicola Murrell.

Following the opening-up to free competition of telecoms markets, such as that of fixed access telecom services, at the beginning of 1998, and with further liberalisation still taking place in countries such as Greece as recently as 2001, the European telecom sector is in a state of transition from a strong public monopoly sector to one that is commercially competitive on a global level, and this requires meeting the increasing current and future demands on European infrastructure.

This chapter discusses the need for greater co-ordination of telecom policies across Europe, as attempts are made to harmonise the regulatory environment of telecommunications, in order to allow member states to benefit from a competitive and innovative pan-European market.

Biotechnology represents the most complex set of public policy issues faced by governments since the nuclear revolution. It is also likely to emerge as the premier high-growth sector of modern economies in the twenty-first century.

States in Western Europe have had particular difficulties in attempting to develop and regulate their biotechnology sectors. On the one hand, they have been forced to deal with increasing competition in biotechnology from the United States and Japan. On the other hand, these states have faced strong domestic opposition to biotechnology due to food scares (such as the BSE crisis) and concerns about protecting the cultural heritage of farmers and the environment. The long periods of testing needed – often many years – to determine potential effects on health of genetically modified foods, have not helped alleviate consumer fears which in turn impact on policy-makers in Europe, apparently more than in the United States. These conflicting pressures are also bound up in the goal of creating the single market project of the European Union. As a result, the EU has had to develop new policies and procedures to govern the industry. In Chapter 15, Smith investigates the recent dramatic changes in EU biotechnology policy by first disaggregating the issue-area into problems such as genetically modified foods, property rights and medical/ethical issues (such as drugs and cloning). Each of these issues involves peculiar collective action problems which require common solutions if EU states hope to develop a viable, competitive biotechnology sector. After examining these problems, he then focuses on the relationship between interest groups, institutions and scientific expertise to explain three major puzzles about biotechnology in the EU:

1 why the EU has been moving toward a more 'pro-biotechnology' regulatory posture;
2 how this move has produced conflicts between scientists, the EU bureaucracy in Brussels and industry groups, on the one hand, and local interest groups and national governments, on the other;

3 and the extent to which these conflicts have been resolved so that the EU can
   fully develop its biotechnology sector yet co-operate with non-European
   states in this area.

Part III and the volume itself close with Chapter 16, which in a sense closes
the loop with which we began by looking at governance and policy-making in
the EU and the handling of – and interacting with – prominent contemporary
areas, such as high technology.

Nixon outlines the part played by technological developments in the process
of integration within the EU. He discusses the potential gains that may accrue
from the reshaping of government services to provide 'Information Age
Government'. He sketches out some of the obstacles to be overcome and
assesses future implications for such a form of governance within the EU.

The chapter seeks to stimulate the further debate needed to evaluate if the
level of co-operation required for such a form of governance exists and the
extent to which such a system of governance is actually desirable or achievable
in the context of the EU of 15 member states, let alone an expanded EU, which
wants to respond flexibly and cohesively, but also with increased participation
and engagement of its citizens, to the challenges of the future.

13

Euratom:
the toothless treaty?

Hazel Dawe

This chapter examines the genesis of the Euratom Treaty, its subsequent development and its efficacy or otherwise in the current political climate. In order to do so it traces the evolution of nuclear energy from its origins in the nuclear weapons programme of the Second World War through the US Atoms for Peace project to the establishment of the European Atomic Energy Community. After establishing the contents of the Euratom Treaty, it then goes on to look at the operation of the Euratom Treaty through two case studies: Austrian membership of Euratom and its relationship to Austria's Nuclear Prohibition Law and the operation of the Euratom monitoring powers on the French nuclear weapons tests at the pacific atolls of Mururoa and Fangataufa.

The political situation at the time the Euratom Treaty was written

Two forces shaped the structure of the European Atomic Energy Community:

(1) The political attitude towards nuclear power: the aftershock of the bombs on Hiroshima and Nagasaki and the wish to develop a peaceful role for nuclear energy to redeem its violent birth pangs.
(2) The political movement towards an integrated Europe around a Franco/German core.

Both of these will be examined in detail.

Attitudes towards nuclear power

Nuclear power has its genesis in the nuclear bombs dropped on Hiroshima and Nagasaki in the Second World War. The nuclear piles made to create fissile materials for bomb making also produced excess heat. Originally an embarrassment, this heat was later used to generate electricity through the medium of steam-driven turbines.[1] The nuclear piles were renamed nuclear reactors. The civilian nuclear industry was a necessary adjunct of the military nuclear

weapons industry. The civilian industry provided some of the materials necessary to bomb making. It also provided a ready-made pool of specialists who
could be enlisted in large numbers at short notice to any military programme.
After the war, the military nuclear programme was scaled down and work
resumed on the civilian nuclear energy project. Great hopes were placed in
nuclear energy. 'The first steps toward the civil use of the energy released by
uranium fission were taken in a world completely disorganised by five years of
war.'[2] The attitude towards nuclear power at this time was such that the term
'Euphoria' is often used to describe the period.[3]

   After the war, partly at the prompting of the Acherson–Lillienthal report on
nuclear proliferation, the US had a declared policy of secrecy in the name of the
prevention of proliferation.[4] Although a report, the Smyth report, on the scientific development of the US nuclear programme was issued, it kept certain
scientific data secret – and stressed that what was not included in the report
would remain secret. A general atmosphere of secrecy pervaded the nuclear
project. Information was concealed. The true effects of the Hiroshima and
Nagasaki bombs were kept secret for some time afterwards. A book of their experiences written by Japanese bomb survivors published in Japan in 1950 was
suppressed and only rediscovered in April 1981.[5] Extensive film shot by US crews
of the disaster was kept in military archives and was not made available to the
public until 1980.[6] During the making of the bomb at Alamo, one of the scientists
working on the project, Harry Dahlian, was exposed to excessive radiation and
died painfully over a period of 24 days of radiation sickness. Project workers who
knew of the accident and its results were instructed not to talk of it.[7]

   This culture of secrecy permeates the nuclear industry till this day. So much
so that even pro-nuclear scientists will now admit to excessive secrecy: '[Nuclear
fusion research] has been undoubtedly assisted by the wholly free international
interchange of information … in sharp contrast to the "commercial secrecy"
with which fission energy was initially shrouded.'[8] Politically, the US government, the keeper of the atom, was concerned that atomic energy should be
publicly accepted. Part of that strategy was to keep any knowledge which might
be alarmist from the general population. Thus the US-run Atomic Bomb
Casualty Commission in Hiroshima attempted to discredit the evidence of a
local medical doctor that people exposed to the bomb suffered disproportionately from leukaemia.[9] Similarly, after the first major nuclear reactor accident at
Chalk River, Canada problems arose because the medical systems were not in
place to deal with accidents of this severity. 'The accident was shrouded in
secrecy in the United States, Canada and Britain for the sake of national security.'[10] The authorities were afraid that knowledge of the problems caused in
nuclear accidents would lower the acceptability of nuclear energy to the population. The secrecy was such that, when an accident occurred 29 years later at
Three Mile Island near Harrisburg in the US, the necessary medical information
had not been passed on to the medical personal who would have to deal with the
new emergency. '[T]here has been the tendency to keep silent about possible

nuclear risks in case, through exaggeration and lack of perspective, these might unduly alarm the public.'[11] This despite evidence that secrecy of this magnitude is ineffective. It simply creates counterbalances. The successful completion by the USSR of a nuclear programme in a short four years – with a little help from US spies – 'was a striking demonstration of the ineffectiveness of the policy of atomic secrecy'.[12]

Eisenhower launched his 'Atoms for peace' initiative in 1953 in an address to the UN.[13] This was designed to propagate the usefulness of nuclear power and to make it politically acceptable to the general public, whose primary impression of nuclear science at this stage would have been of the two bombs which were dropped on Japan. Cynics might also claim that it was a result of the shock caused by the first successful detonation of a Soviet thermonuclear bomb. The first Soviet bomb was detonated in August 1949,[14] the first British bomb on 3 October 1952.[15] The Atoms for Peace project included US dissemination of atomic scientific information; the gradual withdrawal of fissile materials from military programmes to place them into a 'materials bank', which would only be used for peaceful purposes; and eventually the founding of the International Atomic Energy Agency to administer the peaceful use of this fissile material. The Atoms for Peace project included a series of conferences in Geneva[16] and the publication of pro-nuclear material.[17] Nuclear power was seen as the new clean cheap energy which would help rebuild the devastated economies of Western Europe. 'The future trend ... will undoubtedly be for cheaper and cheaper electricity from nuclear power and more and more expensive coal and probably also oil.'[18] 'If this is a new industry, its cleanness, its silence and sheer beauty are all a great advantage on anything we have known before.'[19] Nuclear energy was seen as providing a plentiful bounty of cheap energy. It would be the answer to all the economic problems of the war-torn economies of post-Second World War Europe. 'It is a fact that nuclear produced electricity is the only new energy source that can be expected to make a major contribution to world consumption between now and the beginning of the next century.'[20] 'Yet again, life has made a great discovery, this time nuclear energy, which can open access to an entirely different energy source.'[21] 'What is not in doubt is that nuclear power is a major long term option.'[22]

At the instigation of the US, Britain, Canada and the USSRT, the Atomic Energy Commission of the UN was established in 1946. In 1956 it was disbanded and replaced with the International Atomic Energy Agency (IAEA). The principle objective of the IAEA as stated in its statute is 'to accelerate and enlarge the contribution of atomic energy to peace, health and prosperity throughout the world'.

The politics of European integration

Politically the post-Second World War situation was a time of renewal. Western Europe breathed a collective sigh of relief and set about making sure it could never happen again *'Nie wieder'*. Our basic International and European Human Rights instruments have their origins in this time, with its very special political and social atmosphere. The UN Declaration of Human Rights was adopted by the UN General Assembly in 1948; the European Convention on Human Rights was passed in the Council of Europe in 1950. Many lawyers believe that such legislation was only possible in the political climate of the day, with the impression of the horrors of the Second World War still fresh. It has become successively difficult to get international agreement under rights instruments. For example, the US has refused to sign the 1991 UN Convention on the Rights of the Child. They have genuine objections to parts of the Convention, but this demonstrates that it has become more likely that some countries will not sign up to international rights instruments and more internationally acceptable for them to do so.

Alongside the philosophical and societal renewal of the UN and the Council of Europe negotiating rights instruments came the vital economic renewal. 'The first steps to create the EC were taken against a background of vigorous growth in the capitalist world.'[23] That growth could only take place because industrial growth was promoted by national governments and was seen as a priority by the US, which supported it substantially by means of the Marshall Aid programme. Industrial growth at this pace needed a cheap and plentiful energy supply. Nuclear power was seen as the perfect answer to this need. For Europe to grow and prosper, nuclear power needed to be put on a European footing.

The idea of a United States of Europe predates the First World War. It was used as the title of a peace journal as long ago as 1867.[24] However, it resurfaced both in the inter-war period and in the later stages of the Second World War amongst the idealists of the resistance movement. The resistance movements, with a lead from Italy, actually formed a statement suggesting a federated Europe. A conference in Geneva, organised by the Italien Movimento Federalista Europeo (European Federalist Movement) argued for a 'federal Europe with a written constitution, a supranational government ... with an army under its control with no other military forces being permitted'.[25] However, their absolutist vision of a highly integrated, united Europe, never stood a chance, especially once the exiled political leaders of the political parties started returning to their countries. The first vision of a united post-war Europe was based on an Anglo-French core and was suggested by Churchill in the 1940s. However, he himself later admitted that this had been merely a strategic gambit to bolster French opposition to Nazi Germany.[26] Later the core of European union was to become a Franco-German one, not Churchill's Anglo-French vision.

Rather than political union, it was economic and social rebuilding which topped the agenda. In accordance with this priority, the first actual Europe-wide co-operative effort was the Organisation for European Economic Co-operation (OEEC), which was established to administer Marshall Aid to the ruined economies of Western Europe. The OEEC was governed by the Council of

Ministers. Decisions all had to be unanimous, which led to a somewhat cumbersome decision-making process, but also meant that members were bound by decisions. Its very limited remit meant that it was necessarily of limited duration as an institution, also unanimous decision-making meant that easier issues were dealt with and difficult decisions tended not to be made at all. That was one of the reasons for the founding of the European Coal and Steel Community (ECSC). However, the experience of the OEEC did lead to the countries of Europe becoming accustomed to working together at the intergovernmental level and showed them, by experience, many of the pitfalls they would need to avoid in setting up a more permanent Europe-wide organisation. The OEEC did not entirely disappear; instead it mutated into the Organisation for Economic Cooperation and Development, expanding both its remit and its membership.

The first European Community was the European Coal and Steel Community, showing clearly what the priorities for economic regeneration were. Coal was, at the time, seen as the primary source of energy for Europe, steel had to be completely reorganised from national structures, which had been geared to the needs of the military in war time. However, coal and steel could not be viewed in isolation from the industrial economies of which they were a part. 'The sector by sector approach of the ECSC had proved too problematic. In the end the ECSC was still trying to integrate only one part of complex industrial economies, and could not possibly pursue its aims in isolation from other economic segments.'[27] The attempt was made to expand the ECSC concept to embrace a wider union. The original goal was an energy union of which, however, only nuclear remained by the time concrete negotiations began in Rome.

An instruction from a conference of the ECSC countries in Messina in 1955 initiated the negotiations which led to the Treaties of Rome. This included the instruction that one of the aims of European integration should be the 'peaceful joint development of atomic energy'.[28] The Treaties of Rome founded the European Economic Community and the European Atomic Community. It is the former which attracts far more interest than the latter. This is probably partly because it has been more successful and partly because it is more all embracing. The founders of both communities always saw economic integration as merely the start of true political union *viz.* 'an ever closer union of the peoples of Europe' in the preamble of the EEC Treaty. Continuing the sectoral approach, which had been so problematic for the ECSC, was bound to cause difficulties. Also, Euratom was plagued by diverging national interests from the start. The two treaties were negotiated in parallel, with compromise on the one by any nation being 'rewarded' with concessions on the other treaty. This shaped the negotiations. Germany saw Euratom as an attempt by the French to get Western Europe to subsidise its atomic research programme and the French were wary of having their industry swamped by German exports. 'Of central importance was the counterbalance of French enthusiasm for an atomic community with Germany's preference for an enlarged economic zone.'[29] The horse trading which followed led to the establishment of both communities and was to become a model for future EC dealings.[30]

The Atomic Community is something of a Cinderella in this story: the disreputable sister who is hidden from view. The Economic Community became the star of the show, the most prominent and best known, the Coal and Steel Community is about to leave the stage when it expires in 2002. The Atomic Community has led a shadowy existence in the wings of the theatre. Most of the legal literature on the Communities simply mentions that it was negotiated in Rome at the same time as the Economic Community and then quietly forgets its existence. Even the EU's own website omits the Euratom treaty from the consolidated Treaties.

'Perhaps surprisingly, given the subsequent history of the Community, during this period greater attention was given to creating an atomic community ... rather than an economic common market.'[31] At least one motivation for the creation of a European Atomic Energy Community was the increasing frustration with the excessive US secrecy surrounding their nuclear programme. To the extent that other countries were shut out from nuclear scientific development, Belgium was the victim of a broken US promise to give information in exchange for the uranium from the Belgian Congo. The Belgians were left with a contractual obligation to supply uranium, but with the only information forthcoming from the US being no different from that supplied to all customers of the US nuclear industry.[32] However, the US too had an interest in the realisation of the Euratom concept. 'The United States ... business interests were keen to export the products of their own nuclear industry, but the government was concerned to prevent the spread of nuclear weapons.'[33] The US saw the Euratom agreement as a means to achieve both these aims. 'By ... 1967, the EEC argument for the unrestricted import of cheap energy, and the Euratom argument for the long-term development of atomic energy, were the two dominant elements in Community thinking on energy-supply.'[34]

The conflicting positions of the major political players at the negotiations establishing Euratom were as follows: The US saw Euratom as a convenient customer for its own nuclear plant and materials. At the same time, it felt that Euratom could be used to prevent the development of European atomic weapons. Jean Monnet was president of the High Authority of the ECSC and is credited with being one of the major architects of European integration. Monnet hoped that Euratom would help supply cheap energy. His vision was of an Atomic Community that would be *dirigiste* in nature: very much engaged in central planning and coordination. He believed that this would, of necessity, create functional spill over which would in turn automatically advance integration. He also presumed that it would prevent French development of a nuclear bomb. The French Assembly, in contrast, thought that Euratom would guarantee subsidy for civil atomic research from West Germany and cheap access to other states nuclear know how, whilst allowing France to devote more resources to military atomic research, which would be outside supranational control. The Assembly also hoped for access to high-quality uranium from Belgian Congo.

The German position too was split. The main protagonist here was Franz Joseph Strauss who was the head of the German negotiating team. He tended to back nuclear energy because the resurgent industries of Bavaria needed the cheap energy it could provide. Adenauer was reluctant because of the threat to the German coalfields, but US pressure and his own integrationist sympathies led him to refrain from blocking German participation. This US support was vital.

These competing political agendas shaped the final form of the treaty as compromises were reached. The French did not get exclusive European supply; the opportunity to buy fuel on international markets was included. Therefore Germany could buy from the US. This suited the Germans and the US. The French also did not get joint construction of a European enrichment plant or reprocessing plant. On the plus side for the French, they did manage to achieve a national interest defence for not sharing certain information. In other words, the Assembly was able to develop a French weapons programme: their cherished *force de frappé*. They achieved the desired financial support for their research programme which, at that time, was two-thirds of the total of all nuclear research amongst member states.[35] The next section summarises the final result of these negotiations, the actual contents of the Euratom Treaty.

Contents of the Euratom Treaty

The preamble of the Euratom Treaty claims that the contracting parties are 'resolved to create the conditions necessary for the development of a powerful nuclear industry'. Article 1 defines the task of the Atomic Community as being to create 'the conditions necessary for the speedy establishment and growth of nuclear industries'. The case will be put that this is one treaty aim which has not been fulfilled and, indeed, is no longer pursued. Article 2 summarises the means by which the Community was expected to fulfil that task. The Treaty covers: the promotion of research; the establishment of safety standards to protect the health and safety of workers and the general population; and control of the supply of nuclear fuel, both to ensure regular supply and to prevent it being used for weapons manufacture. Euratom's main remaining duties at the present time appear to be health and safety regulation and the control of fuel. The latter has been made more difficult by the increase in fuel available from Eastern European countries. Instead of ensuring supply in a scarcity situation, Euratom now sees itself involved in policing an oversupply. The case has been made by environmentalist NGOs that Euratom should legitimately confine its remit to health and safety issues and formally end its commitment to the development of a strong nuclear industry.

Changes in the political climate on nuclear power because of problems

The seeds of failure were sown at the time of concluding the Euratom treaty. 'As a viable and functioning "European atomic industry", which would further integration within Western Europe, Euratom was still born.'[36] An inauspicious start included losing its first president to illness and its second president finding that the strength of national interests precluded him from taking a strong supranational lead in the issues. Euratom took a long time to even start work. Developments since then have led to an increasingly cool political climate for nuclear power.

In the UK a major factor leading to public sensitisation to the issue of nuclear safety was a series of accidents at the Windscale reactor in Cumbria. The first accident, which actually caused the escape of radioactivity, occurred in October 1957 when fuel rods caught fire and, after two days, had to be doused with water. The accident appears to have been caused by inadequate monitoring of the reactor pile, which meant that the physicist in charge had insufficient information on which to base any counter measures. The Windscale management was also heavily criticised for not keeping the public properly informed of any necessary precautions. This is yet another example of the continuing culture of secrecy which has dogged the nuclear industry to this day. Because of the accident, the local population discovered for the first time that the reactor had been in danger the previous May, with no information being disseminated to the local population. Inquiries and reports after the October accident exposed serious weakness in the operating safety of UK nuclear reactors, including lack of technical support for the operating staff and a lack of understanding amongst operating staff of the technical processes they were involved in running.[37] Public confidence in the nuclear industry in the UK was on the ebb.

The first major nuclear accident was at Three Mile Island near Harrisburg in the US in 1979. It involved the loss of substantial amounts of contaminated water from a pressurised water reactor. The psychological shock waves were profound. As well as giving a boost to the US anti-nuclear movement, the Three Mile Island accident may well have influenced the Swedish referendum in 1980, which led to the vote to shut down the Swedish nuclear programme over 25 years.

It is perhaps not surprising that it was the Swedish nuclear monitoring system which first detected the fallout from the Chernobyl nuclear disaster in 1986: a disaster of such magnitude that it had consequences, not just for the Ukraine, but for most of Western Europe. Welsh hill farmers were subject to controls and monitoring of their (radioactive) sheep; Austrian dairy farmers lost 100s of tons of milk which were classified as low-level radioactive waste. Health warnings were issued in some countries. In one Austrian province pregnant women and children were warned to stay indoors. All Austrian parents were warned not to let their children play in sandpits. In Sweden it led to an increase in the tempo of the shut down of the Swedish nuclear power programme.[38] The Chernobyl accident was the first intensive experience of European governments with trying to regulate radiation exposure for a general population, especially exposure through foodstuffs. The fact that the accident impacted on the daily life of the majority of Europeans had an immense psychological effect. This extended to the political scene. The most obvious political result was the conference in Vienna, held by the International Atomic Energy Agency later that same year, which adopted international conventions on early warning of incidents to neighbouring countries and cross-border assistance in the case of such incidents – an understandable reaction in crowded Central Europe, home to some of the arguably most dangerous reactors in the world.[39]

After these setbacks for the nuclear industry, a new pro-nuclear argumentation has been deployed. The main argument now used in favour of nuclear power is that it will help reduce carbon emissions and thereby help to combat the greenhouse effect, which is currently leading to global warming.

Practical applications of Euratom: two case studies

The two case studies here illustrate different aspects of the Euratom regulatory regime. The Austrian case study shows the attitude of the European Commission to the application of the Treaty to member states. The Mururoa case study examines the efficiency of Euratom concerning the monitoring of health and safety issues.

Austria: Austria's Nuclear Prohibition law and its membership of Euratom
In 1978, Austria held a referendum on nuclear power. It was the first referendum in Austria since the ill-fated referendum on the *Anschluß* in 1938. [40] The Austrian government had built a nuclear power plant at Zwentendorf, 40km North West of Vienna, which had seemed politically consensual at the time. However, opposition to nuclear power in Austria had been growing.[41] It was in part fuelled by the vehemence and the success of the German anti-nuclear movement. Zwentendorf had become a politically extremely contentious issue. Rather than bear sole responsibility for commissioning an unpopular nuclear power plant, the government first tried to obtain all-party backing through a public inquiry. This went badly wrong and, in 1978, the government finally called a referendum. As a result the referendum was held on 5 November 1978. The actual question posed was whether or not Zwentendorf nuclear power station should be commissioned. The wording on the ballot papers was 'should the law passed by Parliament on the 7 July 1978 pertaining to the peaceful use of nuclear power in Austria (commissioning of Zwentendorf nuclear power station) be implemented?'[42]

The 1978 referendum on nuclear power was decided by a very narrow margin on, what was by Austrian standards, a relatively low turnout of 64.1 per cent. The end result was 50.47 per cent against nuclear power and 49.53 per cent in favour.[43]

As a result the Austrian Nuclear Prohibition Law 1978 was passed. The law was limited in scope, forbidding only the building of nuclear fission reactors on Austrian territory and their use for the purposes of energy generation. The full text of the Law is as follows:

Federal Law No. 676 of 15th December 1978 on the prohibition of the use of nuclear fission for the supply of energy in Austria

The Parliament has decided:

1 Installations which use nuclear fission for the purpose of electricity generation for the supply of power may not be built in Austria. In so far as such installations already exist, they may not be commissioned.
2 The Federal Government is responsible for the operation of this law.

This law did not prohibit the use of the two University research reactors in Vienna and Graz and the government nuclear research establishment in Seibersdorf. Seibersdorf is also the country's only depository for radioactive waste and is only licensed to take low- and medium-level radioactive waste until 2012.[44] The waste stored is mainly from hospitals, but also from the two research reactors. In fact, the law was so narrowly drafted that, when Austria later signed the Euratom Treaty, anti-nuclear groups were dismayed to find that it allowed any nuclear activity other than commercial generation using nuclear fission. This leaves a wide spectrum of nuclear activity which is permissible under the Nuclear Prohibition Law, for example research of all types, fusion (should it ever become a practical proposition) and the transport of nuclear waste. Current EU research programmes include research into radiation protection and reactor safety but also fusion research (Third Framework Programme 1990–94).[45]

After passing the Nuclear Prohibition Law, subsequent Austrian Governments developed an Austrian identity as a 'nuclear free zone' within central Europe.[46] Dr Heinz Holzinger, nuclear spokesperson, Greenpeace Austria describes the genesis of this policy as follows: 'It was actually agreed in the coalition agreement throughout two terms of office that Austria would press for a nuclear free central Europe. It was the pet project of Chancellor Vranitzky and was a further development from "Austria won't commission Zwentendorf" to "We don't want neighbouring countries to turn on their nuclear reactors".'[47]

One possible reason that the Austrian government is keen to have a strong anti-nuclear policy may be a reflection of the fact that some of the most dangerous nuclear power stations in the world are close to the Austrian border: Mochovce, Bohunice in Slovakia, Temelin in the Czech Republic, Klodusy in Rumania, etc. They are now subject to EU intervention to try and make them safer under the PHARE and TACIS programmes.[48] These nuclear reactors are perceived as a threat by the Austrian people.

In support of this policy, Vranitzky went so far as to finance an anti-nuclear lobbying organisation 'Anti-Atom International' under the auspices of the Minister for the Environment, Maria Rauch-Kallat.[49] This meant that this weakly drafted law, which was the result of a narrowly won referendum, attained a political importance out of all proportion to its uncertain genesis.

Environmental groups asked the Austrian government during the membership negotiations how they could sign up to the Euratom Treaty given their anti-nuclear policy. The Austrian government asserted that, 'An explicit exemption from Euratom treaty provisions which are related to promotion would seem to be unnecessary' because 'according to the latest statements of the EU Commission article 1 of the Euratom Treaty is de facto no longer operable'. Article 1 refers to the 'speedy establishment of strong nuclear industries'. The government also referred to the fact that when the Euratom Treaty was concluded, nuclear power was still seen as a positive vision of the future. As proof that this has changed, they cited the fact that six of the 12 member states (at that time) had consciously rejected nuclear power:

> Of the current 12 Member States of the European Community, only two (France and the United Kingdom) continue to follow a policy of expansion in nuclear power, a further four states (Belgium, Netherlands, Spain and Germany) have stopped building nuclear reactors and six states (Denmark, Greece, Ireland, Luxembourg, Portugal and Italy) have no nuclear reactors.[50]

Both the Austrian government and the Commission claimed that Euratom had changed its focus and can now be regarded as defunct as far as its original mission is concerned. The Austrian government repeated the assertion that parts of the Treaty have fallen into disuse in a policy statement, in June 1993:

> Austria welcomes the opinion of the Commission of the European Community as expressed in the 'exploratory talks' that the interpretation of the EURATOM Treaty has changed in the light of socio-political and economic policy developments, and therefore parts of the original goals are no longer pursued by the Community.[51]

This assurance from the Commission that parts of the Euratom Treaty are no longer operable led to the annexation of a declaration to the Austrian Accession Treaty making this explicit. This again reveals the current attitude towards what was supposedly the original aim of Euratom to promote a strong nuclear industry. The wording of the Joint Declaration is as follows:

> The Contracting Parties, recalling that the Treaties on which the European Union is founded apply to all Member States on a non-discriminatory basis and without prejudice to the rules governing the internal market, acknowledge that, as Contracting Parties to the Treaty establishing the European Atomic Energy Community, Member States decide to produce or not to produce nuclear energy according to their specific policy orientation.

A study commissioned by the anti-nuclear group PLAGE (Überparteiliche Plattform gegen Atomgefahren) looked at the relationship between the Nuclear Prohibition Law and the Joint Declaration on the application of the Euratom Treaty which is appendixed to the Final Act on accession to the European Union by Austria, Finland, Sweden and Norway. According to the Austrian government the Joint Declaration clarifies that 'the legal prohibition against constructing or operating nuclear power plants resulting from the 1978 referendum w[ill] not be altered after joining the European Union'.[52] According to the accompanying documentation, this Joint Declaration, although signed by all four applicant countries, was made at the request of Austria during the pre-accession negotiations.[53] It is also the opinion of a senior member of the Federal Environment Agency that, legally, there would seem to be no contradiction between the Treaty and the Nuclear Prohibition Law. The Austrian constitutional department within the Federal Chancellery (*Völkerrechtsbüro*) has also decided that the two legal instruments are compatible.[54] 'Austria will still retain [the Nuclear Prohibition Law] upon accession to the European Union'[55] 'The Nuclear Prohibition Law (BGBl No. 676/1978) is compatible with membership of the European Atomic Community.'[56] This is partly because the law is drafted to cover only a very narrow range of nuclear activity and partly because the Euratom Treaty, whilst having aims which appear to be incompatible with the spirit of the Nuclear Prohibition Law, seems to have fallen into disuse. It has been drafted as a passive empowering Treaty, not a Treaty which actually creates a positive obligation to act. This is not surprising given its genesis as a compromise of conflicting political positions.

The strict legal interpretation remains that, whilst the Austrian Nuclear Prohibition Law forbids the commercial generation of energy using nuclear power plants on Austrian territory, the Euratom Treaty does not in fact force Austria to do just that. However, the argument follows that the Euratom Treaty, with its provisions for the advancement and promotion of nuclear power, is in fact opposed to the spirit of the Nuclear Prohibition Law.

'Euratom has engaged in and continues to undertake a number of useful activities, such as the co-ordination of research and the provision of inspection services. But, in terms of the larger mission for which it was created, there has been little evidence of fulfilment.'[57] Euratom was originally founded in order to develop a 'powerful nuclear industry'.[58] At the time this was seen as feasible and desirable. 'The goal proposed was the achievement of 15 million kilowatt of nuclear electric power over the next 10 years; the investment cost was estimated at US$6,000 million.'[59] In the meantime, the focus of activity within the European Atomic Community would seem to have shifted substantially. Promotion of the nuclear industry, which was to have been the primary focus of Euratom, has been silently abandoned, although no one has been able to amend the Treaty to take account of this. Austria has attempted unsuccessfully to do so; Germany refused to do so at the instruction of the *Land* of Saar, as the Federal government judged that there was no chance of success. The Atomic Community, after an inauspicious start, seems to have retreated even further and is now, according to the Commission itself, no longer operative in its main aims. Further the Declaration states explicitly that each EU member state is free to generate nuclear power or not as it so chooses. The question therefore arises, why have a European Community Agency responsible for Union-wide co-ordination when each member state is acting independently anyway?

Applicability of Euratom to nation states' activities as illustrated by Commission replies regarding French nuclear testing in Mururoa

The Mururoa case study illustrates the attitude of the Commission to its powers to monitor health and safety surrounding nuclear tests in member states. On 13 June 1995, the French President, Jacques Chirac, announced that France would be testing nuclear weapons in the Pacific. As the tests could affect nearby islands, which were British territory, the provisions of the Euratom Treaty applied.[60] This was an issue of the health and safety of the resident population, and, as such, Euratom should have been responsible for ensuring that adequate safety standards were enforced. Article 2(b) of the Euratom Treaty states that the Community shall: 'Establish uniform safety standards to protect the health of workers and of the general public and ensure that they are applied.'

Before the Commission could become involved several questions concerning their competence in the matter had to be cleared up. Firstly both France and the commission agreed that the provisions of the Treaty under Article 35, regarding the powers of the Commission to inspect member states monitoring arrangements, did apply to both military and civil matters.[61] It also had to be established whether the tests were a 'particularly dangerous experiment'. Here Jacques Santer, president of the European Commission, admitted that any explosion of a nuclear device had the potential to be a 'particularly dangerous experiment' in the sense of Article 34, although his language is diplomatically softened with a prevalence of verbs in the conditional tense: 'The Commission is of the opinion that, on occasion, an experiment involving the explosion of a nuclear device could create a risk of the type I have just described, and that it could therefore, in certain circumstances, be considered to be particularly dangerous.'

The statements to the parliament by Santer, showed an interesting picture of the relative power and powerlessness of the European Union when faced with real conflicts between member states. In his declaration to the Commission for Foreign Affairs on 6 September 1995, he made clear the limitations of the Euratom Treaty. 'This is not a right of direct control, but a "control of the controls" carried out by Member States in the specialised installations, which they are obliged to establish, and to which access by the Commission must be assured.'

Article 35 obliges member states in whose territory particularly dangerous experiments are taking place to monitor the radioactivity in air, water and soil. It gives the Commission the right to test the operation and efficacy of the monitoring equipment. Hence with Santer's assertion that it is a 'control of controls', Santer also delineated the competence of the Commission with regard to policy matters of member states concerning nuclear weapons tests:

> I would like to emphasise that the commission has no competence whatsoever to give an opinion on the political or military advisability of this decision of the French Government. It goes without saying that the Commission, as guardian of the treaty, does not give opinions on questions which are the sole prerogative of member states.

Santer made it quite clear that when he spoke of 'control of controls', he meant that the Commission remit was a severely limited one. It could only check that the member state was monitoring radioactivity competently, but could not stop a member state from continuing with any nuclear tests. This is a very narrow interpretation of the Commissions remit under these Treaty provisions. A more proactive Commission president could have interpreted the Commissions remit for the health and safety of workers and the general population as at least including a power to warn when the agreed limits had been exceeded. To do this Santer could have used the second paragraph of Article 34, which provides that the permission of the Commission is needed for 'particularly dangerous experiments' where these affect the territory of other member states. In the case of Mururoa, the effects were acknowledged to extend to nearby islands, which were part of UK territory. Alternatively, Santer could have used the provisions of Articles 30 and 31, which establish basic standards of levels of permissible radioactivity for the EU member states. However, he decided that the Commission would take a more passive role. 'I would like to avoid any misunderstanding at this point. It is not within the competence/remit of the Commission to give a "green light" or a "red light" to a nuclear test. But the commission does have a remit for protective measures for the population and workers against radiation.'

Article 34 seems to be something of a blunt instrument – no action can be taken by the Commission until they are certain that the experiment in question is a 'particularly dangerous experiment'. Although the Environment Commissioner, Mrs Ritt Bjerregaard was ready and willing to send a delegation to Mururoa to check the monitoring equipment, France was able to postpone their arrival and then not allow them access to all the information they required.[62] Eventually, Santer decided that, although he had previously stated that the tests at Mururoa had the potential to be particularly dangerous experiments within the meaning of Article 34, they had not, in fact, reached the threshold required.[63] He therefore refused to take any further action.

If the Commission is limited to an information-gathering role and refuses to actually intervene in any way in what it considers to be a member states prerogative, the question arises as to what use this is to the affected populations. If all the Commission can do is to ask for information and for access for their own scientists to gather information, and that after the event, this is not very helpful to a population which has already been exposed to the radiation caused by the experiments in question. If the radiation levels are dangerous, then the population and the workers have already been exposed before the Commission is in a position to take any action.

Conclusion

International law is a surprisingly fragile creature. Sovereign nation states freely enter into agreements, which they are equally free to leave. There is very little by way of enforcement at all and therefore states tend to be bound by international instruments only as far as it suits their political agenda to be so bound. European Community law or European Union law is a rather more robust animal. As an interlocking network of legal instruments, which permeates the national legal systems of the member states to a high degree and which creates and maintains a complex network of interdependencies, it is harder for a single nation state to escape the consequences of a breach of European law.

However, this study has hopefully shown that European law too is subject to the exigencies of the political system. Law and politics interact in sometimes surprising ways. The validity of laws is subject to the extent to which the political system will allow them to function. If the political climate is adversarial to a certain legal instrument, it will be difficult for that legal instrument to unfold its full potential. The Euratom Treaty, drafted and ratified at a time when nuclear power was perceived as clean, cheap and the best way to fuel the rapidly expanding post-war economies of Western Europe, would appear to have fallen out of favour. The Commission itself – the servant of the treaties – has declared to Austria that Article 1 of the Treaty, its main aim of a strong and powerful nuclear industry, is no longer actively pursued. Is it not therefore time to fully recognise this fact and redraft the Treaty along the lines suggested by environmental organisations and to make it a more efficient guardian of health and safety.

Notes

1 Terence Price, *Political Electricity: What Future for Nuclear Energy?* (Oxford: Oxford University Press, 1990).
2 Betrand Goldschmidt, *The Atomic Complex: A Worldwide Political History of Nuclear Energy* (Illinois: American Nuclear Society, 1982) (French edn, 1980).
3 For example as a chapter heading in Tony Hall, *Nuclear Politics; The history of Nuclear Power in Britain* (Harmondsworth: Penguin books, 1986) and in Goldschmidt, *The Atomic Complex*.
4 Goldschmidt, *The Atomic Complex*, pp. 69–76.
5 Kenzaburô Ôe, *Hiroshima Notes*, translated by Toshi Yonezawa, ed. David L. Swain (Tokyo: YMCA Press, 1981).
6 Rosalie Bertell, *No Immediate Danger: Prognosis for a Radioactive Earth* (London: The Women's Press, 1985) p. 138.
7 *Ibid.*, p. 138.
8 Price, *Political Electricity*, p. 338.
9 Bertell, *No Immediate Danger*, p. 143.
10 *Ibid.*, p. 171.
11 Alan Cotrell, *How Safe is Nuclear Energy?* (London: Heinemann Educational Books Ltd., 1981) p. 4.
12 Betrand Goldschmidt, *The Atomic Complex*, 1980, p. 91.
13 Bertell, *No Immediate Danger*, p. 168.
14 Bertrand Goldschmidt, *The Atomic Complex*, p. 88.
15 Hall, *Nuclear Politics*, p. 13.
16 Price, *Political Electricity*, p. 95.

                                                                           Hazel Dawe

17 Mary S. Goldring, *Economics of Atomic Energy*, (London: Butterworths Scientific Publications, 1957).

18 Derek Wragge Morley, Foreword in Goldring, *Economics of Atomic Energy*.

19 Goldring, *Economics of Atomic Energy*, p. 3.

20 Goldschmidt, *The Atomic Complex*, p. xii.

21 Cottrell, *How Safe is Nuclear Energy?*, p. 114.

22 Price, *Political Electricity*, p. 45.

23 Stephen George, *Politics and Policy in the European Community*, 2nd edn (Oxford: Oxford University Press, 1991), p. 35.

24 Derek W. Urwin, *The Community of Europe: A History of European Integration Since 1945* (London and New York: Longman, 1995), p. 3.

25 *Ibid.*, p. 8.

26 *Ibid.*, p. 11.

27 *Ibid.*, p. 76.

28 Martin Holland, *European Integration: From Community to Union* (London: Pinter, 1994), p. 30.

29 *Ibid.*, p. 29.

30 George, *Politics and Policy*, p. 4.

31 Holland, *European Integration*, p. 30.

32 Goldschmidt, *The Atomic Complex*, pp. 285–6, 292.

33 George, *Politics and Policy*, p. 119.

34 *Ibid.*, p. 119.

35 *Ibid.*, pp. 120–1.

36 Christian Deubner, 'The expansion of West German capital and the founding of Euratom', *International Organization*, 33 (1979), 223.

37 Hall, *Nuclear Politics*, pp. 38, 59–65.

38 Price, *Political Electricity*, p. 74.

39 Convention on Early Notification in the Event of a Nuclear Accident and Convention on Assistance in the Case of a Nuclear Accident or Radiological Emergency.

40 Alexander Tollmann, Geologie von Österreich, 3 Bände, 1977–86, 1983, p. 118.

41 In 1973–75 there were anti-Rüthi nuclear power plant marches by ten thousands of demonstrators from Vorarlberg in western Austria; in 1974–75 massive opposition to the planned St Panthaleon nuclear power plant in upper Austria led to the Austrian government postponing construction and later dropping the plant from their energy plan. Lidia Brandstätter, Michael Grosser and Hannes Werthner, 'Die Anti AKW-Bewegung in Österreich', *Umdenken, Analysen grüner Politik in Österreich* [The anti-nuclear power movement in Austria in 'Re-evaluation, an analysis of green politics in Austria], (Vienna: Junius Verlag, 1984). The book is a study of green politics in Austria with well-known and reputable political academics amongst the authors. The three authors of this particular chapter were all active in the anti-nuclear power movement themselves, although they did not belong to the same groups within the movement.

42 Alexander Tollmann, Geologie von Österreich, p. 123.

43 Total no. of votes: 3,183,147 of which 'Yes' votes: 1,576,839 and 'No' votes: 1,606,308 from *Desaster Zwentendorf*, p. 186.

44 'Austria: General Regulatory Regime: Radio active waste management', from Bundesministerium für Gesundheit und Kunst Abteilung III /11, faxed on 14 March 1996, Ministry for Health and the Arts, Dept. III/11.

45 EC Bulletin 9/1990 quoted in Vrije University, *Energy Subsidies in Europe: An Analysis for Greenpeace*, (Amsterdam: Greenpeace International Climate Campaign, May 1997).

46 Interview with Franz Meister, Energy Department, Federal Environmental Agency, 10 April 1996.

47 Interview with Dr Heinz Holzinger, Nuclear spokesperson, Greenpeace Austria, Vienna 10 April 1996.

48 Vrije University, *Energy Subsidies*, p. 12.

49 Antonia Wenisch and Peter Bossew, Atomenergie für die CSFR? Ökologieinstitut (Nuclear Energy for Czechoslovakia? Ecology Institute), Vienna 1992.

50 Austrian Government, I15, p. 2.

51 Policy paper, Austrian Council of State [Ministerrat], 1993, p. 2.

52 Federal Government report.

53 Geistlinger, 1994, p. 4.

54 Interview with Franz Meister, Environment Agency April 1996, and Interview with Andreas Molin, Federal Chancellery April 1996.

55 Policy paper Euratom, unpublished source from the Federal Chancellery 1996.

56 Answers to 200 Questions on the environment, unpublished source, p. 58 (Questions 132 and 133).

57 John G. Turnbull and Jean Beldon Taber, 'Anniversaries and balance sheets', in R. H. Beck *et al.*, *The Changing Structure of Europe* (Minneapolis, MN: University of Minnesota Press, 1970), p. 20.

58 Euratom Treaty (Rome, 1957), preamble.

59 Political and Economic Planning Research Group, *European Organisations* (London: George Allen & Unwin, 1959), p. 320.

60 Article 198 'Save as otherwise provided, this Treaty shall apply to the European territories of Member States and to non-European territories under their jurisdiction', Euratom Treaty.

61 Intervention of the president of the European Commission, Jacques Santer in the European Parliament, Strasbourg, 24 October 1995 and French Secretary of State for Foreign Affairs in a parliamentary debate quoted in Greenpeace briefing 'French Nuclear testing and the Euratom treaty', 4 October 1995.

62 French nuclear tests: Commission published interim report and Mrs Bjerregaard writes to French Minister, Michel Barnier, Brussels, 11 September 1995. Press release, IP/95/955.

63 Michael Bothe, 'Challenging French nuclear tests: A role for legal remedies', *Review of European Community & International Environmental Law*, 5: 3 (1996), 255.

14

Interest groups, institutions and expertise: the new politics of EU biotechnology regulation

Michael E. Smith

The new industrial revolution represented by modern biotechnology poses special difficulties for Western European states in terms of striking a balance between developing and regulating it. On the one hand, these states have been forced to deal with increasing competition in biotechnology from the United States and Japan. On the other hand, they have also faced strong domestic opposition to biotechnology, due to food scares and concerns about protecting the environment and the cultural heritage of their farmers. These demands are also bound up in the vital single market project of the European Union (EU).[1] As a result, the past decade has seen major changes in the EU's approach to biotechnology. After imposing a set of fairly strict regulations involving genetically modified organisms (GMOs) around 1990, the Commission has worked to amend these policies while also crafting new ones more favorable to the industry. The European Parliament (EP), which stridently opposed the patenting of GMOs ten years ago, has moderated its position. Most dramatically, new agencies to help govern this technology have been developed. These changes should have a positive impact on the EU's biotechnology sector, whose firms show a new dynamism. Yet the new approach still takes place in a fairly unfavorable regulatory climate, which has been dominated by the media's fascination with public protests against biotechnology.

These trends – the EU's changing biotechnology regulations in face of conflicting pressures – are the subject of this chapter. I argue that the EU is finding it increasingly necessary to develop a more nuanced regulatory posture toward biotechnology due to a combination of external and internal factors. Externally, the EU is faced with greater competition from the industry leader in biotechnology, the United States (and to a lesser extent, Japan). It has also had to harmonise its regulations across EU member states, while remaining sensitive to the increasingly dense network of international rules governing the industry, which have tended to be less restrictive than its own. Internally, the EU's policy has been influenced by the evolving relationships between its policy-making institutions, the broader expert policy community surrounding biotechnology and the interest groups concerned about the industry. Explaining the relationships between these factors, and their influence on policy outcomes, is the primary task of this chapter.

The argument is presented in four sections. In the first section, I describe the EU's previous approach to biotechnology, stressing the Commission's first directives governing the industry. This provides a benchmark against which we can measure later changes. In the second section, I examine the external pressures facing the EU in this area, both economic and political. In the third section, I focus on how internal forces in the EU have interacted with the external pressures to influence the policy debates. The outcomes of these debates – the EU's new approach to biotechnology – are the subject of the fourth and final section of the chapter.

The EU's early approach to biotechnology

To what extent has the EU's approach to biotechnology changed in the past decade? To answer this question, we must first establish a reference point. This section will attempt to do so by focusing on the EU's regulatory framework in this area. Although regulations comprise only part of the EU's policies governing biotechnology, regulations tend to have a much greater impact on the development of the industry than other EU policies (such as funding for research and development).[2] In general, these regulations involve three issues. The first is environmental protection, which the EU still considers the dominant policy problem for biotechnology. This area involves everything from lab safety to environmental release of GMOs to liability over environmental damage.[3] The second area involves property rights, primarily in terms of patenting or licensing genes, GMOs or other biotech processes or products, which can yield huge profits.[4] The third category involves the safety of genetically modified (GM) food or medical products. The EU has attempted to devise regulations involving all of these categories, and has changed its approach to all of these issues in the past decade. These regulatory issues also impact the single European market, a more fundamental concern of the EU, and they can be used as trade barriers towards non-EU states as well.

Specific ideas concerning the EU's regulatory framework for biotechnology began to coalesce in the late 1980s; these involved: (1) levels of physical and biological containment, accident control and waste management; and (2) authorisation (as opposed to mere notification) of planned release of GMOs into the environment.[5] Although the EU had tended to follow international guidelines during the early stages of biotechnology development, the Commission's first formal regulations in the two areas above were somewhat more restrictive than those at the global level. The Commission's Director General (DG) XI (Environment, Consumer Protection and Nuclear Safety) assumed the leading role here and it took a more restrictive approach, based on the so-called 'precautionary principle', compared with other states. DG XI was primarily composed of ecologists and other environmental experts, who preferred to regulate biotechnology as a general process rather than govern the unique characteristics of its particular products. This approach was opposed by DG III (Information Market and Innovation), DG VI (Agriculture) and DG XII (Science, Research and Development), who preferred a product-oriented approach.

As a result of the dominance of DG XI, and a failure of the Commission's own inter-agency coordination procedure,[6] the EU's first biotechnology-specific oversight policies (Council Directive 90/219/EEC on the use of GMOs and Council Directive 90/220/EEC on the release of GMOs) were more restrictive than those of its main competitor, the US, which had adopted a product-oriented approach. Under these directives, all products involving genetic modification were subject to the same set of regulations. More specifically, 90/220/EEC required that any firm intending to manufacture or import a GM product must first request approval from the food safety authority of a member state and then forward all relevant information about the GMO to the Commission. If any EU member state objects (whether for scientific or political reasons), the product must then pass a scientific committee (which tends to approve most GM products) and, if necessary, pass a regulatory committee composed of representatives from all EU member states. According to Commission insiders, the regulatory committee was supposed to make the process more flexible by acting as an impartial forum for new information to be introduced into the approval process. However, the regulatory committee quickly became politicised in light of public protests about GMOs, and thus became the chief bottleneck in the EU's approval process. Rather than allow themselves to be outvoted in the regulatory committee, it became more convenient for EU states to place GM products in limbo (in some cases, for years) by not voting at all. In addition, once (or if) this committee reports to the Commission, the EU must then vote again by a qualified majority on whether to approve the product. Even if such a product is approved by these onerous procedures, EU member states still had to pass their own national laws and regulations to accommodate it. Finally, it was difficult to win exemptions from these complex, time-consuming regulations as they tend to be administered by DG XI or its own competent authorities. Amending the directives was also extremely burdensome, often requiring a new Commission proposal, agreement in the Council and approval of the EP.[7]

Pressures for greater restrictions on biotech came from other EU institutions and from European citizens as well. For example, a key European directive on the legal protection of biotechnological inventions, first launched in 1988, quickly became stalled in the EP amid ethical controversies surrounding the patenting of transgenic plants and animals.[8] After failing to win Commission and Council support for most of its 66 amendments to the text (such as prohibiting patents on nearly anything derived from the human body), the EP voted against this directive in 1995, although other states by then had allowed patents on such inventions.[9] Similarly, the European Patent Office (although not an EU institution) in 1989 rejected Harvard's transgenic mouse patent, claiming it was prohibited by the European Patent Convention of 1973. According to the EPO, the mouse did not meet the customary criterion of 'non-obviousness' and patents were forbidden for inventions 'whose exploitation would be contrary to "ordre publique" or morality'.[10] Such refusal to issue or even protect patents in this emerging high-technology sector may have done irreparable harm to the EU's biotechnology industry.

To summarise, by the early 1990s the EU had established strict, 'one size fits all', process-dominant regulations governing the use and release of GMOs, had entered into a series of trade disputes with the US concerning the safety of food products and had failed to harmonise its patent laws (inside and outside the EU) in the face of a growing international consensus concerning intellectual property rights and biotechnology. Although a number of factors were responsible for the differences in approach between the Europe and the rest of the world (such as cultural differences concerning food and medicine, food/medicine safety scares, public trust in science and administrative agencies, styles of media coverage, legal systems and attitudes toward risk[11]), the fact is that the EU seemed to present an increasingly harsh environment, relative to the US and other advanced industrial states, for the development of biotechnology. As we shall see in the next two sections, the EU's attitude toward biotechnology would come under increasing pressures from outside and within.

External forces: the global context of EU biotech reform

It is becoming increasingly difficult for the EU to sustain some of its regulations concerning biotechnology. This is due in part to the international environment concerning biotechnology, in terms of the economic potential of the industry and in terms of international rules governing biotechnology.

Economics: competitiveness and global biotechnology
The EU has long been aware of biotechnology's implications for society and commerce, just as it recognises the powerful linkages between technology and economic growth in general.[12] However, biotechnology is also very capital-intensive, highly interdisciplinary and competitive, and requires years of patience and investment before commercial products are ready for the market. It also involves high barriers to entry and offers potentially lucrative first-mover advantages. Of the thousands of biotechnology firms in the US, Europe and elsewhere, most are private and small (fewer than 150 employees); they often focus on a single product or therapy in the hopes that one blockbuster success will allow them to thrive. For such firms, a stable environment in terms of continued access to large amounts of capital (whether human or financial) and in terms of government policies (concerning research, product approvals and property rights) is essential.

Given the special requirements of the industry, the EU is also highly sensitive to the US dominance of this technology, where firms enjoy a more supportive regulatory environment.[13] This has been so since 1976, when the US National Institutes of Health formed an oversight committee and released the first 'guidelines', not regulations, for recombinant DNA (rDNA) experimentation in the US.[14] The nascent industry passed a major hurdle in 1980, when the US Supreme Court ruled in *Diamond* vs. *Chakrabarty* that genetically altered life forms could be patented. This path-breaking ruling, which created friction with other countries at first, opened up enormous possibilities for the commercial development of genetic engineering in the US, which until that point had rested solely on the ability of companies to protect trade secrets. Since then, other policies (such as state-level funding, tax breaks and specialised biotechnology centers) helped lead to US dominance of the industry as it grew in the 1980s. US government funding of the $3 billion Human Genome Project (with support from the UK and other states as well) further stimulated industry development into the 1990s.

Concerning food safety, the US Food and Drug Administration (FDA), through a 'Working Policy' linked to the 1992 Food, Drug and Cosmetic Act, declared that GM foods were not inherently dangerous and thus did not require special regulation; nor did they require labelling unless the modification resulted in a change to the common or usual name of the food or resulted in a safety or usage issue (the doctrine of 'substantial equivalence'). The Working Policy also provided that any food additives which already exist in the natural food chain are recognised as inherently safe even if they are inserted into other foods using genetic modification. Only the creation of 'a protein, carbohydrate, fat, or oil, or other substance that differs significantly in structure, function, or composition from substances currently found in food as a result of genetic modification requires food additive safety scrutiny'.[15] This legislation, and the approval of over 20 varieties of GM seeds (as well as 40 new biotech drugs and vaccines), helped rejuvenate the US biotechnology sector, as did increased funding for more FDA reviewers. The US also benefited from lower patent costs at this time (about $5,000 per patent), while in the EU they averaged about $30,000.

As a result, biotechnology is still far more developed in the US than the rest of the world, which extends to ties between biotechnology firms and the computer industry to develop gene sequencers and databases, 'biochips', internet-supported clinical trials and other technologies to streamline new techniques and products. Thus, the US leads the EU in biotechnology by a number of measures: major innovations, the number and financial strength of firms, a more supportive regulatory environment and so on (although the UK also has a very highly regarded biotechnology industry[16]). It should also be noted that the Japanese government has taken a very active interest in developing the industry as part of its overall export-oriented economic strategy, and its efforts have brought Japan to a level near to that of the US in terms of the strength of its biotechnology industry,[17] which puts additional pressure on the EU to develop its own firms in this area. As we shall see later, these facts were clearly taken into consideration by the Commission when it began to revise its approach to biotechnology.

Politics: toward a global biotechnology regime

The second external influence on EU biotech policy concerns the emergence of biotechnology regulations at the international level. Although it is not yet possible to speak of a single global biotechnology regime, the international community has been increasingly active in managing the collective action problems created by modern biotechnology. The EU has been closely involved in these discussions and is partly responsible for implementing any global rules in this area. To the extent that the EU's own rules on biotechnology conflict with those of the international community, we can expect pressures for regulatory change.

While the history of this trend is too complex to be detailed here,[18] the main point is that global rules governing biotechnology have emerged (though to varying degrees) for all three major policy categories discussed above: environmental protection, property rights and food/medical safety. A secondary point is that the chief international organisations involved in these efforts (the UN, the OECD and the WTO/Codex Alimentarius food safety rules) generally stress the basic principle that biotechnology generally requires no new or special regulations; the harmonisation of existing regulations should suffice. This position, which is very close to US policy, puts additional pressures on the EU to conform to global standards.

In general, these standards have emerged through two principle mechanisms: international conferences and international organisations, beginning with the June 1973 Gordon Conference on Nucleic Acids and the 1975 International Conference on Recombinant DNA Molecules, or the 'Asilomar Conference' (Pacific Grove, CA). In fact, the Asilomar scientists were exceedingly restrictive at the time, and global guidelines were relaxed a few years after Asilomar.[19] With the emergence of biotech as a commercial industry, by the mid-1980s the OECD had established guidelines for member states engaged in rDNA research and applications. The guidelines followed the basic principle that it was unnecessary, from a scientific standpoint, to regulate the process (rDNA) by which a product was produced. The OECD also recommended further research to improve the prediction, evaluation and monitoring of the outcome of applications.[20] This decision was broadly in line with US government views on the subject. The key provision in these guidelines was a statement that no specific legislation was necessary for rDNA techniques; existing oversight and review mechanisms should suffice. This fundamental principle was later violated by the EU's own biotechnology regulations, which later had to be amended. Later OECD efforts through the mid-1990s promoted the harmonisation of national regulations involving environmental release,[21] which included surveys of national regulatory procedures and regulatory workshops.[22] These efforts are closely linked to the UN's own initiatives in biotech, which involve numerous specialised agencies (such as the World Health Organization, the UN Food and Agricultural Organization, Codex Alimentarius, the UN Industrial Development Organization, UNESCO, the International Council of Scientific Unions, the International Center for Genetic Engineering and Biotechnology and the International Patent Office). A non-governmental organisation, the Human Genome Organization, also helps to coordinate the global human genome project through data collation and workshops to consider ethical, legal, social and intellectual property issues.[23] These coordinated efforts clearly represent the emergence of a global biotechnology regulatory regime.

The most recent international conference took place at the UN Ad Hoc Working Group on Biosafety meeting in Montreal in January 2000. In a rare victory over the OECD and other leading biotechnology states (the 'Miami group'), the EU teamed with the 'Group of 77' developing nations to require mandatory labelling of certain GM grain shipments (but not consumer products) to allow states to prohibit such imports. Assuming this new 'Biosafety protocol' is ratified by the necessary 50 states (out of 130 signatories) and enters into effect, it is likely to be challenged in the WTO's trade court in the near future. Moreover, it does not cover trade in either GM 'commodities' (chiefly maize and soy beans, the two major GM crops) or human pharmaceutical products, making its scope extremely limited.[24]

Internal forces: processes within the EU

Although external factors such as competitiveness and international rules have made the EU more sensitive to its own biotechnology policies, internal forces are more responsible for the specific choices made by the EU. And while certain factors (such as historical context, culture, ideology, etc.) undoubtedly play an indirect role in explaining how the EU formulates its own biotechnology regulations, I argue that policy debates among EU institutions, policy communities and interest groups strongly condition the way the EU responds to global pressures. As a result, the EU does not yet fully conform to these standards and is still finding its way in terms of the simultaneous development and regulation of biotechnology. This section will focus on the interaction between these forces to help explain the EU's recent biotech policy reforms.

EU institutions, particularly the Commission, play a leading role in setting the policy agenda and framing the issue. Since GM product licensing and labelling are also subject to the co-decision procedure, the EP is closely involved in these areas as well; it also has the right to produce opinions on any policy issues. These decisions in turn are acted upon by EU member governments (whether in Council or otherwise), the EP, and other relevant actors. In other words, EU policy creates politics as well, which feeds back into the policy process and influences future decisions. As we saw above, the original EU regulatory framework (1990) included general 'horizontal' directives on the use of GMOs and the research/development/release of GMOs. These were followed through 1995 by more specific 'vertical' directives on the safety and health aspects of biotechnology,[25] additives in foodstuffs,[26] and the marketing of biotech medicinal products.[27] As with the original directive, these later measures were also more restrictive than those of the US, due in part to internal bureaucratic politics in the Commission and strong support for tighter regulations by the EP. The political dynamics created by these regulations, combined with the external influences discussed above, have led all interested parties in the EU to adjust their positions on biotechnology regulation.

For example, one major consequence of the vertical directives is that the Commission's oversight of biotechnology has shifted from the Environmental DG to other DGs, chiefly the new Health and Consumer Safety DG but also those for Agriculture, Market and Enterprise. In fact, only about four people in the Environment DG now deal with biotechnology on a regular basis. Regulation today is thus more fragmented than before and requires far more co-ordination and negotiation among relevant DGs than the original framework directives. Toward this end, the Commission's inter-agency co-ordinating body, the Biotechnology Coordinating Committee (BCC), brings together representatives from all relevant Commission DGs involved in biotech.[28] Although the Committee was established in 1990, its importance has increased as the EU attempted to develop the new vertical directives but also to reform the original horizontal legislation (chiefly 90/220; see below). The new informal rule in the Commission is that the BCC vets nearly all biotech legislation, at the most critical stages of preparation. Interservice communications about biotech regulation at all levels below the political level (i.e., the Commissioners) are common now, and the BCC provides for general information sharing, early warning of potential problems or disputes, screening of everything the EU does regarding biotech and (to a lesser extent) some forward thinking on policy issues.

While the BCC itself does not provide for lobbying by outsiders (although it attempts to balance the interests of biotech stakeholders), the Commission's efforts have also been increasingly influenced by the involvement of Europe's broader biotechnology policy community. The notion of EU policy communities for various issues is well-known;[29] however, the nature of biotechnology means we must also be sensitive to the role of scientific and technical experts in explaining policy choice. The chief entity here is the Commission's Scientific Steering Committee and its system of sectoral-specific Scientific Committees, which were completely reorganised by the Commission in 1997 to help deal with issues such as food safety and medical product approval.[30] These experts have issued over 200 opinions while encouraging the Commission to develop a more nuanced approach to biotechnology than that established by the 1990 directives. The Commission also has its own Advisory Group on Ethics in Science and Technology to help 'bridge the gap' between public opinion and the biotech industry. It deals with questions on labelling, patents, cloning, stem cell research, genetic privacy and similar issues.[31]

However, we must also take care not to overemphasise the role of experts. As I have argued elsewhere,[32] the emergence of a biotechnology epistemic community (at the international and EU levels) has been curbed by several factors: scientific disputes and ethical debates; intense competition over high financial stakes; the multi-disciplinary nature of the industry, which invites regulatory competition among relevant agencies; and the general sensitivity of the topic in that a single discovery or crisis can be explosive enough to prompt a reflexive reaction on the part of both publics and governments. This has happened with the first human protein synthetically manufactured in a bacteria in 1977, with food safety scares in Europe and with the cloning controversy. Even the Commission's own scientific experts express frustration at the constraints placed on their advice by outside political pressures.[33]

Finally, relevant interest groups (beyond scientific and technical experts) have encouraged the Commission to moderate its approach to biotechnology in some areas. These include those in favour of greater regulations and those opposed to it, from both industry organisations and agricultural, consumer, environmental or other groups. In fact, the sensitivity over biotechnology has in fact encouraged competing interest groups to coalesce around the issue (particularly in Europe), thus undermining some of the influence of scientific and technical experts. Pro-biotech groups include EuropaBio (the chief umbrella organisation for EU biotechnology firms), the Senior Advisory Group on Biotechnology (SAGB), the European Secretariat of National BioIndustry Associations, the European Molecular Biology Organization and the European Federation of Biotechnology. These groups compete with environmentalists, consumer and religious groups and political parties of the left and right.

While the scientific community has seen little cause for alarm, opposition groups still tend to dominate the public debate over biotechnology, whether in terms of food safety, fears about environmental contamination and ethical concerns surrounding cloning and other techniques. In interviews, more than one Commission insider noted the continuing strength of an anti-tech movement in the EU, especially compared with the US.[34] Fears over biotechnology have even led to violence and vandalism, and involved the destruction of GM seeds and crops.[35] Animal-rights protestors have also joined the debate (in part by attacking property) in opposing the use of animals for research, prompting the pharmaceutical industry to demand more legal protection from such actions.[36] Although the Commission has made some headway in reforming its biotechnology policies, the influence of these groups should not be underestimated. The EP is a major target for these opposition groups, and it has conducted several high-profile debates over biotechnology (engineered primarily by the Green Group), which have limited the Commission's ability to reform the regulatory process. Although the EP backed certain reforms in recent years (see below), it still intends to play a major role in the EU's discussions on this technology, such as through its Temporary Committee on Human Genetics, in place since January 2001.[37] This will be exceedingly difficult, however, given the inherent political tensions generated by biotechnology and the fact that the EP has no real independent biotech expertise, although a few MEPs are doctors or biologists. The EP's science and technology office is also very small relative to those of national parliaments and the Commission, and it is still finding its way on this issue.[38]

The outcome: the EU's changing approach to biotechnology

Faced with increasing pressures from the global, European and domestic levels, the Commission began to re-examine the EU's regulations in this area several years ago. The key turning point came around 1994–95, when the Commission's directorate general for industry (DG III) produced a draft report on the international competitiveness of biotechnology in the EU. Among other things, this report noted that the US was filing 50 per cent more biotechnology patents than the EU, and that 67 per cent of all biotechnology pharmaceutical patents had been awarded to the US, while the EU's share was 15 per cent. In the late 1960s, Europe's share of new pharmaceutical products was 65 per cent; by 1997 that share had declined to 40 per cent. Other figures showed that the EU's share of biotechnology-derived inventions was 10 per cent while the US had 76 per cent and Japan 14 per cent. The US had also conducted more than four times as many plant field trials than the EU, and by 1994 there had been a net outflow of biotechnology capital investment from the EU to the US as EU biotechnology firms scrambled for alliances with more successful firms in the US.[39]

These trends weighed heavily on the Commission's deliberations. Yet its overall approach is still somewhat erratic, due to conflicting political pressures but also to the inherent uncertainties surrounding the technology and the EU's own internal disputes. For example, due to opposition by EU environmental ministers the Commission issued a moratorium on GM foods in October 1998 after it had approved only a handful of GM seeds;[40] this was later extended indefinitely and 14 GM products remain in regulatory limbo. Still, key changes have occurred, as the rest of this section documents.

One of the most important developments is the establishment of the European Agency for the Evaluation of Medicinal Products (EMEA) in London in February 1995, under the terms of Council Regulation 2309/93/EC. It regulates the standardisation and harmonisation of human and veterinary pharmaceutical applications for marketing authorisation on behalf of the EU, while national authorisation procedures (including price fixing) remain in place for products marketed in one member state. Importantly, where GM medicinal products are concerned, the new agency preempts some of the regulatory provisions of Council Directive 90/220/EEC on the release of GMOs (although the EMEA must also respect the environmental protections of that Directive). In addition to the standard 'mutual recognition' procedure covering most medicines, the EMEA also provides for a new centralised procedure for all medicinal products derived from biotechnology (and by request for other products). This procedure limits the EMEA approval process to about 210 days, which makes it more competitive with the US FDA (although the Commission must then translate the approval into a single market authorisation for the EU, which can be time consuming).

In 1998 the Commission also finally managed to amend its original directive (90/219/EEC) on the use of GMOs to make its risk classifications more compatible with global rules. This was accomplished by the BCC, which brought together all major stakeholders (in the Commission) to forge a compromise. However, this directive still follows the original process-based approach to regulation. The Commission has also proposed reforms to the directive on the release of GMOs (90/220/EEC, the so-called 'biotechnology directive'), although this has been more difficult due in part to the increased public concerns about food safety and environmental protection noted above.[41] The new EU biotechnology directive attempts to refine the scope of the original one by distinguishing between experimental release and release of GM products intended for the market. In doing so it would provide for two harmonised sets of regulations for biotechnology, making the approval process somewhat more flexible. It also provides for periodic license renewals and exempts from labelling requirements products with a GMO content below a certain threshold still blocking the GMO directive.

However, the disputes have not ended regarding revised 90/220 and it has yet to enter into force. Commission insiders argue that the application of the original 90/220 directive was the real problem, not the content of it. One official even admitted that the revised 90/220 is '60–70 per cent window dressing' to make it seem more effective. More problematic, the revised 90/220 Directive was agreed in February 2001, but several EU states (Italy, France, Austria, Luxembourg, Denmark and Greece) added national derogations to the revised directive to interpret it as they saw fit. They also demanded better labelling and 'traceability' of GMOs using containment procedures and genetic markers. These states have since refused to implement the new directive until these questions were addressed by the Commission. In the course of revising 90/220, the Commission suggested an 'interim approach' in mid-2000, which would involve lifting the moratorium on new GM approvals in the expectation that the revision of 90/220 would be successful. Three new GM products were used as test cases by the Commission, but they ultimately failed in the regulatory committee. Biotech firms (and the Commission) could sue member states under the current 90/220 regulations regarding the time period for GM product approvals, but neither are willing to inflame public opinion by doing so. Thus, member states not only continue to prevent product approvals, they also seem to be constantly changing the goalpost regarding the revision of 90/220, even though a text has been agreed.[42] The latest demand involves a liability regime for GM products, yet another highly contentious issue in the

EU. These efforts suggest a series of new political battles regarding the future of EU biotech regulation.

Changes on the GMO patent issue are far more promising. In May 1998 the EP finally approved a new directive to harmonise patent laws across the EU and bring them closer to those of the US and Japan.[43] It allows the patenting of certain products derived from animals and plants but forbids property rights for all or part of a human being at any stage of its development (such as research on human embryos). It also bans human cloning and bans changing human genes in such a way that the changes would be inherited. The directive entered into effect in July 1998 and is now being translated into national legislation, another long and difficult process for EU member states.

Besides regulations concerning pharmaceuticals and the patenting of GMOs, the Commission has spent much effort on the food safety and labelling issue. Here the EU managed to find a compromise for regulations on the approval and labelling of 'novel foods',[44] GM foods,[45] and GM food additives[46] after years of controversy. In this case, the Commission dropped its proposal that foods must use the wording 'may contain GM ingredients' when it is uncertain whether such ingredients are present. Products would be exempt from labelling only if they contained less than 1 per cent GM material by accident. With such wording, virtually every food product would have to be labelled as it is impossible to 100 per cent certify that no GM ingredients are present. Now, food will be labelled only when it is known to contain GM ingredients. However, note that this mandatory labelling requirement still fundamentally differs from the US position, which is that foods do not have to be labelled just because they happen to involve genetic modification (although a few other states have introduced some form of GM labelling[47]). Also, these regulations are still process centered (in line with the Commission's recent thinking on the 'precautionary principle'[48]) and require onerous environmental risk assessments similar to those established by the original 1990 biotechnology regulations.

The Commission, however, is not finished with this issue. In January 2000 it released its White Paper/Action Plan on Food Safety,[49] based on an earlier Green Paper on Food Law.[50] The Paper was a joint effort of the commissioners for Health and Consumer Protection and for Enterprise and Information Society. The centerpiece of the White Paper is a plan for a new 'European Food Authority' (EFA), which will be independent of politics and will follow scientific principles for its decisions regarding standards, labelling, inspections and risk assessment. This 'radical new approach' from 'farm to table,' in the words of the Commission, is necessary to govern a very complex and culturally sensitive area. Its mandate would include the regulation of GM feeds, seeds and foods. Assuming such a body is eventually established (the Commission's goal is by 2002), it could go a long way toward rationalising the regulatory climate for GM foods, provided it co-ordinates its activities with the Commission (chiefly its environmental directorate), with food authorities in EU member states and with relevant international agreements (chiefly the Codex Alimentarius rules).

However, according to insiders, the EMEA is likely to be far more effective than the EFA, for two reasons: the EFA is only advisory (the EMEA can make decisions) and the EMEA has close links to national medicines agencies (the EFA has no links).[51]

Conclusion

Biotechnology represents one of the most challenging regulatory issues that governments will face in the twenty-first century. Like the nuclear revolution, its development involves a major technological breakthrough; a complex network of scientists, firms and governments; an increasingly high public profile; and a number of difficult political and ethical questions. The EU is at the centre of these debates, given its key role in developing a single market among a large (and soon to increase) group of some of the most advanced industrialised states on the planet. Although the EU's approach to biotechnology has become increasingly sophisticated in the last few years, in terms of balancing the interests of firms and consumers, it is still at odds with the US and other biotechnology competitors in some areas. To be sure, the US has its own difficulties concerning biotechnology, and some interest groups have called for more oversight concerning GM foods and medicines, gene therapy, stem cell research and genetic privacy.

Yet, the key point is that the EU still takes a highly restrictive, inflexible and closed approach to biotechnology relative to the US, Japan and other competitors. While the EU won a temporary (even symbolic) victory for its own approach with the Montreal Biosafety Protocol on labelling food shipments, it still lags far behind the US in terms of research and development, patents, commercial products, investment and the general state of the industry. Individual EU member states still attempt to govern certain aspects of biotechnology through bans, regulations or price-fixing, and a true single market in these products has yet to be realised. Finally, the US shows no signs of reconsidering its fundamental approach to biotechnology, which is based on regulating individual products (not processes) and only in cases where risks have been proved with scientific methods. In short, the EU will find itself further behind in the global technology race if it continues to pander to public fears instead of taking a more flexible and nuanced approach to biotechnology regulation. EU research and developing funding will not help in the presence of such an uncertain regulatory environment.

The EU could play a major role in global technological development, as it has shown with its single standard for digital mobile communications, which led to its current dominance of the industry. But its policies and technologies must be fully harmonised at the national level, and be transferable to the outside world as well. There is of course nothing inherently wrong with devising stricter regulations in this area if that in fact is what the majority of Europeans want. Yet, given some of the differences between its regulatory stance and that of its competitors, the EU may at best stifle the economic opportunities offered by this high-growth area, and, at worst, prevent access to the benefits of this technology (particularly in terms of new developments in medicine) to consumers and patients. If successful, the EU could act as a model for other economic regions by showing how regional funding and regulations can improve competitiveness and protect consumers. Perhaps NAFTA and APEC could adopt similar guidelines to intensify their co-operation in this area, while keeping in line with the growing global consensus over biotechnology. In this way the tools of regional and international co-operation may be able to maintain the pace with the growing power of technology.

Notes

I would like to thank the EU Center of the University System of Georgia for their financial support of the research on which this chapter is based, and Chenaz Seelarbokus for research assistance. I would also like to thank the EU officials who agreed to be interviewed for this study.

 1 This paper uses the generic term 'EU' to refer to the current framework of the Treaty on European Union and to its precursor, the European Communities.

 2 On this point, Peterson and Sharp note that EU funding for biotechnology research and development has produced few tangible results in terms of products or firms. It is mostly geared toward academic or other non-profit research. John Peterson and Margaret Sharp, *Technology Policy in the European Union* (London: Macmillan, 1998), p. 197.

 3 W. L. Williams, Jr., 'Transnational legal aspects of biotechnology,' *Law/Technology*, 19 (1986), 23.

 4 David W. Plant, 'The impact of biotechnology on patent law', in Joseph G. Perpich (ed.), *Biotechnology in Society: Private Initiatives and Public Oversight* (New York: Pergamon Press, 1986); U. Wasserman, 'Patents and the biotechnology industry', *Journal of World Trade Law* 20 (November–December 1986), 705–713; and R. S. Eisenberg, 'Proprietary rights and the norms of science in biotechnology research', *Yale Law Journal*, 97 (December 1987), 177–231.

 5 European Commission, 'A Community framework for the regulation of biotechnology', Communication from the Commission to the Council, COM(86)573, final (4 November 1986).

 6 Lee Ann Patterson, 'A comparison of biotechnology regulatory policy in the United States and the European Union', paper prepared for delivery at the Biennial Conference of the European Community Studies Association (Pittsburgh, 2–6 June 1999), pp. 17–18.

 7 Judson O. Berkey, 'The regulation of genetically modified foods', *ASIL Insight* (Washington: American Society for International Law, October 1999); and Patterson, 'comparison of biotechnology regulatory policy', pp. 17–18 and 20–1.

 8 Gordon Lake, 'Scientific uncertainty and political regulation: European legislation on the contained use and deliberate release of genetically modified (micro) organisms', *Project Appraisal*, 6 (March 1991), 7–15; and David Barling, 'The European Community and the legislating of the application and products of genetic modification technology', *Environmental Politics*, 4 (Autumn 1995), 467–74.

9   Such as Argentina, Brazil, Canada, Greece, Hungary, Japan, the Netherlands, New Zealand, Turkey and the US.

10 D. Dickson, 'No patent for Harvard's mouse?', *Science*, 243 (24 February 1989), 1003.

11 Joanna Chataway and Gerald Assouline, 'Risk perception, regulation, and the management of agro-biotechnologies', in Jacqueline Senker (ed.), *Biotechnology and Competitive Advantage: Europe's Firms and the US Challenge* (Cheltanham: Edward Elgar, 1998); and Patterson, 'A comparison of biotechnology regulatory policy', pp. 12–14.

12 Wayne Sandholtz and John Zysman, '1992: Recasting the European bargain', *World Politics*, 42 (October 1989), 95–128; Wayne Sandholtz, *High-Tech Europe: The Politics of International Cooperation* (Berkeley: University of California Press, 1992); and Peterson and Sharp, *Technology Policy in the European Union*.

13 For details, see Senker, *Biotechnology and Competitive Advantage*.

14 'Recombinant DNA: NIH Group stirs storm by drafting laxer rules', *Science*, 190 (21 November 1975); and 'Recombinant DNA: NIH sets strict rules to launch new technology', *Science*, 190 (19 December 1975).

15 US FDA, 'Statement of policy: foods derived from new plant varieties', *Federal Register 57* (Washington DC: Government Printing Office, 29 May 1992), pp. 22984–3005.

16 Clive Cookson, 'Europe's biotech industry "maturing"', *Financial Times*, 16 April 2000. For a more detailed discussion, see Brian Salter and Michael E. Smith, 'The UK's stake in the EU's biotechnology debate', paper delivered at the 4th Pan-European ECPR/IR Conference, University of Kent, September 2001.

17 M. D. Rogers, 'The Japanese government's role in biotechnology R&D', *Chemistry and Industry*, 15 (7 August 1982), 533–7.

18 Thomas C. Wiegele, *Biotechnology and International Relations: The Political Dimensions* (Gainesville: University of Florida Press, 1991); and Michael E. Smith and Craig S. Kim, 'Managing or mis-managing the genetic revolution? International biotechnology policy coordination and the scientific community', paper prepared for delivery at the annual meeting of the American Political Science Association, Boston, September 1998.

19 J. Tooze, 'International and European regulation of recombinant DNA research', *Toledo Law Review*, 12 (Summer 1981), 875–7; B. D. Davis, *Storm Over Biology: Essays on Science, Sentiment, and Public Policy* (Buffalo: Prometheus Books, 1986), p. 297.

20 OECD, *Recombinant DNA Safety Considerations* (Paris: OECD, 1986), pp. 41–2.

21 OECD, '*Report of the OECD Workshop on the Monitoring of Organisms Introduced into the Environment*', OECD Environment Monograph No. 52 (Paris: OECD Environment Directorate, 1992); OECD, *Ottowa '92: The OECD Workshop on Methods for Monitoring Organisms in the Environment*, OECD Environment Monograph No. 90 (Paris: OECD Environment Directorate, 1994); and the companion document, OECD, *Compendium of Methods for Monitoring Organisms in the Environment*, OECD Environment Monograph No. 91 (Paris: OECD Environment Directorate, 1994).

22 OECD, *Commercialisation of Agricultural Products Derived Through Modern Biotechnology: Survey Results*, Environment Monograph No. 99 (Paris: OECD Environment Directorate, 1995).

23 Victor A. McKusick, 'The human genome organization: history, purposes, and membership', *Genomics*, 5 (1989), 385–7.

24 Robert Falkner, 'Regulating biotech trade: the Cartagena protocol on biosafety', *International Affairs*, 76 (2000), 299–313.

25 Council Directive 90/679/EEC, 31 December 1990; 93/88/EEC, 29 October 1993.

26 Council Directive 93/114/EEC, 1 October 1994.

27 Council Directive 93/41/EEC, 1 January 1995.

28 Interviews with various Commission officials involved in Biotechnology, Brussels, 2001.

29 For an overview, see John Peterson, 'Decision-making in the EU: towards a framework for analysis', *Journal of European Public Policy*, 2 (March 1995), 69–96.

30 These include eight scientific committees: food, animal nutrition, veterinary-public health, plants, animal heath/welfare, cosmetic products/non-food products, medicinal products/medical devices, toxicity/eco-toxicity/environment. See Commission Decision 97/404/EC, 10 June 1997 and Commission Decision 97/579/EC, 23 July 1997.

31 Interviews, Brussels, 2001.

32 Smith and Kim, 'Managing or mis-managing the genetic revolution?'.

33 Interviews, Brussels, 2001.

34 *Ibid.*

35 Julia Flynn, John Carey, and William Echikson, 'Seeds of discontent', *Business Week* (2 February 1998), 62–3; and Robert Graham, 'Peasant warriors take up arms against genetically altered corn', *Financial Times*, 27/28 June 1998, p. 2.

36 D. Pilling, 'Appeal over animal rights "terror"', *Financial Times*, 5 April 2000, p. 2.

37 The Committee's mandate generally includes patient's concerns, gene mapping, post-natal genetic testing, pre-natal gene testing, genetics and medicine (embryos/cloning), patents, the pharmaceutical industry, legal aspects, and ethical aspects.

38 Interviews, Brussels, 2001.

39 European Commission, DG-III, 'Draft Report on the International Competitiveness of Biotechnology in the European Union' (Brussels: 11 November 1994), pp. 116–17; European Commission, DG-III, 'Commission communication on the single market in pharmaceuticals' (Brussels: 25 November 1998); and Patterson, 'A comparison of biotechnology regulatory policy in the United States and the European Union', pp. 27–8.

40 These are beets, cotton, maize, soybeans, rapeseed, and rice. Only two of these, soybeans with increased tolerance to the herbicide glyphosate (approved by the Commission in 1996) and maize with insecticide properties conferred by the endoxin gene and with increased tolerance to the herbicide glyphosate (approved by the Commission in 1997), were on the market at the time of writing.

41 See COM85 final (1998) and COM139 final (1999).

42 Interviews, Brussels, 2001.

43 Council Directive 98/44/EC, 6 July 1998.

44 Council Regulation 258/97/EC, 27 January 1997.

45 Council Regulation 1139/98/EC, 26 May 1998.

46 Commission Regulation 50/2000/EC, 10 January 2000.

47 These include Australia, Canada, Japan, New Zealand, Norway, South Korea, and Switzerland.

48 COM1 (2000); also see Michael Smith, 'Washington challenges EU food safety stance', *Financial Times*, 31 March 2000.

49 COM719 (1999).
50 COM176 (1997).
51 Interviews, Brussels, 2001.

15

Deregulation and co-ordination in European telecommunications strategies

Nicola Murrell

With continuing globalisation of commerce, and society's move towards a more information-based economy, the role of advanced telecommunications and information technology networks and services in European competitiveness is becoming increasingly vital. Telecoms is one of the few technological fields in which Europe can be said to outperform Japan and come close to the USA.[1] In November 1998, the European Commission issued an update on telecoms competition, highlighting the US$175 billion European telecoms market as the single most important contributor to economic growth in the European Union.

In addition to being an important part of European commercial activity in its own right, the telecommunications industry also provides the infrastructure over which the rest of European commercial and economic activity is conducted. As Drake highlighted in 1995, the real significance of the telecoms industries may lie in their pervasiveness, underlying and tying together virtually all domains of economic and societal activity. Multinational companies, increasingly use telecoms networks to carry corporate data, email and support multimedia applications across national borders.[2] As greater demands are made on these networks in terms of quality and type of service, as well as in terms of capacity, the successful operation and development of these networks in a transnational context becomes ever-more crucial.

Following the opening up to free competition of telecoms markets, such as that of fixed access telecoms services, at the beginning of 1998, and with further liberalisation taking place in countries such as Greece in 2001, the European telecoms sector is becoming more and more dynamic. The successful transition of European telecoms from an industry that has been traditionally characterised by a strong public service monopoly sentiment, to one that is commercially competitive, is crucial to maintaining Europe's strong position in the telecoms field and ensuring that current and future demands placed on Europe's infra-structure are met.

This chapter discusses the need for greater co-ordination of telecoms policies across Europe as attempts are made to harmonise the regulatory environment of telecommunications in order to allow member states to benefit from a competitive and innovative pan-European telecommunications market. It considers the European Union's policy on telecommunications, and the establishment of effective competition across Europe through the re-regulation of national markets to 'level the playing field' for new and existing network operators and encourage innovation and market growth across Europe. It argues that there is a need for greater co-operation between national and international bodies in the co-ordination of telecoms policy across Europe, in light of some of the issues raised by the progressive and fragmented liberalisation of the European market. It goes on to examine the harmonised inter-operation and development of communications networks across Europe, through co-ordinated technological standardisation and collaboration in the development and deployment of new technologies for communication. Finally, it highlights the transnational nature of the modern telecoms industry and the implications of the resulting increase in interdependence between nations for national telecommunications strategies.

At the core of the European Commission's policy on telecommunications, under DG XIII, are two fundamental 'measures'. Firstly, in 1995, the EC called for member states to liberalise all telecommunications service (i.e. including the previous monopolies in public voice telephony), by 1 January 1998. This has involved the corporatisation and privatisation of state-owned PTTs (programming tools and techniques) – internet service providers – and the establishment of an independent national regulatory authority, such as the UK's Oftel, to create licensing conditions for new entrants to the telecommunications market and also to oversee the negotiation of interconnection agreements to allow them access to the incumbent PTT's infrastructure. This last point is of particular importance with respect to the second EC 'measure', which concerns the setting out of a harmonised framework for interconnection in telecommunications and interoperability of services across Europe for open network provision (ONP). This implies efforts to standardise telecommunications technologies and services across Europe as well as collaborative research and development programmes, such as Advanced Communications and Services (ACTS), to ensure that all regions of the European Union benefit from future technological advances in the telecommunications field. Additionally, European telecoms operators are expected to ensure 'universal service' provision, that is that all potential users, everywhere in the EU, have access to a defined minimum telecoms service of a specified quality at an affordable cost-based price.

The extent to which these policies have been implemented differs across member states. Greece, for example, accepted the option to postpone the liberalisation of public voice telephony services until 2003 due to its telecoms infrastructure's underdevelopment, even though its mobile communications and data communications markets were already open to competition. The process of privatisation of OTE, the Greek PTT, was hampered by national politics. This was also the case in other countries such as France, policies of privatisation not being popular with socialist governments. By February 1996, only 1 per cent of OTE had been sold by the state in preparation for the liberalisation of the sector, and many potential foreign investors to OTE had lost interest due to the inconsistency of government policy on the organisation's privatisation.[3] By 2000, only 49 per cent of OTE had been sold by the state as Greece prepared to open up its public voice telephony market to competition in 2001. However, an independent regulatory authority had still not been established to oversee this transition. On the other hand Spain, which was also granted a five-year period of grace, chose to push ahead with liberalisation and established a duopoly situation between PTT, Telefonica and competitor, Retevision, although the government still retained a considerable stake in both operators. The market was formally liberalised at the beginning of 1999.

Germany and France, among others, followed in the footsteps of the UK, which opened its market to full competition as early as 1991, after a period of duopoly between British Telecom and Mercury, by opening their markets to full competition by the 1 January 1998 deadline imposed by the EC. Despite this, change has been slow in some countries, particularly in Eastern Europe,[4] and the level of competition across Europe has been affected by problems with differing national policies concerning in particular licensing and interconnection which has prevented new entrants from competing effectively with the incumbent network operators.

Towards the end of 1998, in its update on telecomms competition, the EC recognised that there was a need for better regulation of licensing and interconnection, and voiced concerns about onerous licence conditions in some countries, inadequate reference interconnection offers and a general lack of transparency. It also questioned the independence of regulators in Belgium, France, Finland, Ireland and Luxembourg. These issues must be resolved in order for European Union member states to achieve the desired 'state of play' in the European telecoms market and encourage overall market development.

Disparities in licensing conditions also have an effect on the competitiveness of the overall market. New telecoms operators are often competitively disadvantaged early on due to the fees they are made to pay for an operating licence. Early in 1997, the EC questioned the Spanish telecoms licensing conditions under which new mobile operator Airtel Movil had been made to pay a hefty fee for a licence to operate a GSM (Global System for Mobile Communications) network, when rival Telefonica, the Spanish PTT, had paid nothing for a licence when it set up its own GSM services.[5] Similar inconsistencies and weaknesses in licensing policies can be seen in Greece for example, where OTE bypassed licensing regulations when it was not granted a GSM licence using a presidential decree granting it exclusivity in just about everything.[6] The case was similar with licensing processes for third generation mobile services (3G). While in some member states licences were awarded based on a comparative review process, which involved a fixed license fee, other governments chose to auction licences off to the companies willing to bid the highest amount. The auction process led to many companies paying excessively high licence fees, for example BT paid £4 billion for its 3G licence which was awarded via a comparative review process. The inequity in the cost of 3G licences across Europe has left companies with different degrees of debt, or lack thereof, which will effect their ability to invest in actually developing and deploying the next generation of mobile services in each of their respective markets across Europe.

The question of licence awarding is also significant when considering the number of operators a market can support. In Spain, for example, operators are no longer required to bid for licences and merely apply to the CMT. There is no limit to the number of licences to be granted. Although a number of different operators are needed for a competitive environment, too many operators could ultimately undermine the overall competitiveness of each individual company. This would be especially disadvantageous in the context of European or international competition, where such disparities in national policy could undermine the establishment of effective competitiveness in the market as a whole, giving some operators unfair advantages over others.

The differences in licensing policy amongst member states has also obstructed the deployment of pan-European telecommunications services as companies are slowed down by the bureaucracy of applying for multiple licences under differing conditions across the EU. In order to alleviate the problem of differing national licensing conditions as well as the need to apply for separate licences in each nation when attempting to roll out a pan-European network, the EC issued a proposal directive to establish procedures for the mutual recognition of licences in 1992. However, this only covered the provision of value-added and data services, although it was envisaged that it would eventually extend to voice telephony.[7] At this stage, differences in national licensing conditions continue to hamper the development of a fully competitive European telecommunications market and slow down the establishment of truly pan-European networks as networks are rolled out country by country.

Another major barrier to effective competition across Europe has been the establishment of fair interconnection agreements with PTTs, allowing new entrants access to the already constructed national infrastructures held by the PTTs. The negotiation of interconnect agreements is a time-consuming process, holding up the launch of new services and preventing competition in some markets, such as Spain.[8] When Retevision launched in Spain, the interconnection fees that it was made to pay to incumbent Telefonica were so high that the former found it hard to compete.[9] In Germany, in April 1997, Mannesmann Arcor and o.tel.o made a formal appeal to BMPT, the German regulator, concerning among other things Deutsche Telekom's astronomic interconnection fees.[10]

The provision of interconnection services remains a monopoly even if the telecoms market itself is liberalised, as the PTT remains in possession of the nation's primary telecommunications network. Although interconnection with PTTs' networks can be avoided in some cases with the deployment of new networks, it is not completely unavoidable. Even if a company possesses its own national network, if a call terminates with a PTT subscriber then the competing company will be required to pay interconnection charges. While the PTT remains the dominant operator in most markets, this is not balanced out by the fees that the PTT will have to pay for calls made from its network to the competitors. Interconnection is also necessary in the context of ONP. Therefore, the establishment of fair, that is cost-based, and consistent, interconnection terms between PTTs and competing operators across Europe is vital to the EU policies of competition through liberalisation, and ONP through interoperability and interconnection.

Currently, it is only in France, Germany and the UK that interconnect rates fall within the range described as 'best-current-practice', in the rest of the EU all the rates are deemed to be too high, apart from in Ireland which lowered its interconnect rates at the end of 1998 to be one of the lowest.[11] In order to harmonise interconnect rates across Europe to create a fair and competitive environment in European telecoms, greater co-operation will be needed from those countries in which the rates remain high and this will mean greater transparency in revealing actual costs, however difficult it may be to ascertain them.

Such co-operation is likely to be more difficult to obtain where independent national regulatory authorities either do not exist, or where their independence is questionable. Most member states have established an independent national regulatory body to oversee the transition to a competitive market, such as the UK's Oftel. In other countries, however, the establishment of an independent body for the regulation of telecoms has proved problematic, most notable perhaps in Germany where telecoms regulation remains under one of the state ministries. This lack of independent regulation is particularly concerning considering the German government's 47.4 per cent stake in Deutsche Telekom. Such a situation is hardly conducive to a fair, liberalised market.

Even the credibility of the independent regulatory authorities is questionable since they are often based around ex-Ministry personnel used to working in a monopoly environment and not a competitive market. As a result the new authority must make as much of an effort as the PTT to adapt to the new competitive environment and shake off national state-run monopoly sentiments in order to be able to regulate competently. This is likely to be a slow process: 'more than 10 years after first experimenting with competition, the UK is only now beginning to arrive at a situation where regulation and the market … work in tandem'.[12] Even so, in the UK Oftel tends only to intervene when there is an irreconcilable dispute between market players, rather than playing a fully proactive role in guiding competition in these areas. This could imply an approach to government which relies upon the actions of opportunistic operators to guide the development of policy.

Effective regulation at EU (and even international) level can only be based upon effective and transparent national regulation, which heightens the need for these issues to be addressed in all the countries concerned. Regulatory inconsistencies, such as those described above, impede the development of an open and competitive European telecommunications market and, as such, are likely to hinder market development and innovation, compromising the position of the EU as a whole.

In line with the politics of a single European market is the policy of ONP, or open network provision. The so-called Open Network Provision Framework Directive[13] establishes the need for harmonised conditions of access to public networks and services, hence the need for interconnection and interoperability. So in the same way that operators cannot escape interconnection, they are also bound to a certain degree of standardisation in order to harmonise services across the EU. To achieve this, it is necessary for all member states to co-operate in adopting and developing standardised telecommunications technologies.

The practice of mandating standards for use is widespread within Europe, but it is avoided in most other regions, particularly in the US. The EU's commitment to the process of standardisation was reflected in the establishment of the European Telecommunications Standards Institute (ETSI). The clearest benefit to European companies of EU mandated standards, such as GSM, being adopted in Nation States are economies of scale, and a guaranteed market. These factors have meant that the prices of GSM handsets, for example, have fallen considerably encouraging the take up of GSM services by consumers across Europe and driving market growth. The practice also undoubtedly contributes towards the desired harmonisation of the market.

In the context of mobile telecommunications, the mandating of the GSM standard across Europe has led to the creation of a pan-European network in that users can 'roam' across countries and still use their mobile phone. This is a huge advantage to the growing number of people who travel overseas for work purposes, and offers operators a further source of revenue. In contrast, markets without mandated standards, such as the US mobile market have seen their development inhibited by fragmented national coverage due to incompatible standards. The European mobile telecommunications market is considerably more advanced than that of the USA, and Europe has played a leading role in the development of the next generation of mobile telecommunications services.

Nevertheless, mandating standards would seem contrary to the politics of free competition, and is representative of the erection of non-tariff barriers to market entry. It has also been suggested that it may have a potentially adverse impact on innovation.[14] This would be particularly harmful in high technology fields such as telecoms. Loss of benefits arising from product differentiation and increased choice is also a risk with mandated standards, which would further compromise the competitive advantage of European firms.

In order to prevent this from being the case, European government's need to ensure that mandating standards does not lead in effect to monopolistic environments, where competition and innovation are inhibited. This implies collaborative efforts to research and develop new common standards and technologies for harmonised communications networks and services across Europe.

Managed by the EU, common R&D efforts, such as the ACTS (advanced Communications Technologies and Services) provide valuable technological advances, which can be exploited to encourage the development of the European telecommunications market. Indeed, co-operative R&D efforts are not restricted to within the EU itself, and in areas such as mobile communications have involved interested parties from across the globe in the context of such groups as the UMTS Forum. Such co-operation also permits greater economies of scale and less financial risk involved in researching new technologies which may or may not have commercial applications and are likely to involve considerable investment in time and money for research and development before any real financial and economic benefits are seen.

A common strategy for PTT's in the event of market liberalisation has been to branch out abroad as new competing telecoms operators, in attempts to increase revenues as market share is eroded by competition in their national market. The majority of new emerging telecoms companies are often in fact consortia, or the product of strategic alliances between a number of firms, and in this way the ownership nationality of these companies becomes blurred, reflecting the 'europeanisation' of the industry. Germany's Viag Interkom for example is owned by the UK's BT (90 per cent) and Norway's Telenor (10 per cent). France's second operator Cegetel is a joint venture between French media conglomerate Vivendi (44 per cent), BT (26 per cent), Germany's Mannesmann (15 per cent) and the US company SBC Communications Inc. (15 per cent). In effect, Europeanisation becomes globalisation as ownership often extends beyond the EU, and even beyond the continent of Europe. Inter-firm collaboration characterises the industry as markets open up to competition and companies seek to enter foreign markets with the support of local partners.

This trend has intensified as more countries open up their telecoms markets to foreign competition following the signing of a WTO treaty by 61 countries, representing approximately 90 per cent of the world's telecoms revenues, in March 1997. As well as providing further opportunities for European PTTs to expand abroad, this also means that international competition is inevitable and intense.

Another trend has been the formation of global alliances. Large multinational corporations have, for some time, been looking for a single supplier to deal with all their communications needs. In response to this, operators have come together in a series of loose and often shifting alliances, claiming to offer international end-to-end communications services from a 'one stop shop'. However, such alliances have not been without problems. They have often struggled to put together a comprehensive product range and to guarantee service quality. Companies frequently have to rely on partners over whose services and international strategies they have little control.

The joint venture between BT and MCI, Concert, was dissolved following the failure of BT's bid at the beginning of 1998 for 80 per cent of the US's MCI that it did not already own. Friction between France Télécom and Deutsche

Telekom, following the latter's failed attempt to merge with Telecom Italia[15] led to the disbandment of Global One in January 2000. In March 2000, the EC approved France Telecom's purchase of the remaining stakes in Brussels-based Global One from ex-partners Deutsche Telekom and the US's Sprint, for a total equity value of US$3.882 million. Under the agreement, Deutsche Telekom and Sprint are obliged to provide services to Global One customers until at least 2002.

More recently, companies such as the UK's Vodafone and AirTouch from the US have opted for complete mergers. Vodafone AirTouch Plc., the largest mobile telecommunications company in the world,[16] was created in June 1999, following the approval of the relevant regulatory authorities in the US and Europe. Though based in the UK, the company has operations in 25 countries, with a particularly strong presence in Europe where it holds stakes in major mobile operators in Germany, France, Italy, Spain, the Netherlands, Belgium and Greece.

In a similar fashion BT and AT&T the ex-monopolies and strongest telecoms players from the UK and the US have a long-standing relationship. In mid 2001 they were reported to be in talks to pool their telecoms business service units in a separately listed company, which would include their ailing Concert join venture and other business-related telecoms services. This would see the creation of another new 'global' company, which will be independently run. In order to compete with such global players, other national companies are likely to have to link up to create global companies, meaning that the telecoms industry is likely to become more and more transnational in nature.

This tendency towards the 'transnationalisation' of telecoms operators means that it is increasingly difficult to maintain telecoms strategies that are purely national in nature, and even strategies adopted by the European Commission to encourage co-ordination of telecoms strategies across the EU are no longer always relevant. For example, in light of the increasing globalisation of the telecoms industry, European Organisation's such as ETSI (European Telecommunications Standards Institute) have been forced to make concessions to non-European members. The international members of the GSM Association presents a similar picture since the development and deployment of the GSM standard began as a 'European' initiative. Even the name of the standard, Global System for Mobile Communications is indicative of the recognition of the globalisation of telecommunications industry.

International co-operation has been even greater in the development of the next generation of mobile telecommunications. At a meeting of the Operators' Harmonisation Group, in mid 1999, a consensus was reached by leading operators and manufacturers in the US, Europe and the Far East on a single technical standard[17] that will allow the third generation of mobile telephones to be used almost anywhere in the world.[18] This represents a significant concession from the US in the standards-setting arena, showing recognition of the need for international co-operation so that telecommunications services can be standardised across the globe in order to meet the growing demand for international telecommunications services. For such initiatives to be successful, it is necessary for national and regional telecommunications policies to support them.

Also, many of the companies participating in the research and development of new technologies and standards are transnational in nature, with a blurred ownership nationality. It is at best difficult if not impossible for countries to maintain a national policy on telecommunications in terms of research and development to encourage innovation and market growth in the national territory. For example, in France national R&D is carried out at le Centre national d'études des télécommunications, which, despite reorganisation, remains closely linked to France Télécom, which, in turn, has many foreign interests and partners. Indeed, even European R&D programmes such as ACTS, which ran from 1994 to 1998 with a budget representing about 5 per cent of the total funds available for European research under the Fourth Framework, encouraged participation from non-EU countries given the global nature of the communications industry.

In such a context, in order to protect national sovereignty it would be necessary for national organisations to foster the maximum level of transparency possible in telecommunications strategies and to co-operate to ensure that the benefits of collaborative R&D programmes and the adoption of common standards are effectively distributed across all nations concerned. Transparency and co-operation is also vital if we consider the fact that national communications networks, which are crucial to a country's economic growth and development, are no longer nationally owned.

Just as the companies operating international communications networks and supplying services increasingly fail to respect national boundaries, neither does the technology that is being used. Regulation of the telecommunications industry has become increasingly complicated with convergence between telecommunications, media and information technology creating new telecommunications services, such as voice over the Internet, e-mail, data and Internet access over mobile phone networks and data services over digital broadcasting platforms.

In January 1998, the EC was forced to consider whether voice services delivered via the Internet should be considered as falling within the legal definition of voice telephony under the existing legislation. It was decided that the regulatory framework applied to public voice telephony could not be applied to voice over the Internet but that, given the rapid development of the technology, the subject would need to be reviewed periodically. As communications technologies continue to converge, it will be increasingly necessary to resolve the regulatory problem presented by the fact that telecommunications and media have always been a separate, highly regulated area whereas the information technology as a rule has been subject to much less regulatory control. In 1997, the European Commission issued a Green Paper on the convergence of the telecommunications, media and information technology sectors, and the implications for regulation towards an information society approach. It raised the issue of the challenge of globalisation in that the Internet's ubiquity potentially allows it to defy attempts to apply existing regulatory objectives at national level. Due to the global nature of the Internet, the communications platform around which many of these new technologies converge, it will be necessary to adopt an international perspective, establishing a regulatory environment that is relevant and effective.

The European Commission's Green Paper on convergence also highlighted the need to co-ordinate regulation across regions by pointing out that excessive or inadequate regulation in one region could result in a migration of economic activity elsewhere, with adverse consequences on the development of the communications market in the former region. In March 1999, the European Commission published the results of the public consultation on the Green Paper with the key message that regulation needs to be transparent, clear and proportional, distinguishing between transport (transmission of signals) and content. Reforms to regulation of infrastructure and associated services are expected to be proposed by the end of 1999 and will require the co-operation of all member states if a harmonised and competitive market for telecommunications services, promoting the development of the European economy, is to be realised.

The problems experienced with the progressive liberalisation of the European telecommunications market discussed above, whereby inconsistencies in regulation across member states have impeded market development, illustrate the need for a greater level of co-ordination of telecommunications strategies in order to achieve the desired open and competitive market for telecommunications. It is clear that as markets open to competition, the regulatory environment of each member state has implications for the development of the European telecommunications industry as a whole.

Co-operation will be increasingly important as markets in other areas of the world open up to foreign competition and the telecommunications market and the players within it become increasingly global in nature. This increases the urgency for the European telecommunications companies to become more competitive and for national and European policies to become more effective in an international market place.

Convergence will also play an important role in shaping the future regulatory environment of global telecommunications networks and services. Co-ordinated re-regulation will be needed to ensure the path to effective international competition, and to ensure that regulation or regulatory inconsistencies do not impede market development and innovation overall, nor in particular regions of Europe.

As national telecommunications markets are opened to international competition, and communications services are increasingly provided on global platforms such as the Internet, greater co-ordination and convergence of telecommunications strategies across the globe is likely to become unavoidable as nations become ever-more interdependent in terms of communications infrastructures and services.

Notes

1 According to the Observatoire Mondial des Systèmes de Communications, in 1997, the EU held a greater market share in telecoms services than Japan and was just marginally behind the US.
  Key Figures and Indicators for the World Telecommunications Market, OMSYC, 1997.
2 Martyn Warwick, 'Be afraid, be very afraid', *Communications International*, September 1998.
3 M. Taylor and M. Warwick, 'End of the Marathon', *The European*, March 1997.
4 Alistair Harris, 'Taking the Grand Tour', *Communications International*, January 1999.
5 'EC queries Spanish licence conditions', *Mobile Europe*, September 1996.
6 Public Network Europe Mobile Yearbook 1997.
7 Peter Strivens and Andrew Martin, 'Towards a Common Strategy: Telecommunication Regulation in the European Community' (Part 1), *Telecommunications*, February 1993.
8 Vanessa Clark, 'Interconnect proves hurdle to Spanish competition', Total Telecom (www.totaltele.com) 4 December 1998.
9 G. Tremlett, 'Crossed lines', *The European*, 16 February 1998.
10 'Germany stumbles towards 1998', *Public Network Europe*, May 1997.
11 Alistair Harris, 'Taking the Grand Tour'.
12 'Towards 1998', *Telecommunications*, March 1997.
13 Council Directive of 28 June 1990 on the establishment of the internal market for telecommunications services through the implementation of ONP.
14 William Webb, 'Should Spectrum managers be mandating standards?', *Mobile Communications International*, Oct 1996.
15 Alan Osborn, 'EU relaxes restrictions on GlobalOne', *Total Telecom*, 3 August 1999.
16 Vodafone AirTouch PLc. has over 29 million proportionate customers and a combined market capital of approximately £77 billion (US$122 billion).
17 The new common standard will, in fact, have three distinct modes which correspond directly to the technologies and market interests of the three main protagonists. However, handsets will be compatible with all three of them.
18 'When is standard not a standard? When it's 3G', Editorial comment, *Communications International*, July 1999.

Further reading

Bergman, Lars, Chris Doyle, Jordi Gual, Lars Hultkrantz, Damien Neven, Lars-Hendrik Röller and Leonard Waverman, 'Europe's network industries: conflicting priorities, monitoring European, deregulation 1', Centre for Economic Policy Research, London, 1998.

Blackman, Colin, 'Globalization, convergence and regulation', *Telecommunications Policy*, 21: 1 (February 1997).

Curwen, Peter, *Restructuring Telecommunications: A Study of Europe in a Global Context* (Basingstoke: Macmillan, 1997).

Drake, William, J. and Eli M. Noam, 'The 1997 WTO agreement on telecommunications:

big bang or little whimper?', *Telecommunications Policy*, 21: 9/10 (Elsevier Science, 1997).

Key Figures and Indicators for the World Telecommunications Market, Organisation Mondial des Systèmes de Communications, 1997.

Monlouis, J., 'The future of telecommunications operator alliances', *Telecommunications Policy*, 22: 8 (September 1998).

Strivens Peter and Andrew Martin, 'Towards a common strategy: telecommunication regulation in the European Community', (Part 1), *Telecommunications*, February 1993.

Strivens, Peter, and Andrew Martin, 'Towards a common strategy: telecommunication regulation in the European Community' (Part 2), *Telecommunications*, March 1993.

Turner, Colin, *Trans-European Telecommunication Networks: The Challenges for Industrial Policy, Studies in the European Economy* (London: Routledge, 1997).

Ypsilanti, D. and P. Xavier, 'Towards next generation regulation', *Telecommunications Policy*, 22: 8 (September 1998), 643–59.

Press articles and specialist reports and publications

Public Network Europe Mobile Yearbook 1997.

'ETSI makes concessions to non-European members', *Mobile Europe*, October 1996.

'WTO: global agreement at last', *Public Network Europe*, March 1997.

EU Regulation, *Public Network Europe*, March 1997.

V. Shetty, 'Mr Muscle', *Communications International*, March 1997.

'Utility networks: public virtue, private vices', *Public Network Europe*, March 1997.

'Révolution à 1.000 milliards de dollars dans les télécoms', F. Lorenzini, *La Tribune*, 26 March 1997.

'Storming the Fortress', Telekom, J. Coman, N. Moss and D. Brierley, *The European*, 2 February 1998.

'The new era in global telecoms', *Financial Times*, 27 July 1998.

'BT on the verge of an American merger (again)', Simon Reeve, *The European*, 27 July 1998.

Corrigan, Tracy, 'Deal with BT completes reformation of once-lagging AT&T', *Financial Times*, 27 July 1998.

Corrigan, Tracy, 'Partnership founded on friendship', *Financial Times*, 27 July 1998.

Cane, Alan, 'WorldPartners and Unisource to be unravelled', *Financial Times*, 27 July 1998.

Taylor, Roger, 'Lucent and Cisco square up for mismatched combat', *Financial Times*, 17 August 1998.

Hannington, Stephan, 'The political price of liberalisation', *Network News*, 21 October 1998.

Tuckett, Roger, 'There's more to 3G than a choice of technology', *Communications Week International*, November 1998.

Wilson, Richard, 'The gold rush', *Electronics Weekly*, 27 January 1999.

McCormack, David, 'Vodafone AirTouch deal sets the tone for a wireless future', *Network News*, 27 January 1999.

McCormack, David, 'Mobile standard put on hold', *Network News*, 27 January 1999.

Channing, Ian, '3G: Is the end in sight?', *Mobile Communications International*, February 1999.

Horne, Dr Nigel, chairman, Alcatel UK, 'The near future of mobile telecommunications', *Mobile Communications International*, February 1999.

Helme, Susie, 'An early Finnish', *Mobile Communications International*, February 1999.

Osborn, Alan, 'EU relaxes restrictions on GlobalOne', *Total Telecom*, 3 August 1999.

Stohr, Greg, 'AT&T-BT get US approval for $3 billion joint venture', *Totaltele.com*, 29 June 1999.

Scott-Joynt, Jeremy, 'EC revamp boosts telecoms' status', *Communications Week International*, 19 July 1999.

'Progress in the Telecommunications Sector', Background Report, The European Commission, July 1995.

'Commission Confirms Measures Ensuring Full Competition in Telecoms by 1998', The European Commission, 19 July 1995.

'Status Report on EU Telecommunications Policy', The European Commission, 12 April 1996.

'Green Paper on the convergence of the telecommunications, media and information technology sectors, and the implications for regulation towards an information society approach', European Commission, 3 December 1997.

'Summary of the results of the public consultation on the Green Paper on the convergence of the telecommunications, media and information technology sectors; areas for further reflection', DG X and DG XIII, European Commission, 29 July 1998.

'Results of the Public Consultation on the Green Paper on the Convergence of the Telecommunications', Media and Information Technology Sectors, European Commission, 10 March 1999.

'Status report on European Union Telecommunications Policy', Update March 1999, DG XIII, European Commission, 22 March 1999.

Vodafone and AirTouch complete merger, Vodafone press release, 30 June 1999.

Websites

http://europa.eu.int/pol/infso/info_en.htm

www.etsi.org

www.iso.ch/infoe/into.htm

16

J(EU)nesse sans frontières: information age governance, youth and the EU

Paul G. Nixon

This chapter draws on some initial findings from a pilot project which is examining the potential of information communication technologies (ICTs) to provide opportunities for young people to be engaged in the political processes in the EU. It discusses the potential gains that may accrue from the reshaping of EU services to provide 'Information Age Government' and outlines some of the obstacles to be overcome. The chapter seeks to stimulate debate needed to evaluate if the level of co-operation required for such a form of governance exists and the extent to which such a system of governance is actually desirable or achievable in the context of an EU of 15 member states, let alone an expanded EU.

Politics and youth

An overall trend of decline in participation in elections suggests that current political institutions, actors and practice in advanced liberal democracies are in a frail condition and are held in poor public regard. There also is a belief that the current period of rapid social, economic and political change may signal an emergent information age which could provide opportunities to rethink and if necessary, radically overhaul or replace those political institutions, actors and practice,[1] thus providing potential for young people to participate in an information age EU.

If we look at political participation in general we can see evidence of a decline, as illustrated by an examination of voting figures at recent elections. In the 1999 European elections in Britain just 24 per cent of votes were cast – a reduction of over 12 per cent from the previous European election in 1994 (European Parliament Online, 1999)[2] In those same European Elections, voter turnout across the EU has fallen (with one exception being that of Denmark) since 1979. In some instances, the decline has been quite dramatic with a 30 and 32 per cent drop in Finland and Portugal respectively.[3]

However, the decline indicated relates to the electorate as a whole, further evidence has suggested that young people (18–25 year olds) are even less likely to vote, to join a political party or to be politically active. Frazer and Emler argue that it has now become commonplace for a significant proportion of young people in Europe to have no party identification, and to be poorly informed about, and lack interest in, the political process and political issues.[4] The under twenty-fives in Britain are four times less likely to be registered to vote than any other group.[5] This lack of participation has long-term implications for the future of democracy. It suggests a disillusionment with politics generally, or perhaps more specifically, a lack of belief in the ability of individuals to make a difference by their impact on the decision-making process. Coleman sees their involvement as a vital action to restore confidence in politics and political parties.[6] Young people of today are quite literally the future of the EU and thus we argue that any attempt to redraw the EU must take into account their hopes and aspirations, a fact recognised in a recent EU white paper (European Commission, 2001) and also by the setting up of The European Convention to determine how the EU can re-engage its citizens.[7]

In 1995 Wilkinson and Mulgan, conducted a year-long project to identify whether attitudes and experiences of 18–34 year olds were changing in Britain and the implications of any such change for the future. They found that for some young people 'politics has become a dirty word'.[8] The research also found that, although many young people took 'pride in being outside the system', they were nevertheless concerned with many issues: the environment, AIDS, jobs and animal rights. Thus there was a strong sign of discontentment among the young people, with many expressing their distrust of the system, their disconnection with the system and their frustrated ambitions, rejecting traditional politics whilst still being passionate about certain issues.[9] One can see evidence of young peoples perceptions of the EU in Eurobarometer Youth Survey (2002).[10]

A MORI poll (September 1998) on behalf of the Institute of Citizenship, also questioned young people aged between 15 and 24 as to their knowledge of the political process.[11] It showed that:

- 90 per cent of young people claim to know just a little or less about the European Union.
- 81 per cent of young people claim to know just a little or less about the way Parliament works.
- 65 per cent of young people claim to know just a little or less about their rights as a citizen.
- 52 per cent of young people claim to know just a little or less about their responsibilities as a citizen.

The results of the poll suggest that perhaps young people's apathy towards politics may not be as a result of disillusionment with the political process but rather as a result of their lack of knowledge as to how the process works. Accordingly, the need to educate young people to encourage participation in politics seems apparent but this will not address the problem for those young people who have left full-time education or who are, for one reason or another, excluded from full-time education.

These figures are not just unique to Britain. In 1993, 6 per cent of under twenty-fives in Europe said that they valued politics compared to 11 per cent of adults.[12] Acknowledging the principle of subsidiarity we feel that this disillusionment may well be shown to increase with the distance, in terms of geography and participation, between citizen and decision. This must be recognised by the EU in its attempts to forge its identity for the twenty-first century, an identity that must be socially inclusive.

Politics and ICTs

As we move to a situation whereby the characterisation of society as one based upon the traditional notion of production of goods is, at least partially, being replaced by interpretations which foreground the use of information as a product in a service-based economy the structure of our society is being redrafted. The notion of governance is not immune from such change and governments are experiencing a 'paradigmatic shift in thinking, towards an interpretation of the State as being concerned less with provision and more with facilitation, enablement and partnerships in the management and delivery of public services'.[13]

Thus governments too are changing, moving away from the idea of a centralised, bureaucratic government overseeing a physical, productive-based economy towards more fluid, devolved structures and practices, which must also produce, as Chakravarti and Krishnan point out, 'a new model of governance, adaptive to a virtual, global knowledge-based, digital economy and fundamental social shifts'.[14] Peterson and Sharp argue 'that the accelerating pace of technological change in the late 1990s make it a more important determinant of the way in which economies, polities and societies are organised than ever before.[15]

A redesign of existing structures and procedures would be needed in order to re-engineer the EU machine for the information age, in order to provide the EU with what Tapscott calls 'inter-networked government'[16] or as the UK White Paper 'Modernising Government' terms it 'joined up government'.[17] This re-engineering of the EU machine of governance would lead to a redrawing of boundaries, responsibilities and competencies, which may well come under challenge from within the existing hierarchies.

Existing power bases in the political arena combined with a restructuring of bureaucracies may also lead to potential power loss by political actors. This could be further exacerbated by a move away from the traditional model of public service in which a divide exists in that officers inform, explain and interpret, and elected representatives debate and decide towards a more participatory, responsive and reflective system in which the users interact and their experiences are acknowledged at all levels.[18] Thus substantial socio-cultural shifts may be required to encompass the requirements of the information society.

As access to digital technologies enable more and more people to transcend geographic boundaries and access vast quantities of information from an ordinary personal computer terminal, the notion of traditional democratic participation is being questioned by cyber-libertarians. Loader[19] has discussed the limitations of the cyber-libertarian approach. However, Hague and Loader[20] note that there are key features of interactive media that are claimed to offer the potential for the development of a new variety of democracy:

- Interactivity: users may communicate on a many-to-many reciprocal basis.
- Global network: communication is not fettered by nation-state boundaries.
- Free speech: users may express their opinion with limited state censorship.
- Free association: net users may join virtual communities of common interest.
- Construction and dissemination of information: net users may produce and share information that is not subject to official review or sanction.
- Challenge to professional and official perspectives: state and professional information may be challenged.
- Breakdown of nation-state identity: users may begin to adopt global and local identities.

Perhaps ICT adoption and the creation of a digital democracy can allow the EU both to modernise its procedures and practices and also to re-engage with its citizens. Thus forging new relationships, which may help to address the criticisms of the EU as a political entity suffering from a democratic.[21] It could be argued that the young possess the most flexibility in order to adapt to new technologies.[22]

The EU and the information society

The EU has been somewhat slow to encourage the use of ICTs, particularly when related to governance. Whilst politicians and officials have been eager to provide answers to economic questions throughout the development of the EU, they have been more reticent in putting forward an agenda for political change. This reluctance to think the unthinkable has been primarily due to the need to convince member states' governments, and perhaps more importantly their electors, that it was they and not the bureaucrats in Brussels that were in charge. Thus one finds integrative measures talked down and the outward nature of the Union is one characterised, in many respects, overtly at least as inter-governmental.

If one examines the thrust of previous programmes designed to create an information society in the European Union one can see that the emphasis has concentrated firstly on the market, secondly on society and only relatively recently upon the EU machine itself, although it is now broadly accepted that innovation and restructuring are necessary components of successful European integration.[23] If one looks at the efforts to encourage and target research and development into new technologies one can argue that from the First Framework Programme, designed to arrest Europe's declining competitiveness and dependence on imported expertise and technology, there have been a plethora of initiatives. Some have been specifically focused on ICT developments, for example R&D in Advanced Communications Technologies in Europe (RACE) and the Advanced Communications and Services (ACTS) programme, whilst others were more generalised, although contributory to ICT developments, such as the European Strategic Programme for Research in Information Technology (ESPRIT) and Basic Research in Industrial Technologies – European Research in Advanced Materials (BRITE-EURAM). These sought to bring together divergent research and development (R&D) competencies in order that researchers and commercial interests could build partnerships of mutual benefit, leading to the development and successful marketing of products that could compete in the EU markets and also in competitor markets, for example the US and Japan.

The rise of internet use in Europe in the early 1990s spurred the EU into action. Building upon the broad themes of initiatives such as the *US National Information Infrastructure* (NII), which was championed by Clinton and Gore,[24] the EU launched an *Information Society Initiative* (ISI), which sought to outline the conditions needed to enable the member states to compete in the global information market. The publication of the Bangemann Report in 1994, espousing the rhetoric of competition within free markets, attempted to create confidence in an information society,[25] which was to be embedded in European society at the EU level and also within individual member states in all applicable areas and sectors of the economy. This was to be brought about through a series of funded programmes and projects, which would produce what the report saw as a 'virtuous circle of supply and demand'.[26] As a consequence of the Bangemann Report and subsequent updating, the EU has sought to formulate a network of instruments, ranging from publicity programmes to promote the notion of an information society, whilst fostering social and cultural cohesion in Europe, through to regulatory frameworks designed to seek to control ICTs and in particular the Internet and its applications.

The 'G7 Government Online Project' (now G8) as part of its recommendations urged governments to champion the information age by demonstrating at first hand how it could revitalise organisations. It posited governments as having the opportunity to lead instead of following commercial activity by demonstrating how ICTs could assist in a 'reinvention of government'[27] transforming many of the ways in which governments and citizens interact. National Information Strategy positions have also been espoused, such as the UK Government's 1999 White Paper 'Modernising Government', Denmark's 'Info-Society 2000', or Germany's 'Info 2000: Deutschlands Weg in die Informationsgesellschaft'.[28] Whilst these are of course national answers to the problems of informatisation the increased co-operation between EU member states implies a logic of complimentarity. Although whilst initially these initiatives seem to be offering potential solutions to similar, if not identical, questions posed by informatisation and that those proffered solutions appear to be based upon similar values, it is vital to recognise the diversity of cultures and values under which such proposals were formulated.

The benefits of information age government in the EU

It should also be remembered that the definition of an information society is a contested one.[29] So too are the responses to it. Most government responses detailing potential future strategies have largely been predicated upon a business or commercial analysis of the information society as shown above. The notions of political and democratic impacts of the information society have been some-what in the background of these strategies.[30] However these questions are now being asked as a digital democracy moves from the hitherto realms of science fiction and the futurists towards being a realistic possibility, underpinned by the potentiality of evolving social structures and norms as identified by Castells[31] as many governments embrace ICTs as an enhancing and empowering tool for governance within Europe. Let us then examine the basis for change.

The first question to ask when considering changes to the way in which the EU (and thus the member state governments themselves) operates, is why change at all? What outcomes do we seek? What do we want it to do, what do we want it to be? If for the sake of argument one accepts the logic of political inte-gration within the EU, a logic that if one takes account of the largely accepted notion of subsidiarity whereby policy competencies could potentially be trans-ferred either upwards or downwards to the most appropriate level, then one could make a case for certain tasks or competencies to be dealt with at EU level. Indeed this is already the case in certain policy domains, for example agricul-ture. Does the adoption of ICTs and the potential that they facilitate for re-shaping governance allow us to suggest that this process should be extended and if so to what?

Perhaps this can be split into two categories which are by no means mutually exclusive

1 Improving the machinery of governance and the way government activity is undertaken to improve the central bureaucratic machine of the EU, its administration and, potentially, its service delivery.
2 Increased participation in many areas of governance enabling citizens to interact with officials and politicians in the decision-making process, creating a more open and direct style of interface between those who govern and the governed, offering a digitally based element to governance and democracy.[32] It is this category that appears to hold the most scope to adapt to the needs of young people.

So let us briefly examine what potential could be offered. The following bene-fits could be suggested.

Better co-ordination of EU policies and legislation. The new business environment evidenced in the private sector will also be necessary in the public and third sectors. This re-orientation would require a re-evaluation of structures, which in itself would provide the potentiality to redefine the ethos of governance as well as facilitating new forms of policy-making and service delivery via better use of information. As Taylor notes 'once this point of view [the need to re-orient] is taken, new arguments are brought forward to reinvent and re-engineer government organisation through bringing about alterations in these [information] flows and domains'.[33]

More efficient use of resources could be engendered via a utilisation of ICTs and a streamlining of costly property portfolios. Although whilst initially suggesting cost savings it is more likely that the type of use of ICTs undertaken by an information age EU would be linked to a political move to take the institutions of the EU closer to the people and could therefore potentially cost more to operate than the present system.

Dissemination and consultation could be facilitated by the use of ICTs allowing greater participation and easier access to information about, and produced by, the various organisations and agencies of the EU.

Enable more efficient quantitative and qualitative auditing of dispensers and recipients of EU funds, a function which the EU is in dire need of at present. Although it must be pointed out that whilst ICTs can be used to monitor and audit and reduce the potential of certain criminal activities they can also be used to facilitate new forms of crime and corruption.[34]

Bring equality of treatment to each citizen. At present each citizen's information rights in terms of access are determined by national governments and this can lead to inequalities of access to information throughout the differing member states. In the interests of equality between citizens this would need to be rectified by EU-wide legislation concerning the freedom of information.

Reconfiguration of interfaces between citizen and the EU, thus implying new relationships between government, agencies, civil servants, businesses and citizens, via a co-ordinated information and service delivery interface. One-stop shops could replace the traditional organisation forms in numerous locations, thus bringing the notion of subsidiarity out of its institutional settings and into the physical localities of the EU's citizens

Increased communication with, and between, European citizens and the EU. The EU could publicise its profile and work through websites and live interactive broadcasts by European Union and national government officials on the Web, in the hope of dispelling perceptions of remoteness, thus improving popular support. One of the ways in which this could be strengthened in relation to young people is via youth parliaments. The notion of youth parliaments is one that is gaining ground as a way of empowering or giving voice to young people, although it must be said that this idea is in its infancy and requires further effort if such parliaments are to play a serious role in the information age EU. Our initial research shows that young people, even those who are otherwise socially excluded (where they are aware of the existence of initiatives such as the UK Youth Parliament) are interested in contributing and that this could well apply to similar initiatives taking place in other member states. To build upon this interest it is vital that the youth parliament does not simply replicate the national Parliament which, as has been demonstrated, does little to engage young people. Youth parliaments need to ensure that the issues of all young people are addressed and that representatives from across the country and from all socio-economic backgrounds are facilitated to participate.

As part of the furthering of the integration process a move towards a more direct digital democracy may be possible via ICT use. ICT use could afford the EU the opportunity to address the charge of democratic deficit in an innovative manner, by re-engineering its institutions and revolutionising the interface between governance and citizens to create a joined up EU. Such technologies are becoming, relatively, cheaper and easier to operate, although inequality of access is still a problem. Whilst an increasing proportion of the population within the EU have access to technologies enabling them to access information from anywhere in the world, full implementation of internet governance is constrained by the potential social exclusion of those who do not have such access. There is a danger that '[t]echnological change in government could deepen inequalities in access, and further distance the public from government and politicians'.[35]

Whilst technological advancement may produce solutions to a number of the problems of governance it will not provide solutions to them all and may be a contributing factor to the new problems within governance, such as privacy, freedom of information, cybercrime and surveillance to name but a few. As '[t]he rhetoric of technological shifts are not always translated into successful implementation. Technology is a tool that can aid us in improving society but it does not, of itself, provide solutions to questions such as inequality, power, democracy and justice.'[36]

The notion that any form of modern government, and leaving aside the protestations of certain politicians, that is one of the things that the EU undoubtedly is, can control its activities when those activities are delivered via a myriad of institutions and agencies is debatable. The adoption of new technologies merely relocates the political issues that lie behind the recognition of a need for change. The contesting and debating of political differences over a plethora of multifaceted and often interlinking issues are essential grounding forces within highly complex democratic institutions.

We will now move on to an examination of the barriers and obstacles to information age government in the EU.

Potential barriers and obstacles to information age government in the EU

The most immediate political barrier that the EU would appear to face is that the member states would be most wary of giving up their powers to a European level of governance, although it must be said that the degree of political, social and cultural cohesion achieved under the auspices of the EU would have been thought unlikely at its post Second World War inception. Just because the political imperative is not present today does not mean that it may not appear in the future. A common currency for the EU was being derided as unattainable only ten years ago and we now stand on the threshold of its adoption in 11 of the member states. Clearly the degree of antipathy to further integration varies from state to state and it would be difficult to predict the level of future convergence, particularly in an enlarged EU.

A further barrier to an information age EU would be that at present its citizens owe allegiance to, and identify themselves as citizens of, the member states. The EU needs to create a trust relationship with its citizens in order to allow them to transfer, at least part of their allegiance, from the member states to the EU. This would probably involve a twin track or 'dual nationality' approach to identity that would allow one to retain affinity to one's social and cultural heritage. Interestingly, it is perhaps the young, who have less 'national baggage' to bring with them, who may be persuaded to define their identity increasingly in European rather than national terms.

In terms of young people, in particular, the EU will need to create the political conditions that allow informed participation and a new form of interaction between politicians and young people. The problems to be addressed were outlined in a survey of 150 young people, which sought their views of politics, social exclusion and policies that effect them.[37] The young people who took part in the project had direct or related experience of the most severe forms of disadvantage, adversity and exclusion from mainstream society. They have experienced at first hand what it is like to be homeless, to be part of the care system, abuse, school exclusion, drugs, unemployment and family conflict. However, although these young people were all experts in these areas, which had directly impacted on their lives, they had never before been consulted about them.

The research found that despite the widespread and deeply held mistrust of politics, the young people in the sample were motivated by a wide range of social and political issues. Again, research in other European nations suggests that despite low interest in party politics, the majority of young people in Europe are interested in a variety of social issues, for example in Finland, for young people the most important issue was unemployment.[38] The young peoples' more general sense of alienation and distance from mainstream institutions and communities certainly affects their view of formal politics, but they also have specific and detailed criticisms to make:

- Politicians use irrelevant and evasive language.
- These young people are not ready to engage with politics unless they see it making a tangible difference to the circumstances they face.
- They do not feel that they are listened to or are taken seriously by politics or politicians.

- Gimmicks are not appreciated, and politicians should not attempt to sound 'hip'.
- Politics is not perceived to make a difference, and these young people distrust the use of statistics.
- The school curriculum should include more about practical citizenship and current political issues.

Of course, young people are not a homogenous group. They do not all have the same life experiences or opportunities. Potentially, educating for citizenship would improve participation rates but this is only useful or appropriate for young people who are still in the education system, have not been excluded or have some sense of their own self worth. For many young people, the key to their lack of interest relates to the observations that politics seems so remote from them or their experiences and politicians are not interested in them or in changing their lives. This can be evidenced in the Eurobarometer Youth Survey (2002), which shows a worrying lack of concern for issues such as enlargement.

Leaving aside the notion of political change in order to operate a system of information age governance across the EU there would need to be standardised systems for data collection in each member state. The agencies of governance would be driven towards data sharing which could potentially undermine organisational effectiveness if there is insufficient flexibility to enable the data to be used by a diverse range of Departments and agencies. As Taylor notes 'whilst there may be a strategic case and desire for changes in the collection and sharing of information across a system, there is also a case to be made against it in favour of constitutional separations and separate information domains'.[39]

In order for any such system to operate there must be increased training initially in keyboard and mouse skills, although new developments such as voice command, touch screens, video-conferencing and other developments will enable easier interaction in the future. This means that education policies in schools, in the workplace, and across the community must be geared to meet the needs of information age government. Skills are needed by the users but also by the agents of governance. Whilst placing extra reliance upon champions of technology and thus elevating the status of the IT expert within government, many officer-level tasks are de-skilled. This would seem to suggest a flattening out of organisational hierarchies, which in itself brings both advantages and disadvantages to the implementing agency.[40]

For reasons of simplicity, as well as affording real equality of opportunity within the government machine, there is a case to be made for the adoption of a common administrative language to be used throughout the EU, although this would be politically unacceptable at the time of writing. This would most probably be as part of a twin track linguistic approach, with citizens retaining their own language, at least at first, in order that regional cultural sensitivities are accommodated. At present a reliance on internet technology is a reliance on the

English language, with the majority of information on the net being in English, the 'lingua franca' of the net.

In order to use the new technology, whichever language is spoken, easy access to electronic services, perhaps via interactive TV, will need to be guaranteed. If possible this should be at household level but there may also be a need for public access points, with technical support and advice on hand. It is imperative that the EU 'ensure that the Information Society does not lead to exclusion, adding to the divisions that still exist in society'.[41] Although it is almost inevitable that access would be stratified with those having personal access to a computer terminal being able to access most if not all government information and services from the comfort and privacy of their own home.

Anyone not having private access would have to use public terminals, with a lack of privacy and may well have to queue to utilise them. Public access terminals would involve people travelling to interact with government, and for people in rural areas this could involve long distances, in order to use 'public' terminals adding to the problems that rural dwellers face due to their geographic location.[42] Thus one would have an information age, class system with tiers of access. Those with private means would enjoy a superior citizen to government interface. Those using the public services may find demand exceeding supply at certain times and thus be denied access. Of course, the pace of technological change could mean that costs of upgrading and updating technology could be a great burden on both the provider, in this case the EU, and the users, of whom poorer users would suffer disproportionately. Although one could argue that major inequalities in access to information exist under the present system there is a strong case, on the grounds of social inclusion, for de-commodifying internet access.

Such problems can be particularly exacerbated for young people who may lack the resources to be able to provide equipment and access. Indeed there are particular problems for socially excluded young people, who may suffer from the 'double whammy' of not having sufficient resources to enable them to afford private access and of being unable to utilise public access technology in public places, such as libraries, schools and colleges from which the young people may be formally excluded.

The initial indications of our ongoing research show that the location of technology is important to young people. In many instances, young people are not happy using technology in open public environments. They preferred the technology to be sited in a known place in which they feel comfortable, their own defensible space. This coincides with other research undertaken by CIRA, which shows a preference for the provision of access to computers at existing community locations and facilities, where people attend and interact in relation to other non-computer related activities and interests. This stands in contrast to more centralised provision of purpose-built 'telecentres' or 'electronic village halls'.

The young people we have interviewed to date support this approach to provision. Many felt that, whilst they would at some time in the future use or indeed had already used the computers at their 'home' location, they would not consider using them elsewhere, or would not feel welcome elsewhere. Many said that having computers in their own 'home' locations improved the quality of use, as there was far greater scope for young people to pursue their own interests.

A potential barrier to young people exploring the new technology relates to gate-keeping by local workers. It was apparent that some workers were extremely concerned by the fact that the young people had access to an on-line facility; this concern was deepened by a move to now introduce video-conferencing into some of the projects. The workers seemed to assume that the young people would be rude and offensive in on-line communications or that they would down-load what might be considered as inappropriate material from the Internet

A further barrier is that there would have to be a system of digital identification perhaps through the use of an ID card system based upon smartcards with which citizens can identify themselves, use services, safeguard their privacy and, increasingly, make and receive payments. The cards would be multi-functional and contain encrypted digital signatures. This could cause problems for the UK where there is strong resistance to the idea of identity cards, particularly amongst the young. The UK has no real standardised system of identification numbers, unlike other member states, and the UK government would need to seek a system allowing the government/citizen interface to benefit from the opportunities offered via ICT adoption.

These outside agencies (banks, the Post Office, supermarkets, accountants, interactive broadcasting companies, the information technology industry and others) could also become key partners in the delivery of information and services within the EU in that it is possible to envisage EU one-stop shops being set up in locations where they are easily accessible and could provide 'a co-ordinated group of information and services to support their needs ... across related programs at a particular level of government, across local, and state government levels, and between public and private sector providers.'[43] Thus citizens accessing EU services or information at such locations will be able to deal with different agencies via one transaction, which would enable them to share data such as change of address, simply and electronically, therefore saving time and the duplication of effort.

However such schemes need to gain and maintain the trust of the citizens and thus must be a fully inclusive system in order for that trust to occur. Also there is a danger that the technology, whilst facilitating information age government, could also threaten civil liberties as it offers unscrupulous groups and individuals, or even perhaps the state, the capacity to undertake covert surveillance of citizens. In order to safeguard the citizen against such abuse, once more the need can be seen for an EU-wide freedom of information act, which must include the ability for an individual citizen to scrutinise and challenge the information held upon them.

If the EU is to truly adapt to the information age then, along with individual member state governments it will have to shake off the shackles of traditional thinking and create a future where the institutional ethos is one built upon the notion of internal entrepreneurialism. It will need to use ICTs as a valuable tool in meeting the varied needs of individual citizens, groups and business, and be in the forefront of technological advancements. This implies further moves towards sharing the burden of research and development with other partners in order to achieve this. The EU must seek to engender full public and private membership of the information society. It must encourage an adoption of the information age, at all levels of corporate life from SME's upwards, in order to maintain the EU's commercial position in the world and through a revitalising of its activities, structures and processes place itself in the vanguard of the information age. Leading by example and not necessarily always trailing behind private corporations.

Conclusions

There appears to be a growing over reliance upon technology as the answer to the problems of governance. We would contest that only in alliance with radical political changes, particularly where linked to issues of social inclusion, can information age government within the EU become a valid goal. The rhetoric of technological shifts has not always been translated into successful implementation and one can see the gap between rhetoric and reality, exemplified in some of the past experiences. There can be little doubt that technology can be a tool that can aid us in improving society, but it does not of itself provide solutions to questions such as inequality, power, democracy and justice. Thus the issue of inclusion must be dealt with prior to the achievement of an information age EU. This appears to posit a conundrum in that, it could be argued, such issues can only be resolved by an EU wide government. In an update of the chicken and egg question we must ask which comes first: inclusive democracy or information age governance?

The future of democracy in both the nation state and in Europe generally will depend on the participation of a greater proportion of the electorate. To this end, engaging young people in the political process is beneficial to ensuring future participation and the development of ICTs allows young people to gain practical skills and, through the gaining of those skills and their interaction with others, they learn self-respect, community building and hope for the future. The European Union as an organisation will have to rise to meet the challenges of a changing environment.

Of course there would be strong resistance to change from what might be termed 'the forces of conservatism'. Even if one discounts the distinct possibilities of inter-departmental rivalries or the desire to protect one's own department or organisation or country from radical change, etc., one is still left with the problem of policy co-ordination. It is difficult to effectively implement policy if there are potential differences, albeit small, surrounding the perception of policy goals and the ways in which those goals should be implemented at the government citizen interface. There is a potential that the decentralisation of services via a form of quasi-privatisation, as noted above, may indeed re-enforce rather than deconstruct individual institutional identity. Thus creating a scenario of a government machine that is joined-up, perhaps, but not seamless. In governance, concepts such as decentralisation and one stop shops are not new and their use has, to date, failed to break down institutional barriers to radical change within government. The fear would be that the actors and organisations would effect change at the pace of the slowest participant. This would suggest the need for an enforcer or leader who can take decisions based upon the needs of the EU as a whole.

The notion that the EU could, given the diffuse nature of modern governance, plan and control the future development of the services delivered via structures employed either directly, but more likely indirectly, by national governments or their agents, on behalf of the EU and *de facto* only nominally under its control remains one that is open to challenge. As democratic institutions are, by nature, highly complex in that, amongst other things, they provide spaces for the contestation of views, that is the expression and debate of political differences. It is this democratic nature that threatens the rationalistic progression of information age governance, as rationalistic information systems do not lend themselves to operation under constantly evolving, competing perspectives on what is to be achieved, when, how and by whom.

The creation and recognition of an EU identity by citizens, perhaps as suggested earlier in collaboration with national identity, is vital to moving forward the EU project.[44] We would contest that it is amongst the young that the drive for re-identity may take place and that they could become the grass roots champions for information age government in the EU. However the price of their efforts is greater inclusion within the political and social system along with mechanisms that would deal with problems of privacy and data verification, most probably by an EU-wide Freedom of Information legislation.

The type of government needed will change with government becoming more entrepreneurial, seeking to lead and not follow developments in the information age. The development of information age government may facilitate a concomitant shift to a more direct style of politics/democracy, which may be more participatory and inclusive.

The improved transparency from such initiatives in governance and democratic accountability vis-à-vis EU institutions and European citizens could act as a component part of a solution to problems of image and identity. Adoption of information age government could allow the EU to present itself as a modern organisation, which is ready to meet the challenges of the twenty-first century and to assume a role as a world leader in the political arena, as a real competitor to the US on the world stage. The one certainty of the future in EU governance is change. For modern governance change will be the only constant as '[r]einvention is only the latest initiative in the enduring cycle of reform'.[45]

Notes

1 B. N. Hague and B. D. Loader, *Digital Democracy* (London: Routledge, 1999).
2 For more information visit http://europa.eu.int/futurum/index_en.htm.
3 European Parliament Web Site, *European Elections Facts and Figures* (1999), BBC News Onlne, 'Apather winner in Euro poll', 10 June 1999. For more information visit http://europa.eu.int/futurum/index_en.htm.
4 E. Frazer and N. Emler, 'Participation and citizenship: a new agenda for youth politics research?', in J. Bynner *et al.* (eds), *Youth, Citizenship and Social Change in a European Context* (Aldershot: Ashgate Publishing Ltd., 1997).
5 H. Wilkinson and G. Mulgan *Freedom's Children: Work, Relationships and Politics for 18–34 Year Olds in Britain Today* (London: Demos, 1995).
6 S. Coleman, 'Can the new media invigorate democracy?', *Political Quarterly*, 70: 1 (1999), 16–22.
7 'A new impetus for Europe's youth', White Paper, European Commission, 2001, http:/europa.eu.int/comm/education/youth/ywp/whitepaper_en.pdf. For an interesting analysis of the new potential for crime see D. Thomas and B. D. Loader (eds), *Cyber Crime: Law Enforcement, Security and Surveillance in the information Age* (London: Routledge, 2000).
8 Wilkinson and Mulgan, *Freedom's Children,* p. 17.
9 D. Rucht, 'Political Participation in Europe', in R. Sakwa and A. Stevens *Contemporary Europe* (Basingstoke: Palgrave, 2000).
10 Eurobarometer, *Youth Survey* (2002), http://europa.eu.int/comm/public_opinion/index_fr.htm.
11 'Natwest State of citizenship in Britain Survey', Institute for Citizenship, MORI Poll, September 1998.
12 H. Helve 'Perspectives on social exclusion, citizenship and youth', in Bynner *et al.* (eds) *Youth, Citizenship and Social Change in a European Context.*
13 J. A. Taylor, 'Governance and electronic innovation: whither the information polity?', *Information Communication* and *Society*, 1: 2 (London: Routledge, 1998), p. 145.
14 A. K. Chakravati and A. S. A. Krishnan 'Electronic government and the international scenario', Seminar on Electronic Governance, 27 January 1999, Jaipur, Rajcomp.
15 J. Peterson and M. Sharp *Technology Policy in the European Union* (Basingstoke: Macmillan, 1998), p. 1.
16 D. Tapscott, *Digital Economy* (New York: McGraw Hill, 1996).
17 'Modernising government', Government White Paper, CMnd 4310, 1999.
18 P.G. Nixon, 'Joined-up government: Whitehall on-line', in R. Gibson and S. J. Ward (eds), *Re-Invigorating Democracy: British Politics and the Internet* (Aldershot: Ashgate, 2000).
19 B. D. Loader, *Cyberspace Divide* (London: Routledge, 1998); B.D. Loader, *The Governance of Cyberspace* (London: Routledge, 1998).
20 Hague and Loader, *Digital Democracy*, p. 9.
21 P. Lynch, N. Neuwahl and W. Rees *Reforming the European Union* (Harlow: Pearson, 2000).
22 I. Hutchby and J. Moran-Ellis (eds) *Children, Technology and Culture. The Impact of Technologies in Children's Everyday Lives* (London: Routledge, 2001).
23 V. Koutrakou and P. Nixon 'Integration, communication and transparency in

Europe: innovating integration or integrating innovation?', in V. N. Koutrakou and L. A. Emerson (eds), *The European Union and Britain: Debating the Challenges Ahead* (Basingstoke: Macmillan, 2000).

24 C. Bellamy and J. A. Taylor, *Governing in the Information Age* (Buckingham: Open University Press, 1998), p. 133.

25 C. D. Raab, 'Electronic Confidence: Trust, Information and Public Administration', in I. T. M. Snellen and W. B. H. J. van de Donk, *Public Administration in an Information Age: A Handbook* (Amsterdam: IOS Press, 1998).

26 M. Bangemann, *Europe and the Global Information Society: Recommendations to the European Council* (European Commission Brussels, 1994).

27 Osborne and Gaebler 1992, cited in Taylor, 'Governance and electronic innovation'.

28 'Modernising government', Government White Paper; Danish Ministry of Research, 'Info-Society 2000', Report from the Committee on the Information Society by the year 2000, November 1994; German Federal Ministry of Economics, 'Info 2000: Deutschlands Weg in Die Informationsgesellschaft', www.info2000.de/gip/programme/info2000/html.

29 F. Webster, *Theories of the Information Society* (London: Routledge, 1995).

30 G. Bennehard, 'Democratisation under influence', Information Society Research Centre Working Papers 5/1998, INSOC, 1998, Tampere.

31 M. Castells, *The Information Age: Economy Society and Culture, Vol. 1, The Rise of the Network Society* (Oxford: Blackwell, 1996); M. Castells, 'The *Information Age: Economy Society and Culture, Vol. 2, The Power of Identity* (Oxford: Blackwell, 1997a); M. Castells, *The Information Age: Economy Society and Culture, Vol. 3, End of Millennium* (Oxford: Blackwell, 1997b).

32 P.G. Nixon and H. Johansson 'Transparency through technology: a comparative analysis of the use of the internet by political parties', in B. Hague and B. D. Loader (ed.), *Digital Democracy: Discourse and Decision Making in the Information Age.* (London: Routledge, 1999)

33 Taylor, 'Governance and electronic innovation', p. 150.

34 The UK Government issued a discussion paper on the introduction of ID cards at the time of writing.

35 W. H. Dutton, *Society on the Line: Information Politics in the Digital Age* (Oxford: Oxford University Press, 1999), p. 176

36 P. G. Nixon, 'Joined up government'.

37 T. Bentley and *et al.*, *The Real Deal: What Young People Really Think about Government, Politics and Social Exclusion* (London: Demos, 1999).

38 H. Helve, 'Perspectives on social exclusion'.

39 Taylor, 'Governance and electronic innovation', p. 149.

40 A. Zuurmond, 'From bureaucracy to infocracy: are democratic institutions lagging behind?', in I. T. M. Snellen and W. B. H. J. van de Donk, *Public Administration in an Information Age: A Handbook* (Amsterdam: IOS Press, 1998).

41 S. Micossi 'By the people, for the people?', *I and T Magazine*, no. 19 (April 1996), p. 1.

42 J. C. Allen and D. A. Dillman *Against All Odds: Rural Community in the Information Age* (Boulder, CO: Westview Press, 1994); Also: H. Helve, 'A comparative sudy of living conditions and participation of rural young people in changing Europe'.

43 Chakravarti and Krishnan, *Electronic Government*.

44 D. Beetham and C. Lord *Legitimacy and the European Union* (Harlow: Addison

Wesley Longman, 1998); C. Lord, *Democracy in the European Union* (Sheffield: Sheffield Academic Press, 1998).

Further reading

BBC News Online (1999) *UK politics: who does not represent me?* 7 May 1999.

Buckingham, D. *After the Death of Childhood: Growing up in the Age of Electronic Media* (Cambridge: Polity Press, 2000).

DG XIII (1999) *Measuring Information Society: Report by INRA*, Brussels, EU.

European Commission (1994) *Europe's Way to the Information Society*, Brussels, European Commission.

Koutrakou, V. N., *Technological Collaboration for Europe's Survival* (Aldershot: Avebury, 1995).

Muxel, A., 'Entry thresholds to politics: between inheritance and experiment', in A. Cavalli and O. Galland (eds), *Youth in Europe* (London and New York: Pinter, 1995).

Conclusions

Vassiliki N. Koutrakou

Since the end of the 1980s, commentators and writers of international relations and European affairs have lost count of the times they announced the arrival of a new post-Cold War world order and tried to define and encapsulate it, only to be contradicted the very next week, or year, by a continuing roller-coaster of politico-economic developments, which defy all prediction and refuse to conform with any neat new construct attempted. This shortens the life-cycles of usefulness of most articles and books, and sends scholars out to constantly seek the most up-to-date, informed analysis on the shelves.

It is not sufficient for literature to be post-1989 or post-Maastricht to capture the basic post-Cold War trends in international relations or in EU policy-making. The 1990s brought with them a sea-change of promise towards co-operation and interdependence bathed in ample, positive light, but the experiences of Bosnia, Kosovo, the mass graves and trails of refugees, did not allow this euphoria to last long. While the East–West barriers appeared to crumble, those who were traditionally 'on the same side' and presumably had every reason to be so still now, more than ever, appeared anxious to define their own distinctive positions and identities more clearly, with the EU beginning to test its wings in the foreign and security policy fields, and an unspoken competition with a NATO, which celebrated its fiftieth anniversary while searching for a new role, starting to simmer.

While the EU financed cross-border transport and easier access and mobility, it began to forge tighter immigration legislation, giving rise to accusations of a 'Fortress Europe'. While it sponsored East European economies to accelerate efforts towards meeting a catalogue of standards included in the 'Acquis Communautaire', not least in terms of environmental legislation, to make these countries eligible for EU entry, it could only sit back and watch NATO's depleted uranium bombs litter the Balkans, impotent to offer an alternative effective policy to stop the conflict.

The late 1990s also brought Monetary Union, and an unprecedented appreciation of the globalisation movement in the world of business and communications, as well as the EU's position as a major trading bloc. With power came more constraints however, and the EU found itself both driving and being driven doggedly along the process of market liberalisation and deregulation, as were its major trading partners, within the context of a more interdependent than ever, international economic order, symbolised, over this latest period, most recognisably by the rise in influence of the World Trade Organisation and other international financial and trade institutions like the G8. A symptom of the times, the rapid evolution of high technologies and their applications revolutionised speed, efficiency and diversity in traditional trade and opened up new areas, accentuating competition but, at the same time, intensifying the move towards joint ventures and greater interdependence in a war for economies of scale. Their desirability as a massively important ingredient of any conceivable international economic standing, was matched only by their pervasiveness in political and social discourse over the role, existing and potential, in the conduct of democratic processes (as with the Internet) and sustainable societies (as with the debates over genetically modified foods or the prospects of nuclear energy).

In a climate where all discourse, not to mention economic wealth, appeared to be concentrating ever more on the triad of wealthy nations and their satellites, the anti-globalisation movement gathered pace and came to vocalise the plight of a Third World, which was increasingly sensing that it was being frozen out; after a period of neglect with the non-ratification of the Kyoto Treaty by the US and a series of more restrictive, less generous and more conditional aid-to-trade development schemes offered to the world's poor by the EU and other world donors at the turn of the century, the anti-globalisation movement and environmental imperatives were hitting the headlines once again.

Meanwhile, domestically, calls for a more democratic and flexible EU, which after its 1995 Scandinavian enlargement was preparing to admit several new members in this decade, predominantly from eastern Europe, in quick succession, warranted the reforms to institutions and procedures, initiated by the intergovernmental conferences, which resulted in the Amsterdam and Nice Treaties, another couple of important milestones one cannot afford to miss out in studying the post-Cold War EU.

However, even if at the turn of the century one was tempted to suggest that the unsettled period of post-Cold War readjustments had thrown up as many major surprises as it was likely to for a few years to come, the events of the 11 September 2001 in the US once more turned the tables on political analysts and those keen to predict trends and shapes in the world order. Since then we have experienced the rather controversial war on Afghanistan, the even more bizarre renewed Iraqi crisis, which cast a damaging shadow over the credibility of many international organisations such as the UN, NATO and the EU, in view of their potential for open manipulation, and threw into question, among other things, once more the validity of interdependence and co-operation. We also saw nevertheless mounting co-operation in security intelligence sharing and the

co-ordination of immigration policies. We also witnessed contradictory policies, which, on the back of the Yugoslavian experience, tended to favour the
hitherto unacceptable justification of violation of state border sovereignty in the
name of human rights, at the same time as legitimising national governments
across Europe curbing civil liberties in the name of the war on terrorism. The
environment and the plight of the Third World once again unsurprisingly and
very quickly lost the spotlight, and the EU and NATO, with their new foreign
policy and security persona as much in question as in the previous decade,
embark on new waves of enlargement.

Surely by the time this volume hits the first bookshelf, many interesting
events, that none of us could possibly anticipate, will have occurred, lending
their own different light to the analysis of contemporary international issues in
EU policy. We have tried in the preceding chapters to highlight the new parameters of interaction, and areas of international policy-making within which the
European integration process is carving its continuing path, constantly
responding, adapting, regrouping, given the milestones outlined just above.
Some of these areas are still very young and give ample opportunity for further
research, as do indeed all areas, subject as they are still, to the unpredictable,
daily developments in our as yet unsettled, and unidentifiable twenty-first
century world order.

Index

QM LIBRARY
(MILE END)